NUNC COGNOSCO EX PARTE

THOMAS J. BATA LIBRARY
TRENT UNIVERSITY

PARSONS AND POLITICS

PARSONS
&
POLITICS

The rôle of the Wesleyan Methodists in Upper Canada and the Maritimes from 1780 to 1855

GOLDWIN FRENCH

THE RYERSON PRESS, TORONTO

© 1962, by The Ryerson Press, Toronto. All rights are reserved. No part of this book may be reproduced in any form, except by reviewers for the public press, without written permission from the publishers. Printed and bound in Canada.

ACKNOWLEDGMENT

Grateful acknowledgment is given to Clarke, Irwin and Company for permission to quote from *Egerton Ryerson: His Life and Letters*, Vol. I, by C. B. Sissons.

To Iris

PREFACE

In the winter of 1781, William Black, an immigrant from Yorkshire, went forth on foot to bring the gospel according to John Wesley to the people of Nova Scotia. Nine years later William Losee, an American Methodist preacher, crossed the St. Lawrence on a similar mission to the scattered settlers of Upper Canada. By 1850 the labours of these and a host of other faithful men had been productive of large Wesleyan Methodist churches in the Maritime Provinces and Upper Canada.

As members of an evangelical group with few social pretensions, the Methodists of Upper Canada and Nova Scotia were from the outset objects of suspicion to the conservative and predominantly Anglican ruling circles of British North America. In short order, however, the Methodists in the eastern provinces gained the esteem of the political if not the religious authorities. The bishops might grumble but these Methodists retained an aura of respectability never wholly obscured by their participation in the secular world.

The Upper Canadian Methodists, in contrast, were distrusted as lower class enthusiasts and as carriers of that most virulent infection —American ideas! When, in the eighteen-twenties, they became involved with the rising reform element in the province, their enemies freely asserted that they were now appearing in their true guise as republican termites in the body politic. To the reformers the Methodists appeared as powerful allies in a time of great need. But their apparent changes of front in the ensuing decades convinced many that the Methodists were really concerned only for their own interests. Many more concluded that the Methodists were a group to be reckoned with in any political calculation.

Subsequent commentators have kept alive the belief that the Methodists were an important factor in Upper Canada's political evolution. In 1882 Egerton Ryerson, the so-called Methodist "pope" and an active participant in Methodist political controversies, asserted that the Methodist ministers "taught doctrines which lay at the foundations of a country's freedom." Methodism was "the first and the most effective promoter of civil and religious liberty for the entire country."[1] Years later W. P. M. Kennedy argued that in the great tory electoral victory of 1836 "the controlling force . . . was the Methodists under the direction of Egerton Ryerson."[2] More recently S. D. Clark has suggested that "the radicalism of early Canadian Methodism had no strong roots in a

[1] E. Ryerson, *Canadian Methodism; Its Epochs and Characteristics* (Toronto, 1882), 129.
[2] W. P. M. Kennedy, *The Constitution of Canada* (Oxford, 1922), 152.

liberal political philosophy.... Nineteenth-century Canadian conservatism (and twentieth-century Canadian socialism) owe much to Methodist inspiration and Methodist leadership."[3]

These differences of opinion concerning the Methodist rôle in Upper Canadian politics, and the outwardly peaceful history of the Methodists in the Maritime Provinces, suggested to the present writer the need for a careful re-examination of the place of Methodism in our history. Since I have had no wish to emulate the prolixity of the Methodist preachers themselves, I have considered for this purpose only the political and educational policies of the Methodists. Education has been included because much Methodist politics was the politics of education and because the Methodists' political outlook was often illuminated by their educational interests.

Within this general framework my primary concern has been to analyze what the Methodists sought to accomplish and to indicate why they pursued certain courses of action to the exclusion of others. Since the evidence about the extent and depth of Methodist influence is neither impartial nor adequate I have treated this aspect of the matter as secondary. In this area the "educated guess" seems to me far more appropriate than blunt affirmation.

In dealing with this subject I have adhered to certain conceptual, chronological and institutional limits. I have assumed that the theological and ethical attitudes and the type of polity of any religious organization will affect significantly the reactions of its members to secular issues. This is to say, for example, that a church with a liberal gospel and a representative system of government will be more likely to display sympathy and understanding toward corresponding elements in the social order than one which does not have such features. Its members, when acting as such rather than as members of a class or group, probably will be unwilling to go much beyond what is implicit in their religious circumstances. Equally, they will be reluctant not to relate the logic of their beliefs to their political behaviour.

Accepting this as at least a plausible assumption, I have sought to interpret the Methodists' response to worldly challenges in the context of the climate of opinion within their community at successive stages in its development. But in this process of analysis it has been necesssary, firstly, to stress that from its inception the Wesleyan movement incorporated elements derived from two distinct religious and ecclesiastical traditions, and therefore had no precise affinities with any one type of social or political system

[3] S. D. Clark, "A Review of C. B. Sissons, Egerton Ryerson: His Life and Letters, volume two," *Canadian Journal of Economics and Political Science* XIV (1948), 257.

Secondly, particular attention has been drawn to the fact that the Methodist heritage was transmitted to British North America by the parent Wesleyan Conference and by its powerful offspring the Methodist Episcopal Church in the United States. The adaptation of the peculiar Methodist system to the conditions of the Maritime Provinces was accompanied by no significant clash between the two great Methodist bodies, whereas in Upper Canada progress toward this same goal was marred by persistent conflict. In these divergent applications of an ambiguous tradition is to be found, I believe, much of the explanation of Methodist action in the secular realm.

My decision to approach the Methodist question in this way largely dictated the other limits to be imposed on this study. Since the history of those who were or who came to be known as Wesleyan Methodists is very extensive, no detailed consideration has been given to the Methodist Episcopal Church founded in Upper Canada in 1834, or to other Methodist groups that were active in British North America. Similarly, the growth of the Wesleyan Methodist interest in Lower Canada and Newfoundland has been mentioned only incidentally, because in my judgment it would not alter materially the argument that is presented here. This work begins with the earliest Methodist missions in British North America; it concludes in the eighteen-fifties, the point at which the old struggles within the Methodist fold and its traditional difficulties were becoming insignificant or were taking on a new and distinctive guise.

2

The number of those to whom I owe much for help and encouragement in the writing of this book is indeed great. The administration of McMaster University has provided me with financial assistance, understanding, and congenial working conditions. Principal E. T. Salmon, the former head of the Department of History, and its present chairman, Dr. H. W. McCready, have done everything in their power to make possible the successful completion of this task. My colleagues, Professors C. M. Johnston, J. H. Trueman, W. M. Kilbourn and F. N. Shrive, have shared with me their own wide historical and literary knowledge and have saved me from many errors and omissions. To Professor D. G. Creighton I owe inspiration, good counsel, and above all a helping hand at a critical juncture. To all these I am most grateful.

It gives me great pleasure to record my thanks for assistance given by several archival institutions and libraries. The Public Archives of Canada and the Ontario Archives have greatly facilitated my research. Mount Allison University Library put at my disposal its valuable accumulation of material relating to Methodism in the eastern provinces. The staff of McMaster University Library has borne with great patience my depredations on its time and resources.

I owe a special tribute to the Library of Victoria University and to its librarian, Miss Margaret Ray. At Miss Ray's suggestion I was given full access to the Library's manuscripts and rare books. Moreover, the Victoria Library generously procured microfilm copies of the records of the Wesleyan Methodist Missionary Society. This splendid collection, which I have used most extensively, is now in the Archives of The United Church of Canada.

The Rev. George Boyle, first archivist-historian of The United Church of Canada, his successor, Dr. A. G. Reynolds, and Mr. Boyle's former assistant, Mrs. Dorothy Nicholson, have been kindness itself. At their instance the facilities of the Archives were placed fully at my disposal. I should like to record here as well my gratitude to the Committee on Archives of The United Church of Canada, which has given me a full measure of support in this undertaking.

Although Dr. Lorne Pierce, the former editor of The Ryerson Press, is no longer with us, I should like to say how much I appreciated his kindly interest and his willingness to encourage a young author. His successor, Dr. John Webster Grant, following Dr. Pierce's example, has given much time and thought to preparing this manuscript for publication.

My platoon of typists, Mrs. M. Winder, Mrs. Y. Cruft, Miss J. Inglehart and Miss O. Di Francesco are especially deserving of mention in this place. They have toiled faithfully over crabbed handwriting and the intricacies of footnotes and have thereby gained a just reputation for charitable deeds. My former student, Mrs. Nancy Vichert, has prepared the index in her usual competent way and has spared me much tribulation, for which I am most thankful.

I am most happy to acknowledge that the Humanities Research Council of Canada is giving financial assistance in the publication of this book, with funds provided by the Canada Council.

Finally, to my mother and other members of my family who have given me sympathetic encouragement I am very grateful. To my wife, who has been at all times a source of inspiration and who has borne with me most patiently, I am especially indebted.

McMaster University,
180th anniversary of William Black's
mission to the people of Nova Scotia

Goldwin French

CONTENTS

CHAPTER ONE	1
CHAPTER TWO	29
CHAPTER THREE	54
CHAPTER FOUR	86
CHAPTER FIVE	101
CHAPTER SIX	134
CHAPTER SEVEN	171
CHAPTER EIGHT	196
CHAPTER NINE	217
CHAPTER TEN	248
CHAPTER ELEVEN	278
Note on Sources	288
Index	291

ONE

"Let thy religion be the religion of the heart."

In the evening of May 24, 1738, John Wesley, a young Anglican clergyman, went "very unwillingly" to a religious meeting in Aldersgate Street, London.[1] During the meeting someone read from Luther's commentary on Romans, at which point Wesley felt his "heart strangely warmed."[2] In this simple fashion he described his acceptance of a new insight into the Christian faith, which he felt impelled to share with all those who could be induced to hear him. Perhaps with astonishment, but surely not with dismay, he soon found himself the leader of an expanding religious movement.

Thirty years after Wesley's conversion the Methodist Connexion, the community of those who accepted his teaching and pastoral direction, had emerged as a distinct and, in many ways, unique religious organization.[3] The Methodist bodies that developed between 1770 and 1800 in the United States and British North America were offshoots of English Methodism and long maintained various relationships with it. Even when the ties of formal association were loosened, indeed, the teaching and example of Wesley continued to be a living tradition in North American Methodism. It is therefore of the utmost importance to grasp the essence of Methodism, and of Wesley's place in it, at the point when it began to expand beyond the narrow confines of Great Britain.

John Wesley was the product of a distinctive family, educational and religious background. His father, the Reverend Samuel Wesley, was a diligent, unimaginative, and scholarly parson who engendered in his son a certain respect for learning.[4] Wesley's mother, Susanna, however, was the dominant personality of the Wesley household. From her he acquired the principal ingredients of his early education and his original religious ideas. Mrs. Wesley firmly believed that, since wilfulness is the principal source of sin in the world, the first duty of an educator is to break the child's will. All her children were raised according to a rigid system which so stressed regularity, order and discipline as to ensure the elimination of impulse.[5] Wesley's will was not broken by this procedure, but certainly he acquired orderly habits and he learned to repress his natural emotions.

Equally, if not more, important in the formation of John's character were the religious principles upheld by Susanna. He was taught that he must believe in order to be saved, faith being defined by Mrs. Wesley as "assent to whatever God has revealed to us, because He has revealed it."[6] It was not enough, however, simply to believe. Mrs. Wesley attempted to implant a pattern of godliness in all her children. They were told that unless they at all times tried to follow the will of God they would not be saved. "Heaven or Hell depends on this alone."[7] In effect, Wesley learned as a child that works are the path to perfection.

The religious influences to which Wesley was exposed as an Oxford undergraduate strengthened these early religious impressions and led him down a path that proved unrewarding. In 1725 Wesley came upon Jeremy Taylor's *Rules and Exercises of Holy Living and Holy Dying*, which affirmed that the Christian must strive so to purify his intentions as to serve God at all times. "Regard not, how full hands you bring to God, but how pure. Many cease from sin out of fear alone, not out of innocence or love of virtue; and they, as yet, are not to be called innocent but timorous."[8] William Law's *Christian Perfection* and *Serious Call to a Devout and Holy Life* "convinced me, more than ever," so Wesley said, "of the absolute impossibility of being half a Christian; and I determined, through his grace (the absolute necessity of which I was deeply sensible of) to be all-devoted to God, to give him all my soul, my body, and my substance."[9] "And by my continued endeavour to keep his whole Law, inward and outward, to the utmost of my power, I was persuaded that I should be accepted of Him and that I was even then in a state of salvation."[10]

Once having accepted this high standard of Christian living, Wesley began a frantic struggle to reach it, a struggle that ended in failure so long as he held to the beliefs of 1725. At first he drew up a general rule: "Whenever you are to do an action consider how God did or would do the like, and do you imitate His example."[11] This entailed constant attendance upon the ordinances of the Church, private devotions, the avoidance of idle people and idle thoughts. In 1729 he joined and soon took over the leadership of a small group of students devoted to the study of the Bible and to charitable works.[12] The Holy Club, however, proved no answer to Wesley's problem. He remained so uncertain of himself, that in 1735 he left for Georgia as a missionary, not so much to help the natives as to restore his own peace of mind.[13] In Georgia the young cleric attempted to apply to his congregations the religious standards that he had set for himself, a policy that earned for him some respect and much hearty dislike. To many Wesley seems to have appeared a bigoted hypocrite rather than a Christian minister.[14] Harried from the colony, he returned to England with his self-assurance shattered and with his urgent desire for religious certainty still unrequited.[15]

There can be no doubt that in 1738 Wesley was a better Christian than most people ever become, but it is equally clear that his faith was of little value to others or to himself. At this point, however, he became acquainted with a group of Moravians whose beliefs would work the revolution in his own life that became the basis of the Methodist movement. Impressed by their serene behaviour under stress, he found that their principal belief was that salvation comes to man through faith alone. By April, 1738, Wesley was convinced of the logical and Biblical validity of this doctrine but had not yet attained spiritual certainty.[16] His Moravian friends also persuaded him that faith could be acquired instantaneously. The acceptance of these new convictions no doubt prepared him for the experience of May 24, of which he wrote: "I felt I did trust in Christ, Christ alone, for salvation; and an assurance was given me that He had taken away *my* sins, even *mine,* and saved *me* from the law of sin and death."[17]

The significance of this spiritual experience has been the source of much controversy.[18] Surely the striking fact is that whereas before May 24, 1738, Wesley had been torn and driven by spiritual doubts and fears, his writings after this time mirror a life rarely qualified in its serenity. The Wesley who up to this point had been a mediocre preacher, one who by his own account had little influence over others, was transformed into one who ministered with overwhelming power and authority to a flock of increasing dimensions. Henceforth "he called with the authority of a prophet to the dirty colliers who worked in the coal mines of Bristol, to the filthy rakes who hid in the dens of London, and to the barbarous mobs who inhabited the wild moors of Northumberland."[19] One must agree with Lecky that "the conviction which then flashed upon one of the most powerful and most active intellects in England is the true source of English Methodism."[20]

If this is so, it is most important to determine what took place at this stage in Wesley's life. As early as June 11, 1738, in his sermon on "Salvation by Faith" he attempted to explain this crisis in his spiritual development.[21] It is clear that the first lesson Wesley learned at Aldersgate was that man can do nothing to unlock the gates of heaven. He is saved only by the grace of God, which comes through faith; but, for Wesley, faith was no longer rational assent. "Christian faith is then, not only an assent to the whole Gospel of Christ, but also a full reliance on the blood of Christ; a trust in the merits of his life, death and resurrection; a recumbency upon him as our atonement and our life *as given for us* and *living in us.*"[22] This faith is not of man's creation. "Of yourselves cometh neither your faith, nor your salvation: 'It is the gift of God;' the free, undeserved gift; the faith through which ye are saved, as well as the salvation, which he of his own good pleasure, his mere favour annexes thereto. That ye believe, is one instance of his grace, that, believing, ye are saved, another.... He who is ... saved by faith is indeed *born again*. He is *born again of the Spirit* unto a new life which 'is hid with Christ in God'."[23] In effect, Wesley was one of those passionate seekers after God who was rewarded by the direct intervention of the Holy Spirit in his life.

Although Wesley's fundamental religious conviction was profoundly altered by the Aldersgate experience and the spiritual travail that had preceded it, his personality, his attachment to the Church of England and his views on secular issues remained unchanged. Despite or perhaps because of Mrs. Wesley's careful training, Wesley was an obstinate autocrat with a staggering sense of mission.[24] Until his death he continued to regard himself as a faithful member of the Church of England and to uphold many of the beliefs and practices of that institution.[25] As a public man he was a tory gentleman with a marked lack of respect for individual politicians and a profound sympathy for those disinherited and unhappy masses so largely neglected by his favourite institutions, the Church and the monarchy.[26] So deeply rooted, indeed, were these personal traits and beliefs that it was only with difficulty that Wesley accommodated them to the implications of his new religious outlook. That he was able to do so accounts in large measure for his success, but the reluctance with which he did so explains in part the persistent contradictions within the movement that he founded.

One must remember, too, that Wesley's teaching was assimilated largely by those for whom it might have been expected to have little appeal. Although he began by preaching to Anglican congregations, Wesley quickly wore out his welcome and had no option but to bring his message to the people, in fields, houses and other improvised places of worship.[27] Soon his ministry became largely confined to those who could be reached in this way, the working poor of England.[28] Inevitably, however, the predilections and prejudices of these people affected the careful balance which he tried to maintain between his Anglican and evangelical interests. The result was the Methodist Connexion, a body difficult to classify or describe.

To the casual observer the essence of Methodism, even in Wesley's day, might appear to be its organization; to a trained observer such as Leslie Stephen it was a "moral and philanthropic" movement, "cast in a theological mould."[29] In fact, neither of these insights is correct. The Methodist community was from its inception an association of those who accepted and applied Wesley's teaching about the beginning, the development and the end of the Christian life. The structure of the movement was directly related to the dissemination and application of his religious views, as were the social and political attitudes that he prescribed for his people.

In seeking to make his own experience meaningful and significant for others, Wesley had to clarify his views of human nature, of justification, and of the end of the Christian life. The result constituted the doctrinal foundation of Methodism.

Wesley, like all evangelical Christians, had an essentially pessimistic view of human nature. He believed that man, created in the natural and moral image of God, was originally furnished with immortality, understanding, free will and the capacity to love unselfishly.[30] Through the Fall, however, man's position was transformed. Corruption was substituted for perfection, and the moral image of God in the human heart was replaced by a spirit "altogether corrupt and abominable," full of pride and self-will, "sensual appetites and desires."[31] Man's wickedness, then, was to Wesley not the product of a poor environment or unsatisfactory education, but a natural attribute of all men, who were children "of wrath, liable to death eternal."[32]

Wesley was convinced, nevertheless, that the corrupt man can experience "a present deliverance from sin, a restoration of the soul to its primitive health, its original purity." His soul can be renewed "after the image of God, in righteousness and true holiness, in justice, mercy and truth."[33] But no man can save his soul by his own works, for "only corrupt fruit grows on a corrupt tree."[34] The cleansing and invigorating grace of God comes only as a "free undeserved gift."[35] Still, Wesley did not share the Calvinist view that this gift would be bestowed upon the unwilling few. "Grace," he insisted, "is free in all and free for all."[36] Man can and must seek God through the agency of prevenient grace, that "measure of free-will" which has been "supernaturally restored" to him.[37] Thus the constant emphasis in Wesley's preaching was that man must reach out to God; he must "cry unto him day and night who 'while we were without strength died for the ungodly' until [he] knowest in whom [he] hast believed."[38]

According to Wesley, justification or forgiveness marked the mere beginning of the religious life, the end being sanctification, or Christian perfection. The way to perfection is opened by the new birth, which accompanies forgiveness in an intimate manner. The regenerated or reborn man has power over "outward sin of every kind." In him, "love of the world is changed into the love of God; pride into humility; passion into meekness; hatred, envy, malice, into a sincere, tender, disinterested love for all mankind."[39] Nevertheless, the spirit of the justified man is not entirely pure. His obligation is to seek so diligently the purification of his soul through good works that he may become a fit object of that second intervention of the Holy Spirit in his life, by which he attains Christian perfection or holiness.[40]

Convinced as he was that the imperfect Christian cannot see God, it was natural for Wesley to assert that the doctrine of perfection "is the grand depositum which God has lodged with the people called Methodists and for the sake of propagating this chiefly he appeared to have raised us up."[41] Christian perfection he described as "that habitual disposition of soul which, in the sacred writings, is termed holiness; and which directly implies, the being cleansed from sin, 'from all filthiness both of flesh and spirit'; and, by consequence, the being endued with those virtues which were also in Christ Jesus; the being so 'renewed in the spirit of our mind' as to be 'perfect as our Father in heaven is perfect'."[42] To put it even more simply, Christian perfection meant for him purity of motive, the entire elimination of the inherent tendency of the human spirit to sin. Wesley was never so innocent, of course, as to think of perfection in its absolute sense. The man who has reached this stage will still commit acts that have an immoral impact on others; he will still make mistakes; in effect, he will still be burdened by the limitations and frailties of this existence. But he will also be aware of "love, joy, peace, always abiding," and he will be deeply conscious of his entire dependence on God.[43]

Such, in substance, was Wesley's doctrinal position, which was accepted without qualification by his followers and whose essentials were kept to the fore by their familiarity with his works.[44] Clearly it was an ingenious combination of elements drawn from the Catholic and Reformed traditions. Wesley could not deny the evangelical implications of his own religious experience, but his religious practice emphasized his equal reluctance to give up the Anglican ideal of holiness.

Believing as he did that all men stood naturally by the yawning pit of Hell, but that all might be rescued and transformed by the Holy Spirit, Wesley had established a distinctive pattern of religious and moral activity for his followers. To begin with, the Methodist Connexion was intensely evangelical. No effort was spared to bring the Gospel to all who could be induced to hear it, especially through simple services that were held at any convenient site, and later in Methodist chapels.[45] Following Wesley's example, these services consisted of fervent hymn singing, vigorous prayer, and enthusiastic preaching. It was his intention that decency and order should prevail, and that the preacher should attempt to reach constructively the minds and hearts of his listeners.[46] As his work was generally carried on by men often less capable than himself amongst people whose responses were crude and simple, the Methodist service tended at an early date to become more enthusiastic and often less positive in its appeal.[47] In effect, the evangelical approach became somewhat stereotyped.

Since gathering souls was in a way less important to him than keeping spiritual novices on the path to perfection, Wesley laid down a set of rules governing the moral and spiritual development of all his adherents. They were "to evidence their desire of salvation, first by doing no harm, by avoiding evil in every kind." Methodists were forbidden to profane the Sabbath; to use or sell "spirituous liquors"; to buy or sell "uncustomed goods"; to wear "costly apparel" or to sing "those songs" and to read "those books which do not tend to the knowledge or love of God." Rather, they were to seize every opportunity of "doing good of every possible sort, and, as far as is possible, to all men," by which Wesley meant helping the poor, the ill, the criminal, and those "of the household of faith." In all they must run "with patience the race that is set before them" and "bear the reproach of Christ."[48]

The observance of moral rules depending ultimately upon the quality of the Methodist's spiritual life, Wesley attached much greater significance to attendance "upon all the ordinances of God."[49] Every Methodist was expected to set aside a part of each day for prayer, reading the Bible and other devotional works.[50] He was to attend regularly the Methodist services and those of the Church of England, the former being so arranged as not to interfere with the latter.[51] Wesley, the high churchman, held the Holy Communion in the highest esteem. In his sermon on "The Duty of Constant Communion" he affirmed that "we must neglect no occasion" to participate in this rite. "This," he declared, "is the food of our souls: This gives strength to perform our duty, and leads us on to perfection."[52] The feeling of fellowship with the whole Church was further enhanced by the love-feast, a simple meal combined with testimony of spiritual experience, which, among the Methodists, became in time a pre-communion service.[53] In all this, Wesley sought to ensure that his people would reach a level plainly described in one of his sermons: "Let thy religion be the religion of the heart. Let it lie deep in thy inmost soul. . . . Be serious. Let the whole stream of thy thoughts, words and actions flow from the deepest conviction that thou standest on the edge of the great gulf . . .

just ready to drop in, either into everlasting glory or everlasting burning. . . . Be thou a lover of God and of all mankind."[54] If any man did not seek this kind of religious life, he was to be admonished "of the error of his ways; we will bear with him for a season: But then if he repent not, he hath no more place among us."[55]

The organization of the Methodist community was directly related to Wesley's desire to secure converts and to lead them along the path to perfection, but its shape was affected by his temperament, prejudices, and affection for the Church of England. In consequence, it had certain ambivalent features that plagued his successors for many years.

At first, Wesley seems to have given no serious thought to matters of organization. His intention was simply to preach the gospel as he understood it as often as he could. Within a short time, however, those who heeded his words urged him "to give us the advices which you well know we need and to pray with us, as well as for us. . . . So I told them, 'If you will all of you come together every Thursday, in the evening, I will gladly spend some time with you in prayer, and give you the best advice I can.' Thus arose without any previous design on either side, what was afterwards called, *a Society*."[56] The Society soon became the basic element in the Wesleyan organization. Wherever he had adherents, one or more Societies were organized. Meetings of the Society were open to all, the condition of membership being "a desire to flee from the wrath to come," but continued membership involved acceptance of Methodist discipline.[57]

Finding that he could not adequately supervise the spiritual and moral growth of the Societies, Wesley divided them into classes under class leaders.[58] The leader was to "see each person in his class, once a week at least, in order to inquire how their souls prosper" and "to receive what they are willing to give, toward the relief of the poor."[59] The class meeting became the principal instrument for religious and moral instruction and reproof, as well as a means of procuring regular contributions for the work of the Connexion. Each member was examined quarterly by the minister as to the state of his soul. To each of those whose seriousness was evident was given or reissued a membership ticket; for generations this was to remain the principal credential of the faithful Methodist.[60]

Useful as the class and the class leader proved to be, Wesley was obliged at an early date to consider broader problems of organization. His preaching had proved far more popular than he had perhaps anticipated and, despite ceaseless activity on his part, he had been unable to provide for all the needs of his growing flock.[61]

He had secured the aid of a few clerical sympathizers but these could reach only the Societies adjacent to their parishes.[62] Being unwilling to separate himself from the Church of England and to recruit, train and ordain a separate ministry, Wesley fell back upon the circuit system and a peculiar kind of lay ministry.[63] Each of the Societies formed part of a circuit, within which one or more of Wesley's helpers itinerated according to a regular schedule, preaching and visiting the classes. In each circuit an experienced preacher designated as the Assistant was responsible for the supervision of the other preachers and for the quarterly examination of the classes. Each preacher was removed to another circuit at three-year intervals, to prevent the growth of local attachments and to make possible the efficient use of what was in many cases a limited stock of knowledge.[64] The itinerant preachers in their turn were assisted by the local preachers, men who felt called to preach but not to desert their secular vocations. These faithful men provided a sense of continuity and a degree of intimate supervision which the itinerants themselves would have found it difficult to provide.[65]

In selecting, training, and using his itinerant preachers, Wesley exercised great care and consideration. Those who were "called of God to preach" had to possess "three marks":

1. Have they the love of God abiding in them? Do they desire and seek nothing but God? And are they holy in all manner of conversation?

2. Have they gifts (as well as grace) for the work? . . . Have they a right judgment in the things of God? . . . Do they speak justly, readily, clearly?

3. Have they fruit? Are any truly convinced of sin and converted to God by their preaching?[66]

Those who passed this test were placed on probation for four years, before being received into full connexion with Wesley and his brethren. Meanwhile they were enjoined to improve their abilities by wide reading, for Wesley felt that learning did not diminish religious zeal.[67] Upon being received into full connexion, all Wesley's associates had to adopt as their code of conduct "The Twelve Rules of a Helper," in which piety and common sense were cleverly combined in Wesley's characteristic fashion. His helpers were to be diligent and were to be employed at all times at useful tasks. They were to be serious. They were not to slander others, but were to "tell every one what you think wrong in him, and that plainly, as soon as may be." "You have nothing to do but to save souls," he emphasized, "to bring as many sinners as you possibly can to repentance, and with all your power to build them up in that holiness without which they cannot see the Lord." Finally, he instructed:

> Act in all things, not according to your own will, but as a son in the gospel. As such, it is your part to employ your time in the manner which we direct; partly, in preaching and visiting from house to house; partly, in reading, meditation and prayer. Above all, if you labour with us in our Lord's vineyard, it is needful that you should do that part of the work which we advise, at those times and places which we judge most for his glory.[68]

Although the saving of souls was the primary task of these helpers, they were evidently to do it only on Wesley's terms.

Although he much preferred his own judgment to that of anyone else, Wesley fortunately had provided his people with two institutions, the Quarterly Meeting and the Conference, through which they could be consulted and by which their activities could be effectively governed. The Quarterly Meeting arose naturally out of the system of quarterly visitation of classes by the principal circuit preacher. It soon became a regular meeting of the itinerant preachers, the local preachers, the class leaders and stewards, at which the work of the circuit was reviewed.[69] Although the class leaders and stewards were chosen by the preachers, their presence injected into the government of Methodism at this primary level a significant element of lay participation and consultation that grew stronger as the Societies grew in numbers and wealth.

The Conference had begun in a similar casual fashion and in a form in which it did not seem likely to flourish. In 1744 Wesley summoned several of his colleagues to London, "to give me their advice concerning the best method of carrying on the work of God."[70] Soon the Conference, composed of all the itinerant preachers, came to meet annually to admit and discipline the itinerants, to settle doctrinal issues, and to examine the work of the Connexion as a whole. Although decisions were taken by mutual agreement, as long as Wesley lived the Conference was essentially a consultative body. This arrangement accorded neatly with his determination not to lead a schism in the Church of England, and with his conviction that as the burden of supervising the Methodist Societies had been laid on him by God, he could on no account lay it down.[71] Those who had joined his Connexion as preachers had agreed to serve him "as sons in the gospel."[72] So long as they wished to do so, he felt they should accept the terms of service willingly. Those who were dissatisfied might leave at any time.

While Wesley succeeded in stifling discontent among his followers, he did not effectively inhibit the development of the Methodist Connexion and Conference as self-conscious entities. By 1770 the Conference had come to think of itself as the real governing body of an independent religious community. Wesley himself would reluctantly admit this in the Deed of Declaration of 1784 and in the ordinations of that and subsequent years.[73] But the institutional climate of opinion in the Conference and in the Connexion generally was not clearly defined. For many years Wesley's autocratic temper would continue to affect the attitude of the Conference towards its members and lay Methodists. His establishment of the Legal Hundred, in whom were vested his own powers, helped to strengthen this attitude.[74] At the same time, the Conference was a kind of parliamentary body, which would come to elect its own officers. Outside the Conference were the numerous lay preachers and other lay officials, in close contact with the outlook of the Societies. Both preachers and people worked within the context of a liberal gospel. In consequence the spirit of Methodism was neither wholly conservative nor wholly liberal. It was a subtle compound, very susceptible to such pressures as might be exerted by those who sought power and by those who sought to give Methodism a government related to its faith and the composition of the Societies. In this situation, Wesley's churchmanship and his devotion to the Church of England were additional complicating influences which militated against those who desired innovation and independence.

Unlike many religious leaders, Wesley was not content simply to provide his adherents with the appurtenances of the religious life. He gave them specific, if somewhat contradictory, advice about the rôle that they ought to play in the secular world, especially in matters of political and social responsibility.[75] Here, as in the doctrinal sphere, Wesley enunciated principles, unoriginal in themselves, but to which he gave a distinctive quality in accordance with his background and experience.

Born a gentleman, raised in a conservative atmosphere, and apparently unaffected by the radical political and social thought of his time, Wesley was disinclined to innovate wherever his religious interests were not directly involved. In any case, he was convinced that collective political or social action would not result in social improvement. Political and social evils were the consequence of individual wrongdoing and could only be eliminated by the progressive alteration of the moral attitudes of individual men and women.[76] Wesley was a radical only in his determination to bring this lesson and its implications home to his followers in his comments on political, economic and other issues.

Wesley's political opinions were characterized by the rejection of the doctrine of government by consent and by certain positive assertions about the nature and function of government. For him there was no evidence of "any original compact" and as, in practice, the "people" meant "scarce a tenth part of them," to talk about the will of the people was mere political cant.[77] Wesley was certain, too, that the average man is incapable of wielding political power properly. To make political decisions required "not only a good understanding but more time than common tradesmen can spare and better information than they can possibly procure."[78] Given this fact, popular control was likely to facilitate the rise of the corrupt and the incompetent whose actions would "unhinge all government."[79]

If the compact theory is unhistorical and if popular government is undesirable, what then is the basis of authority? In company with most orthodox divines, Wesley believed "there is no supreme power, no power of the sword, of life and death, but what is derived from God, the Sovereign of All,"—"rulers are God's ministers, or delegates."[80] Realizing the danger implicit in this concept, Wesley urged the limitation of the functions of government to the maintenance of public order. In addition, he affirmed that the liberty of the subject must not be curtailed. "Liberty is the right of every human creature, as soon as he breathes the vital air."[81] Liberty, wrote Wesley, is "either religious or civil." Religious liberty "is inseparable from humanity," for "every man must give an account of himself to God."[82] Civil liberty is "a liberty to enjoy our lives and fortunes in our own way; to use our property, whatever is legally our own, according to our own choice."[83] In effect the free man is one who has liberty of conscience and economic independence. If he is accorded these rights, the chances of tyranny will be greatly reduced.

Yet, if the government stepped outside these limits, was the citizen forbidden to challenge it? Was he supposed to leave it to God? On the contrary, Wesley's lieutenant, John Fletcher, asserted that "all governing power is delegated from the King of Kings, and therefore it is subordinate to Him and it is limited by the bounds which He has fixed—that is by reason, scripture and the apparent good of the people."[84] Consequently, "subjection must be in everything required by the civil power that can be done with a good conscience. . . . God allows . . . our withdrawing from a Government undeniably and capitally tyrannical."[85] In keeping with this attitude Wesley frequently criticized English politicians. "Members of parliament, in their capacity of legislators, are no more authorized by the people to make laws and bound to vote according to the directions of their constituents" than ministers receive authority from their "flocks to preach the gospel."[86] They were to act in the best interest of the community, remembering always their ultimate responsibility to God.

Wesley, then, was essentially a conservative who would not, however, hesitate to bring individuals and governments before the bar of moral judgment. In his dealings with his followers it was his conservatism that appeared most prominently. Methodists who had the vote were to avoid corrupt practices, stay out of party politics, and assess candidates solely according to their moral qualities. Those Methodists who had no vote and the itinerants were not to engage in politics. The latter were to support established authority and were to leave political judgments to Wesley himself.[87] In consequence, even in the minds of its adherents Methodism came to be associated with political quietism. Nevertheless, neither Wesley's teaching nor his practice were without liberal implications. Any religious community that placed so much stress on the effective maintenance of moral standards and on the worth of the individual could become a powerful and radical political force.

While forbidding certain social and political activities to his followers, Wesley tried to instil in them a sense of concern for the ills of society. His point of view was perhaps most clearly revealed in his discussion of the acquisition and use of wealth.

Characteristically, Wesley noted in his sermon on "The Use of Money" that "it has . . . been the manner of poets, orators, and philosophers, in almost all ages and nations, to rail at this [money] as the grand corrupter of the world." But he asked, "is not all this mere empty rant?" The fault lies in the use of money. "It is therefore, of the highest concern, that all who fear God know how to employ this valuable talent," a question which he felt "may be reduced to three plain rules": "Gain all you can"; "Save all you can"; "Give all you can."[88]

Although in using the phrase "gain all you can" Wesley clearly accepted participation in the existing economic and social order, he was equally determined to prevent Methodists from making money improperly. They were on no account to indulge in pursuits harmful to their bodies or minds. They were never to harm their neighbour "in substance," "in his body" or "in his soul." Not to harm one's neighbour in his substance meant, for Wesley, to refrain from such normal business practices as exorbitant interest, price-cutting, excessive charges and speculation. To avoid hurting one's neighbour "in his body" one must not produce or sell what would impair health. The distillers, especially, were murdering "His Majesty's subjects by wholesale. . . . A curse is in the midst of them." Likewise, those who ministered to unchastity or intemperance, or who provided "natural inlets to sin" would have "a sad account to make" to God.[89]

Having gained all they could, while observing these severe limitations, Wesley's followers were encouraged not to waste their substance in purchasing fine food, expensive clothing and elegant surroundings. "Daily experience shows," he added, that the more our desires are indulged, the more they increase.[90] In fact, one should be frugal not only with oneself but with one's children as well. Wesley would set no traps in the way of their sensuality or vanity. If they showed no prudence, they should be deprived of everything but the necessities of life.[91] To put it bluntly, Wesley would let no man dissipate his wealth in vain diversions.

Ultimately, of course, men were to gain and to save because they had a higher responsibility. "But let not any man imagine that he has done anything, barely by going thus far. . . . If . . . you would indeed 'make yourselves friends of the mammon of unrighteousness,' . . . then 'give all you can'."[92] Aligning himself firmly with the spirit of the New Testament, Wesley insisted that every Christian must regard himself as a steward who, having spent prudently for his family, must employ all else "in doing good, all possible good . . . to the household of faith, to all men!"[93] "The Gospel of Christ," he concluded, "knows of no Religion but Social, no Holiness but Social Holiness."[94]

In his teaching and practice Wesley ended, then, as he had begun with a plea for the disciplined and responsible Christian life. It is not surprising, therefore, that when he was asked to describe a Methodist, he replied: "A Methodist is one who has 'the love of God shed abroad in his heart by the Holy Ghost given unto him'; one who 'loves the Lord his God with all his heart and with all his soul, and with all his mind, and with all his strength'." He "does good unto all men . . . in every possible kind . . . but much more does he labour to do good to their souls. . . . These are the principles and practices of our sect; these are the marks of a true Methodist. . . . If any man say 'why, these are the common, fundamental principles of Christianity!' Thou hast said; . . . this is the very truth."[95]

To call the Methodist Connexion simply a community of fervent Christians would not, however, be in any sense the whole truth. On the contrary the religious outlook, the organization, and the attitude toward secular issues of the Societies were characterized by an ingenious blend of often divergent features, based ultimately on Wesley's beliefs and his conception of how they should be propagated. Wesley was dedicated to the dissemination of an original interpretation of the Christian gospel in which were combined the best elements in the Protestant and Catholic traditions. On the one hand he revived the Protestant conviction of the necessity for divine intervention in the process of salvation, although he dropped the idea of divine prescription, contending that every man has to play a part in determining his religious destiny and will receive positive evidence of God's interest in him. On the other hand he could not give up his belief in the importance of each man's growth in holiness through those individual and corporate means of grace, hallowed by long usage in the various branches of the Catholic Church. For Wesley the true Christian was one who had, after intense spiritual travail, felt the divine spark kindled in his soul and who, through the grace of God, dedicated his life to the search for holiness.

Out of these religious principles developed a distinctive religious community. In Wesley's day, at any rate, the Methodists were a group of people vigorously engaged in the attainment of Christian perfection. They met together for simple, emotional services; they followed meticulously the rules of behaviour laid down by their leaders; the majority of them participated in the services of the Church of England. They were known throughout the land for their religious fervour, their industry, their sobriety and the extraordinary extent of their charitable endeavours. But they had begun to show signs of discontent with Wesley's blend of evangelical and churchly Christianity. They were becoming increasingly desirous of the type of emotional service that would produce dramatic conversions; their version of sanctification was another emotional upheaval, preceded only by the reformation of external behaviour; they were becoming less willing to share in the services of the Church. They had in fact started to upset the careful balance which Wesley had established between the evangelical and the ethical aspects of the Christian religion.

The organization of Wesleyan Methodism, like its religious outlook, was a fusion of two distinctive conceptions of church government, one of which was much in evidence, the other almost latent in Wesley's lifetime. In it were combined autocracy and incipient democracy. So long as Wesley was in command, his Societies were effectively centralized around him. He appointed all those in authority; he directed the deliberations of the Conference. He never rested in his efforts to determine how people were doing their tasks. His followers were trained in habits of obedience and orderly government, and he bequeathed to them a central organization that retained his authority in commission. Other influences, however, were likely to produce a leaning towards a more democratic form of church government. Throughout his career Wesley had to depend on lay assistance, for he allowed laymen to take charge of the financial problems of his Societies, and his religious teaching was individualistic and egalitarian. Consequently it was to be expected that the constitutional development of Methodism would be marked by frequent attempts to work out a new balance in its organization. Such efforts would be significant not only in themselves, but also for the manner in which they would shape the secular political leanings of those who participated in them.

In the long run the political implications of Wesley's religious and ecclesiastical views were likely to be of more importance than his attitude towards secular politics. Still, one should not overlook Wesley's legacy of conservatism and moral criticism. The former, in combination with his prohibition of political action on the part of the clergy, was likely to produce a reactionary outlook that would reinforce the autocratic influence of the Wesleyan organization. Even so, Wesley's insistence upon the moral responsibility of government could produce men fit to act in some sense as the conscience of the community, men who would hew a middle road between the extremes of political partisanship. Which of these attitudes would prevail would depend in part upon external conditions, in part upon the general development of Methodism itself.

If Wesley's political views were ambiguous, his position on social issues was precisely formulated. Here again one must remember that Wesley was no innovator and that he was not interested in broad schemes of social reform. Nevertheless, his insistence upon the relevance of practical Christianity in the attainment of holiness and upon individual responsibility for the problems of the community gave Methodism an absorbing interest in the welfare of others. From the outset no Methodist was likely to forget that if he took no interest in his fellows he would not see God. Eventually Methodists would come to see that man and society cannot be sharply differentiated and that Christian charity must assume corporate forms. This inherent impulse towards moral endeavour was to affect Methodism in ways that could not be foreseen in Wesley's time.

2

In response to reiterated pleas from the small Methodist Societies that had been formed spontaneously in New York, Philadelphia, Virginia and Maryland, Wesley sent two missionaries, Richard Boardman and Joseph Pilmoor, to America in 1769.[96] Their arrival in Philadelphia in October, 1769, marked the formal extension of the Methodist Connexion to this continent.[97] Fifteen years later, at a conference in Baltimore, Thomas Coke, one of Wesley's principal lieutenants, presided over the establishment of the Methodist Episcopal Church of America, an autonomous organization that acknowledged Wesley's primacy over it.[98]

Among those present at the Baltimore Conference was William Black of Nova Scotia who, with Coke's help, persuaded the new church to send missionaries to that province.[99] The relationship thus formed was not severed until 1800 when the Societies in eastern British America came under the direct control of the English Conference.[100] A decade earlier the Methodist Episcopal Church had begun in Upper Canada a mission that was to lead to the growth of a large Methodist community. That body of Methodists remained within the American fold until 1828.[101] Since the formative years of Methodism in British North America were so intimately connected with the early history of the Methodist Episcopal Church, it is of particular importance to determine how faithfully the latter reproduced in America the characteristic features of the English inheritance.

Methodist missionaries brought to America a form of Christianity that was distinctive in its spiritual quality, in its organization and in its political and social attitudes. Methodism was evangelical but catholic, autocratic but democratic, conservative in politics but highly critical of individual politicians, vitally interested in the spread of Christian charity but with no desire to attempt the direct transformation of society. The transplantation in the new and different American soil of a form of religion so filled with inner tension and so firmly controlled by its founder was a formidable task. Inevitably certain adjustments were made through which Methodism in America took on a distinctive character. Despite the absence of Wesley and the pressure of circumstances, however, the Methodist Episcopal Church preserved much of the spirit of the original Connexion in its polity, its religious outlook and its attitude towards the secular world.

When the American Revolution ended in 1783, the Societies in America had some fifteen thousand members under the care of eighty-three preachers, of whom the majority had been recruited in the former colonies.[102] Since 1773, the preachers, meeting frequently in conferences, had maintained the circuit system and other elements of the Methodist discipline. They felt keenly the lack of an ordained ministry, however, and there were among them strong advocates of presbyterian ordination.[103] Now, working as they were in a society in ferment, which had secured its political independence and in which the Episcopal Church was disorganized, they were determined to establish an independent form of Methodism in America.

Although Wesley was perhaps not fully aware of the sentiments of his followers, he realized that they were "now totally disentangled," from the state and from the English hierarchy and concluded, "We dare not entangle them again."[104] In consequence, nothwithstanding his devotion to the Church of England and his appreciation of the complexity of the task that faced his American brethren, he resolved to assist them to "stand fast in that liberty wherewith God has so strangely made them free."[105] To provide for a regular succession in ordinations, Wesley set apart Dr. Coke as superintendent and requested him to ordain and set apart Francis Asbury, the leading preacher in America, as co-superintendent of the Societies. Coke and Asbury were then to ordain those preachers of sufficient age and experience who were already at work in the United States. In addition, Wesley provided Coke with abridged versions of the Thirty-Nine Articles and of the Anglican liturgy for the use of the new church.[106]

Arriving in America in November, 1784, Coke hastened to meet Asbury and to summon the American ministers to a conference.[107] A large and representative group met under Coke's chairmanship in Lovely Lane Chapel, Baltimore, December 24, 1784.[108] The Conference proceeded with remarkable unanimity to regulate the affairs of the American Methodist Societies. It was agreed that the new body should be known as the Methodist Episcopal Church of America and that in it *"the Liturgy* (as presented by the Rev. John Wesley) *should be read"* and the sacraments should be "administered by a superintendent, elders, and deacons, who shall be ordained by a presbytery." Those preachers to be ordained were "to be nominated by the superintendent, elected by the Conference . . . the superintendent [having] a negative voice."[109] At Asbury's instance the superintendents themselves were elected by the Conference before he was ordained as a minister and subsequently set apart for that office. The Conference then drew up a discipline based on English practice and arranged the ordination of several of its members.[110] Thus, when the sessions ended on January 2, the scattered Methodist Societies had transformed themselves into an independent church possessed of a body of doctrine, a liturgy, an ordained clergy and a superintendency.[111]

Although much had been accomplished at the Baltimore Conference, the lines along which the Methodist Episcopal Church would develop were still indefinite. Within two decades, however, its principal structural features had emerged and the spirit in which the system would be worked had been defined.

For many years, the general superintendency or episcopate was one of the most vital elements of the Methodist polity. Following the precedent set by Asbury, the bishops were elected by the Conference and ordained by bishops and elders, but they were in many respects not amenable to the Conference. With the right to veto the election of any ministerial candidate and the right to station all the itinerants without appeal they were placed in a formidable position relative to their colleagues. Moreover, since the Methodist episcopate was itinerant rather than diocesan, all areas of the church's work came under its immediate supervision and authority.[112] Even so, the character of the office was largely determined by its original occupants. In the absence of Bishop Coke, Francis Asbury was until 1800 the sole bishop in America.[113] Although he lacked Wesley's scholarship and his breadth of view, Asbury was unquestionably devoted to the essentials of Methodism and was an indefatigable workman for the Lord. Above all he possessed in full measure the determination to rule so conspicuous in Wesley's own career.[114] He ruled himself and his brethren with an iron if charitable hand, being abetted in this policy during his last years by William McKendree, a rugged Virginian of equally autocratic temper.[115] In such hands the executive branch of the Methodist system acquired and retained a powerful, if not preponderant, rôle in its operation.

In addition, the position of the bishops was strengthened by the presiding eldership, which gained formal recognition in 1792.[116] Shortly after the Christmas Conference it was realized that in a growing church the bishops alone would be unable to provide the degree of supervision required. Besides, the shortage of adequately trained preachers made it unsafe to ordain enough clergy to supply the sacraments with sufficient frequency. The appropriate solution seemed to be the appointment of ordained men of experience, each of whom would be responsible for an area served by several preachers. The elder watched over the itinerants in his district, presided over the circuit quarterly meetings and, where necessary, administered the sacraments. In time he would assist the bishop in the allocation of preachers to the circuits.[117] Bishops like Asbury naturally selected for this office men who shared their views and in this way powerfully reinforced their own authority, a situation that very early became a source of complaint to the more independent itinerants.[118]

From the beginning, however, the influence of the episcopate was at least partially balanced by the authority of the Conference. In contrast to the English Conference, with its somewhat ambiguous position, the Methodist Episcopal Conference assumed in 1784 the right to legislate for the whole church.[119] This first Conference was composed exclusively of ministers as were all subsequent Conferences for many generations, but a distinction soon came to be made between General and Annual Conferences.[120]

Six Annual Conferences were organized in 1796 to group the Methodist Societies into convenient territorial units.[121] Originally both legislative and disciplinary gatherings, they became at an early date essentially regulatory assemblies of the preachers. Their principal duties were in fact the admission of candidates, their advancement to election as ordinands, the examination of character and the disbursement of Conference funds. The conclusion of the Conference was invariably marked by the reading of the appointments by the bishop, an event that emphasized his authority over the destinies of the preachers.[122]

The legislative needs of the church were met by the institution of the General Conference, which met in 1792 and at four-year intervals after that date.[123] By 1808, however, the church had grown to such an extent that it was no longer possible for all the itinerants to attend, and in consequence the General Conference became a delegated body. At the same time limitations were imposed on its authority.[124] It was forbidden to alter the Articles of Religion, to alter or abolish the itinerant episcopate, or to change the rules of the Societies without the concurrence of all the Annual Conferences and of two-thirds of its own members.[125] Within these severe limits it was empowered to take any steps consonant with the welfare of Methodism.

Powerful as the episcopate and the Conferences were, no analysis of the Methodist Episcopal system of government would be complete without reference to the rôle of the laity. As in England, the circuit minister was obliged to rely mainly on lay assistance and support. His salary, such as it was, was supplied by the Societies. He was assisted by local preachers, exhorters, class leaders and stewards, all of whom were laymen, closely identified with the interests of the Societies.[126] Both the presiding elders and the itinerants met these lay personnel regularly in the Quarterly Conferences, at which the financial and disciplinary affairs of the circuit were regulated and through which subtle pressures might be brought to bear on the Conferences and the bishops.[127] The likelihood that lay demands would be put forward was much greater in the flexible American community than in the still hierarchical social conditions of England.

Such, in brief, was the Methodist Episcopal system of government in the period when its influence was greatest in British North America. In large measure it maintained the balance that Wesley had sought to achieve between centralization, efficiency, and the consultation of lay and clerical interests. Under Asbury, indeed, it was run almost as autocratically as the English Connexion had been under Wesley. After Asbury, however, the episcopate would lack the kind of prestige that Wesley and he had enjoyed in their respective spheres. The Conference had from the outset a secure function as the legislative arm of the church as a whole, but it too was limited in its activities by episcopal influence, by its self-imposed rules and by the pressure of lay opinion. In effect, the American Methodist system was very much a limited polity—neither episcopal nor conference tyranny was really conceivable. Its mode of operation, with its inner tensions, was likely to be conducive to the development of a sympathetic attitude towards limited, constitutional government in the secular realm.

Ultimately, of course, the kind of influence that emanated from the Methodist community depended as much, if not more, upon the quality of its religious outlook as on the nature and functioning of its government. In this respect too there occurred a subtle shift of emphasis as Methodism became firmly established in American society. In seeking to develop among his followers a form of religious life in which were blended the Evangelical and Catholic traditions, Wesley relied upon the traditions and the actual presence of the Church of England. Indeed, he always thought of Methodism as essentially a movement within that church, an identification that was abandoned with some reluctance by many of his successors. But after 1784 the Methodist Episcopal Church was a church in its own right, with no real interest in its Anglican background.[128] It was, moreover, a church that lacked leaders with the breadth of insight and education possessed by Wesley, Coke and Fletcher.[129] The unsophisticated and often ill-educated Methodist itinerants sought converts in a community equally lacking in refinement and affected by all the pressures of a society constantly on the move along the perimeter of an expanding frontier.[130] The largely latent religious tradition of this society was a diluted form of evangelical Calvinism in which were compounded a fear of hell, the association of religion with emotional upheaval and an implicit rejection of the Calvinist doctrine of election.[131]

In these circumstances the American Methodists quietly jettisoned the liturgical and formal side of the Wesleyan tradition and sought to present their gospel in as appealing a form as possible.[132] Their preaching was marked by a most vigorous espousal of the Arminian position, and by vivid emotional appeals to the consciences of those who came to hear them.[133] Only a hardened crew of sinners could resist the onslaught of a preacher who paused dramatically in his sermon and said: "I feel an impression that there is some young man or woman in this house who will be tramping in hell before this time next year."[134] But although the threat of damnation was thus freely voiced the preachers also emphasized the doctrine of assurance in its simplest form — the dramatic experience of conversion, followed by a continuing sense of transformation and exultation.[135] The doctrine of sanctification was pressed in a similar way—its ethical demands being replaced in considerable part by the second blessing, another visitation of the Holy Spirit, whose emotional consequences were similar to those of conversion.[136] In effect, the American itinerants stressed the evangelical aspect of Methodism rather more than the Wesleyans. Thus their services were marked by extreme simplicity and occasionally by excessive fervour, especially in the camp meeting, that great agency for the rescue of lost souls.[137]

Even so, these Methodist preachers were rarely content simply to rouse pious emotions. They were concerned to disseminate sound doctrine (a policy that was facilitated by the effective use of hymns) and to stimulate moral and spiritual growth in the Societies. To that end the classes were regularly assembled, and from these were excluded those who persisted in drunkenness, disorderliness, gambling and frivolity—the characteristic activities of an uprooted society.[138] With the enforcement of the discipline went a positive stress on the love-feast and the Lord's Supper, celebrated humbly, frugally and solemnly at every Quarterly Meeting.[139] In this way, the Methodists were at least kept in touch with Wesley's ideal and with the spirit of the Church as a whole.

In these early decades, then, the religious outlook of American Methodism was a rather simplified version of the Wesleyan position. The principal emphases were never entirely obscured, but the balance had shifted: in the American Societies it was perhaps easier to mistake emotion for piety, the form of holiness for sincere moral improvement. This adjustment, in conjunction with concern for the independent growth of the Methodist Church, tended to narrow the range of Methodist interest. At the same time the Methodist zeal for souls operated as a more powerful egalitarian force in America than in England, and as one that would in time be associated with a broader understanding of Wesley's concern for social holiness.

For some time, however, the Methodist Episcopal Church was not moved to look intently at the political and social implications of its doctrine and government. In political questions the position of the Conference was undistinguished. All were free to subscribe to different political opinions, but participation in political controversy was deprecated.[140] One of the first acts of the new church was to present an address of loyalty to President Washington, not an improper act but one that was not accompanied by an affirmation of the moral accountability of government.[141] Only in the Conference sessions themselves was there any serious political discussion, and it was confined to matters of church government. One must conclude that formally, at least, the Methodist political position was conservative and quietist.

In contrast, the Conference demonstrated from the outset an interest in education. The Christmas Conference enforced regular study on the preachers, urged them to preach on education, and resolved to found what became Cokesbury College in Maryland.[142] This early effort failed, as did others, but although the series of events pleased some of the ministers[143] the Methodist leaders did not glory "in ignorance."[144] Asbury vigorously promoted the establishment of academies, and in 1820 the General Conference adopted a comprehensive educational policy.[145] Indeed, despite the tremendous task of evangelizing the frontier and the educational limitations of preachers and people, the early Methodist Church kept alive a concern for education in a Christian environment.

On the whole, in those years when it was laying the foundations of Methodism in British North America, the Methodist Episcopal Church was not an unworthy replica of the English Connexion. Although profoundly evangelical, it sought to preserve a balance between religious experience and the achievement of moral perfection. Its rejection of the Church of England, while not in keeping with Wesley's convictions, secured for it a degree of flexibility and an ease of adaptation that the Wesleyans lacked. Similarly, although the Methodist Episcopal polity was highly centralized and autocratic in principle, it was, if anything, more liberal in implication than the Wesleyan system and perforce had to develop in an atmosphere saturated in religious individualism. The political and social attitudes of this new body were even narrower than those of English brethren, but the Wesleyan concern for the shape of society was not dead: the American Methodists were as convinced as the Wesleyans that the transformed individual is the key to the transformation of the social order. It remained to be seen what impact this Methodism, Wesleyan and yet not Wesleyan, would have in the distinctive circumstances of British North America.

REFERENCES TO CHAPTER ONE

1. John Wesley, *The Works of the Reverend John Wesley, A.M.*, ed. T. Jackson (3rd ed., London, 1829), I, 103. This will be cited hereafter as *Works*.
2. *Ibid.*, 103.
3. The Methodist Connexion did not become a legal entity until Wesley made in 1784 the Deed of Declaration, the terms of which were to become operative at his death.

4. M. Piette, *John Wesley in the Evolution of Protestantism* (New York, 1937), 220-221.
5. *Ibid.*, 541-544.
6. L. Tyerman, *The Life and Times of the Rev. John Wesley, M.A., Founder of the Methodists* (New York, 1872), I, 39.
7. Piette, *op. cit.*, 542.
8. J. Taylor, *The Whole Works of the Right Rev. Jeremy Taylor, D.D.*, ed. R. Heber (London, 1828), IV, 30.
9. *Works*, XI, 367.
10. *Ibid.*, I, 99.
11. John Wesley, *The Journal of the Reverend John Wesley, A.M.*, ed. N. Curnock (London, 1909), I, 48.
12. Tyerman, *op. cit.*, I, 66-74.
13. *Works*, I, 17.
14. Wesley's romance with Miss Sophie Hopkey had much to do with his abrupt departure from Georgia. The grievances of his parishioners are outlined in *Works*, I, 56-59.
15. *Works*, I, 101.
16. *Ibid.*, I, 102.
17. *Ibid.*, I, 103.
18. See Piette, *op. cit.*, 305-309; U. Lee, *John Wesley and Modern Religion* (Nashville, 1936), 90-109; J. E. Rattenbury, *The Conversion of the Wesleys* (London, 1938), 36-37.
19. W. R. Cannon, *The Theology of John Wesley* (New York, 1946), 77.
20. W. E. H. Lecky, *History of England in the Eighteenth Century* (New York, 1883), II, 607.
21. *Works*, V, 7-16. The date in the heading of this sermon is June 18, 1738. Apparently this is an error, for Wesley's Journal indicates that he left for Germany on the 13th.
22. *Ibid.*, V, 9.
23. *Ibid.*, V, 13, 12.
24. R. A. Knox, *Enthusiasm* (Oxford, 1950), 455-458.
25. Piette, *op. cit.*, 433; *Works*, VIII, 30-36; XIII, 263.
26. M. Edwards, *John Wesley and the Eighteenth Century* (New York, 1933), 13-19.
27. Piette, *op. cit.*, 349-350.
28. Wesley was usually to be found in London, Bristol, Leeds, Staffordshire, Cornwall and Durham, areas in which the industrial poor were concentrated.
29. Quoted in E. R. Taylor, *Methodism and Politics* (Cambridge, 1935), 28.
30. *Works*, VI, 66-67.
31. *Ibid.*, V, 7; VI, 68.
32. *Ibid.*, VIII, 277.
33. *Ibid.*, VIII, 47.
34. *Ibid.*, V, 7.
35. *Ibid.*, V, 13.

36. *Ibid.*, VII, 373.
37. *Ibid.*, X, 229-230.
38. *Ibid.*, V, 24.
39. *Ibid.*, VI, 71.
40. For a clear discussion of this question see H. Lindstrom, *Wesley and Sanctification* (Stockholm, 1946), 120-125.
41. *Works*, XIII, 9.
42. *Ibid.*, V, 203.
43. *Ibid.*, XI, 422-423.
44. The four volumes of Wesley's Sermons and his Notes on the New Testament were required reading and were considered as the doctrinal basis of Methodism. W. J. Townsend, H. B. Workman, G. Eayrs, *A New History of Methodism* (London, 1909), I, 306 n.
45. *Ibid.*, I, 281-283; 290-291.
46. For descriptions of Wesley as a preacher see *ibid.*, I, 209-212; Knox, *op. cit.*, 513-517. For the services see Townsend *et al., op. cit.*, I, 306-307.
47. Knox, *op. cit.*, 520-534; Lee, *op. cit.*, 298-299.
48. *Works*, VIII, 270-271.
49. *Ibid.*, VIII, 271.
50. *Ibid.*, 322-323.
51. *Ibid.*, VIII, 320-322; Piette, *op. cit.*, 466.
52. *Works*, VII, 148.
53. *Works*, VIII, 258-259; Townsend *et al., op. cit.*, I, 246.
54. Quoted in Lee, *op. cit.*, 209.
55. *Works*, VIII, 271.
56. *Ibid.*, VIII, 250.
57. *Ibid.*, VIII, 270.
58. *Ibid.*, VIII, 252-253.
59. *Ibid.*, VIII, 253.
60. *Ibid.*, VIII, 256-257.
61. Townsend *et al., op. cit.*, I, 291-294.
62. Among those who helped Wesley were Charles Wesley, Samuel Taylor, Vincent Perronet, William Grimshaw, John Fletcher and Thomas Coke.
63. Wesley's intention was to establish a movement inside the Church of England. See *Works*, VIII, 320-322. For a discussion of this question see Lee, *op. cit.*, chapter X.
64. Townsend *et al., op. cit.*, I, 294, 297-298.
65. *Ibid.*, I, 291-294.
66. *Works*, VIII, 324-325.
67. *Ibid.*, VIII, 315.
68. *Ibid.*, VIII, 309-310. During Wesley's lifetime, his preachers were not ordained. It was not until 1746 that Wesley abruptly rejected the doctrine of apostolic succession. Only in 1784 did he begin ordinations, principally to meet the special needs of the American Methodists. For a discussion of this subject see Lee, *op. cit.*, 256-272.

69. Townsend *et al., op. cit.,* I, 299.
70. *Works, VIII,* 312.
71. Townsend *et al., op. cit.,* I, 307-310; *Works,* VIII, 312-313, 320-322, 326-327.
72. *Ibid.,* VIII, 313.
73. The Deed of Declaration is printed in Townsend *et al., op. cit.,* II, 551-556. For the ordinations see Lee, *op. cit.,* 259-272.
74. For a discussion of this question see *ibid.,* I, 381-384.
75. In so doing Wesley was moved in part by his own keen interest in questions of this kind.
76. In general, there were few figures in the eighteenth century who had a collectivist outlook.
77. *Works,* XI, 97, 102.
78. *Ibid.,* XI, 19.
79. *Ibid.,* XI, 98.
80. *Ibid.,* XI, 47-48, 105.
81. *Ibid.,* XI, 79. This remark was elicited by the slavery controversy, but it is indicative of Wesley's general position.
82. *Ibid.,* XI, 37.
83. *Ibid.,* XI, 41.
84. W. J. Warner, *The Wesleyan Movement in the Industrial Revolution* (London, 1930), 111.
85. *Ibid.,* 111-112.
86. *Ibid.,* 96-97.
87. Warner, *op. cit.,* 102-103; *Works,* XI, 154-155.
88. *Works,* VI, 125-126, 131, 133.
89. *Ibid.,* VI, 127-130.
90. *Ibid.,* VI, 131.
91. *Ibid.,* VI, 132-133.
92. *Ibid.,* VI, 133.
93. *Ibid.,* VI, 136.
94. Warner, *op. cit.,* 212.
95. *Works,* VIII, 341, 346.
96. *Minutes of the [British] Methodist Conferences* (London, 1862), I, 91. The organization of these societies is discussed in W. C. Barclay, *Early American Methodism* (New York, 1949), I, 14-23. See also W. W. Sweet, *Virginia Methodism; A History* (Richmond, 1955), 44-46.
97. A. Stevens, *History of the Methodist Episcopal Church in the United States of America* (New York, 1864), I, 98.
98. A brief sketch of Coke's career may be found in Barclay, *op. cit.,* I, 104-120.
99. See below, chapter 2, pp. 32-33.
100. See below, chapter 2, p. 39.
101. See below, chapter 2, p. 39.
102. N. Bangs, *History of the Methodist Episcopal Church* (New York, 1838-1841), I, 162-163.

103. *Ibid.*, I, 130-131; Stevens, *op. cit.*, II, 59-65.
104. John Wesley, *The Letters of the Rev. John Wesley, A.M.*, ed. J. Telford (Standard Ed., London, 1931), VII, 239. See also for the preceding exchange of letters between Wesley and the Americans, W. W. Sweet, *Religion on the American Frontier*, IV, *The Methodists* (Chicago, 1946), 12-16.
105. *Wesley's Letters*, VII, 239.
106. Wesley's explanation to "Our Brethren in America" is in *ibid.*, VII, 238-239. For discussions of Wesley's actions see Lee, *op. cit.*, 264-272; Barclay, *op. cit.*, 1, 92-96, and J. U. Faulkner, *Burning Questions in Historic Christianity* (New York, 1930), chap. 13.
107. See F. Asbury, *Journal* (New York, 1852), I, 484; Stevens, *op. cit.*, II, 169-170.
108. There is no definitive list of those present. See Barclay, *op. cit.*, I, 97; Asbury, *Journal*, I, 486 f.; Sweet, *Religion*, 19 n.
109. Stevens, *op. cit.*, II, 183-184, quoting the *Journal* of Richard Whatcoat.
110. Barclay, *op. cit.*, I, 97-98.
111. Apparently Wesley expected to exercise more than moral authority over the Methodist Episcopal Church, but it is evident that this was all that its leaders were prepared to tolerate. See Stevens, *op. cit.*, II, 199, 496-498.
112. For the powers and responsibilities of the episcopate see Bangs, *op. cit.*, I, 176-177.
113. Francis Asbury came to America in 1771, was appointed General Assistant in 1772 and was superseded by Thomas Rankin in 1773. Rankin left America in 1778 and Asbury soon assumed the leading rôle among the itinerants. Asbury, *Journal*, I, 11, 45 ff. On Rankin see *The Life of Mr. Thomas Rankin, Written by Himself* in T. Jackson, ed., *The Lives of Early Methodist Preachers* (London, 1866), V, 135-213. Richard Whatcoat, a saintly and modest man, was Asbury's colleague from 1800 until 1806. Barclay, *op. cit.*, 130-131; Sweet, *Religion*, IV, 73-74. The term "bishop" was adopted in the Discipline in 1787. Stevens, *op. cit.*, II, 497.
114. E. S. Tipple, *Francis Asbury: The Prophet of the Long Road* (New York, 1916), 242-243.
115. See Sweet, *Religion*, IV, 60-61, 263. For McKendree's general attitude see his statements quoted in Barclay, *op. cit.*, I, 252, 255.
116. The term was first used in 1789. Stevens, *op. cit.*, II, 501; III, 18-19; Sweet, *Religion*, IV, 40.
117. Bishop McKendree made this change in the organization.
118. The first clash occurred at the General Conference of 1792. Stevens, *op. cit.*, III, 16, 21-28. There were several subsequent clashes over proposals for an elective presiding eldership and lay representation in Conference.
119. Sweet, *Religion*, IV, 38.
120. See Stevens, *op. cit.*, II, 219-220; III, 17.

121. *Ibid.*, III, 339. On this matter see N. B. Harmon, *The Organization of the Methodist Church* (New York, 1948), chapters 7 and 11.
122. Stevens, *op. cit.*, II, 221-222. Until 1792, all matters of legislation were dealt with in turn by the Annual Conferences and such legislation did not take effect until all agreed.
123. Harmon, *op. cit.*, 99-100; Barclay, *op. cit.*, I, 161.
124. J. M. Buckley, *Constitutional and Parliamentary History of the Methodist Episcopal Church* (New York, 1912), 110.
125. *Ibid.*, 111-112.
126. Sweet, *Religion*, IV, 47-48. The exhorter was an apprentice local preacher whose duty was to emphasize the principal points made in the sermon.
127. Stevens, *op. cit.*, 223.
128. Only one member of the Baltimore Conference voiced opposition to its assumption of independence from the Church of England. Barclay, *op. cit.*, I, 98. Subsequently Bishop Coke tried on his own to reach an understanding with the Protestant Episcopal Church. Sweet, *Religion*, IV, 25-30.
129. Asbury had an elementary school education which he augmented by wide reading. See W. W. Sweet, *Men of Zeal* (New York, 1935), 150.
130. E. K. Nottingham, *Methodism and the Frontier* (New York, 1941), chapter 2; W. W. Sweet, *Religion in the Development of American Culture, 1765-1840* (New York, 1952), 96-99; 129-137.
131. Nottingham, *op. cit.*, 22-23; Sweet, *Religion in American Culture*, 210-219.
132. Stevens, *op. cit.*, II, 197-198.
133. See, for example, Benjamin Lakin's sermons on predestination. Sweet, *Religion*, IV, 722-725; Nottingham, *op. cit.*, 188-189.
134. Sweet, *Religion*, IV, 54.
135. It is only fair to record that few of the Methodist preachers were interested simply in emotional manifestations. Sweet, *Religion in American Culture*, 153. Asbury himself was very cautious on this point. *Journal*, III, 113.
136. Bangs, *op. cit.*, II, 74-75.
137. The camp meeting, however, was never recognized formally by the Methodist Episcopal Church.
138. See Stevens, *op. cit.*, II, 235; Bangs, *op. cit.*, I, 198-214; Sweet, *Religion*, IV, chapter 13.
139. Stevens, *op. cit.*, II, 223.
140. Bangs, *op. cit.*, II, 149-150.
141. *Ibid.*, I, 284-285.
142. *Ibid.*, I, 196, 204, 230-240. The early conferences showed a keen interest in the temperance and slavery issues.
143. Asbury evidently thought Cokesbury too ambitious a venture. Tipple, *op. cit.*, 274.
144. Sweet, *Religion*, IV, 65-66.
145. Tipple, *op. cit.*, 275; Stevens, *op. cit.*, IV, 469.

TWO

"Dear bro. go on—
Do all you can for poor souls droping into Hell."

In the spring of 1779, when the Methodists in the American colonies were still beset by the scourge of war, a revival began among the Yorkshire Methodists who had settled in Cumberland County, Nova Scotia.[1] Among those converted was William Black, who two years later began a voluntary itinerancy among the scattered communities of the province.[2] Encouraged no doubt by his correspondence with Wesley, and daunted by the magnitude of the work which he had begun, Black journeyed to the Baltimore Conference in 1784.[3] Here, through the influence of Coke and Wesley, he secured two missionaries for Nova Scotia, and inaugurated a relationship of some duration between the Methodists in the eastern provinces of British North America and the newly established Methodist Episcopal Church in the United States.[4] In this quiet way were laid the foundations of a Methodist community that came to differ in many respects from that of Upper Canada, established six years later by missionaries from the United States.

The sources of the distinctive character and influence of Methodism in the Maritime Provinces are to be found in the peculiarities of the environment and of the religious forces to which it was subjected. When William Black began to itinerate as a Methodist preacher in 1781, this whole region, with the exception of Newfoundland, comprised the province of Nova Scotia. Scattered over its vast expanse, although concentrated in what is now Nova Scotia, were some seventeen thousand settlers. Among these the largest group were New England farmers and fishermen who had come to this area in 1758 and subsequent years.[5] Reproducing the characteristic social and religious institutions of their native colonies, they made Nova Scotia for a time almost an extension of New England,[6] although from the outset their position was challenged by the original English settlers and by English and Scots colonists who arrived after 1770.[7]

In 1783, however, the arrival of at least thirty thousand Loyalists transformed the position of Nova Scotia.[8] The fifteen thousand Loyalists who settled in the Saint John valley laid the foundations of what became in 1784 the province of New Brunswick.[9] This

Loyalist influx greatly affected the social and political climate of both provinces. In New Brunswick they sought to establish "the most Gentlemanlike" colony "on earth," in which there would be a marked preference for an aristocratic social order, an established church and oligarchic political institutions.[10] In Nova Scotia, too, despite the presence of the New Englanders, the position of those who sought to keep the colony loyal, conservative and Anglican was greatly strengthened.

Unfortunately, from the standpoint of those who sought stability and order in church and state, Nova Scotia was undergoing a religious revolution before the Loyalists arrived. Formally, the Church of England was established in this province, as it would consider itself to be in New Brunswick, and efforts were made at an early date to provide Anglican missionaries for the region.[11] In practice, however, religious diversity prevailed. Among the most influential religious groups were the Congregational churches, formed by the New England colonists, but decay had begun to affect them at an early date. Separated as they were from New England, these congregations had found it difficult to secure a regular supply of ministers. Those who came were often not the most worthy representatives of a religious community that had in any case lost much of its vitality. The disruptive impact of the American Revolution on the lives of the clergy and their congregations completed the process of disintegration.[12]

In 1776 there came into this scene of desolation Henry Alline of Falmouth, a man of extraordinary personality and religious ideas, who was to revolutionize the religious situation in the Nova Scotia settlements. Like so many great religious figures, Alline had an unusually sensitive and mystical temperament. As a youth he lived in great fear of his physical surroundings and of the perils of an irreligious life. "Often while on the floor in my dance . . . I could hardly contain myself . . . with such dreadful views of the gulph of perdition beneath my feet and the danger of being cut off and dropping into an irrevocable state."[13] Disturbed by pangs of conscience, he sought an answer to the riddle of life. "All the conception I attained to at last, was to find myself a mystery of unhappy existence, between two inconceivable eternities or as an inextinguishable spark of life hanging over or fluctuating in an infinite, unbounded abyss or bottomless ocean."[14] His way was not made clear until he realized that nothing he could do would commend him to God. "When I gave up all to Him to do with me as He pleased . . . redeeming love broke into my soul with repeated scriptures with such power that my whole soul seemed to be melted down with love; the burden of guilt and condemnation was gone."[15] Almost at once, he tells us: "The Lord discovered to me my labour in the ministry and call to preach the gospel."[16]

Although he lacked education and ordination, Alline began to preach on April 18, 1776, and continued at his self-appointed task until his death in 1784.[17] The gospel that he expounded had a very mixed parentage. In a fervent and uninhibited fashion Alline denounced the lifeless, formal practice of the existing churches and offered in its place to his delighted hearers the hope of universal salvation through faith alone. Believing in the guidance of the inner light and the perseverance of the saints, he seems to have deprecated concern for moral improvement as an essential part of the Christian life.[18] "Mr. Alline himself told several persons one day, that 'a believer is like a nut thrown into the mud, which may dirty the shell but not the kernel'."[19] Questionable as such doctrines might be, they appealed to people emotionally starved and possessed of a residual Calvinism. Alline's preaching resulted in the disruption of the Congregational churches, their replacement by several Newlight congregations and the recruitment of a number of preachers who kept alive for many years the tradition of vigorous, informal gospel preaching in a highly individualistic context of church government and doctrine.[20]

In retrospect, it is evident that the condition of Nova Scotia at this point was by no means wholly favourable to the propagation of Methodism. Although Alline's success had clearly demonstrated the need for a simple, enthusiastic presentation of the gospel, an English anti-Calvinist form of religion with a strong ethical emphasis was unlikely to have as strong an appeal as an indigenous, informal and outwardly Calvinist movement. Likewise it was certain that to the Loyalist-reinforced governing group Methodism would be suspect as a form of dissent, although among the rank and file Loyalists it would probably find support if its English identity were stressed. In any event, to found and develop an effective religious organization in the far-flung and poorly integrated settlements of Nova Scotia and New Brunswick would assuredly require great faith, skill in organization, and an adequate supply of personnel.

To William Black, however, the essential fact about Nova Scotia in 1781 was its religious destitution. This he felt he could overcome in part by the energetic exposition of Methodist doctrine, for Methodist preaching had already brought about a radical transformation in his own life.

William Black had been born in 1760 into a moderately prosperous family of Huddersfield, Yorkshire. As a boy he had secured a sound elementary education, upon which he later improved by systematic study.[21] His formal education was interrupted in 1775 when his family migrated to Cumberland county, Nova Scotia, to join other Yorkshiremen who had already settled there.[22] Some of these who were Methodists soon began to hold class and prayer meetings. In 1779 there was a religious revival, and William Black was one of the converts.[23]

An impressionable and sensitive individual, Black had as a child been greatly moved by his mother's assiduous efforts to focus his attention on the state of his soul. On coming to America he took the lead in gay and frivolous amusements, but like Alline he was never entirely free of disgust for his mode of life. In consequence he was greatly moved by the prayers and exhortations of his fellow settlers and "determined never to rest until [he] found rest in Christ." At last, during a meeting at a certain Mr. Oxley's, "it pleased the Lord to reveal His free grace" to him and "a sweet peace and gladness were diffused through [his] soul." He "now longed vehemently that all should know the sweetness and preciousness of Christ," and began "to pray and exhort at almost every meeting." Though his "body trembled" and his "knees smote one against another," he found he "could speak with confidence, freedom, and tender affection."[24]

Driven as he was by this urgent concern for the salvation of his neighbours, it was natural that when he came of age in 1781 Black should embark on a preaching career. To his self-appointed task he brought a fine combination of determination, selflessness, moderation and good sense, and a firm conviction that Methodism was the finest form of evangelical Christianity. He lacked, however, that holy ruthlessness in dealing with others that was so conspicuous in the careers of Wesley and Asbury. This was a serious defect, for in no other place would this quality be so necessary as in the intractable mission field of Nova Scotia.

Although Black's initial preaching tours were remarkably successful, he was no doubt conscious of his need for assistance and recognition. This concern was heightened by Alline's skill in breaking up the Societies founded by Black and by the arrival of the Loyalists in 1783.[25] When Black hastened to Shelburne in June of that year to greet the new settlers he met Robert Barry, a Methodist from New York, who reinforced his determination to seek help from Wesley.[26] Wesley had already demonstrated a keen interest in Black's work but, being unable to send missionaries to Nova Scotia, he urged him to look to the American Societies for assistance.[27] Before this suggestion reached him Black had set off "to visit the States, intending to get some help from our brethren there."[28]

The contact that Black made in 1784 with Dr. Coke and his American brethren was the prelude to a period of confusion in the affairs of the Nova Scotia Methodists that persisted until the end of the century. Coke persuaded the Baltimore Conference to allow two able preachers, Freeborn Garrettson and James Cromwell, to go to Nova Scotia.[29] Probably it was assumed that as a result the Nova Scotia mission would become an integral part of the Methodist Episcopal Church. If this arrangement was to be successful, that church had to supply an adequate number of workers and maintain control over the new field as it would in Upper Canada. Time, however, was to show that these conditions would not obtain.

For the moment Black must have felt greatly encouraged by Coke's sympathy and the acquisition of two energetic itinerants. In October, 1786, the first quasi-official Conference, meeting in Halifax, stationed six ministers on four circuits: Halifax, Liverpool, Cumberland and Shelburne-Barrington, and introduced the Methodist system to Nova Scotia.[30] Unfortunately, the prospects of this new branch of the Methodist Connexion were soon obscured by the difficult problem of leadership and personnel.

Of the two itinerants sent to Nova Scotia by the American Conference, Freeborn Garrettson was the more outstanding. His missionary tours throughout Nova Scotia were marked by great acclaim. Not unnaturally, Coke and Wesley decided that he should be appointed superintendent of the work in British North America and the West Indies, but his initial reaction to this proposal was unfavourable.[31] Writing to Asbury at about the same period he remarked: "The Lord knows I am willing to do everything in my power for the furtherance of the gospel; but as to confining myself to Nova Scotia, or any part of the world, I could not; a good God does not require it of me."[32] Under pressure, however, Garrettson agreed to try it if the people in his charge proved willing to have him, but at the American Conference of 1787 the plan was suddenly dropped.[33] Clearly he felt unhappy about leaving a familiar field for one that was alien in many respects, an attitude that was reinforced by Asbury's unwillingness to lose so valuable an assistant.[34]

When Garrettson left Nova Scotia the natural thing would have been to appoint William Black as superintendent, but as he was not yet ordained this was not done. Instead Wesley sent out James Wray, a member of the British Conference, to supervise the work in Nova Scotia. Wray moved too quickly to impose the Methodist system on preachers and people, thereby creating dissension in the Societies,[35] but fortunately Black's ordination in 1789 made possible his removal to the West Indies.[36] From 1789 until 1800 Black acted as presiding elder of what was in effect the Nova Scotia District of the Methodist Episcopal Church.[37]

Curiously enough, the association of the Methodists in Nova Scotia with their American brethren was never as satisfactory as the contemporary arrangement in Upper Canada. Throughout the decade a number of American preachers volunteered to work in Nova Scotia, but in 1799 only two remained.[38] In that year the district comprised ten circuits for which only six preachers were available. Black had tried repeatedly to secure additional preachers from the United States, but he had found the preachers reluctant to volunteer and Bishop Asbury unwilling to let them go to a land from which they returned "not so humble and serious as when they went."[39] Faced with a constant shortage of able men at home, the bishop and his colleagues were not really interested in the distant and detached Nova Scotia mission. Probably the preachers too could see little merit in going from the United States, where Methodism was a flourishing and accepted form of Christianity, to a country in which they would be aliens, potentially if not actually suspect to the authorities and people.[40]

Despite the disheartening shortage of missionaries, in the years from 1786 to 1799 Methodism acquired a firm foothold in Nova Scotia and New Brunswick. During the same period its peculiar features began to emerge. As the preachers were perhaps the most influential factor in this process, one must turn to their meagre records for insight into it.

In this interval at least twenty men came to help Black in his momentous and sacrificial labours,[41] but the majority of these are shadowy figures who passed too quickly through the field to leave a significant imprint on it. Of those who stayed for some time, William Jessop and Daniel Fidler were of some importance. The former, the son of a prosperous New Jersey Quaker, joined the itinerant ranks in 1784 and was in Nova Scotia intermittently from 1788 until his death in 1795.[42] Evidently he was a man of intense piety and deep charitable instincts. Asbury declared that he had his "difficulties in speaking of a man so well known and so much beloved. He was always solemn; and few such holy, steady men have we found among us."[43] To his friend Fidler, Jessop wrote: "Dear bro. go on— Do all you can for poor souls droping into Hell." In Halifax he was "a Messenger of Peace to many souls" and it was thus "a trying dispensation" for them to part with him.[44]

For Black it was a sore trial to part with Daniel Fidler, who preached in Nova Scotia from 1792 until 1798. A native of New Jersey, he entered the itinerancy at eighteen and laboured on the American frontier until he heeded Black's call for volunteers.[45] Unlike Jessop he was a cheerful Christian, who after fifty years of ministerial vicissitudes could speak "of mercies past and present, and of his brightening prospect of a certain and glorious immortality."[46] His papers testify to the affection in which he was held by Black and his colleagues, a feeling that was justified by his uncomplaining attention to the needs of several extensive circuits.

Apart from such men as Fidler and Jessop, three men, John and James Mann and Duncan McColl, were, with Black, primarily responsible for the establishment and the quality of Methodism in these provinces. The brothers John and James Mann of New York had both played an active part in the Methodist life of that city before joining the Loyalist migration to Shelburne in 1783.[47] John Mann began to preach almost at once, and in 1786 James was enrolled by Garrettson. They were ordained along with William Black by the Philadelphia Conference of 1789 and from that date toiled unceasingly until 1812, after which time they preached as they were able.[48]

John Mann, who became the father of Methodism in Newport, was probably the less successful of the two. "After hearing Mr. Jessop so long," Simeon Perkins found "Mr. Mann's voice and Manner is Still more uncooth than usual."[49] Some years later one of the Halifax brethren reported that "Brother Jn° Mann is with us, Thundering away with all his might and [I] hope he will prove a special blessing at least to the Society."[50] To another, "he was not eloquent, yet he possessed a sound judgment, and clear understanding. He was well acquainted with all the Methodist doctrines and was a great lover and admirer of Mr. Wesley's writings."[51] In any event, borne down though he was by domestic cares and a meagre income, he served the Methodist cause in Newport "as long as he could sit on his horse."[52]

James Mann impressed himself much more forcibly on his contemporaries. His early life was said to have been marked by a lack of responsibility for which he made ample penitence in his years as an itinerant. A large dark man who dressed with great care, he had a stern mien, as befitted the rectitude of his behaviour. His preaching, especially in later years, was "chaste, edifying and usually unimpassioned." He was "exceedingly prudent and circumspect in all his associations with saints and sinners," yet "even the ungodly would fight for him." His devotion to the Methodist cause was of the highest order, being marked by the most arduous travels over the roads and seas of Nova Scotia and New Brunswick. Christmas Day, 1820, the last day of his life, was the occasion of his final sermon, which he gave after a hard ride through the snow, a fitting end to a difficult ministry.[53]

Ten years later Duncan McColl, the third member of the little band who worked so faithfully with Black, preached his last sermon and made his final diary entry at St. Stephen, the scene of the greater part of his career.[54] A Scot who had been raised in the Episcopal Church, McColl came to America as an army pay-sergeant. While in the army he began to have qualms of conscience by which his early religious impressions were revived. Gradually he came to realize that salvation depended on faith, but it was only after intense inner conflict that " his chains fell off" and "his heart was free." "This peace of soul," he continued, "remained with me. . . . Although I had some temptations God did not leave me."[55]

Settling in St. Stephen in 1785 he began to preach with great success. On one occasion his "mind was carried up from the world and a power came down like an earthquake: some fell on their faces. . . . Others adored the Lord."[56] Threatened by the magistrates as an unlicensed preacher he laid his "case before the Lord. And the prophecies of Jeremiah XX, 8, 11, came with such force to my soul as to remove all scruple."[57] He then gathered his people into a Methodist Society and in 1790 built a church for them in St. Stephen. Two years later he placed himself under Black's direction, but he was not ordained until 1795.[58] From then until 1826 he served Methodism unremittingly but independently, confining his ministry largely to southwestern New Brunswick. At his death in 1830, "many of his converts thoughtfully walked in the long procession which followed his body to the grave."[59]

Although the most striking feature of this group of early itinerants was the individuality of its members, it had some important common attributes. Most of its members were apparently men of some education and social status. The leading figures were either from the United Kingdom or Loyalists with Anglican sympathies. In most cases they were steady, cautious men, but they were seemingly not very susceptible to discipline. Men such as Jessop slipped back and forth between the United States and Nova Scotia; others such as John Mann and McColl settled in specific areas from which they could not be dislodged. It is likely that they were rather more formal in their religious practice than their American brethren, but in their own way they were as fervent exponents of Methodism as any.[60]

Whatever was distinctive about Nova Scotia Methodism reflected the attitudes of this faithful band of men, for before 1800 the organization of this field was rudimentary. From 1786 onward, unofficial conferences met regularly to station the preachers, but these were often sparsely attended and their decisions were not always heeded.[61] In fact, as each of the leading preachers had an established base of operations, the itinerancy did not attain the flexibility customary in England and America.[62] As presiding elder, Black strove energetically but with limited success to overcome this defect and to make the most effective use of the inadequate supply of preachers.

By 1800 Black and his brethren had established the Methodist cause in a number of places: Halifax, Liverpool, Shelburne, Windsor, Annapolis, Cumberland, Saint John and St. Stephen. These were the centres of large circuits. The Windsor circuit, for example, included Horton, Cornwallis, Falmouth, Windsor and Newport; the Cumberland stretched for forty miles from the Nappan to the Petitcodiac rivers; there were Societies in Sheffield and Fredericton that were nominally part of the Saint John circuit.[63] In most of these places churches had been built, but in all there were only eight hundred and fifty members with some three thousand adherents. Of these less than two hundred were in New Brunswick, while Prince Edward Island had disappeared from the records.[64] The fact that Methodism was spread so thin over the scattered settlements of the two mainland provinces is to be accounted for not only by the scarcity of preachers, but by the powerful attraction of the Newlight churches and the general social instability of the area.

Although this small Methodist community was the object of unfriendly attention from Loyalist magistrates and some of the Anglican clergy led by Bishop Inglis, it was neither socially, religiously nor politically extreme.[65] It counted among its most faithful supporters such prominent figures as Alexander and Joseph Anderson of Halifax, Robert Barry of Shelburne, and Joshua Newton and Simeon Perkins of Liverpool, although the majority of its members were humbler folk.[66] That many Methodists were friendly towards the Church of England was made evident by their acceptance of the services of Thomas Twining, the missionary at Cornwallis.[67] On the other hand the Methodists of Halifax decided in 1792 to hold their services during "Church" hours, a move that was rightly regarded as a declaration of independence on their part.[68] In fact, the Methodist Societies were drawn from a broad section of the population and were more concerned with their own spiritual needs than with criticism or defence of other groups.

If men such as James Mann and McColl were sober rather than enthusiastic preachers, the spirit of Methodism in the Maritime Provinces was none the less fervently evangelical. Services were held anywhere, in barns, homes and schools, and were often marked by great outpourings of the spirit. On Monday, June 2, 1783, Black preached near Liverpool: "The power of the Lord was eminently present. . . . I think there were about fourteen crying out in great anguish of soul; while others were shouting for joy. Such affecting heart-piercing cries as were uttered by one, my ears never heard."[69] In 1795 Colonel Perkins noted: "At evening Mr. Frank Newton Preaches at his Brother's. A Lively time among the people after Meeting. Two that had professed to be converted Some time ago, were in a wonderful extisay. . . . Hetty Draper that Lives in my Family was in great distress & Seemed in a Manner to Swoon & remained in that State a long time."[70]

But the object of the preachers was always greater than the behaviour of their hearers might attest. Mindful of the alleged antinomian tendencies of their Newlight brethren, they sought to achieve the transformation of the whole man. Their faces were set "against all such diversions as cannot be used in the name of the Lord Jesus; such as gambling, dancing, etc."[71] Beyond that, as Black so finely expressed it: "Let us endeavour to draw forth their expectations of a present salvation. Let us preach up and press after entire holiness. We shall never be right while God is not in possession of the whole heart."[72]

So intent were the preachers on the spiritual welfare of their followers that the secular world had almost no significance for them. They could see no reason for the mingling of secular and religious considerations in the work of the church. "What," asked Black "have the ministers of Christ to do with the administration of civil government? Christ's kingdom is not of this world. We are neither magistrates nor legislators."[73] Nevertheless their influence was thrown behind constituted authority. Whatever may have been the views of the American missionaries, there is no evidence that the leading preachers were anything but loyal in the Loyalist sense. It was "a point of some consequence" to John Mann, for example, that the missionaries be "sound with respect to their attachment to our good King and Happy Constitution."[74] It should come as no surprise, therefore, to learn that in contrast to the Newlights the Methodists were much "esteemed by those in authority for their quiet and orderly lives, good morals and strict loyalty."[75]

At the turn of the century, indeed, Methodism had become a quiet but modestly influential force in the life of Nova Scotia and New Brunswick. Although its adherents were not numerous and its organization was not remarkable, it had become acclimatized to these new provincial societies. Native leadership had been secured and the Methodist outlook had been adapted in a way that rendered it acceptable to a considerable section of the community. Seemingly, though, this branch of the Connexion lacked that dynamic spirit of initiative which would have enabled it to deal in a masterly fashion with the spiritual and moral challenge presented to it by this part of British North America.

2

While Black and his brethren were earnestly trying to disseminate the Methodist gospel in the eastern provinces, the bounds of the Methodist Connexion were being extended over the distant province that was in 1791 to become Upper Canada.[76] In 1789, the year of Black's ordination, William Losee was admitted on trial for the Methodist Episcopal ministry.[77] His presiding elder was Freeborn Garrettson, lately returned from his arduous toils in Nova Scotia and now engaged in the equally difficult task of establishing new circuits in the Lake Champlain region.[78] At Losee's request Garrettson permitted him to visit Upper Canada in the winter of 1790. He appears to have travelled along the St. Lawrence from the St. Regis to the Bay of Quinté, preaching with such success that he was asked to petition the New York Conference for a regular missionary.[79] Losee's reappearance in Upper Canada in 1791 with the approval of that Conference marked the acceptance of the province as a mission by the Methodist Episcopal Church.[80]

Upper Canada differed and would continue to differ in several respects from Nova Scotia and New Brunswick. These differences, in combination with a somewhat different type of Methodist leadership, facilitated the growth of a Methodist community whose qualities were by no means identical with those of the Nova Scotia District.

Upper Canada in 1791 was a vast and impressive wilderness with a population of ten thousand people, most of whom were concentrated along the upper St. Lawrence and in the vicinity of the Bay of Quinté, Niagara, and Detroit.[81] Twenty-one years later, when the outbreak of war with the United States brought a crisis in the life of the province, there were nearly one hundred thousand inhabitants, the majority of whom had come to Upper Canada as part of the great westward movement of the American people. In 1812 eight out of every ten Upper Canadians were of American origin, and of these not more than one quarter were Loyalists or their children.[82] Most of the new arrivals were settled in the western region, especially in the Niagara Peninsula, the Lake Erie townships and the Thames Valley.[83] Yet, in 1812 as in 1791, Upper Canada consisted really of a string of widely separated settlements along the international boundary.

This new provincial society, primitive and immature, presented both opportunities for and obstacles to the effective preaching of Methodist doctrine. Throughout this period Upper Canada was a society on the move, with little to spare in energy or resources for other tasks than the establishment of a basis for living in the all-encompassing forest. It was, too, a region with no significant urban areas and almost no institutions.[84] The people of Upper Canada had, in concert with the imperial authorities, to create for themselves out of nothing a viable social and political framework.[85] Inevitably this was a slow process, and for some time the individual settler was left largely isolated, uneducated and uncivilized.

The Loyalist migration included few who had been socially or professionally prominent in the old colonies.[86] The provincial élite remained distinctly minute until it was reinforced by some New Brunswick Loyalists and by such men as John Strachan from the United Kingdom.[87] The bulk of the Loyalist and post-Loyalist settlers were very ordinary folk—artisans, tradesmen and farmers—a cross-section of the people who had been moving out from the seaboard colonies for some time. Certainly it cannot be said that there was among them anything comparable to the sense of continuity and cohesion that marked the New England migration to Nova Scotia.

Nevertheless, there was almost from the outset a latent clash of ideals within the poorly integrated Upper Canadian settlements. Whether the settler was a Loyalist or a post-Loyalist he came from an area and a social level where a free society was coming increasingly to be preferred to a privileged one. He was likely, therefore, to be sympathetic to ideas of self-government and of social and religious equality. If he were a Loyalist, however, especially if he had been socially prominent before the Revolution, he had to take another factor into account. He was committed to rejection of the Revolution and its consequences and to fervent or professedly fervent loyalty to the British Crown.[88]

Unfortunately, but not surprisingly, this conflict between the Loyalist and the North American outlook that was often present in the mind of the individual Loyalist was sharpened by the actions of the British government and its representatives. The political institutions given to Upper Canada were intended to provide representative government and to make possible the establishment of a stratified social order.[89] They were given concrete form by Governor Simcoe, who was enthusiastically devoted to monarchy, aristocracy and the established church, and equally antagonistic to democratic and republican principles. Simcoe's zeal stimulated the prejudices of the ardent Loyalists and their English supporters. At the same time, his willingness to countenance large scale immigration from the United States resulted in the reinforcement of the cause to which he was most opposed.[90]

In religion, as in matters social and political, Upper Canada began with a rather chequered heritage. Apparently the Loyalist and post-Loyalist settlers were drawn from a variety of religious traditions.[91] As members of a society on the move they had few strong associations, but they shared the conviction that some form of Christianity was essential. They were, therefore, potentially susceptible to any group who were prepared to present the Christian faith vigorously, and in a form that would meet their religious needs and deliver them from the isolation imposed by the forest. But, as in the political sphere, someone else knew what was good for them. The British government, its representatives, and the Anglican leaders in Quebec designed to impose the Church of England on Upper Canada so that it might serve the same religous and social ends as in England.[92] For some time establishment was more a threat than a reality, but so long as it was mooted non-Anglican forms of religion, apart from the Church of Scotland, were neither politically nor socially acceptable in the province.[93]

The Methodist circuit-riders who came to Upper Canada were, as in Nova Scotia, often too unworldly to appreciate the complexity of the context within which they worked, but it is clear now that it contained favourable and unfavourable elements. Their simple, evangelical faith was certain to have a strong appeal, an appeal uninhibited in Upper Canada by the Congregationalist and Newlight tradition that was so effective in slowing Methodist expansion in the Maritime Provinces. As Americans, they were in a strong position when speaking to American immigrants. They were highly suspect, however, to those who stood for either the Loyalist or the imperial tradition. In their case, too, the suspicion was not balanced, as it was in part in Nova Scotia, by the presence of men comparable to Black and Mann, or by the friendliness of some influential figures, including the governors themselves. Above all, to reach the isolated and steadily growing settlements of Upper Canada would require a large number of men willing to accept poverty and toil as their lot. If the Methodist Episcopal Church should fail to develop a real interest in its Upper Canadian mission, that mission was not likely to grow significantly.

Fortunately for the future of Methodism in this province, the American Methodists never regarded their work here in the same dubious light as their contribution to the cause in the Maritime Provinces.[94] The circuits in Canada became a separate district within the New York Conference in 1794, and in 1810 the Upper Canada District was incorporated within the newly organized Genesee Conference.[95] By this means the work in Upper Canada was subjected to the same administrative arrangements as in other parts of the church. Through the channel thus dug there flowed a steady stream of volunteer itinerants who were selected and supervised in the same manner as all the preachers in the Methodist Episcopal fold.[96] By this means, the Methodist Societies in Upper Canada acquired at an early date a sense of order and coherence, and an awareness of participation in the growth of a great religious body.

In the years from 1790 to 1812 seventy-six missionaries were sent to Canada. Of these not more than seven were born here, the remainder being drawn largely from Connecticut, New Jersey and New York, those states which were providing settlers for the American northwest and Canada.[97] Most of them were of humble social background and few if any had been extensively educated. Their manners and their interests were, no doubt, those of the social level from which they came, a circumstance that enabled them to deal effectively with those whom they sought to reach.

It would be incorrect, however, to consider these men as a homogeneous group. Some of those who stayed long enough to make their mark in Upper Canada stood out above the rest. The first missionary, William Losee, who probably had Loyalist sympathies, was a singularly energetic traveller and preacher. His fervent sermons, marked by frequent injunctions to the Lord to smite the sinners, greatly endeared him to the inhabitants of the Cataraqui circuit.[98] Regrettably, after two years of thunderous activity Losee was smitten by mental illness and was obliged to cease preaching. His first colleague, Darius Dunham, a former physician from New York, was in charge of the Canadian mission from 1792 to 1798.[99] Dunham was a man of outspoken opinions and some administrative ability. A disciplinarian rather than a preacher, he became notorious for his dislike of slovenly living and his firm resistance to opposition.

After he left the itinerancy in 1800, he continued as a local preacher for the rest of his life.[100]

Among Dunham's colleagues, Calvin Wooster, who began his ministry as a sanctified person, was an unusually fervent preacher. He was remembered by the people as "a man of mighty prayer and faith," whose voice was often heard "in the night season when, rising from his bed while others slept," he would engage "in earnest prayer for the salvation of souls." His appeals were so "bold and pointed," especially "to the wicked, that few of these could stand before him—they would either flee from the house, or, smitten with conviction, fall down and cry aloud for mercy."[101] While thus employed Wooster contracted consumption, and in the last part of his life he had to use an interpreter to transmit his whispered sermons to the people.[102] His selfless life stood in marked contrast to that of Samuel Coate, also a man of frequent prayer but sufficiently vain to dress his hair every night. A polished orator, he "swept like a meteor over the land and spellbound the astonished gaze of the wondering new settlers.... He was the heaven-anointed and successful instrument of the conversion of hundreds."[103]

Among those who came for longer periods, Nathan Bangs, Henry Ryan and William Case stood out above the rest. Bangs, an Anglican from New England, became a Methodist convert while working as a surveyor near Niagara. His conversion was preceded by a period of spiritual indifference followed by a long struggle with himself. When he first became acquainted with Methodism, he poked fun at it, but at this point, he assures us: "My conscience ... awoke; all the sins of my life seemed vividly brought to my recollection ... I felt as if I should sink into perdition. For the first time in my life I began to call upon God."[104] Subsequently he felt "such awful apprehensions of God's just displeasure" that he wished "for annihilation." Thus, when a Methodist preacher spoke to him "his words came like a dagger to [his] heart." "I could make no reply, but turned from him, begging him to pray for me." In due time, he continues: "The Spirit of God bore witness with mine that I was adopted into the family of His people."[105] Reluctantly and hesitantly he agreed to enter the itinerant ranks, becoming one of the first preachers to be recruited in Upper Canada. As the evangelist of the Thames valley, then the most remote and primitive area in the province, he testified to the depth and the quality of his faith.[106]

Henry Ryan, who played a more powerful rôle than Bangs in early Canadian Methodism, was a man of far different character. Little is known of his career before he came to Canada in 1805. A large and exceptionally energetic man, he had probably been a professional boxer before his conversion, a supposition borne out by the roughness of his actions. Nevertheless he was "a very pious man, a man of great love for the cause of Christ and great zeal in his work as a minister.... His favourite exhortation [was] 'Drive on, brother! Drive on! Drive the devil out of the country! Drive him into the lake and drown him!' "[107] To this task he brought considerable organizing ability, the instinct of the disciplinarian and a hearty manner that led others to overlook his deficiencies. Within five years he became presiding elder of Upper Canada, a post which he filled with success during a troubled era.[108]

To William Case, who came to Upper Canada with Ryan, Canadian Methodism owes much. Born in Swansea, Massachusetts, in 1780, Case grew up in moderately prosperous circumstances and apparently secured a good primary education.[109] Converted in 1803, he was admitted on trial in 1805 and was appointed to the Bay of Quinté circuit.[110] A handsome, amiable youth with some musical ability, Case quickly achieved popularity. Yet he was a reticent man, about whom even his biographer seemed hesitant to speak.

The brief journal that Case kept during his second tour in Canada reveals a humble, sensitive, conscientious and rather credulous personality. When he was asked to come again to this province he agreed unwillingly because of his fear of war and his desire not to leave his friends. He was also disturbed by feelings of spiritual inadequacy that were occasionally accompanied by the conviction that he was becoming puffed up with his success as a preacher. Despite these alternations of feeling, he was a faithful itinerant. In Albany, for example, he had an impulse to preach to the dock workers, selecting as his text: "Why will ye die?"[111] In York, with a few hours to spare, he thought of applying for permission to preach to the soldiers, but was fortunate in securing congregations at one and five o'clock.[112] These were but two of the four hundred sermons he gave in one year, many of which were marked by urgent appeals "to flee from the wrath to come."[113] In the midst of these labours he found time to read and to ruminate on his portentous dreams.[114] But it is unlikely that to his people he appeared in any other guise than that of a passionate, prayerful missionary who upheld the Methodist system in a kindly but firm fashion.

Such were some of the men who first gave coherence to the Methodist cause in Upper Canada. Of humble background and attainments, they were at the same time men whose intense conviction that they had a message of vital interest gave them a sense of assurance and of mission through which they overcame these deficiencies. They presented their message with all the simplicity, vigour, and frequency of which they were humanly capable, undeterred by the traditions or the ideals of others.

In presenting the gospel to the people of Upper Canada, these early preachers, like their brethren in Nova Scotia, must have uttered much jargon. Probably, indeed, they often mistook exhortation for argument. Nevertheless, their teaching had at least two themes, which were not unfaithful to the Methodist tradition:

> The doctrine more especially urged upon believers was that of *sanctification, or holiness of heart and life,*—a complete surrender ... to the service of God,—and this was pressed upon them as their *present* privilege, depending for its accomplishment now on the faithfulness of God who had promised to do it. It was this *baptism of the Holy Ghost* which fired and filled the hearts of God's ministers at that time.

The unconverted were told of "the necessity of immediate and instantaneous conversion or a present justification by faith." They were warned "in the most faithful and affectionate manner of the imminent danger of delaying one moment to repent of their sins and surrender their hearts to God." In "pointed language" they were reminded of "the past judgments of God against impenitent sinners" and were urged "with the most affectionate and pathetic strain of eloquence to accept of pardon and salvation without a moment's delay."[115]

To many, no doubt, the process of justification and sanctification consisted simply of a series of emotional upheavals. It is clear, however, that despite their emphasis on the working of the spirit, the preachers did not neglect the disciplinary side of Methodism. Through the class meeting they upheld a high standard of behaviour. William Case has recorded his participation in a trial for intoxication. On other occasions he stopped a local feud, inculcated a reverent attitude at services, and urged charity upon his flock, actions which were apparently characteristic of his brethren.[116]

Apart from this stress on personal morality, there is no indication that the itinerants attempted to relate their faith to the life of the settlements as a whole. As Americans, they may in many cases have been unsympathetic to the local system of government, but they were certainly not vocal in their opposition. Case's conviction that political disputes were undesirable was symptomatic of the real attitude of the preachers.[117] Their outlook was essentially unworldly; their primary concern was the preparation of the soul for eternity. They sought to make each man realize, as one layman put it: "I am bound for Heaven, although I meet with some conflicts which is nothing strange, I dispair ever getting read of trials & afflictions till I am sheltered in that house out of sight to the mortal eye."[118] In that perspective, secular issues took a secondary place, especially at a time when the community was too immature to have a keen interest in other matters than survival.

To bring their message to as many as possible, the American missionaries relied upon the same means that had proven so effective in England and America. Under the firm hand of the Conference and the presiding elders, the itinerant system quickly took shape in Upper Canada, complete with class leaders, exhorters and local preachers. The business of all these men, with the exception of the class leaders, was to hold or to assist in simple services as frequently as possible. Special attention was paid to the quarterly meeting and the camp meeting, occasions when unusually large numbers could be gathered for preaching and the administration of the sacraments. Often it could be said with Bangs: "Our Quarter M. is over and we had the shouts of a King in the Camp. The Glory of our God rested upon the Tabernacle. Now and then a sinner gets converted, about 30 have turned out for volunteers for Jesus here lately."[119]

On the whole the "volunteers" were most effectively secured in the camp meeting, of which the first in Upper Canada was held by Case and Ryan at Hay Bay in 1805. Two hundred and fifty people gathered in September for this great event, which began with "singing, prayer and a short sermon on the text: Brethren, pray!" After an intermission of about twenty minutes another sermon was delivered on "Christ, our wisdom, righteousness, sanctification and redemption." Later "a prayer meeting was held and towards its close the power of God descended on the assembly and songs of victory and praise resounded through the forest." The next day, Bangs tells us, "I felt an unusual sense of the divine presence and I thought I could see a cloud of divine glory resting upon the congregation." He and the other preachers then went down among the crowd, gathered the weeping sinners "in little groups" and "exhorted God's people to join in prayer for them and not to leave them until he should save their souls. O what a scene of tears and prayer was this!" On Sunday "the Lord's supper was administered to multitudes." He concludes: "I will not attempt to describe the parting scene for it was indescribable.... [The people] wept, prayed, sang, shouted aloud and had at last to break away from one another as by force. As the hosts marched off in different directions the songs of victory rolled along the highways."[120]

The ceaseless activities of the circuit preachers between 1790 and 1812 resulted in a considerable victory for Methodism in Upper Canada. First Losee and Dunham organized two enormous circuits, the Cataraqui and the Oswegatchie, which included the whole region from the Bay of Quinté to the border of Lower Canada.[121] To these the Niagara circuit was added in 1795.[122] From these three bases the lines of Methodist influence were gradually extended throughout the settlements. In 1810 there were ten circuits in Upper Canada: three along the St. Lawrence, three along Lake Ontario, three in the Niagara Peninsula and one around Detroit—an arrangement that roughly reflected the distribution of population in the province.[123] Within these circuits there were twenty-six hundred members, but it may be supposed that thousands more had at least been exposed to Methodist teaching.[124]

This scattered band of converts gathered by the unending labour of the itinerants doubtless consisted largely of ordinary folk, drawn, it may be supposed, from the ranks of the Loyalist and post-Loyalist settlers.[125] In their willingness to support their preachers and to erect chapels they gave evidence of a sense of responsibility for the promotion of Methodism in Upper Canada. As yet, however, they had not thrown up a native leadership in the itinerancy itself, being content rather to rely upon the assistance of their brethren in the United States. That they were willing to do so indicates that they felt no strong sense of conflict between their religious and political allegiance.

For them, as for their spiritual guides, worldly matters in the sense of a broad concern for the shape of society were secondary. Apart from the sheer problem of existence, their eyes were fastened not on this world but on the next. In their simple fashion they really believed that the experience of conversion and sanctification could open the road to heaven and that failure to live in a sober and upright fashion would block that road with equal facility. Hence they gloried in their somewhat tempestuous services and were in general markedly moral in their behaviour. To the superior their attitude smacked of the "most deplorable fanaticism."[126] Nevertheless, in their profound concern for the individual soul, in the egalitarianism of their meetings and in their absorption in moral issues they were laying the foundations of a more constructive outlook on the secular world that would be enlarged by changing conditions and different leadership.

3

Twenty years of missionary activity in the Maritime Provinces and Upper Canada had resulted in the establishment of two new branches of the Methodist Connexion, of which the latter seemed to be the more flourishing. In Upper Canada the Methodist system of government was perhaps more firmly grounded than in the east, although its organization was more clearly dependent than its Maritime counterpart. Social and religious pressures inhibiting the propagation of the Methodist gospel had been at least partially overcome, although in contrasting ways in the two areas. The Methodists of the eastern provinces had acquired a broad base of social acceptance, whereas in Upper Canada Methodism was becoming the characteristic creed of the common man. In the quality of their spiritual outlook, moreover, subtle differences had begun to emerge. Although for both groups one's destiny in the next world was the ultimate consideration, the necessity of salvation was on the whole urged more enthusiastically by the Upper Canadian preachers than by Black and his associates. Similarly the latter, despite their unworldliness, were more willing to uphold the existing political order than were their brethren in Upper Canada. At the outset it was easier for the Upper Canadian itinerants, most of whom were citizens of another state, to affirm that the gospel is not of this world and that political considerations are irrelevant to its spread. Ultimately, however, it would be more difficult to maintain this stand in Upper Canada than in the eastern provinces.

For the moment neither group was greatly aware of the implications of its position. The most important issue in the Maritime Provinces was the survival of the Connexion, and in Upper Canada its extension in a steadily expanding society. But the steps taken to achieve these ends, in conjunction with altered circumstances, would soon change the course of Methodist history in both regions and would lead each body to follow a distinctive path.

REFERENCES TO CHAPTER TWO

1. For details of this settlement see T. W. Smith, *History of the Methodist Church . . . of Eastern British America . . .* (Halifax, 1877), I, 83-88. See also M. Campbell, "English Emigration on the Eve of the American Revolution," *American Historical Review,* LXI (1955), 9-20. For the revival see *The Life of Mr. William Black, Written by Himself* in T. Jackson, *The Lives of Early Methodist Preachers,* V, 244.
2. Cited in Jackson, *op. cit.,* 258-262; M. Richey, A *Memoir of the Late Rev. William Black* (Halifax, 1839), 47.

3. Cited in Jackson, *op. cit.*, 283-284.
4. *Ibid.*, 284; Asbury, *Journal*, I, 487; A. Stevens, *History of the Methodist Episcopal Church in the United States of America*, II, 378-379.
5. E. McInnis, *Canada* (New York, 1959), 147; M. L. Hansen and J. B. Brebner, *The Mingling of the Canadian and American Peoples* (New York, 1940), 29-35.
6. J. B. Brebner, *The Neutral Yankees of Nova Scotia* (New York, 1937), chapter 7.
7. *Ibid.*, 119, 110.
8. M. L. Hansen and J. B. Brebner, *op. cit.*, 54-55.
9. E. C. Wright, *The Loyalists of New Brunswick* (Fredericton, 1955), 167; C. Martin, *Foundations of Canadian Nationhood* (Toronto, 1955), 84.
10. Wright, *op. cit.*, 126.
11. H. H. Walsh, *The Christian Church In Canada* (Toronto, 1956), 90-91, 102-108. In New Brunswick, the Church was highly favoured but was not legally established. J. Hannay, *History of New Brunswick* (Saint John, 1909), I, 169.
12. M. W. Armstrong, *The Great Awakening in Nova Scotia* (Hartford, 1948), 39-59.
13. H. Alline, *The Life and Journal of the Rev. Mr. Henry Alline* (Boston, 1806), 15.
14. *Ibid.*, 10.
15. *Ibid.*, 32-35.
16. *Ibid.*, 36.
17. Armstrong, *op. cit.*, 65, 86.
18. For an objective analysis of his teaching, see *ibid.*, 93-107.
19. Cited in Jackson, *op. cit.*, 271.
20. Armstrong, *op. cit.*, 65-85, 119-138.
21. Cited in Jackson, *op. cit.*, 242; Richey, *op. cit.*, 5, 7; Smith, *op. cit.*, II, 241. He was most anxious to enter Wesley's Kingswood School.
22. Cited in Jackson, *op. cit.*, 243, 244.
23. *Ibid.*, 244-251.
24. *Ibid.*, 247; 249-250; 258.
25. *Ibid.*, 266.
26. *Ibid.*, 275-276; Smith, *op. cit.*, I, 135-137, 144.
27. Black began to correspond with Wesley in 1781. The latter held out hope of assistance in February, 1783, but in October, 1784, he suggested that Black look to the American societies for help. Wesley's *Letters*, VII, 168-169, 244.
28. Cited in Jackson, *op. cit.*, 283.
29. N. Bangs, *The Life of the Rev. Freeborn Garrettson* (New York, 1838), 150; S. Drew, *The Life of the Rev. Thomas Coke* (New York, 1818), 119.
30. Richey, *op. cit.*, 163-164; Smith, *op. cit.*, I, 180-181.
31. Bangs, *op. cit.*, 174.
32. *Ibid.*, 178.

33. *Ibid.*, 184.
34. W. C. Barclay, *Early American Methodism*, I, 171.
35. G. G. Findlay and W. W. Holdsworth, *The History of the Wesleyan Methodist Missionary Society* (London, 1921), I, 295-296; Wesley's *Letters*, VIII, 68-69.
36. Richey, *op. cit.*, 243, 253-254. Wray left for St. Vincent in 1791. Smith, *op. cit.*, I, 214.
37. Black is first listed as a presiding elder in the American Minutes of 1791. *Minutes of the Methodist Conferences Annually Held in America* . . . (New York, 1813), I, 105. The Societies in Nova Scotia do not appear to have been formally annexed to the Methodist Episcopal Church, a situation whose origin probably lay in Coke's ambiguous relations with that church. Certainly he assumed that the work in Nova Scotia ought to be supervised by the American Conference. See Mount Allison University Library, Black Papers, T. Coke to W. Black, September 7, 1792; Barclay, *op. cit.*, 172-173. Black was out of office for a brief period, December, 1792, to April, 1793, when he was appointed to the West Indies. Richey, *op. cit.*, 291-297. Fidler Papers, microfilm copy. Black to Fidler, July 2, 1793. The original letters are in Drew University Library.
38. Between 1784 and 1799 thirteen preachers came from the United States to Nova Scotia.
39. For example, at the General Conference of 1796 some preachers professed fear of French privateers off Nova Scotia. The Bishop refused to let two volunteers return with Black. Fidler Papers, Black to Fidler, December 26, 1796; September 23, 1795.
40. Barclay, *op. cit.*, I, 174-175.
41. This figure is based on all the available records.
42. Smith, *op. cit.*, I, 196-197, 217, 275, 304, 310.
43. *Ibid.*, 311.
44. Fidler Papers, Jessop to Fidler, January 3, 1793; Alexander Anderson to Fidler, March 20, 1793.
45. Smith, *op. cit.*, I, 271-272. For his appointment to Nova Scotia see Fidler Papers, Black to the Methodist Society in Liverpool, November 15, 1792. Black's last plea that he remain is dated August 31, 1798.
46. Smith, *op. cit.*, I, 330.
47. On John Mann see the *Methodist Magazine* (U.S.A.), II (1819), 13-18. On James see Smith, *op. cit.*, I, 170-173.
48. Smith, *op. cit.*, I, 208; Simeon Perkins, *The Diary of Simeon Perkins 1780-1789*, ed. D. C. Harvey (Toronto, 1958), 480-481. Perkins reports having seen John Mann's certificate of ordination. Their superannuation is noted in *Records of the Wesleyan Methodist Missionary Society,* microfilm copy. Reel 1, Black to the Missionary Committee, June 8, 1812. (The original manuscripts are in the Society's headquarters, London, England.) This source will be cited as *W. R.*

49. Perkins, *op. cit.*, 436.
50. Fidler Papers, Joseph Anderson to Fidler, October 19, 1796.
51. *Methodist Magazine* (U.S.A.), II (1819), 18.
52. *Ibid.*, 17.
53. Smith, *op. cit.*, I, 107-108, 106. For examples of his practical yet friendly letters see the Fidler Papers.
54. *Ibid.*, II, 246-247.
55. *British North American Wesleyan Methodist Magazine*, I (1841), 293.
56. *Ibid.*, 299.
57. *Ibid.*, 300.
58. *Ibid.*, 302, 332, 415.
59. Smith, *op. cit.*, II, 247.
60. See McColl in *B.N.A. Wesleyan Methodist Magazine,* I (1841), 458. "I do not encourage a noise or crying out in meetings, yet in cases where convictions are very strong and terror great it is difficult to restrain it."
61. Black's letters in the Fidler Papers provide a record of some conference sessions.
62. Black generally resided in Halifax; John Mann was usually at Newport; James Mann favoured Liverpool and Shelburne; McColl lived in St. Stephen.
63. The best summary is found in Smith, *op. cit.*, I, 332-342.
64. *Ibid.*, I, 343, 341.
65. See McColl's account of his difficulties in Saint John. *British North American Wesleyan Methodist Magazine,* I (1841), 335-336; S. D. Clark, *Church and Sect in Canada* (Toronto, 1948), 66.
66. Joseph Anderson was a Halifax merchant; his brother Alexander was an official of the naval yard. Joshua Newton was the customs collector at Liverpool, Simeon Perkins its most prominent citizen.
67. *W.R.*, Reel 1, Black to the Committee, October 10, 1804. It was the Loyalist element that favoured the Church. See Smith, *op. cit.*, I, 349. Black, though friendly to the Church, was very willing to defend the principle of religious equality. Richey, *op. cit.*, 299.
68. Smith, *op. cit.*, I, 350. It may be that this step was taken in the light of the agitation in the English Conference regarding its relationship with the Church of England. Separation from the Church took place in 1795. Townsend *et al., A New History of Methodism,* I, 384-386.
69. Richey, *op. cit.*, 103.
70. Public Archives of Canada, The Diary of Simeon Perkins. Typescript. January 17, 1795.
71. *British North American Wesleyan Methodist Magazine,* I (1841), 458.
72. Fidler Papers, Black to Fidler, September 14, 1796.
73. Richey, *op. cit.*, 310.
74. *W.R.*, Reel 1, John Mann to the Missionary Committee, September 18, 1804.

75. *Ibid.*, Reel 1, Black to the Committee, September 17, 1804. He added that Governor Wentworth proposed to grant land to him and the Methodists in Halifax. He was also cordially received by Governor Fanning of Prince Edward Island. Richey, *op. cit.*, 305-306.
76. The old province of Quebec was divided by an order-in-council, August 24, 1791. W. P. M. Kennedy, *Documents of the Canadian Constitution* (Toronto, 1918), 207.
77. *Minutes of the Annual Conferences*. . . I, 80.
78. Bangs, *op. cit.*, 155.
79. G. F. Playter, *The History of Methodism in Canada* (Toronto, 1862), 21, 22-23. There were already Methodist classes in Augusta and Adolphustown. J. Carroll, *Case and His Cotemporaries* (Toronto, 1867), I, 6.
80. There is no record of his appointment by the New York Conference of 1790. For his work see Playter, *op. cit.*, 23-25. In 1791 he was appointed to Kingston. *Minutes of the Annual Conferences*. . . I, 105.
81. J. J. Talman, ed., *Loyalist Narratives from Upper Canada* (Toronto, 1946), lix; Hansen and Brebner, *op. cit.*, 59-64.
82. *Ibid.*, 90. F. Landon suggests a figure of 75,000. *Western Ontario and the American Frontier* (Toronto, 1941), 1. The land policy of Upper Canada and perhaps Loyalism were factors in bringing American settlers to this province. Hansen and Brebner, *op. cit.*, 78-82.
83. *Ibid.*, 85-90.
84. In 1815 Kingston had a population of 2,800; York had fewer than a thousand inhabitants.
85. In this respect Upper Canada and New Brunswick were much alike.
86. Talman, *op. cit.*, xxiii. There were only two clergymen in the group.
87. The Ryersons and the Robinsons came from New Brunswick to Upper Canada at the end of the century.
88. For a discussion of this question see Talman, *op. cit.*, xxiii-xxvii.
89. W. P. M. Kennedy, *The Constitution of Canada* (Toronto, 1922), 85.
90. A. R. M. Lower, *Colony To Nation* (Toronto, 1946), 162-163.
91. This is a matter about which little is known. Some of the Loyalists were Methodist Palatines. Others probably had a Lutheran background. There were, in addition, Quakers, Anglicans and Presbyterians. Evidently there were no strong Congregationalist or Anglican groups as in Nova Scotia and New Brunswick.
92. T. R. Millman, *Jacob Mountain, First Lord Bishop of Quebec* (Toronto, 1947), chapters 2 and 3.
93. For example, the marriage legislation was designed to exclude Methodists and other dissenters.

94. At any rate no evidence has appeared to suggest that the Canadian work was regarded as a drag on operations in the United States.
95. *Minutes of the Annual Conferences. . .* I, 145, 485.
96. Bishop Asbury did not visit Upper Canada until 1811. Playter, *op. cit.*, 103-104.
97. These figures are based on Playter and Carroll.
98. Carroll, *op. cit.*, I, 8, 10-12.
99. Playter, *op. cit.*, 42-43.
100. *Ibid.*, 41-42, 48-49, 65-66.
101. *Ibid.*, 51.
102. *Ibid.*, 57-58.
103. *Ibid.*, 55; Carroll, *op. cit.*, I, 20.
104. A. Stevens, *The Life and Times of Nathan Bangs* (New York, 1863), 29.
105. *Ibid.*, 32, 39, 48.
106. Playter, *op. cit.*, 80-83.
107. Carroll, *op. cit.*, I, 23-25.
108. Playter, *op. cit.*, 99. Ryan succeeded Joseph Sawyer who was instrumental in bringing Bangs into the ministry. He was presiding elder throughout the War of 1812-1814 and in 1815 was appointed to the same office in the Lower Canada District.
109. Carroll, *op. cit.*, I, 1-2.
110. *Ibid.*, I, 9-10, 112.
111. Victoria University Library, *Manuscript Journal of William Case*, 1808-1809, 3.
112. *Ibid.*, 28.
113. *Ibid.*, 46, 23.
114. *Ibid.*, 10, 30.
115. N. Bangs, *History of the Methodist Episcopal Church*, II, 74-75.
116. W. Case, *Journal*, 11, 12, 8.
117. *Ibid.*, 8.
118. Victoria University Library, James Dougall Letters, James Dougall to Andrew Prindle, January 26, 1810.
119. Victoria University Library, Nathan Bangs Letters, Nathan Bangs to James Dougall, March 7, 1805.
120. Stevens, *Bangs*, 151-154.
121. Playter, *op. cit.*, 42.
122. *Ibid.*, 45.
123. *Ibid.*, 98. There were also seven circuits in Lower Canada.
124. *Ibid.*
125. It is significant that the greatest concentrations of Methodists were in the Loyalist areas of Augusta, the Bay of Quinté region and Niagara.
126. Ontario Archives, Strachan Papers, John Strachan to Dr. Brown, July 13, 1806. He added: "You can have almost no conception of their excesses. They will bawl twenty of them at once, tumble on the ground, laugh, sing, jump & stamp, and this they call the working of the spirit."

THREE

*"The chapel sounded with outcrys...
'I am a true Britton'."*

For the Methodists of British North America the first two decades of the nineteenth century were a critical period in which decisions were taken that greatly affected the future development of their Connexion. In the Maritime Provinces the nominal control of the Methodist Episcopal Church was replaced by the real control of the English Conference. In Upper Canada the situation was more complex. At the conclusion of the War of 1812 the American Methodists reaffirmed their determination to retain direction of the work, but the Upper Canadian leaders soon made it clear that they preferred independence from both English and American Methodism. These steps led to divergent patterns of growth in the two branches of Methodism in British North America and in consequence to the exertion of distinctive kinds of influence on their respective communities.

Despite heroic efforts by the missionaries, the first twenty years of Methodist activity in the Maritime Provinces had produced a meagre return, a result that could most easily be attributed to the shortage of preachers. As it was clear that the Methodist Episcopal Church had no intention of supplying the deficiency, the Methodists of Nova Scotia and New Brunswick were faced with the choice of finding an adequate supply of itinerants within their own ranks or of seeking the guidance and help of the English Conference. Apparently Black felt that there was no hope in the first alternative. Because of his excessive toils he was now growing old in spirit, if not in years, and he had no young and vigorous lieutenant to whom he could bequeath the responsibility of providing for the needs of the Societies. In any case, his feeling for his native land and for its Methodist associations was still strong, so that it may have been with alacrity rather than reluctance that he hastened to England late in 1799 to seek the aid of his brethren there.[1]

As in 1784, Black was successful in his quest. At the sessions of the English Conference in 1800 he was cordially received, especially by his old friend Dr. Coke.[2] With the encouragement of the Conference, four preachers—James Lowry, William Bennett, Joshua Marsden and Thomas Olivant—volunteered for Nova Scotia.[3] It was apparently assumed then that the association thus begun would continue indefinitely, and in fact it was not significantly altered until the Conference of Eastern British America was organized in 1855.[4]

At this stage English Methodism had begun to acquire those attributes that would distinguish it throughout the first half of the nineteenth century. Since Wesley's death the Conference no longer had to defer to his Anglican sympathies, and the whole Connexion had come to think of itself as an independent and important religious community. It was not really prepared to challenge the national claims of the Church of England, however, unless these constituted a direct threat to its own existence, and indeed many, especially among the ministers, still felt a marked affinity with the Church.[5]

Within the Connexion itself the ambiguities of Wesley's position had been similarly resolved. His benevolent dictatorship had been replaced by the less amiable tyranny of the Legal Hundred within the Conference and of the Conference over the Societies. The first attempt to give concrete form to the liberal elements in the Methodist system had been foiled. The liberals had departed; those who supported authority in church and state remained.[6] Throughout the first part of the century the Wesleyan Conference was, except when challenged, a powerful conservative agency.

In a way, too, the spiritual quality of the Wesleyan Connexion had changed. Formally, Methodism was no less evangelical and no less concerned with the achievement of perfection than in the past, but some of the original spontaneity and freshness had disappeared. The religious practices of the Methodists were becoming more conventional as they became a stable religious body.[7] On the other hand, the first years of the new century witnessed a tremendous rise in missionary interest, through which the Christian needs of the world overseas came to be regarded with as much lively concern as had been those of the English people in the past.[8]

Given this movement of opinion amongst the Wesleyans there was every reason to believe that they would pay devoted attention to the needs of the eastern provinces, but the introduction of their missionaries was certain to create new problems for the Societies under Black's care. The Methodists would acquire greater respectability in the eyes of colonial ruling circles, yet it would be no easy task to assimilate the English missionaries into colonial society. Moreover, it was to be expected that the English authorities would resist any serious effort to uphold local autonomy and any attempt to handle social and political issues in a way that would challenge their conservative and pro-Anglican outlook. By turning from the American to the British Conference, indeed, the Nova Scotia Methodists had merely given the problem of religious dependency

55

a new shape, made more tolerable only by the ostensibly close ties between the eastern provinces and the United Kingdom.

At the outset, the establishment of a direct link between the English Conference and the Societies in America involved little more than the dispatch of missionaries to their assistance. The energetic, enthusiastic, and erratic Dr. Coke was still personally responsible for the Methodist missions and would continue to be until his death in 1814.[9] The Conference, alarmed at the jumbled condition of the missionary accounts, appointed a Committee of Finance and Advice in 1804, but as Coke was president and the membership of the Committee changed frequently, very little was accomplished.[10] Between 1800 and 1812 only ten preachers were sent to the Maritime Provinces, and the detailed letters which the Committee required after 1804 were used principally as the basis of the annual reports issued by the Conference.[11]

Coke's sudden death while on a voyage to India coincided with the growth of intense concern for the missionary enterprise in the English Societies. In consequence, the Conference of 1815 appointed an executive committee with two secretaries for the management of the missions.[12] This committee was superseded when the General Wesleyan Methodist Missionary Society was founded in 1818.[13] The Society consisted of all who contributed annually to the support of the missions, the funds thus collected being entrusted to a large lay and clerical committee (referred to henceforth as "the Committee"). The routine management of the Committee's work was entrusted to three secretaries, of whom one lived at the Mission House and devoted his time exclusively to the missions. To facilitate the Committee's task, the relationship between the Conference, the Committee and the missionaries was clearly defined at the outset. The missionaries were to be stationed by Conference in accordance with the recommendations of the Committee, and they remained subject to its doctrinal and disciplinary authority. Each mission station was to become a circuit and the circuits were to be embodied in districts, whose chairmen were also to be appointed by the Conference.[14] In practice, the secretaries became the executive directors of the Wesleyan missions; the Committee made policy; the Conference confirmed the Committee's dispositions.

From its inception the Committee sought to assimilate the Societies in British North America to the English pattern. Following the precedent of the 1815 Executive Committee, societies and circuits were to be formed as in England and particular attention was to be paid to the securing of regular contributions from the members.[15] The preachers were kept under close supervision as were the District Meetings, the latter being sharply criticized for deviations from the prescribed forms.[16] Those preachers recruited by the District Chairman as probationers were carefully scrutinized and confined to British North America.[17]

The Committee's second main concern, the orderly extension of the missionary enterprise and its efficient maintenance, called above all for a prudent financial policy. With no source of support except the voluntary donations of English and colonial Methodists, the Society sought to encourage a combination of frugality and self-help. Accordingly, in 1819, a schedule of allowances for missionaries was approved, but unfortunately British North America was excepted. In this field the circuit preachers were allowed to draw on the Society and the District Meeting was required to check the accounts, a procedure calculated to engender friction between the Committee and its representatives.[18] On the other hand the Committee encouraged the Societies to help themselves, questioning disparities between the contributions of individual circuits, insisting on the rental of pews, and refusing to occupy any station that would cost the Missionary Society more than £50 a year.[19] Evidently not all these injunctions were heeded, but they indicate the Society's determination to bring the missionary districts fully into line with English practice and its willingness to rule them vigorously and firmly.

In the end, of course, the extent and depth of the influence exerted by the Conference and later the Missionary Committee over the development of Methodism in the Maritime Provinces depended on the number and the type of men sent to that region. Throughout the first decade of the century Black and the Mann brothers continued to be the dominant group in the Nova Scotia District. Apart from a brief period in 1803 when he was in the United States, Black remained chairman until 1812.[20] In that year he was accompanied into the ranks of the superannuated by John and James Mann.[21] Meanwhile a new generation of preachers was growing up, all but one of whom were English missionaries. The outstanding figures among them were William Bennett, Stephen Bamford, William Croscombe and James Priestley.

A native of Manchester, William Bennett had reached the age of thirty and had acquired considerable preaching experience before his arrival in Nova Scotia on October 22, 1800.[22] He impressed Colonel Perkins as "a good Speaker," "very Distinct and Methodical" and sound in doctrine.[23] Bennett proved to be an unusually devoted and self-sacrificing preacher, whose basic conviction was stated in an early letter to the Missionary Committee: "I view myself as no longer my own but Christ's, his creature, Purchase and Servant & now as your Missionary I look up to you, invested with authority in the church of Xt for Guidance, Commands & Support while in these climes, according to the order of Methodism."[24] Although he was subsequently treated rather shabbily by the Committee, he continued for many years to be a faithful and withal an independent itinerant.

In 1806 the Nova Scotia Conference placed on probation Stephen Bamford, who since his arrival in 1802 had combined local preaching with his military duties.[25] A man who never lost his military bearing, he had a "quaint, broad face, that beamed with happiness as if his heart were overflowing with joy." Bluff, naïve and eccentric, a preacher who was sometimes eloquent, and sometimes lost "the thread of his discourse" entirely, Bamford was one by whom "humor was sanctified and employed in the furtherance of the Gospel."[26] His faith was unsophisticated as was his simple acceptance of the existing religious and political order. To many Methodists he became a beloved figure.

William Croscombe of Devon, who was for many years associated with Bamford, was first persuaded by some militant local preachers to consider Methodism. After much hesitation "an inward impression" led him again to a Methodist prayer meeting at which, he says, "I rose from my knees, lightened of my load of sins and happy in His precious love." He soon began to preach and to study, much of the latter being done in the peace of the local cemetery.[27] Taken on trial in 1810, he arrived after many mishaps in Nova Scotia in 1812, to begin a ministry in British North America that continued until 1855.[28] A man in whose character "humility and dignity" were "delightfully blended," he proved to be a conservative and yet enterprising emissary of the Society.[29]

In 1811 the Nova Scotia Conference witnessed the arrival of James Priestley, whose assistance they welcomed but whose smart appearance aroused their distrust.[30] A genial person and an eloquent preacher, Priestley quickly attained popularity in the district. To the Committee he confided that the office of preacher was one "in which the most happy angel in heaven might covet to be employed for ten thousand years to come."[31] It was his "constant endeavour," he added, "to honour [God] by well doing and by patient suffering as a professor of the Religion of the Holy Jesus ought to do."[32] This he did until he was suspended from preaching for drunkenness.

These men of diverse talents and qualities soon came to occupy positions of responsibility in the Nova Scotia District. When Black retired in 1812 he was succeeded by Bennett as district chairman, the latter being replaced by Priestley in 1821.[33] Priestley's fall from grace in 1824 necessitated his replacement by Bamford.[34] These changes were, however, only the outward symbol of the new order.

At the 1823 District Meeting more than half of the preachers present had come to British North America since 1812. Only two were native Nova Scotians; six out of eighteen had been recruited to the ministry in the district.[35] Clearly the itinerancy was dominated at this point by men close in spirit to English Methodism. Among the younger preachers in this group were three—Robert Alder, William Temple and Matthew Richey—who in various ways would exert great influence over the development of the Nova Scotia mission.

Robert Alder, a printer's apprentice, was taken on trial by the English Conference in 1816 and appointed to Yarmouth, Nova Scotia.[36] As later events would amply demonstrate, he had keen intelligence and great ambition as well as the shrewd ruthlessness of the successful politician. His early letters reveal a man of strong religious feeling and of highly conservative opinions. Writing from Horton in 1817, he assured the Secretaries:

I attempt to increase in grace & holiness, and in order that I may be a workman that needeth not to be ashamed, I bend all the powers of my mind & employ my leisure hours in the acquirement of useful knowledge, well knowing that Ignorance is not devotion . . . & that instead of being a proof of superior piety it is one of the concomitants of sin.

He believed that the history of the preceding thirty years testified to the working of Providence:

It is well known that the poisonous principles scattered in France before & during the revolution threatened to subvert monarchy & Xtianity. . . . But, tho' they vainly expected to see the glorious system which had withstood the wisdom of Greece & the power of Rome, falling before the wit of Voltaire & the ribaldry of Diderot, Jehovah laughed them all to scorn . . . & stirred up his servants of every denomination to associate together for the purpose of defending the divine doctrines of Xtianity.[37]

His evident antipathy to liberal opinions was combined with great friendliness toward the Church. He soon became friendly with the vice-president of King's, whose students attended evening service at Alder's chapel when he was stationed in Windsor.[38] He was moved to Montreal in 1826 and thence to England, where he was soon elevated to secretarial rank.[39]

On the other hand William Temple, who arrived in Saint John in 1820, was to remain in the Maritime Provinces for the rest of his life. Before he came to America his lameness had led to his employment at the Mission House rather than on a circuit.[40] In this country, however, he was a most indefatigable itinerant who in one year travelled nineteen hundred and twenty miles over the roads and seas of Nova Scotia to preach two hundred and ten times.[41] Independent in his attitude toward the Committee, he was at the same time a shrewd, vigorous and level-headed exponent of Methodist doctrine.

In length of service to the Methodist cause Matthew Richey can be compared with Temple. Born in 1803 into a family of Donegal Presbyterians, Richey emigrated to New Brunswick in 1820 and became an assistant master in the Saint John Grammar School. In the same year he attracted Priestley's attention and was persuaded to enter the itinerant ranks, where he served with distinction for many years.[42] His first sermon before the District Meeting, delivered at six in the morning, was given "in a most pleasing, systematic and devout manner, and without apparent effort," a performance that foreshadowed "a preacher never to be forgotten by any who listened to him."[43] Richey's eloquence was sustained by strong, if narrow, religious and political convictions. He assured the Secretaries that he had "once thought that Methodist and enthusiast were convertible terms but ... grace has conquered the prejudice of education and given me to see that a Methodist can be more unlike nothing than an enthusiast, for he does not expect to attain the end without the use of the means; he does not expect regeneration or sanctification without *faith*, nor heaven without *holiness*."[44] His preference for an orderly and decorous type of Methodism was accompanied by great reverence for monarchy and empire, characteristic of the Orange atmosphere of his childhood environment.

Such were some of the men upon whom the Missionary Committee relied in the eastern provinces and who for a considerable interval replaced native preachers in positions of leadership. Diverse as they and their colleagues were in character and outlook, as a group they had certain features that deserve particular emphasis. Although they were evidently men of humble background, they appear to have had some education and even some pretensions to scholarship.[45] Their salaries were always inadequate, but they tried to live in a respectable fashion, a practice that may have set them apart from some of their hearers.[46] Indeed, although they were energetic exponents of the faith, theirs was not exactly the kind of Methodism to which the people of these provinces had previously been exposed.

The teaching and practice of the Wesleyan missionaries reflected the growing moderation of English Methodism. Bennett used Wesley's Liturgy in Saint John; others such as Alder complained that it was not in general use.[47] The preachers were suspicious of excesses. When, for example, Temple found that the people in

Port Mouton had strange notions he remarked that "fanaticism is nearly allied to infidelity." He approved, if his hearers did not, when the steward stopped a man who, "imagining he was influenced by the Divine Spirit addressed the Congregation. He was mistaken. He bawled out in a dreadful manner, repetition upon repetition."[48]

It would be inaccurate, however, to underestimate the evangelical zeal of the English missionaries. The eminently sensible Temple noted on one occasion: "Almost as soon as I began I forgot myself and was lost in my subject. I preached with all my might for an hour and ten minutes which was very unusual for me. . . . Never did a congregation appear more to eat the word."[49] George Jackson deprecated "the idea of spending my years and strength without being of use to my fellow-creatures. Oh, for an increase of every qualification essential to real usefulness! The Lord preserve me from *playing* with the awful truths of the Gospel, the consciences and the souls of men and the realities of eternity!"[50] To this one may add the testimony of John Snowball who, ill with what he feared was consumption, continued to preach, contrary to his doctor's orders: "I would rather die a martyr in the cause than live and not be useful."[51] Clearly the missionaries were men of deep conviction, even if they preferred to present their faith in a more restrained manner than other Methodists in North America.

There is no doubt, too, that although the Wesleyan itinerants vigorously insisted upon the observance of the Methodist discipline as an essential part of the achievement of Christian perfection, they were not as yet prepared to consider the broader social and political implications of their moral principles, continuing to regard the personal salvation of their followers as an objective far more significant than all others. Nevertheless, because of the Committee's policy and their own sympathies, they exercised a particular kind of political and social pressure. They were expressly forbidden to engage in political activity, but they were also expected to support established authority.[52] Simeon Perkins noted that Mr. Marsden "took occasion to explain the nature of Government and our Excellent Constitution etc." Priestley assured the Committee, "I understand it to be my duty to exhort the people to be piously loyal to their God and then there will be no doubt but that they will be loyal to their King."[53] Stephen Bamford lamented later that "there is a kind of Republican independent spirit which runs thro' the whole of religion and politics in this land,"[54] an attitude which the missionaries sought to combat, without becoming directly involved in secular issues.

Moreover, as one might expect, the Wesleyan itinerants looked with favour on that other essential feature of the status quo, the

Church of England. Alder's friendly contacts with the clergy reflected more than an amiable disposition. His friend Temple likewise preferred Anglicans to dissenters, whom he found "ignorant and bigoted."[55] Thus, when in 1825 a committee for the protection of religious rights was being formed, the Nova Scotia District refused to be associated with it. "Above all," said Temple, "as we entertain a sincere esteem for the venerable Establishment of our country and believe that we are called to promote real religion & not mere political views, we of course declined all connection of the kind"—a noteworthy decision, considering the hostile attitude of Bishop Inglis and other clergy in Nova Scotia.[56]

Still, whatever the qualities and opinions of the Wesleyan preachers might be, the shape that Methodism would take in the Maritime Provinces depended as well on the environment in which their work was done. During the first quarter of the century a number of developments occurred in this area that had some bearing on the growth of the Methodist community. Of these, the increase of population was not the least important. Between 1806 and 1827 the population of Nova Scotia rose from 65,000 to 123,360; the population of New Brunswick increased from 35,000 to about 90,000; Prince Edward Island acquired some 10,000 people between 1815 and 1827.[57] These immigrants, who were principally from Scotland and Ireland, filled in the good lands in Nova Scotia and Cape Breton, pushed on up the St. John valley, and began to settle the north shore of New Brunswick. In these years the Maritime Provinces, especially New Brunswick, continued to be a land of new settlements, and persistent emigration to the United States was an additional unsettling factor.[58]

Although there was a constant movement of population in this region, by 1825 each of the three colonies had emerged as a distinct economic and social entity. Nova Scotia, concentrating upon fishing, shipping and trade, became an important part of an international economy that linked it particularly with England and New England. As such it achieved a degree of stability and social maturity, marred somewhat by the fluctuations of the world economy and by the pressures of war.[59] New Brunswick, although also closely linked through the timber trade with Great Britain, remained a raw community, afflicted with the restlessness of the seasonal worker and the sense of instability induced by the changing fortunes of the timber trade.[60] It was very different from Prince Edward Island with its relatively simple farming and fishing economy.[61]

These movements of people and distinctive patterns of economic development inevitably affected the political and social climate of all the provinces. In Nova Scotia the progressive dilution of the New England element combined with the establishment of profitable trading connections to soften past animosities and allay present discontents. After 1815, in particular, this province began to take on an identity of its own in which pro-British feeling was not seriously mingled with anti-American attitudes. Politically it was more peaceful than it had been before the war.[62]

In contrast, New Brunswick presented a rather bewildering pattern of internal division. The relatively stable settlements of the St. John valley had little affinity with the frontier region to the north and east. At the same time the increasingly close connection with the United Kingdom tended to strengthen the position of the Loyalist element, who further consolidated their position by a partial accommodation with the commercial group in Saint John.[63] In consequence, social and political animosities continued to be felt more strongly here than across the Bay of Fundy, but given their situation there was little that the majority could do to overcome their frustrations.

Considered in retrospect the disparate conditions of the eastern provinces provided a difficult background for the spread of Methodism in an increasingly English guise. The preachers were, of course, aware of the challenge presented by the persistent advance of the frontier of settlement, the constant fluctuation of the population, and the continuing poverty and backwardness of large areas.[64] They were greatly perturbed by the survival of the Newlight outlook, with its overly emotional and anti-moral characteristics.[65] They did not realize, however, that Newlight attitudes survived because they accorded most neatly with the religious background or present condition of many people. Similarly they were not really alert to the fact that although in Nova Scotia the policy of assimilation to English practice was superficially attractive, it ran counter to the inner logic of that province's growth, nor were they aware that in New Brunswick Methodism would be regarded as a form of dissent regardless of the shape it assumed. They were unknowingly presenting Methodism in a form that was likely to appeal principally to those who were moderately prosperous, to those for whom the imperial tie still meant something, and to those, such as the Irish, who felt most at home with preachers from the old land.

To the Wesleyan missionaries, however, "Methodist doctrines were [the] best," and sustained by that conviction they went out courageously to battle.[66] To their regret and dismay the engagement was more protracted and the results less decisive than they had perhaps anticipated. At the Conference of 1804 seven preachers were stationed and nine hundred and fourteen members were reported in ten circuits. Among the circuits, Halifax, Liverpool, Annapolis and Sheffield had the largest numbers of members.[67] In 1812 the number of active preachers was unchanged; the membership stood at eleven hundred and fifty-three.[68] The District Meeting of 1825 stationed seventeen preachers in twenty-two circuits, which included some twenty-two hundred members.[69] Among the new circuits were Yarmouth, Wallace, Petitcodiac, Bedeque, Lunenburg, Parrsboro, Charlottetown and Murray Harbour, clear evidence that with more missionaries and assured financial support the Connexion had been extended along with the lines of settlement. Even so, there had been no significant change in the proportion of Methodists in the total population of the region, a situation that was no doubt the result in part of a continuing shortage of personnel and in part of the limited appeal of Methodism among considerable segments of the population.

Whatever the disappointments, the influence of the missionaries in conjunction with the pressures exerted by the local environment had produced a community distinctive in composition, in organization, in religious outlook and in approach to the outside world. The Societies and their adherents were probably composed of those who remained of the original nucleus of Loyalists, Yorkshiremen and New Englanders, and their descendants, and of recent English and Irish immigrants. Socially they continued to represent a cross-section of the population, excluding, in Temple's words, "the most wealthy and the most ignorant."[70] Thomas Roach and John Barry, members of the Nova Scotia Assembly, were Methodists, the former being a local preacher; in Saint John, members of the Assembly attended service.[71] No doubt the majority of the members were ordinary folk, but the atmosphere of respectability evidently thickened around the Societies in this period, as it did among their fellow-Methodists in England.[72]

The organization of the Nova Scotia District did not, however, come up entirely to the standards set by the Missionary Committee. Certainly after 1812, and more especially after the establishment of the Society in 1817, a greater degree of order and regularity was achieved in the Methodism of the eastern provinces than under Black's régime. Outwardly at least the district ran smoothly: a reasonably sure supply of money and preachers provided a greater sense of stability, the itinerancy was at last put in proper working order, and the circuits were more carefully organized. On the other hand, the relationships between the Committee and the missionaries and between the missionaries and the Societies were not wholly satisfactory.

The basic source of disagreement between the Committee and the missionaries was the former's contradictory insistence on obedience and encouragement of local initiative. The Committee's determination to uphold its authority reflected in part the prevailing temper of English Methodism, in part a well-founded suspicion that the missionaries were inclined to go their own way, and in part a real unwillingness to admit that conditions in America were not identical with those in England. But when the missionaries took the initiative, as for example in trying to raise money in ways convenient to their people, and in the nomination of a district chairman, they were chastised.[73] Naturally the preachers gradually came to fall back on the Committee and to work only indirectly against its orders.

Unfortunately, this feeling of dependence was reflected in the attitude of the Societies. Temple was not alone in his complaint that "a missionary must be ostler—chapel keeper, —class leader, —circuit steward, etc., besides a pastor over his flock."[74] He could have added that the preacher as steward often had great difficulty in wringing contributions from his followers, at least in the form and quantity stipulated by the Society.[75] That this happened in the more prosperous as well as the poorer circuits suggests that the dependent relationship was not wholly beneficial and also that the native sense of independence was at work.

When one turns to the religious outlook and religious practice of this group of Methodists one finds a similarly ambiguous situation. In keeping with the attitude and teaching of the missionaries the atmosphere in the Societies was deeply evangelical, but zeal was kept within bounds. Before 1812 several revivals occurred, particularly in Liverpool and Saint John; in 1817 and 1818 great public meetings took place at Nictaux Plains and Granville.[76] The repetition of these was forbidden by the District Meeting of 1820 but they were not replaced by any other similar agency until the eighteen-thirties.[77] It is evident, however, that some preferred a more lusty type of religion. Alder asserted that "because we oppose their enthousiastick excesses & do not permit people to rise up & speak, alias to rant & rave in our solemn assemblies ... they [the Newlights] would endeavour to persuade our people that they are in bondage."[78] In all probability this is what some Methodists did think, for when Temple had a "bawling" man stopped "it was thought by some to be a mighty wicked thing."[79]

Similarly, although there is every reason to believe that most Methodists were as careful to observe the rules of the Societies as their brethren elsewhere, Bamford complained, "It is difficult to enforce the Methodist Discipline in this country as we do in England."[80] When George Dunbar insisted on the proper use of class tickets, "some said it was popery & told the people they ought to plaister the Ticket against the Backs of their *chairs* & then kneel down & worship it. Others said I was after making money."[81] In contrast, the charming woman who was assured by Temple that the ticket was not for sale, stated: "I always thought the Gospel was free."[82] Some of this resistance to discipline may be put down to ignorance, but it may have been aggravated by the rigidity of the preachers and by the unwillingness of their followers to accept controls.

To the casual observer, the social and political attitudes of these Methodists were very straightforward, although the appearance may have been rather misleading. The twofold emphasis of the missionaries on the need to prepare for eternity, and on loyalty and obedience to established authority was designed to produce a quiet and peaceable body of people. The District Meeting of 1820 asserted: "To enlarge on the loyalty of our societies would be superfluous.... It is an important part of our religion to fear God and while they do this they cannot but honour the King seeing the two duties are indissolubly united in the Word of God and they as well as ourselves are subject to the powers that are, not for wrath but for conscience sake."[83] Although when John Barry ran for the Assembly the Methodists were said to be involved, the local missionary reported that "Methodism had nothing to do in it."[84] Certainly there is no evidence of marked social interest even in connection with such questions as religious liberty. The last noteworthy clash between Anglicans and Methodists occurred when Black was at Saint John in 1810.[85] In the twenties, seemingly, no one questioned the unwillingness of the ministers to associate themselves with other religious bodies in defence of their privileges.

Although the Methodists were apparently regarded with some justice as a politically harmless people, it would have been unwise to assume that this inertness would continue to be unquestioned. As the Maritime Provinces were until 1830 relatively free from acute political or social tension, the atmosphere was not conducive to bringing out the latent qualities and opinions of their people. In any case the Missionary Committee and its agents had gone a long way toward shifting the balance in the Methodism of the Maritime Provinces towards acceptance of the otherworldly and conservative elements in the Methodist tradition. Nevertheless, elements of a more liberal approach existed within the Societies. The Arminian gospel was still proclaimed, if in a somewhat modified form. The Methodist system of government continued to be one that could not easily function without the recognition of popular interests. The persistent if muted conflict between the missionaries and the Committee and between the preachers and the Societies was also a potentially explosive factor in the formation of new political and social attitudes.

Twenty-five years of devoted preaching and pastoral work had created in the eastern provinces a Methodist community, more firmly based and more widely spread than it had been in 1800, but still one of the smaller religious bodies in this area. In the intervening period this group of Methodists had been dominated by the Wesleyan Conference more effectively than it had been before or would be in the future. Although missionary aid had enabled Methodism to gain support in some places the dependent relationship had increased the difficulties in others, and had to some extent inhibited the adaptation of its peculiar system to the specific conditions of the environment. The Methodists remained a deeply evangelical people, if rather more conventional than in the past in the outward form of their religion. As citizens they were to all outward appearance an orderly and loyal body, more intent upon their salvation than upon the things of this world. In the words of a contemporary observer: "Wherever the Methodists abound, vice and immorality are made to hide their heads and every man and woman is taught to pray."[86] Herein lay the quality of their real influence in the Maritime Provinces.

2

The War of 1812-1814 was a great turning point in the development of Methodism in Upper Canada. Its immediate result was the partial disruption of the Methodist missionary campaign, and ultimately it altered markedly the conditions under which the preachers had to work. Until 1812 neither ministers nor people had been concerned about the implications of American control over the Canadian Methodists, but when no itinerants from Canada were able to attend the Genesee Conference in July, 1812, it became evident that the issue could no longer be avoided. For the ensuing year the Conference stationed only preachers of British or Canadian origin in Canada; only two new men were appointed, and only one of them made his way across the border.[87] Cut off as they were, the Canadian leaders valiantly attempted to maintain Methodist organization and preaching, but they were greatly hindered by the dislocation incidental to the war and the location of seven circuit-riders.[88] Inevitably it was "extremely difficult, at times, and especially in some of the circuits, to get many together for the purpose of religious instruction" and thus the advance of Methodism was perceptibly retarded. Nevertheless, "the preachers . . . were enabled to preserve most of the societies; and when the waring tempest would for a season subside, not a few, here and there, were brought to God as the fruit of their painful and unremitted exertions."[89] It would not be surprising, however, if in these circumstances some in the itinerant ranks and the Societies began to wonder about the future of Methodism.

More serious in the long run than this temporary dislocation of the Methodist system was the marked alteration in Canadian conditions effected by the war. Before 1812 only the governing group in Upper Canada showed any great dislike of American influences and people, and their attitude did not result in the erection of barriers to American settlement. By 1815, however, the situation was entirely transformed. Upper Canada had become a self-conscious society and one of the primary elements in its new sense of identity was a virulent suspicion of all things American. The Loyalist tradition, partially dormant in preceding years, had come to life with a new bitterness and sharpness to strengthen the conservative elements in the colony—a process that was abetted by a powerful tide of reaction in the United Kingdom itself.[90]

This alteration in the Upper Canadian climate of opinion was furthered by movements of population incidental to and following the war. During its course many American settlers had left the province, probably depriving it thereby of those who had taken the lead in spreading American ideas. At its conclusion the flow of American immigrants was not resumed, and their places were taken by a steadily increasing number of immigrants from all parts of the United Kingdom.[91] Among the English were many lesser gentry who, if they survived the rigours of pioneer life, reinforced the conservative outlook of the provincial governing class. The Scots settled in close-knit communities in which they established Roman Catholic or Presbyterian churches. The Irish, who were in the majority, usually arrived destitute and frequently gravitated to the fringes of society in town and country. To the conservatism of the English and the steadiness of the Scots they added the bigotry and the violence of their native land.[92] But whatever their specific attitudes might be, the presence of these new settlers greatly strengthened the intellectual and social ties of Upper Canada with the old world.

This vast influx of immigrants prolonged the pioneer period in Upper Canada for at least three decades, as the newcomers gradually filled gaps along the lake front, extended the lines of settlement to include the second tier of townships and infiltrated the great central region bounded by Lake Huron and Yonge Street. By 1830 half the people of the province were living in regions that had been virgin forest in 1820.[93] When one recalls how inexperienced the average immigrant must have been, in contrast to his American predecessor, it is easy to visualize how unsettled and primitive life must have been throughout the province.

Despite the instability attendant upon rapid settlement under new auspices, and in part because of the experiences of the war years, post-war Upper Canada gave evidence of growing social and political awareness. The remarkable interest that was shown in Gourlay's campaign against the local oligarchy demonstrated clearly that at least the older settlers were conscious of the need to take decisions about the kind of society and government that ought to be established in the province.[94] That Gourlay's particular agitation failed is not surprising, but it is clear that it was not forgotten. Throughout the twenties there was a growing concern among Upper Canadians about a number of practical political issues that would soon be sharpened into a concerted if erratic battle over the destiny of their land.

In most respects, then, the end of the war of 1812-1814 opened up new prospects and problems for the Methodist community in Upper Canada. As a body governed by an American institution, staffed in the past largely by American citizens, and suspect incidentally because of the alleged vulgarity of its religious beliefs and practices, it was certain to be strongly distrusted in a society given over in part to the nurture of anti-American and conservative prejudices. Besides overcoming this fundamental antipathy, the Methodist preachers would have to cope with a radically unfamiliar situation. Could they appeal to the hordes of new settlers from the United Kingdom? Could they secure enough recruits to their ranks to maintain the impetus of Methodist expansion? Most vital of all, would they be able to meet the forthcoming challenge of political and social controversy among the Upper Canadians themselves?

At the conclusion of the war, however, these formidable difficulties were not yet wholly evident. The Genesee Conference, meeting in Lyons, New York, in 1815, "resolved to go on with the work in Canada; but to be careful in the choice of preachers, that offence, as far as possible, might be prevented."[95] The two districts of Upper and Lower Canada were retained and staffed with fourteen preachers, with William Case and Henry Ryan as presiding elders respectively.[96] Their first task was to rebuild the circuits and to regain the thousand members lost during the war.

Evidently the Conference chose its representatives wisely, for within a year the membership increased and great interest was shown in Methodist teaching. This was stimulated by a revival that began at the Conference of 1817, held at Elizabethtown and attended by the newly appointed Bishop George.[97] His vigorous sermons awakened "more than one hundred persons" and "ten persons found peace in believing."[98] The spirit of revival spread rapidly throughout the neighbouring townships and eventually to the Bay of Quinté and Niagara regions. William Case reported that "like a devouring fire it spread through the neighbourhood [Bay of Quinté]; thence it travelled east,—thence north . . . sweeping in its irresistible course almost all the families in its way." He continued: "It is most delightful to hear the solemn praises of the happy converts, especially as they sail across the Bay, to and from the place of worship. . . . The drunkard's song is changed into loud hosannahs, and blasphemies are turned to praise. . . . They seem to hang upon the preacher's lips as if feasting on every sentence."[99] Not surprisingly, more than forty-seven hundred members were reported in 1818.[100] Despite altered circumstances, Methodism was clearly on the march again in Upper Canada.

Unfortunately, the re-establishment of the Methodist Episcopal Church in the province coincided with the adoption of a new policy by the Wesleyan Conference that raised in a very dramatic way most of the issues posed to American Methodism by the new situation in Upper Canada. As far as is known, no Methodists in Upper Canada sought the services of the Wesleyans before 1812. In the Montreal Society some members had wanted an English preacher as early as 1807, but at the time Coke had suggested that they look to the American Conference for assistance.[101] The imminence of war in May, 1812, spurred the loyal members of that Society to write again to Coke. They asserted that the American preachers were not anxious to travel several hundred miles to a miserable, cold country with a despotic government, and that it was customary for the preacher to arrive some ten weeks after Conference with "a long account of his travels and a long string of Expence." They added that the preachers "are in general bitter enemies to our good old King & Government. . . . Therefore we are often stigmatized as a set of Jacobins, when in fact only our spiritual guides are so; but they being our head, we the body are supposed to be defiled and corrupted in the Sorbonian Bog of Democracy which we abhor."[102] No preacher being available, their request was refused and they contented themselves with the services of Thomas Burch who, despite the war, arrived from the United States.[103]

Two years later, however, John B. Strong, an agent of the Committee, reached Quebec, which had been without a minister during the war.[104] When Burch left Montreal in the same year he apparently turned over the Society to Strong. In the following year Mr. Montgomery, representing the Genesee Conference, arrived on the scene, only to be driven out by Strong and the local leaders.[105] This event led the Committee to appoint William Bennett to investigate the religious condition of the Canadas.

Sharp controversy followed when, as presiding elder, Henry Ryan visited Montreal in September, 1815.[106] Ryan asserted that, before coming to Montreal, he found that Bennett had visited the Ottawa circuit (a discovery that doubtless did not improve his temper). He was then locked out of the Montreal chapel, which was opened only after he threatened the missionary, Richard Williams, in a particularly blunt way. When he met the Society he proposed that the question of ecclesiastical allegiance be referred to the two Conferences, but the people refused. "The Chapel sounded with outcrys from one and another 'I am a true Britton.'" He added: "If national lines are agoing to be the bounds of our feloship, the Upper Province will be wrested from us likewise." But, he argued: "Who has ever proved any of us to be rebels? . . . Can it be proved that any of us has not been conscientious in praying for Kings and all that are in authority? . . . Therefore Manhood, *Religion, Justice, Mercy, Truth and* Every Thing that is *sacred* calls aloud for you to step forward in the real characters of men that fear God and call your Preachers immediately out of Canada."[107]

From Bennett the Committee received another version and different advice. Finding that there was some dissatisfaction with the American preachers he urged that an effort be made to develop the Canadas as a new mission field.[108] Unfortunately, perhaps, Black's considerable influence was thrown behind Bennett's recommendation. The English preachers would, he thought, be of superior ability and more acceptable politically. "Would it not be a kindness to thousands yet unborn," he asked, "to supply the Canadas with *able, judicious* and *faithful* Methodist missionaries?"[109]

Assaulted by these contradictory suggestions, the Committee wrote to Asbury in December, 1815, that "considering the relative situation of the inhabitants of Montreal and of Canada to this country; and particularly as a principal part of the People appear to be in favour of our Missionaries it would be for their peace and comfort . . . for our Brethren to occupy those stations," especially the former. "We are conscious," they added, "that their general habits and prejudices are in favour of English preachers. . . . We cannot but hope, that from the contiguity of the labours of the Brethren belonging to the two conferences, that the spirit of love and unity will be promoted by this measure." To facilitate a settlement Black and Bennett were asked to attend the next General Conference of the Methodist Episcopal Church as agents of the Wesleyan Conference.[110]

As might have been expected, the General Conference did not feel that the "spirit of unity" would be stimulated by Methodist competition in the Canadas. After hearing the views of Case and Ryan for Canada and of Black and Bennett for the English the Conference concluded: "We cannot, consistently with our duty to the societies of our charge in the Canadas, give up any part of them . . . to the superintendence of the British connexion."[111] Regrettably the English Conference, disregarding this pointed statement, decided to send additional missionaries to the Canadas, but enjoined them to concentrate on religiously destitute areas and the Indians.[112] If the English missionaries had confined their labours to Lower Canada it is probable that the Canadians would have carried the matter no further. When, however, itinerants appeared in Kingston, Cornwall, Stamford and York, the issue could no longer be ignored.[113] The American preachers, feeling that Upper Canada was peculiarly their own sphere of responsibility, fought back vigorously.

For their part the Wesleyan missionaries and their adherents averred that Upper Canada was religiously neglected and that the representatives of the Methodist Episcopal Church were individually and politically unsuitable. The Rev. Henry Pope, who arrived at Cornwall in December, 1816, found that "a general inattention to Divine things" was ."deplorably manifest." The American preachers were "by no means acceptable, partly owing to the late war . . . and partly owing to their extensive ignorance and uncouth conduct."[114] His colleague, Thomas Catterick, was much more explicit. The preachers were "so ignorant & enthusiastic as to render their discourses ridiculous in the ears of respectable and well informed People." He added: "Much of their religion consists in a great noise at the house of God & then all is over till their next meeting. . . . They believe unless they can set their hearers a-shouting, no good is done; hence at their Quarterly Meetings, tumbling, clapping their hands, praying loud and shouting with all their might are common." Elder Youmans smoked in the pulpit and preached on such foolish texts as: "Look not on me because I am black," and "Set on the large pot."[115] Worst of all, the preachers in Canada were disloyal. William Case, a most unworldly man, was alleged to have said:

"As they [the Wesleyans] were English men he would give them red hot balls, this he has done in the true spirit of a republican Methodist." "This Mr. Case," continued his detractors, "is a Bitter and Bold Enemy to this government and he has been heard to say in his Publick preaching when across the lines, the British is a tyrannical Government and he thanked God he was from under their galling yoke."[116] It may be supposed that if statements of this kind were made to the Missionary Committee they were also made in Upper Canada itself.

In response the Canadian Societies let it be known that they would not accept the Wesleyan "yoke." The leaders of the Yonge Street and Ancaster circuits felt that the Wesleyans "must have had many wrong statements given to [them]." "Why," they asked, "should we cast off our preachers that God has owned in the Salvation of our Souls and be to a vast expense in fetching over Preachers from England barely because they were Brittish born?" Their preachers had worked faithfully and loyally with them and they hoped that the Wesleyans would be recalled to England.[117] Subsequently Ryan issued a printed statement in which the Canaadian case was squarely put. "It must be something very singular," he began, "that has caused these men to swarm out of England . . . and express by their practice a desire to croud themselves upon the people in the Canadas where a large majority of the Methodists are in pointed opposition to their procedure." The loyalty plea was false. In any case, he went on: "God forbid that I should harbour such a thought that we Canadians have such a tyrannical government that a man from any part of the world has not a right to be instrumental of saving souls in this Province." The English missionaries were, he felt, most interested in settled areas and the better people. As their real intention was to "rend the flock of Christ with whom we have laboured in tears for years," it was the duty of the Societies "to hold them at a distance." He concluded: "Should any of them undertake to answer this by way of burlesque I shall treat their arguments as they treat the people in the back settlements—pass them at a distance."[118]

Confronted with this uproar the Committee urged the missionaries to avoid conflict with their American brethren, but its "resolutions were as water spilt upon the ground."[119] Thus, when in 1820 the General Conference sent a delegate to confer with the Committee, agreement was soon reached to divide the work in the Canadas, Lower Canada being left in Wesleyan hands, Upper Canada in the hands of the Genesee Conference.[120] To its representatives the Society emphasized that Upper Canada was not in such need of ministers as had been supposed. The political argument was also discounted:

> We cannot lay it down as a principle that those whose object is to convert the world shall be prevented from seeking and saving souls under a foreign government.... To act upon this principle would be to cast an odium upon our American brethren as though they did not conduct themselves peaceably under the British government, which is, we believe, contrary to the fact.... Upon any political feeling which may exist, either in your minds or in the minds of a party in any place, we cannot therefore proceed. Our objects are purely Spiritual and our American brethren and ourselves are one body of Christians, sprung from a common stock, holding the same doctrines, enforcing the same discipline and striving in common to spread the light of true religion through the world.

The missionaries were therefore enjoined not to heed local prejudices and to get on with their proper task, a plea which was reiterated by Bishop McKendree in his letter to his preachers.[121]

Although this settlement was greeted by violent protests from Wesleyan sympathizers in Upper Canada it was promptly put into effect, except that contrary to the original understanding, Kingston was retained by the Wesleyans.[122] But though the immediate conflict was thus stilled, its implications were serious. There was no disguising the fact that to some Upper Canadians, Methodism in its American guise had little appeal. Similarly, a willingness to suspect the worst of preachers drawn from the United States was manifest among leading citizens and the colonial government. To Governor Maitland, writing in great alarm to Bathurst, it was "obvious" that "if to preserve the allegiance of the people to the government of the Mother country be held an object of importance," the presence of American preachers could not be "too strongly discountenanced."[123] In this situation only one constructive course appeared open to the Canadian Methodists, that of establishing an independent Methodist connexion in the province. It was by no means certain, however, that in a population whose complexion was steadily changing, independence itself would satisfy the pro-British element. The Wesleyans remained nearby with their pro-Anglican and conservative tendencies, ready for exploitation by interested elements in the province. Their outpost in Kingston stood as an ominous warning of an intra-Methodist conflict that was still to come.

For the moment, however, the more prescient, doubtless with an eye to future independence, suggested to the General Conference of 1820 that an annual conference be established in Upper Canada. This was not immediately granted, but the bishops were authorized, subject to the consent of the Genesee Conference, to take this step within four years.[124] This decision was the prelude to a new phase of unsettlement in the Upper Canadian Societies, related in part to external conditions and in part to their internal situation.

The 1820 General Conference had been the occasion of a spirited battle concerning the election of presiding elders, in which a majority of the preachers were resolutely opposed by the aged Bishop McKendree. Despite his opposition the Conference accepted the principle of election but suspended the resolution for four years, that it might be tested in the Annual Conferences. Subsequently the Bishop dissuaded a majority of the latter from accepting the elective principle but in so doing kept the subject clearly in the foreground.[125] In the interval, too, the elective eldership issue was gradually obscured by a much broader agitation for the election of lay delegates to annual and general conferences.[126] This controversy, which reflected a deepening conviction that the Methodist Episcopal Church should be run on more democratic lines, was a matter of concern to itinerants and lay Methodists in Upper Canada as in other parts of the church. Moreover, they could use as the focus of discussion the District Conference of local preachers, authorized as a palliative to local interests by the General Conference of 1820.[127]

In Upper Canada the lead in keeping the uproar going was taken by Henry Ryan, a presiding elder from 1810 to 1824. His temper was especially aroused by the failure of the Genesee Conference of 1823 to elect him as a delegate to the forthcoming General Conference.[128] An imperious and ambitious autocrat, Ryan urged the Societies in Upper Canada to seek independence as a means of forestalling reform in the Methodist constitution, a move which he probably hoped would ensure his emergence as head of an independent church in Upper Canada.[129] He was supported by David Breckenridge, a local elder and a pronounced tory.[130] This curiously assorted pair went unofficially to the General Conference of 1824 bearing petitions from the eastern circuits asking for immediate independence.[131]

After much discussion the Conference rejected the elective presiding eldership and lay delegation, thereby precipitating the establishment of the Methodist Protestant Church.[132] At the same time it refused to hear Ryan's case, although agreeing to set up a Canadian Conference.[133] Angered at this turn of events, Ryan hastened home and called an enlarged District Conference at Elizabethtown. From this gathering issued the "Declaration of Independence of Certain Methodists" in which the General Conference action was noted. The question now was: "Does reason or religion require us to submit to them and thereby expose ourselves to ruin? Doth not the word of God require us to yield to the wishes of the Government we are under as far as we can without weakening Grace or wounding conscience? It certainly does." It was proposed, therefore, that the "Wesleyan Methodist Episcopal Canadian Church" be formed, and that it admit only those ministers who would become British subjects. The new church was to retain the substance of Methodist Episcopal doctrine and organization but was to give up the delegated general conference and allow no changes in the rules without the consent of two-thirds of the local preachers.[134] The Declaration was signed by Darius Dunham, Joseph Sawyer, and Sylvanus Keeler, located preachers long resident in Upper Canada, by Breckenridge and his son, and by James Richardson, a veteran of the war who would soon become a prominent figure in Canadian Methodism.[135] It appears to have been widely circulated and thoroughly discussed, especially in the Bay of Quinté district.

Confronted by this formidable agitation the bishops hastened to prepare the ground for the inception of the new Canada Conference. Its first session was preceded by a general visitation conducted by Bishops George and Hedding, accompanied by Nathan Bangs, a veteran of the Canadian itinerancy.[136] The tension was eased by these means, but the Conference, meeting in Hallowell, hastened to draft a memorial for independence, looking towards the establishment of a Canadian church by the General Conference of 1828.[137] With this the majority was evidently content.

One of the steps taken by the Conference was the demotion of Henry Ryan to the rank of missionary, which was followed by his superannuation in 1825.[138] Now growing old and embittered, he was not long in renewing his charges of 1823 and 1824. He would not admit that independence was likely to come in 1828. Also he laid many other complaints at the door of people and preachers. The latter were, he said, "ambitious, foppish, proud, covetous and persecuting." The church "was falling"; it had "no revivals of religion," rather "both preachers and people were following the fashions of the world." The bishops, he asserted, were hypocrites "having no desire to lessen their power and jurisdiction, disregarding the people and denying their fervent wishes and sacred rights."[139] Brought to account for this by the Conference in 1827 he withdrew to form the Canadian Wesleyan Methodist Church, which was a source of anxiety, if not of great numerical loss, to the Canada Conference in the first years of independence.[140]

It would be easy to put down the disturbed condition of the Upper Canadian Societies in the years 1820 to 1828 to the intervention of a few interested and misguided individuals. Ryan, in particular, may well have felt that he was out of step with events and that his long and heroic services had been inadequately rewarded. But in fact this entire episode, far from being an exercise in frustration, was symptomatic of important changes in Upper Canadian Methodism.

To begin with, the Methodist community was becoming increasingly identified with Upper Canada, rather than the United States or the United Kingdom. Thirty-five years of Methodist preaching, the continuous residence of men such as Dunham, Sawyer and Ryan, the isolation of the war years, and the recent clash with the Wesleyans had stimulated the growth of this sense of identity. In consequence, the itinerant ranks were being gradually filled by Upper Canadian natives and by immigrants from the old country, whose presence, in turn, lent emphasis to the Canadian orientation of the episcopal branch of Methodism.[141]

This development was accompanied by less tangible changes in the quality of the itinerancy and in the general character of the Societies. The itinerant ranks continued to be filled by men of the most diverse backgrounds, but the preachers, working in a community becoming somewhat civilized and facing the possible competition of the more urbane Wesleyans, were more willing than before to admit that zeal alone was not the passport to an acceptable ministry.[142] A sense of mission was still, of course, the vital prerequisite to entrance into the itinerancy, but education began to appear important. The Conference of 1825, following the earlier lead of the General Conference, noted with regret "the want of intellectual improvement among our young preachers generally." Declaring "our young men should have more advantages for the improvement of their minds in order to meet the wants of society, now improving in literary acquirements," it enjoined presiding elders and senior ministers to assist junior preachers in improving their minds. In future, admission to full connexion was preceded by an examination based on such works as Wesley's *Sermons*, Watts' *Logic*, Mosheim's *Church History*, Murray's *English Grammar* and Morse's *Geography*.[143] It would appear that these examinations were not strenuous, but that this step should have been taken was in itself significant.[144]

Although the preachers were becoming more aware of the demands likely to be imposed by their position, they continued to be a most diversified body of men, united by their conviction that the gospel of conversion and holiness must be spread widely and that it must be preached in the simplest and most positive terms. Similarly, the societies to whom they ministered were powerfully infused with the evangelical spirit. On the whole, indeed, the direct influence of

Methodism in Upper Canadian society after 1815 continued to be essentially religious. The gathering of converts and the quest for personal holiness were the principal preoccupations of preachers and people. They were in the world but, at their best, they were not of the world. It was in the atmosphere of their religious and ecclesiastical life rather than in formal statements or acts that they were likely to sense the secular significance of certain features of that life.

Nevertheless, most Methodists were likely not of exactly the same mind as they had been two decades earlier. Ryan's complaint that they "were following the fashions of the world" should not be dismissed as the invective of an old man. In all likelihood the Societies in settled areas were becoming rather more conventional, at least in contrast to those which were still being formed in the new settlements. This change was accompanied by a broadening of concern for the rôle of Methodism that was best exemplified by the remarkable Methodist interest in Indian missions.

In fact, by 1825 the Methodist community in Upper Canada had become closely integrated with the life of the province in personnel and in outlook and had matured sufficiently to realize that its responsibilities might include more than the simple preaching of the gospel in its Wesleyan form. The long controversy with the Wesleyans had presumably heightened Methodist awareness of the unexpected dangers that lay in the way of the most detached preaching. In the same way, the discussion of independence and of church organization had probably given most Methodists a better grasp of the working of their polity and the political significance of their religious beliefs, although as yet these insights had not been brought to bear directly on the place of Methodism in society. Throughout this period, in any event, the continued expansion of the territorial boundaries and of the membership of the Methodist Connexion ensured that whatever kind of influence it came to wield it would be no negligible factor in the future development of Upper Canada.

3

To the casual observer of 1825 the Methodist groups in Upper Canada and the Maritime Provinces would have appeared very much alike. In reality, however, the passing years had perceptibly deepened the differences in their outlook and position. They were akin in their devotion to the Wesleyan tradition and in their search for lost souls, a task which they felt to be more important than any worldly concern. But whereas the Methodists of the eastern provinces had come to accept a rather conventional approach to their evangelical task, their Upper Canadian brethren were still a band of enthusiasts. Then, too, the latter had come to think of themselves and to act as Canadian Methodists. They were more closely identified with the Canadian scene than their distant fellow-workers in Nova Scotia, who had largely adapted themselves to a dependent rôle. Above all, this process of adaptation had stirred the Methodists of Upper Canada to a kind of creative turmoil that would lead them to deal rather more constructively than the Methodists in the east with the questions posed by the secular world.

REFERENCES TO CHAPTER THREE

1. T. W. Smith, *History of the Methodist Church* ... I, 331.
2. Findlay and Holdsworth, *History of the Wesleyan Methodist Missionary Society*, I, 307.
3. *Minutes of the Methodist Conferences* (London, 1813), II, 52. Their arrival was noted in Perkins's diary for October 12, 1800.
4. From 1855 until 1874 the Conference of Eastern British America was united with the Wesleyan Conference.
5. W. J. Townsend, *et al.*, *A New History of Methodism*, I, 385-388.
6. On this development see E. R. Taylor, *Methodism and Politics*, chapter 3.
7. *Ibid.*, 108-109.
8. Townsend, *et al.*, *op. cit.*, I, 397-398.
9. W. C. Barclay, *Early American Methodism*, I, 120.
10. In 1799 and 1800 the Conference explicitly established controls over Coke's operations. See Findlay and Holdsworth, *op. cit.*, I, 66-69.
11. See *An Account of the Progress of the Methodist Missions in the West Indies and the British Dominions in America, in Ireland and in North-Wales* (London, 1805), and subsequent reports published under a variety of titles. The figure of ten is based on these reports.
12. *Minutes of the Methodist Conferences*, IV, 124-126.
13. For the background see Findlay and Holdsworth, *op. cit.*, chapter 2.
14. *Minutes of the Methodist Conferences*, IV, 448-456.
15. *Records of the Wesleyan Methodist Missionary Society* (outgoing). Microfilm copy. Reel 1, Regulations for the Methodist Missions, November 18, 1815. This source will be cited in future as *M.R.*
16. The preachers could not marry while on probation. They were expected to correspond regularly with the Secretaries.
17. *M.R.*, Reel 2, Secretaries to James Priestley, September 3, 1821; *ibid.*, Reel 1, Committee Minutes, July 7, 1819. Colonial preachers could, in principle, be moved to England by the Committee.
18. *M.R.*, Minutes of Sub-Committee on Finance, March 31, 1819. How much individuals were allowed to draw is not clear. In 1815

the Committee stipulated that a maximum of £50 could be drawn at one time. *Ibid.*, Regulations for the Methodist Missions, November 18, 1815. In that same year, Bennett had established a scale based on the English allowances plus 35% for the higher cost of living. *W.R.*, Reel 4, Bennett to the Committee, December 17, 1820.

19. *M.R.*, Committee Minutes, July 7, 1819. The Committee noted that at Horton the average contribution was 28/-, at Annapolis, 10/-. *Ibid.*, Reel 2, Secretaries to Priestley, September 3, 1821; Reel 1, Committee Minutes, September 24, 1823; September 20, 1820.
20. Black left Nova Scotia in the hope of returning to England. He was impelled by nostalgia for his own land and by a bitter personal attack by some members of his circuit. See *W.R.*, Reel 1, Complaint of Halifax Class Leaders, March 22, 1802; Black Papers, A. Anderson to D. Fidler, May 22, 1803. In 1804 Black went as far as New York on his way to the West Indies at Coke's behest. *W.R.*, Reel 1, Black to Coke, August 26, 1804.
21. *W.R.*, Reel 1, Minutes of Conference, 1812.
22. Smith, *op. cit.*, I, 369-370, 373; *W.R.*, Reel 1, Bennett to the Committee, November 16, 1804.
23. S. Perkins, *Diary*, October 12, 1800.
24. *W.R.*, Reel 1, Bennett to the Committee, November 16, 1804. He preferred to use his wife's money rather than draw heavily on the mission funds. *Ibid.*, February 22, 1817.
25. *Ibid.*, Reel 1, Black to Coke, May 19, 1808; Smith, *op. cit.*, I, 380-384, 400-401.
26. *Ibid.*, II, 353-354.
27. *Ibid.*, I, 427-431.
28. *W.R.*, Reel 1, Black to the Committee, June 8, 1812.
29. Smith, *op. cit.*, II, 357.
30. *W.R.*, Reel 1, Priestley to the Committee, November 20, 1811.
31. *Ibid.*, January 27, 1813.
32. *Ibid.*, Reel 4, July 10, 1819.
33. *Ibid.*, Reel 1, Black to the Committee, June 8, 1812. At that time the title of superintendent was still in use. *Minutes of the Methodist Conferences*, V, 226.
34. On the first point, see *W.R.*, Reel 3, Bennett and Alder to the Committee, March 17, 1824; Priestley to the Committee, March 20, 1824. For Bamford's appointment see *ibid.*, Bamford to the Committee, December 13, 1824; *Minutes of the Methodist Conferences*, V, 498.
35. The two Nova Scotians were R. H. Crane and A. Desbrisay, the latter being the son of the Rector of Charlottetown.
36. *W.R.*, Reel 1, Alder to the Secretaries, June 12, 1818; *ibid.*, Black to the Secretaries, December 1, 1816; *M.R.*, Reel 1, Committee Minutes, September 3, 1816.
37. *W.R.*, Reel 1, Alder to the Secretaries, February 15, 1817.

38. *Ibid.*, Reel 3, Alder to the Secretaries, April 1, 1824. Before his death he took orders in the Church of England.
39. *Minutes of the Methodist Conferences*, VI, 36. Alder's appointment appeared in the 1825 Minutes, but he did not take up his work in Montreal until 1826. He became a missionary secretary in 1832.
40. W.R., Reel 4, Temple to the Secretaries, November 2, 1820.
41. *Ibid.*, Reel 5, July 1, 1823.
42. *Ibid.*, Reel 4, Richey to the Secretaries, October 17, 1820.
43. Smith, *op. cit.*, II, 98.
44. W.R., Reel 4, Richey to the Secretaries, October 17, 1820.
45. In 1824 Temple ordered the following books for his colleagues: Walker's *English and Classical Dictionary*, Schneider's *Concordantia*, Rollin's *Ancient History*, Chalmers' *Sermons* and standard Wesleyan works. W.R., Reel 3, Temple to the Secretaries, December 4, 1824. Their journals and letters testify to the level of their education, as did, for example, Richey's publication of Black's biography.
46. W.R., Reel 5, George Jackson to the Secretaries, December 21, 1822. He remarks in this letter that he has yet to see a properly furnished parsonage.
47. W.R., Reel 5, Alder to the Secretaries, December 2, 1822.
48. *Ibid.*, Temple's Journal, January 4, March 4, 1823.
49. *Ibid.*, September 14, 1823.
50. *Ibid.*, Jackson to Secretaries, August 28, 1822.
51. *Ibid.*, Snowball to the Secretaries, October 26, 1825.
52. This point is explicitly covered in the "Instructions" of 1834, but these were in effect long before that date. Findlay and Holdsworth, *op. cit.*, I, 161-162. See *Report of the General Wesleyan Methodist Missionary Society*, 1822, 6.
53. Perkins, *Diary*, December 16, 1803; W.R., Reel 1, Priestley to the Committee, January 27, 1813.
54. *Ibid.*, Reel 4, Bamford to the Secretaries, July 4, 1821.
55. *Ibid.*, Temple to the Secretaries, April 12, 1821.
56. *Ibid.*, Reel 3, October 17, 1825.
57. J. B. Brebner, *Canada, a Modern History* (Ann Arbor, 1960), 168, 193, 182-183.
58. In Nova Scotia, for example, between 1815 and 1833, 22,000 Scots, 13,000 Irish and 2,000 English arrived. New Brunswick also continued to receive settlers until later in the century. The figures on emigration are indefinite, but it was a subject of constant lament by the Methodist preachers.
59. See Brebner, *op. cit.*, chapter 12.
60. *Ibid.*, 192-195.
61. After 1830 fishing became a secondary industry in the Island.
62. For a good description of this situation see S. D. Clark, *Movements of Political Protest in Canada, 1640-1840* (Toronto, 1959), 239-242.
63. *Ibid.*, 242-243. Brebner, *op. cit.*, 197, is not so certain that this accommodation took place.

64. See Black's reports to the Committee, *W.R.,* Reel 1, September 17, 1804; October 10, 1804.
65. *W.R.,* Reel 1, Bennett to the Committee, November 16, 1804; Priestley to the same, November 20, 1811; Reel 5, Alder to the same, December 2, 1822.
66. *W.R.,* Reel 5, Temple's Journal, January 4, 1823.
67. *Ibid.,* Reel 1, Minutes of Conference, 1804.
68. *Ibid.,* Minutes of Conference, 1812. Black and the Mann brothers were technically retired.
69. *M.R.,* Reel 5, District Minutes, 1825. Black and Bennett were still available as occasional preachers.
70. *W.R.,* Reel 5, Temple's Journal, January 4, 1823.
71. *Ibid.,* Reel 4, Priestley to the Secretaries, July 10, 1819; Reel 3, George Miller to the Secretaries, December 2, 1824; Reel 4, Temple to the Secretaries, November 2, 1820.
72. The missionaries often spoke of the inadequate resources of their flocks, but inability to pay subscriptions could have reflected the shortage of currency or simply unwillingness to pay.
73. *W.R.,* Reel 5, Temple to the Secretaries, April 3, 1822; *M.R.,* Reel 2, Secretaries to Priestley, September 3, 1821. Bamford, among others, objected to a motion carried by one vote to elect the district chairman annually. *W.R.,* Reel 4, Bamford to the Secretaries, July 4, 1821.
74. *Ibid.,* Reel 7, Temple to the Secretaries, August 8, 1828. See also Reel 1, Croscombe to the same, June 24, 1818; Reel 3, Alder to the same, April 1, 1824.
75. *W.R.,* Reel 4, Alder to the Secretaries, February 15, 1820.
76. *W.R.,* Reel 1, Black to W. Jenkins, May 16, 1807; Smith, *op. cit.,* II, 88-91.
77. *Ibid.* Such meetings were to be held only with the permission of the Committee.
78. *W.R.,* Reel 5, Alder to the Secretaries, December 2, 1822.
79. *Ibid.,* Temple's Journal, March 4, 1823.
80. *Ibid.,* Reel 4, Bamford to Committee, July 4, 1821.
81. *Ibid.,* Reel 1, Dunbar to James Buckley, June 17, 1816.
82. *Ibid.,* Reel 5, Temple's Journal, January 4, 1823.
83. *Ibid.,* Reel 4, Address of Loyalty, 1820.
84. *Ibid.,* Reel 3, George Miller to the Secretaries, December 2, 1824. He admitted, of course, that Methodists at Shelburne had voted for Barry.
85. Mount Allison University Library, McColl Papers, Black to McColl, September 4; October 3, 1810. *Methodist Magazine* (U.K.), XXXIII (1810), 407. Temple took care to defend his colleagues to the Secretaries against the allegations of Bishop Inglis and Archdeacon Best. *W.R.,* Reel 3, Temple to the Secretaries, October 17, 1825.
86. Smith, *op. cit.,* II, 97.

87. G. F. Playter, *The History of Methodism in Canada,* 109.
88. *Ibid.,* 138.
89. *Methodist Magazine* (U.S.A.), II (1819), 33, W. Case to J. Soule, November 3, 1818.
90. A. R. M. Lower, *Canadians in the Making* (Toronto, 1958), 184-185; S. D. Clark, *Movements,* 250-252.
91. Severe restrictions were placed on land grants to American citizens. E. McInnis, *Canada,* 199-200. The population rose from about 90,000 in 1815 to 150,006 in 1824. In 1837, it had risen to 397,489. Brebner, *Canada,* 228.
92. Lower, *op. cit.,* 194-195.
93. J. J. Talman, *Life in the Pioneer Districts of Upper Canada* (Ph.D. Thesis, Toronto, 1930), 1-2.
94. For a detailed analysis of Gourlay's career see Clark, *op. cit.,* 331-348.
95. Playter, *op. cit.,* 143.
96. *Ibid.,* 143.
97. *Ibid.,* 158. This was the first occasion on which the Genesee Conference met in Canada.
98. *Methodist Magazine (U.S.A.),* II (1819), 33.
99. *Ibid.,* 36-37.
100. There were 4,731 members in Upper and Lower Canada. Of these, 87 were from Lower Canada. In contrast 1,765 members were reported from Upper Canada in 1815.
101. *W.R.,* Reel 1, James Booth and Richard Pope to the Committee, August 12, 1817.
102. *Ibid.,* Richard McGinnis, Alex Reid, *et al.* to Coke, May 26, 1812. (Copy).
103. *Ibid.,* McGinnis, Reid *et al.* to the Committee, November 11, 1815. Burch was an Irishman. J. Carroll, *Case,* I, 260. See also *Annual Report of the State of the Missions* ... (London, 1814), 13.
104. Playter, *op. cit.,* 140; *Annual Report of the State of the Missions* ... (London, 1815), 15.
105. *W.R.,* Reel 1, Henry Ryan to A. Clarke, October 9, 1815. Richard Williams took Montgomery's place. *M.R.,* Reel 2, James Buckley to Strong (n.d., but probably February, 1815).
106. *W.R.,* Reel 1, Bennett to the Committee, October 6, 1815.
107. *Ibid.,* Reel 1, Ryan to Clarke, October 9, 1815.
108. *Ibid.,* Bennett to the Committee, October 6, 1815.
109. *Ibid.,* Black to Joseph Benson, November 12, 1815.
110. *M.R.,* Reel 2, James Buckley and James Wood to Asbury, December 31, 1815.
111. Playter, *op. cit.,* 149.
112. *M.R.,* Reel 2, Buckley to Bennett, August 22, 1816.
113. *The Report for the Year 1817* ... (London, 1817), lists Wesleyan missionary appointments at Kingston, Cornwall and Fort Wellington. Henry Pope came to York in 1820. Carroll, *op. cit.,* II, 282.

See also *W.R.*, Reel 4, T. Catterick (Stamford) to the Committee, September 10, 1820.

114. *W.R.*, Reel 1, H. Pope to James Wood, February 11, 1817.
115. *W.R.*, Reel 4, Catterick to Temple, September 13, 1820.
116. *W.R.*, Reel 4, *The Remonstrance of the Private and Official Members . . . in the Bay of Quinty Circuit* (no date, but probably January, 1821). See also a letter from Mr. Paul Glassford of Matilda: "The political sentiments of the American Preachers frequently slip out, Shewing their inveterate hatred of the British Government." *Ibid.*, P. Glassford to J. Taylor, November 23, 1820.
117. *W.R.*, Reel 1, Peter Bowman, Daniel Cummins *et al.* to the London Methodist Missionary Society, December 4, 1816.
118. *W.R.*, Reel 2, Printed statement signed by Henry Ryan, April 14, 1818.
119. *M.R.*, Reel 1, Committee Minutes, January 27, 1819; Playter, *op. cit.*, 171. The Committee was advised in 1818 that Upper Canada was not destitute of preachers and that the political argument was not important. "The morals of the people in general are better, and their religious views less exceptionable than the generality of even the protestants of our own country." *W.R.*, Reel 1, Edward Johnston to the Committee, April, 1818. Johnston was the district chairman.
120. *Journals of the General Conference of the Methodist Episcopal Church, I, 1796-1836* (New York, 1836), 215; *M.R.*, Reel 1, Committee Minutes, July 10, 1820. The delegate was the Rev. John Emory. The decision was confirmed by the English Conference in the same year.
121. *M.R.*, Reel 2, Circular to the Missionaries, August 23, 1820. For McKendree's letter see Playter, *op. cit.*, 186-189.
122. The Committee was deluged with memorials, some of which were of questionable inspiration. For example, one Kingston petition was signed by those eminent non-Methodists, Thomas Markland and C. A. Hagerman. *W.R.*, Reel 4, "The Petition of the Magistrates, Householders and other Inhabitants of the Town of Kingston in Upper Canada." (Date of covering letter, January 6, 1821). For the Kingston issue and the Committee's negative reply to the various petitions, see *M.R.*, Reel 1, Committee Minutes, June 20, 1821.
123. Public Archives of Canada, *Q.329*, 3, Maitland to Bathurst, January 4, 1821. In reply Bathurst suggested that the only immediate remedy was to increase the number of Anglican clergy in Upper Canada. P.A.C., *G. Series*, Upper Canada Supplement, Bathurst to Maitland, July 24, 1821.
124. *Journals of the General Conference*, 214-215.
125. Barclay, *op. cit.*, I, 251-252, 254.
126. *Ibid.*, 254-255.
127. *Ibid.*, 253. The District Conference was composed of the local preachers under the chairmanship of the presiding elder.

128. Case, the other presiding elder, was not elected. The intention was to send delegates prepared to consider seriously the interests of preachers and laymen. Playter, *op. cit.*, 234.
129. *Ibid.*, 234-235.
130. Breckenridge was an ordained local preacher, magistrate and militia officer, Carroll, *op. cit.*, I, 128.
131. Playter, *op. cit.*, 234-235; A. Green, *The Life and Times of Anson Green* (Toronto, 1877), 38.
132. Barclay, *op. cit.*, I, 255-257.
133. *Journals of the General Conference*, 302.
134. The meeting concluded on June 16, 1824. For the Declaration see *W.R.*, Reel 3. Ryan was apparently not present. E. Ryerson, *Canadian Methodism: Its Epochs and Characteristics* (Toronto, 1882), 251.
135. Sawyer began to preach here in 1800; Keeler, a Canadian resident, was first called out in 1795. James Richardson, a native of Kingston, would become the editor of the *Christian Guardian* and bishop of the secessionist Methodist Episcopal Church in Upper Canada.
136. Green, *op. cit.*, 40; Ryerson, *op. cit.*, 252-254.
137. United Church Archives, Journal of the Canada Conference, (MS), 1824, 4-7.
138. *Minutes of the Annual Conferences of the Wesleyan Methodist Church in Canada* (Toronto, 1846), 3, 6.
139. Playter, *op. cit.*, 298.
140. Green, *op. cit.*, 106-107; Ryerson, *op. cit.*, 258-269.
141. In 1815, 83% of the preachers were Americans, in 1820, 58%, in 1824, 45%. In 1824 more than half of the remainder had been born in British North America.
142. Among those recruited after 1815, William Ryerson was a farmer, George Ferguson a soldier, David Youmans a blacksmith.
143. *Minutes of the Canada Conference*, 8; Playter, *op. cit.*, 260. The list also included Fletcher's *Checks*, Goldsmith's *Rome*, Rollin's *Ancient History*, the works of Milton and Cowper, and biographies of Wesley, Coke and Xavier.
144. Green, *op. cit.*, 101-102.

FOUR

"A Methodist can be more unlike nothing than an enthusiast."

In May, 1826, the preachers of the three eastern provinces met in Halifax for the last session of the Nova Scotia District Meeting.[1] Although they had had little warning of it, their principal task was to implement the decision of the British Conference to divide the district into two parts.[2] With some reluctance the assembled missionaries created the Nova Scotia and New Brunswick districts, including in the former Prince Edward Island, in the latter the Annapolis valley.[3] Bamford continued as chairman of the Nova Scotia District with Temple as secretary.[4] Richard Williams, since 1815 a missionary in Lower Canada and Henry Ryan's former adversary, became chairman of the New Brunswick District.[5] He was, in Carroll's words, "a man of strong sense and equally strong will, . . . of sterling integrity and unquestionable piety."[6] With these veteran preachers were associated twenty missionaries, of whom three—McColl, Black and Bennett—were in semi-retirement, and two—James Hennigar and William Harrison—were put on probation at this point. As a group they were responsible for twenty-one stations or circuits and some twenty-two hundred members.[7]

Although the formal division of this small group of itinerants and laymen had some geographical advantages, it coincided with changes in the local situation and in the Committee's policy that could have been met more effectively by a single organization. In the ensuing decade, as in the previous ones, the potential field of Methodist activity continued to expand. Thirty-seven thousand people came to New Brunswick between 1825 and 1840; in the same interval eighty thousand flowed into Nova Scotia.[8] In both cases older communities became more populous and the new settlements in eastern Nova Scotia and north-eastern New Brunswick continued to expand. This inflow was accompanied by persistent emigration to the United States and by economic fluctuations which, as in the past, made it difficult to maintain continuity in the Societies and to secure adequate financial support from them.

Accompanying these continuing material and physical pressures were changes of even greater significance in the climate of opinion of the mainland provinces. Here, as in the Canadas, the eighteen-thirties saw the attainment of a degree of stability and maturity of outlook that made possible a comprehensive if sometimes erratic examination of the existing social and political structure. As a consequence there emerged in Nova Scotia and New Brunswick a growing determination to make the political system more amenable to popular pressure or at least to a wider range of interests.[9] In addition the church-state issue contributed much to what has been aptly described as an "era of ill feeling,"[10] with education the principal focus of controversy.

In dealing with the spiritual, social and political issues with which they were faced the Wesleyan preachers were if anything more restricted than in the past. November, 1832, saw the appointment of Alder as a missionary secretary; three years later he was charged with the oversight of the British North American districts.[11] With him were associated Jabez Bunting, the most influential and autocratic member of the British Conference, and John Beecham and Elijah Hoole,[12] firm but rather more charitable men. This energetic group imparted new life to the missionary cause, but by pressing simultaneously the need for local initiative and the importance of having their orders obeyed, they undermined the confidence of the preachers themselves. Only in the forties did they admit, albeit reluctantly, that their representatives must have more freedom of action in order to carry out their responsibilities.

The special concern of the Committee and the Secretaries, apart from their general insistence upon discipline, was utilization of men and money in a thrifty way. Faced as they were with a constant gap between the supply of volunteers and the demand for more men they paid increasing attention to the establishment of a "native agency." By this was meant the systematic recruitment of potential preachers from the local Societies.[13] After 1833, however, such men were called assistant missionaries, a title formerly used only for coloured recruits.[14] To the ministers in British North America the term was offensive because it suggested a difference in kind between English and colonial candidates.[15] Then, too, it reflected the Committee's calculation that it could secure local people for less money.[16] This did not happen in British North America, but the missionaries there were discriminated against in that they were not allowed to participate in the English pension fund.[17] "The feelings thus aroused having all the excitability of Nationality" were not conducive to the "spiritual prosperity" of these districts and probably made it more difficult to enlist native preachers.[18]

In addition to this source of controversy and distrust, a change in financial policy did little to improve relations between the North American districts and the Committee. In 1825 the Committee evidently decided to stop payments to individuals and instead to make to each district an annual grant that would be apportioned by the District Meeting to the various circuits.[19] This step produced consternation in the two eastern districts, whose members contended that the preachers' allowances were already inadequate and that the circuits were contributing as generously as those in England. As contributions were frequently received in kind, the Committee's cash grants were of particular value in providing servants, laundry and stationery. In general the missionaries felt that this new scheme would lower their standard of living and indirectly hamper the spread of the Gospel.[20] To this plaint the Committee apparently replied so sharply that in 1828 the New Brunswick District took "strong exception" and refused to comply with the new regulations.[21]

Eventually the two eastern districts accepted the new system, but they frequently over-spent their allocations. The Committee generally paid the deficits, but was naturally led to interfere incessantly in the management of the districts.[22] Again and again the preachers were enjoined to procure regular contributions from their flocks. The chairmen were asked why some ministers preached more frequently than others, presumably in the hope that if all worked equally hard no more men would be required.[23] Pointed remarks were made about the comparative costs of parsonages and travel. In fact the Secretaries' queries were so minute that on occasion the District Meetings were moved to reply quite bluntly, and to suggest that if their members were so bad as to deserve the Committee's censures they ought not to be retained in their posts.[24] Nevertheless the Committee generally had the last word: "I have been directed by the Committee," said Alder, "to admonish the Brethren to cultivate a better spirit . . . a spirit more in accord with the meekness and gentleness of Christ, and I may add . . . more in unison with your general character."[25]

Actually the Secretaries would have been better advised to urge their brethren to cultivate a more self-reliant rather than a meeker spirit. The dependent relationship which they sought to maintain was unhealthy for preachers and circuits. The former were constantly concerned about their financial position, but neither preachers nor people were really encouraged to accept full responsibility for their own welfare.[26] Attention was diverted from constructive projects while they justified their actions to London, yet conversely they were slow to develop a genuinely independent attitude of mind that would have led them to throw off the Society's authority.

Slow though they were in reacting to pressures from without and within, the two districts were developing perceptibly after 1830.

Growth was largely due to the work of new leaders. Though his authority was limited the chairman could, if he wished, give a sense of coherence and direction to the work of his district. Unfortunately Bamford and Williams, under whom the districts began their separate existence, proved unsatisfactory. Now becoming too old-fashioned for the larger circuits, Bamford was replaced by Croscombe in 1829. When the latter was transferred to Lower Canada in 1833,[27] Richard Knight was brought from Newfoundland, where he had laboured with great devotion.[28] A Devonshire man of Anglican background, he was alert to the spiritual needs of the circuits and soon gained the respect of his colleagues. His strong sense of duty, profound distrust of popular movements and limited imagination also secured for him the confidence of the Secretaries.

In New Brunswick, too, it was some years before a chairman acceptable to the Committee and the district was found. Richard Williams, appointed to that office in 1826, was soon declared "utterly unfit" to supervise its finances and was superseded in 1832 by J. B. Strong, his former associate in Lower Canada.[29] Strong retained his position until 1837 but did not enjoy the support of his brethren. To their consternation, fear of shipwreck led him to miss the district meeting of 1837. Then, in Temple's words, the enemies of Methodism said: "Their very chairman is frightened . . . no ties of family nor calls of duty . . . could overcome his terror." "I say not," he added, "Tell it not in Gath! No! Tell it Nowhere."[30] Fortunately Strong's absence led the Committee to appoint Temple in his place, thus giving New Brunswick as chairman a man high in their esteem, and one who was becoming closely identified with North American Methodism.[31]

The work of these able chairmen and indeed the general growth of Methodism in the eighteen-thirties was greatly assisted by some important additions to the itinerant ranks. In New Brunswick, especially, the impact of instability at the top was lessened by the presence of Enoch Wood, who came to the province from the West Indies in 1829. "From the first," in Carroll's words, "he impressed all his friends . . . with the average completeness of his talents for the pulpit and the platform, and the even balance of his character on all sides, combining as he did a vigorous intellect with an emotional nature—pastoral adaptation, with a capacity for connexional business."[32] Wood was "a business man" or, more politely, an able and energetic administrator who, in his influential circuits—Fredericton and Saint John—and later as district chairman, contributed greatly to the institutional growth of Methodism in New Brunswick.[33]

With this English recruit, whose viewpoint was becoming increasingly colonial, were associated three young North Americans—

Alexander McLeod, Humphrey Pickard and S. D. Rice—each of whom would contribute particular talents to the development of these eastern districts. Born at Saint John in 1808 into the family of Alexander McLeod, who was a close friend of Daniel Fidler and was formerly an aspirant to the itinerancy, McLeod grew up in a deeply Methodist environment. He was educated at the Saint John Grammar School and subsequently began the study of law. Converted in 1829, he entered the itinerant ranks during the following year, and would in time become the leading journalist among the eastern Methodists.[34]

Humphrey Pickard and S. D. Rice, candidates for the ministry in 1836, were in their way equally if not more valuable additions to the ranks. Each came from a Congregationalist background, but Pickard was born to a Methodist family in Fredericton, Rice to that of a Maine physician. The former was educated at Wesleyan schools in New England, the latter at Bowdoin College, Maine. They were, in effect, typical products of the close relationship between New England and the Maritime Provinces and of the second generation of Methodism in New Brunswick. To the ministry Pickard brought an urbane yet deeply moral interest in education; Rice displayed courage and administrative ability that would lead him to the highest position in Canadian Methodism.[35]

The acquisition of these men was indicative not only of steady growth in the number of preachers, but probably of a subtle alteration in their calibre and in their outlook.[36] They were becoming a body of men either native to the Maritime Provinces or identified with the area by long residence in it.[37] As such they showed a greater inclination than their predecessors to view the Methodist situation in local terms. They remained devoted to the evangelical ideal of Methodism—in some ways they were more enthusiastic than the first generation of English Wesleyans—but they had a broader vision of the rôle which the Methodist Societies might play in the world.

Under the impulsion of such preachers the Methodist community in the eastern provinces grew from 2,200 to 6,800 in little more than a decade.[38] New interests mingled with the traditional ones, but the implications of the Methodist system were still not clearly perceived. For preachers and people the dissemination of the Methodist version of the Gospel was still the paramount task.

Apart from shortages of men and money and difficulties set by the physical environment itself, sectarian opposition was the impediment that gave greatest concern. Although there were occasional complaints of Anglican opposition, the real threat was said to be posed by the Baptists, the inheritors of the worst features of the

Newlight tradition.[39] Writing from Shubenacadie in 1831, Thomas Crosthwaite complained that his circuit swarmed with believers in the unconditional perseverance of the elect, some of whom accused the Methodists of teaching the doctrine of purgatory.[40] For George Miller in Bridgetown, adult baptism was the great obstacle to Methodist progress. With characteristic Irish exuberance he exclaimed:

When Baptism by immersion is proclaimed as the Great Diana of modern times in this land, and preached as essential to salvation, the subjects being encouraged after the ordinance is administered to believe they had parted with the load of their sins in some liquid pool, probably with a turbid bottom, and that unconditional perseverance is the subsequent result, it is not a matter of wonder that many weak minds are led away, either by the attractions of popularity or of finding an easier way of going to heaven.[41]

To impress those who believed there was an easier way to heaven and those who gave it no thought, the missionaries travelled unremittingly around circuits that were still very large, preaching frequently on Sundays, less frequently during the week.[42] To make a special appeal to potential hearers they introduced, at the instance of the Secretaries, the "protracted meeting," a genteel version of the Canadian camp meeting.[43] Six were held in the New Brunswick District in 1836, the first year.[44] After the fashion of the camp meeting the protracted meeting was held in a central chapel, usually for four days. Charles Churchill, a newly arrived missionary, vividly describes one of these at which he preached in 1839. He found outside the chapel "forty vehicles" and "a dense crowd . . . a prelude to the throng within, where the people were so closely packed that it was with the utmost difficulty they could give way sufficiently for [him] to pass through to the pulpit." While he was preaching "a breathless silence, interrupted only by deep sobs, hung over the assembly; but when this part of the service was succeeded by exhortation and appeal . . . a heaving was visible in the whole assembly, and presently individuals . . . with difficulty pressed forward until they were bowed three deep around the altar, kneeling in prayer, and weeping bitterly, though accompanied with no extravagance of expression." The next evening, he continued, "was the most extraordinary time for the outpouring of God's Holy Spirit that [he] ever witnessed. . . . During the after portion of the meeting the effects produced baffle all description. . . . At one time ten or twelve persons arose at once, as though one gust of the Holy Spirit's quickening power had simultaneously burst their bonds, their places being quickly filled with others as they retired."[45]

A similar meeting held at Charlottetown in 1837 roused such enthusiasm that meetings continued for two months, resulting in the conversion of two hundred people, including some notorious sinners.[46]

Not only was popular response to this new form of revivalism a significant indication of the need to broaden the Methodist appeal but the willingness of preachers and people to take this step was symbolic of a rising determination to make their voices heard in other ways. The most conspicuous result of this change of mood was the foundation of the *Nova Scotia and New Brunswick Wesleyan Magazine* in 1832.

The decision to publish an inexpensive Wesleyan periodical, made apparently without the knowledge or the concurrence of the Committee, was taken in the light of prevailing conditions. The Methodist community, it was said, was constantly assailed by Baptist and Presbyterian magazines. Besides, the people required more instruction than could be given by the preachers and they were too poor to purchase English Methodist literature, which was often unsuitable in any case. The Committee, however, more impressed by the disobedience of the ministers than by the needs of the Societies, immediately suppressed the magazine.[48] Still convinced that the need was great, the Nova Scotia District laid its case before the Committee in 1833, but no reply was made.[49]

Two years later the inaction of the Committee impelled the District Meetings and some of the preachers to press for a quick decision.[50] "The poor Methodists," lamented William Leggett, "have no public instrument wherewith to repel the attacks of their assailants and to disseminate their doctrines in circles whereunto their missionaries have no access."[51] As silence continued to prevail in London, the first number of *The Wesleyan* appeared in February, 1838, under the editorship of Alexander McLeod. It was to be a fortnightly magazine designed to "afford the Wesleyan Methodists in the Provinces of Nova Scotia and New Brunswick an opportunity of stating and defending their doctrines and discipline and of employing the powerful instrumentality of the Press in doing good," and was to include articles covering biography, divinity, literature, history, science, missionary and general intelligence.[52] Until 1840 *The Wesleyan* continued to appear without official sanction.

Passing through Nova Scotia in July, 1839, Alder met the preachers in a special session at Halifax, *The Wesleyan* being the first order of business. Agreement was reached to discontinue it and to request permission to publish the *British North American Wesleyan Methodist Magazine* under the joint editorship of Temple and Wood.[53] The Committee acceded to this proposal with the understanding that editorial appointments must be submitted to Conference and that no political articles were to be published.[54] Not surprisingly the prospectus stated that "its principles will be expected to be denominational; but in its pages it will never be overlooked that there is a general Christianity whose interests are to be promoted. . . . Careless indifference and sectarian exclusiveness will be studiously avoided and the improvement of the reader in faith and love . . . as carefully sought."[55] To these standards the magazine adhered until it was supplanted by a new version of *The Wesleyan*.

While the two districts were engaged in securing this reluctant concession from the Committee, their members were becoming deeply concerned about the policy which they ought to adopt in the widening educational controversy of that era. In Nova Scotia and New Brunswick, as in Upper Canada, the provision of an educational system that would adequately cater to the needs of a poor and scattered population was complicated from the first by the determination of the provincial oligarchies to impose Anglican control over the system. The College of New Brunswick, which became King's College, Fredericton, in 1828, excluded dissenters until 1829.[56] It served and for a time continued to serve as a vehicle for the training of Anglican aristocrats, whereas the province was very slow to develop primary and secondary institutions useful to the majority.[57] In Nova Scotia, similarly, primary schools were largely neglected, while King's College served only the wealthier Anglicans.[58]

To provide for their own people in this situation, the Presbyterians had established Pictou Academy in 1816; requests for government grants for this institution precipitated a conflict between the two branches of the legislature.[59] As unfortunately the Academy was rather isolated and was as strongly Presbyterian as King's was Anglican, the Baptists founded Horton Academy in 1829, thereby adding an additional irritant to the business of the Nova Scotia legislature.[60] In 1830, then, both provinces, and especially Nova Scotia, had sectarian systems of higher education, but primary education and the interests of those who might wish a non-sectarian scheme of secondary education had been overlooked.

Although they were not one of the largest religious groups, the Methodists could perhaps have played an outstanding part by taking up the cause of non-denominational education. They were as convinced as their opponents, however, that a sectarian educational system was essential. In 1828 the Nova Scotia District proposed the establishment of a classical seminary.[61] So many offers of suitable sites were received that the Committee evidently decided not to act.[62] The question was raised again in 1832 by Croscombe, who pointed out that, in view of the rigid attitude of the Baptists and Anglicans, there was great need of a grammar school in which Methodist children could secure sound instruction.[63] In reply the Committee suggested that the two districts consult about the matter. The result was a decision to found Methodist academies at Fredericton, Halifax and Horton; these would be supported, it was hoped, by private subscription and government grants.[64] Early in 1834 the Committee sanctioned the establishment of "Christian and Methodistical" schools in both districts, but would of course provide no financial assistance. There for the moment the matter rested.[65]

Meanwhile, in Nova Scotia the university question was reaching a critical stage. Dalhousie College, founded by Lord Dalhousie in 1817, had formally opened its doors six years later but had languished for lack of students and public support.[66] By 1838, however, a rising demand for a non-sectarian university led to the appointment, as Dalhousie's president, of Dr. McCulloch, the former head of Pictou Academy. At the time it was anticipated that his assumption of office would be followed by the provision of adequate public support and the selection of staff by merit rather than for religious considerations. The breakdown of this scheme was followed by the foundation of the Baptist Acadia College and a prolonged educational dispute.[67]

In the ensuing agitation the Methodists did not participate actively, but there is no reason to suppose that they were enthusiastic about the proposed provincial university. They were much more attracted by an offer conveyed in a letter to Temple, in January, 1839, from Charles F. Allison, a prominent Sackville Methodist. "The establishment of schools in which *Pure Religion* is not only taught but *Constantly* brought before the youthful mind and represented to it as the basis and ground work of all the happiness which man is capable of enjoying here on Earth" was, he said, "one of the most efficient means in the order of Divine Providence to bring about the happy result spoken of by the Wise Man." He continued: "I now propose . . . to the British Conference and to the Wesleyan Methodist Missionaries . . . to purchase an Eligible site and erect suitable buildings in Sackville . . . for the establishment of a school of the description mentioned . . . to be altogether under the management and Control of the British Conference." If this offer were accepted, he was prepared to build the school in one year and for ten years to contribute £100 a year to its maintenance.[68]

Allison repeated his "providential" offer at the joint district meeting held in July, 1839. The preachers affirmed "that the necessity of an Institution in which the children of our Members and others desiring it might receive an Education on Wesleyan Principles has been long and painfully felt by the brethren of the Nova Scotia and New Brunswick Districts."[69] Allison's proposal was accepted with alacrity and Alder was asked to use his influence with the Committee in securing its permission for this venture. The prominent New Brunswick Methodists, Wilmot and Fisher, were to be asked to devise a deed incorporating arrangements for a board of trustees composed of the missionary secretaries and treasurers, the district chairmen, five preachers and five laymen from each district.[70] Alder also presented to the preachers a statement of the Committee's views on church-state relations in which the principle of church establishment was accepted and the responsibility of a Christian government to provide for the religious and moral welfare of its people was stressed. They found this position acceptable, thereby saying in effect that they would not molest the Anglican educational institutions and affirming that they were right in seeking state support for their proposed academy.[71]

The special district meeting of 1839 broke up in a thankful mood, for at last the Wesleyan Methodists of this area were within measurable distance of securing their own press and secondary school. The inception of these agencies, in 1841 and 1843 respectively, symbolized the beginning of a new era that would end in the establishment of the Conference of Eastern British America. It is clear that the two districts, despite the difficult conditions under which they functioned, had since 1826 become more closely identified with the Maritime community and more aware of the critical issues faced by that region.

On the whole, however, the quality of the Methodist response to the Maritime situation was not remarkable. If Methodists wanted a journal it was in large measure to defend themselves in an atmosphere of flourishing bigotry. Their educational plans sprang from a determination to educate Methodist youth in a Methodist environment rather than from the conviction that in a Christian society a religiously based educational system is essential. Working as they were, too, in an increasingly tense political situation, they apparently gave little thought to the possible political significance of their own position.

The typical Methodist posture continued to be a *non-political* loyalism. Probably with an eye on events in Upper Canada, Bamford assured Alder that the American Methodists were ignorant and enthusiastic politicians but that "among all the loyal subjects of

Great Britain, the Wesleyan Methodists are the top for loyalty."[72] Speaking of the 1836 Nova Scotia election Robert Cooney exclaimed: "Our little agitators are sounding the war-cry of the Radicals and Straining every nerve to form a democratic majority. But I hope the Lord will rebuke the company of spearmen, the multitude of the bulls with the calves of the people till everyone submit himself!"[73] Two years later *The Wesleyan* printed with approval Alder's letter about the disturbances in Lower Canada. In this, Croscombe, the district chairman, was warned against "all unnecessary intermeddling with political affairs," and was urged "to inculcate upon [his] people those great lessons of loyalty to our Most Gracious Sovereign and . . . a cordial obedience to the laws. . . . You should . . . exhort all to whom you have access to be subject to the higher powers and constantly urge upon those who are in danger of being seduced from all allegiance that ancient and sound precept 'Fear thou the Lord and the King and meddle not with those that are given to change.'" Finally, Alder added: "Wherever it is practicable, meetings for social prayer should be held and the divine blessing . . . be implored . . . especially for those who are placed in authority over them."[74] This statement breathed the same spirit as a letter from "A Methodist" who expressed the hope that *The Wesleyan* would not forget that "God's design" in raising up the Methodist preachers "was to spread Scripture holiness over the land." "Methodism," he continued, "has always maintained a firm and decided ground. It has been decidedly loyal and attached to the principles of the British constitution."[75] William Leggett, likewise, felt that "were all men Wesleyan Methodists . . . all would love old England, venerate her laws and honour her Queen."[76]

These admittedly fragmentary pieces of evidence, taken in conjunction with the educational policy of the two districts, suggest that the political outlook of the preachers and, presumably, of the Societies, continued to be conservative. Certainly there is no clear indication that any substantial group of Methodists in this region felt strongly about the liberal implications of their doctrine and system of church government. Even so, it does not follow that they were opposed to the budding reform movements in Nova Scotia and New Brunswick. The same Methodist who upheld the loyal tradition reminded his readers that Methodism had been "a warm advocate for . . . civil and religious liberty."[77] To many Methodists, no doubt, there was no contradiction between loyalty to the British constitution and to the principle of civil and religious liberty, in part because the loyalty cry had not the same violent emotional overtones here that it had in Upper Canada. Probably, therefore, many individual Methodists were to be found in the ranks of those who opposed many aspects of the existing political and social system. Nevertheless, as a body the Methodists of the eastern districts were more nearly identified with the existing order than with its opponents, and they were encouraged by their spiritual guides not to meddle with it as Methodists.

This inner ambiguity of the Methodists' political position was, it would appear, symbolic of their place in the Maritime Provinces during the eighteen-thirties. Essentially they constituted a small but growing religious minority, in process of assimilation to the local environment. This situation did not compel Methodists to undertake a thorough scrutiny of the part they might or ought to play in the political and social reform of the Maritime Provinces. They proved to be unwilling or unable to take more than tentative steps towards the development of a sense of responsibility for secular issues, continuing rather to insist, explicitly or implicitly, that their real function was to spread "Scripture holiness" throughout the land. In effect they added to the numbers of those earnestly religious people who, although accepting the elementary obligations of citizenship, disliked the distractions of the world and avoided involvement in them. Their acceptance of a more positive rôle in the life of their society was yet to come.

REFERENCES TO CHAPTER FOUR

1. *M.R.*, Reels 5 and 6. Minutes of Nova Scotia and New Brunswick District Meetings, 1826.
2. T. W. Smith, *History of the Methodist Church* . . . , II, 186. Apparently the missionaries were not generally cognizant of the Committee's plans. *W.R.*, Reel 3, Temple to the Secretaries, November 15, 1825.
3. See the protest of the Nova Scotia District in *M.R.*, Reel 5, Bamford and Temple to the Secretaries, June 1, 1826. The original plan was to include Prince Edward Island in the New Brunswick District, but to strengthen that district the missionaries decided to attach the Annapolis valley to it instead. *W.R.*, Reel 6, W. Burt to the Secretaries, January 12, 1826; *M.R.* Reel 6, New Brunswick Minutes, 1826.
4. *M.R.*, Reel 5, Nova Scotia Minutes, 1826.
5. *Ibid.*, Reel 6, New Brunswick Minutes, 1826.
6. J. Carroll, *Case and His Cotemporaries*, II, 75-76.
7. *M.R.*, Reels 5 and 6, District Minutes, 1826. In 1827 there were 9,408 Methodists and adherents in Nova Scotia. Public Archives of Nova Scotia, *Report of the Board of Trustees . . . for the Year 1947* (Halifax, 1948), 21.

8. W. T. Easterbrook, H. G. J. Aitken, *Canadian Economic History* (Toronto, 1956), 239; J. B. Brebner, *Canada: A Modern History*, 168.
9. C. Martin, *Foundations of Canadian Nationhood*, chaps. 6 and 7.
10. H. H. Walsh, *The Christian Church in Canada*, 151.
11. *M.R.*, Reel 1, Committee Minutes, November 21, 1832.
12. Bunting was a secretary from 1818 to 1820, 1821 to 1824, and 1833 to 1851; Beecham from 1831 to 1856; Hoole from 1834 to 1872. Findlay and Holdsworth, *History of the Wesleyan Methodist Missionary Society*, I, 107-108.
13. *M.R.*, Reel 2, Alder to J. B. Strong, March 2, 1835.
14. Findlay and Holdsworth, *op. cit.*, I, 333.
15. *M.R.*, Reel 5, Nova Scotia Minutes, 1836; *W.R.*, Reel 24, W. Leggett to the Secretaries, November 6, 1837.
16. *M.R.*, Reel 2, J. Beecham to chairman of New Brunswick District, February 27, 1834.
17. *Ibid.*, Alder to the same, April 2, 1836. Temple pointed out that, as retired preachers could not be allowed to starve, it would be cheaper to let them participate. *W.R.*, Reel 24, Temple to Alder, November 27, 1837.
18. *Ibid.*, Reel 11, Temple to the Secretaries, March 5, 1838. In the forties the title "Assistant Missionary" was dropped. Findlay and Holdsworth, *op. cit.*, I, 334.
19. *M.R.*, Reel 1, Committee Minutes, January 4, 1832.
20. *Ibid.*, Reels 5 and 6, New Brunswick and Nova Scotia Minutes, 1826.
21. *Ibid.*, Reel 6, New Brunswick Minutes, 1828.
22. See *M.R.*, Reel 2, Beecham to the chairman of the Nova Scotia District, February 22, 1835.
23. In 1835 Fredericton was not allowed an additional preacher because the incumbent preached only five times each week. *Ibid.*, Alder to New Brunswick chairman, March 2, 1835.
24. *Ibid.*, Reel 6, New Brunswick Minutes, 1835.
25. *Ibid.*, Reel 2, Alder to New Brunswick chairman, April 2, 1836.
26. In 1840 Halifax had two chapels, one of which was elaborately furnished, but the circuit still drew on the Society's grant. For a description of the chapels see Charles Churchill, *Memorials of Missionary Life in Nova Scotia* (London, 1845), 26-27.
27. In 1828, "A Methodist" wrote from Halifax that two years of Bamford's preaching was enough; three years would be too much. *W.R.*, Reel 7, "A Methodist" to the Committee, July 6, 1828; *M.R.*, Reel 2, Beecham to Croscombe, March 30, 1833.
28. Smith, *op. cit.*, II, 211.
29. *W.R.*, Reel 24, Secretaries to Strong, July 13, 1832.
30. *Ibid.*, Reel 24, Temple to Alder, September 8, 1837.
31. *Ibid.*, Reel 24, Temple to Alder, November 27, 1837. Temple noted in an earlier letter that he was regarded by some as a spy for the Committee.

32. Carroll, *op. cit.*, V, 9.
33. The phrase is Bamford's. *W.R.*, Reel 11, Bamford to Alder, December 31, 1838. Except for a term in the Miramichi circuit, Wood shuttled between Saint John and Fredericton.
34. See the Fidler Papers for letters written by McLeod senior. On McLeod see his statement for the Committee. *W.R.*, Reel 7, May 31, 1830.
35. Smith, *op. cit.*, II, 269-273. Subsequently Rice became general superintendent of the Methodist Church in Canada.
36. In 1840 there were forty-two preachers in the two districts.
37. The presence in the districts of McLeod, Pickard, Rice, A. McNutt, Bamford, Richey, Henry Pope, Knight and Temple justifies this statement.
38. The figures are based on district minutes. Circuits increased from twenty-one to thirty-two.
39. See *W.R.*, Reel 8, Henry Daniel to the Secretaries, February 26, 1832.
40. *Ibid.*, T. Crosthwaite to the Secretaries, June 28, 1831.
41. *Ibid.*, Reel 10, Miller to the Secretaries, May 8, 1836.
42. This statement is based on a variety of reports concerning sizes of circuits and preaching schedules.
43. Smith, *op. cit.*, II, 275; *M.R.*, Reel 5, Nova Scotia Minutes, 1835.
44. *M.R.*, Reel 6, New Brunswick Minutes, 1836.
45. Churchill, *op. cit.*, 76-77, 79-80.
46. *W.R.*, Reel 24, Knight to Alder, August 15, 1837.
47. *M.R.*, Reel 5, Nova Scotia Minutes, 1833.
48. *W.R.*, Reel 8, Alder to the Secretaries, May 8, 1832. Four issues were printed. Smith, *op. cit.*, II, 407.
49. *M.R.*, Reel 5, Nova Scotia Minutes, 1833; Reel 2, Beecham to the Nova Scotia chairman, February 27, 1834.
50. See *Ibid.*, Reels 5 and 6, Nova Scotia Minutes, 1836; New Brunswick Minutes, 1837.
51. *W.R.*, Reel 10, Leggett to the Secretaries, June 20, 1837.
52. *The Wesleyan*, I, February 28, 1838.
53. *M.R.*, Reel 5, Minutes of a Joint Session of the New Brunswick, Nova Scotia and Newfoundland Districts, July 12, 1839.
54. *Ibid.*, Reel 1, February 12, 1840.
55. *The Wesleyan*, II, February 3, 1840.
56. J. Hannay, *History of New Brunswick*, I, 398-400.
57. See K. F. C. MacNaughton, *The Development of the Theory and Practice of Education in New Brunswick, 1784-1900* (Fredericton, 1947), 53, chapters 4 and 5.
58. The King's College Act was passed in 1789; the royal charter was granted in 1802. In 1803 the statutes of the College were issued, prohibiting any form of dissent within it. F. W. Vroom, *King's College: A Chronicle* (Halifax, 1941), 21, 34, 36. On education in Nova Scotia see Brebner, *Canada*, 174-175.

59. D. C. Harvey, "The Intellectual Awakening of Nova Scotia," *Dalhousie Review*, XIII (1933-34), 14; Walsh, *op. cit.*, 155.
60. R. S. Longley, *Acadia University* (Wolfville, 1939), 22.
61. M.R., Reel 5, Nova Scotia Minutes, 1828.
62. Smith, *op. cit.*, II, 389.
63. W.R., Reel 8, Croscombe to the Secretaries, December 31, 1832.
64. M.R., Reel 5, Nova Scotia Minutes, 1833; Minutes of an Extra District Meeting, 1833.
65. *Ibid.*, Reel 1, Beecham to New Brunswick chairman, February 27, 1834. In New Brunswick extensive preparations were made, but these were not completed. See Smith, *op. cit.*, II, 389-390; W.R., Reel 9, W. Murray to the Secretaries, October 17, 1833.
66. D. C. Harvey, *An Introduction to the History of Dalhousie University* (Halifax, 1938), 18; Walsh, *op. cit.*, 157.
67. Walsh, *op. cit.*, 156-158; Longley, *op. cit.*, 25-37. The act to incorporate Acadia College was approved in 1841.
68. W.R., Reel 11, C. F. Allison to W. Temple, January 4, 1839.
69. M.R., Reel 5, Minutes of Joint Meeting, 1839.
70. *Ibid.*
71. *Ibid.*
72. W.R., Reel 9, Bamford to Alder, May 6, 1834.
73. *Ibid.*, Reel 10, Cooney to the Secretaries, September 1, 1836.
74. *The Wesleyan*, I, May 6, 1838.
75. *Ibid.*, March 14, 1838.
76. W.R., Reel 11, Leggett to the Secretaries, October 10, 1838. In 1837 the New Brunswick District assured Sir John Harvey that its members taught loyalty to their people and had no desire to meddle in politics. See *M.R.*, Reel 6, New Brunswick Minutes, 1837.
77. *The Wesleyan*, I, March 14, 1838.

FIVE

"Shall then this 'night-mare upon our constitution'
... be tolerated and sanctioned in Upper Canada?"

When the Canada Conference met at Switzer's Chapel near Kingston, October 2, 1828, many of its members must have felt that this was an historic occasion, for they knew that their principal task was the establishment of an independent Methodist Church in Upper Canada.[1] Perhaps only the most prescient among them suspected that this step would be the prelude to years of controversy, the consequences of which would be vital in the development of the Methodist Connexion.

When the Canada Conference had been formed in 1824 its first act was to draft a memorial for independence. It was felt that a separate conference would become necessary because of the anti-American prejudices excited by the war, "the insulated and extended situation of the societies in this Country from the General superintendency," and, above all, the objections of the local government to a religious body subject to a foreign jurisdiction. Until they became independent there was no hope of securing those civil privileges of which the Methodists were deprived.[2] In the interval the position of the Conference had not improved. The political atmosphere of Upper Canada had become increasingly embittered, and among the Methodists Ryan was actively proclaiming that independence must be secured at all costs. In any event, the changing complexion of the Conference itself heightened the pressure for independent status. It was not surprising that the Conference of 1827 appointed a delegation to attend the General Conference of 1828 and to seek its permission to establish a Canadian Methodist church.[3]

Nathan Bangs and the committee appointed to consider the Canadian request were opposed to the separation of the Canada Conference from the parent church, but as John Ryerson exuberantly declared: "Blessed be God for ever. Amidst all the painful & trying scenes through which we have passed in this conflicting business, the God of David has stood by us & has given us a desided victory."[4] By a majority of sixty-two the Conference acceded to the Canadian proposal. The Canada Conference was empowered within the next four years to elect a general superintendent, to be ordained by one or more of the American bishops. In addition a generous financial settlement was made and the Conference undertook to persuade the British Conference not to break the division agreement reached in 1820.[5] The way was now clear for the momentous step which would be taken by the Conference of 1828.

Since the independence movement had not been prompted by dissatisfaction with the general character of the Methodist Episcopal Church, the Canadian preachers in large measure followed the precedents established by that body. In the new Methodist Episcopal Church in Canada, the Conference, in its dual aspects of general and annual conferences, retained supreme authority over preachers and people. Conscious, however, of the lay agitation in the United States and the Ryanite threat, the Conference agreed that

> No new rule . . . or alteration of any rule or regulation now in force respecting our temporal economy . . . [nor] . . . any new rule . . . respecting the doctrines of our Church, the rights and privileges of our members . . . shall be considered as of any force . . . until such rule . . . shall have been laid before the several Quarterly Conferences throughout the whole connexion and shall have received the consent . . . of two thirds of the said Conferences.[6]

The quarterly meeting, thus significantly strengthened, was retained as the agency of local government throughout the church.

Despite its willingness to give more authority to the laity the Conference maintained the episcopate and the presiding eldership but the informal consultation between the bishops and the elders, customary in the United States, was made obligatory, especially in the stationing of the preachers.[7] In practice, however, the episcopate did not develop within the new framework. The Conference of 1828 selected the Rev. Wilbur Fisk, a noted American Methodist, as the first bishop but he and other candidates refused the post. The Conference had to appoint a temporary superintendent.[8] William Case was elected to this office and retained it until the abolition of the episcopate in 1833.[9] Since Case did not resemble Asbury and McKendree the episcopal office did not become very important in Upper Canadian Methodism. This development served to strengthen the position of the presiding elders and other powerful individuals in the Conference.

Considering the limited veto acquired by the quarterly meetings and the decline of the episcopate it is clear that after 1828 the distribution of power in the Canada Conference was different from that in the Methodist Episcopal Church. If anything, the position of the Conference was stronger and within it there was a greater degree of freedom. Nevertheless, the Conference had accepted much more explicitly than had the parent conference the need for more than self-imposed limitations on its actions. It could not be forced to act in a certain way, but it could be prevented from acting in an unpopular manner. Essentially this was a limited system of government that at least admitted the right of the lay majority to be consulted. It pointed not toward democratic rule, but to a constitutional form of government operated with a sense of restraint and responsibility.

The changes that were made in the Canadian Methodist polity by the Conference of 1828 were not accompanied by any alterations in doctrine. The new church remained committed to the doctrinal formulation of the Methodist Episcopal Church and to the practical teaching of conversion and sanctification.[10] Unfortunately the secular significance of this teaching was no more evident than that of the Methodist system of church government. In principle the strong Methodist conviction that salvation was "free in all and free for all" could and perhaps should have involved an equally fervent commitment to social and political individualism. Indeed, according to Egerton Ryerson, "the early Methodist preachers . . . taught doctrines which lay at the foundation of a country's freedom."[11]

In practice, however, the secular inferences, if any, drawn by Methodists from their religious outlook, would depend upon the kind of emphasis laid on different aspects of it. If they were encouraged to accept an individualist and other-worldly approach to the achievement of holiness, they were likely to separate themselves, as Methodists, from the world. If, on the other hand, they were urged to think of themselves as free men, equal in the sight of God, committed to seek their own salvation in accepting responsibility for the needs of others, they might willingly develop a broad concern for social and political equality. The willingness with which one attitude or the other was espoused by the Methodist community would be determined by the attitudes of its leaders, the character of its membership and by secular conditions.

In 1828, the Canada Conference included forty-eight itinerant preachers, a number that in four years would increase to sixty-four.[12] Among this growing body of men there was agreement on certain basic principles but in background and general outlook they were remarkably diverse, a fact of great importance in assessing their conceptions of the rôle of Methodism. This can be most effectively demonstrated by an examination of some representative figures in the Conference.

To many observers, the Ryerson brothers, especially Egerton, were the only Methodist preachers who counted in this period. They were men of great influence but the leading ranks also included

William Case, his protégé Anson Green, and James Richardson. Colonel Joseph Ryerson, an Anglican Loyalist, had five sons who entered the Methodist ministry.[13] Of these, John, William and Egerton were the most influential. William Ryerson, a graduate as he quaintly said of the college of "Buck and Bright," was admitted on trial in 1823.[14] A "large ... rather coarse featured" man, "he possessed," said Carroll "those feelings of strong sympathy with his subject for the time being and the power of transferring his own realizations and emotions, whether of fear, hate, indignation, scorn, or tenderness, to his hearers, to such a degree, that for the present they were not under the control of their sober second judgment."[15] Despite his lack of opportunity William was a "man of some little learning ... and of a rare order of genius." His mind was "unceasingly active" and his gift for conversation was unusual.[16] In short, William Ryerson was a great, if unpolished preacher, who would acquire broad liberal sympathies in political and religious matters.

At the Conference of 1821 John Ryerson, "aged twenty-one, single, not in debt," was admitted on trial.[17] He had "a good degree of intelligence; a genteel appearance and manner, great gravity of demeanour ... a sound judgment and strong will; ... and certain spasmodic bursts of fervor ... made his ministrations effective and noticeable."[18] Unlike some of his colleagues he was "very studious, especially in sermon-making."[19] John Ryerson would become an ecclesiastical statesman rather than a great pastor or preacher. Within six years he had been appointed a presiding elder and continued to occupy leading positions in the Conference. His letters and actions amply demonstrate that his judgment was shrewd, but that his sympathies were essentially conservative. For him the preservation of the Methodist Church as an institution was of the first importance.

John's younger brother Egerton has remained a rather elusive figure. When he entered the ministry in 1825 he had already laid the foundations of an education that would make him one of the most scholarly men in Upper Canada.[20] A nimble mind and an equally nimble pen, great courage, tenacity, and self-confidence would make him a formidable defender of every cause he espoused. He generated fierce loyalties and strong antipathies that were relieved by his ability to command the friendship and the respect of his colleagues. To many he seemed a man of little faith, but no impression could have been more misleading. Throughout his entire career Ryerson clung to a simple evangelical conviction, whose significance he construed more broadly than did many others. In ecclesiastical and secular matters his position was subtle and many-sided, a characteristic which reflected the powerful cross-currents of Canadian religious and political life and which fitted him to deal effectively with them.

In marked contrast to the powerful Ryerson triumvirate was William Case, acting general superintendent from 1828 to 1833. A mild and humble man whose beliefs and habits probably seemed somewhat archaic, his influence was waning in 1828, a development hastened by his increasing preoccupation with Indian missions.[21] With Case would go an influential embodiment of the former intimacy with the American Methodists, and of that detachment from secular things that had characterized Methodism in the past.

Case's close friend, Anson Green, however, was on the verge of a considerable career in Canadian Methodism; he would be the last American to occupy a position of real importance in the Conference. Born in rural New York in 1801, Green was "born again on the 27th of October, 1819." "The former," he emphasized, "was an important event, but would have proved an endless curse without the latter."[22] His conversion was preceded by a period of "halting and temporizing between the Church and the world"; its sequel was a decision to enter the Methodist ministry, made after he had emigrated to Upper Canada as a teacher.[23] Green entered the ministry in 1825 with a disciplined and well-stocked mind, dignity and decorum that would endear him to prosperous congregations, sympathy for Canadian needs, and liberal inclinations. Yet this man, the epitome of the respectable minister, was driven by a zeal so fearless that his exertions as a presiding elder gravely impaired his health.

James Richardson, who was a probationer along with Egerton Ryerson and Green, also became a distinctive figure in the Conference. He was a former naval officer of English and Anglican background who had lost an arm at Oswego. Richardson had become a man of influence before he was converted in 1818; as a local preacher he had signed Ryan's 1824 manifesto, an indication of the independence of mind he would later display. In Carroll's words: "His manners were easy, and made him free of access; there was an air of the most unmistakable piety about him—not asceticism or grievance, but simple goodness. . . . His preaching was truly Wesleyan: sound, simple, clear and unctious. It stood not in the wisdom or device of men, but in the power of God."[24] Appointed assistant preacher on the York circuit in 1824 he became the senior preacher in the following year and rose rapidly in the esteem of his brethren. As editor of the *Guardian*, following Egerton Ryerson, he revealed great liberality of mind but his range of vision was more narrow than his predecessor's.

Behind this diverse group of leading figures, to which might be added Franklin Metcalf and David Wright, stood the growing ranks of those who never attained the limelight, but on whose actions in conference and circuit much of the welfare of Methodism depended.[25] Among the latter were George Ferguson and Robert Corson. When independence came in 1828, George Ferguson had been an active preacher for many years; he would serve on outlying circuits until 1843.[26] Born in Londonderry to an Anglican family, Ferguson was exposed to Methodist influences at an early age and soon developed pangs of conscience. Unfortunately the attention that was paid by kind friends to his spiritual needs was not matched by his parents, who neglected his education. He entered the army in 1809, a convinced Methodist but one inadequately equipped for a preaching career.

In Canada he met Henry Ryan who persuaded him to enter the itinerancy. He soon came to epitomize the legendary Methodist evangelist—one who sought by disciplined study to remedy his lack of knowledge, who was blessed with a large family and cursed by poverty, who maintained discipline with a firm hand and whose preaching was marked by great simplicity and enthusiasm. The meeting at which a shout was not raised was a disappointment to George Ferguson. Nevertheless, he had a keen appreciation of the qualities of others such as Egerton Ryerson and of the difficulties with which his church was faced. He preferred, however, to emphasize the need for holiness and thus to divert his people from worldly extremes. In humility he began; in humility he ended his account of his life: "I am much humbled in retracing God's mercy and grace to me, an unworthy worm."[27]

For Carroll, Robert Corson was the typical itinerant of the 1830's. Born in Upper Canada in 1793, Corson's "hard heart was softened" by Case's preaching in 1807.[28] After his conversion he became an exhorter and subsequently a local preacher and farmer. A simple, energetic and intelligent man, he soon attracted Case's attention and was put on trial with William Ryerson in 1823.[29] His enthusiastic sermons and his jovial demeanour won many converts and friends. Yet Corson was not simply an evangelist. He was aware of the broader responsibilities of his Church and would intervene frequently in Conference on behalf of what he felt to be Canadian and popular interests.[30] Indeed, although he was regarded as a rather rustic figure, Corson's appreciation of worldly and other-worldly things was representative of the rising generation of preachers.

Assuredly, if those preachers who have been described were characteristic of the Methodist itinerancy as a whole, it would be unreasonable to anticipate from them any simple or uniform pattern of reaction to the complex environment in which they laboured. A body of men predominantly North American in background, of humble antecedents and modest learning, they were likely to identify themselves with local and popular interests.[31] Perhaps a majority of them agreed with Ferguson or Corson that their main task was to lead men into the way of holiness. To some, therefore, the world was a hindrance and a distraction; to others it was an area of limited concern. Politically, men of this type were often drawn for the sake of peace to the side of authority, rather than to an examination of the secular implications of their creed. In the minority were some, of whom John Ryerson was possibly the most outstanding, whose primary objective was the institutional growth of Methodism. Faced with political and social issues, men of this kind could be expected to form independent attitudes instead of aligning themselves consistently with any political group. Egerton Ryerson, and to a lesser degree William Ryerson, Green and Richardson, stood apart from both groups. They had a deeper, broader understanding of what it meant to be an Upper Canadian Methodist in 1830 and supported Canadian and majority interests. They too were limited, however, not only by the sense of moderation and independence of mind so marked, for example, in Ryerson, but also by their conviction that ultimately Methodism would be judged on its effectiveness in leading men to salvation.

The Methodist community consisted of a host of lesser leaders and ordinary members as well as preachers. In this newly independent body a large number of local preachers, exhorters and class leaders assisted the itinerants in caring for the spiritual needs of some thirty thousand Methodists and adherents.[32] The Methodist Societies were scattered from the eastern to the western end of the province and included people in most of the settled areas. Probably a majority of them were of either American or Irish origin, but of the former a substantial number must have been native Upper Canadians.[33] The Methodists were predominantly rural-dwellers but it is not certain that they were generally from the lowest level of the social order. On the contrary, Methodist congregations likely represented a wide cross-section of the Upper Canadian populace, excepting those in government and those who classified themselves as gentlemen. Methodists doubtless were as literate and intelligent as the overwhelming majority of their fellow-citizens.[34]

With these antecedents the Methodist membership presumably had an incipient sympathy for the popular or reform cause. Moreover, as persons who had voluntarily entered the Methodist fold, they had a stronger and more easily aroused sense of loyalty to their leaders than the members of some religious bodies. There were, however, limits to their willingness to respond to suggestion. To begin with they had a keen interest in making their own voices heard and would resist any important proposal about which they had not been consulted. But the kind of policy that would appeal to the old American would not always be attractive to the Loyalist or his descendant, nor to the Irish immigrant with no historic stake in North American quarrels. With even less opportunity to consider the implications of his faith than the itinerant had, the average Methodist was in all likelihood religiously conservative—that is, principally concerned with his place in eternity rather than in time. For him, active intervention in secular affairs might be a dangerous pastime, or more commonly, he failed to relate his religious and his secular opinions in any coherent way.

When viewed in the broad framework of its polity, its doctrines, the qualities of its ministers and of its members, the new Methodist Episcopal Church appears as a body with uncertain potentialities. Clearly, many within its ranks would interpret the Methodist task narrowly, whether for institutional or religious reasons. At the same time, others, probably a minority, were prepared to examine the secular implications of the Methodist polity and of the Methodist ethic and to apply their insights to the secular realm. In so doing, they were unlikely to adopt an extreme position and, ultimately, as Methodists, rather than as citizens, they were certain to conclude that the spiritual order must not be endangered by devotion to temporal needs.

Left to themselves, the Methodists as a body probably would not have become involved in the political life of Upper Canada. But two years before the coming of independence they were caught up in the growing controversy over the place of the Church of England in the province, a dispute which in itself was but one facet of a complex battle about the future development of Upper Canadian society. Without an understanding of the nature of this conflict the Methodist part in it can, however, scarcely be appreciated.

2

In the eighteen-twenties and thirties, Upper Canada was a heterogeneous collection of settlements with few common interests and little sense of identity.[35] Over this fragile social order had been set a system of government designed to grant the form but not the substance of power to the majority. In combination with prevailing social and economic conditions, this arrangement had facilitated the emergence of the so-called Family Compact.[36] The Compact never was an association linked by family ties; rather it was a clique composed of those who had secured political power at either the local or provincial level. It was held together partly by the natural reluctance of those who had power to relinquish it, and in part by its adherence to certain political and social principles.[37] Its members believed that only those who had wealth, education and, if possible, a family tradition, should exercise political authority—in effect that the existing oligarchic system of government should be continued. To consolidate and strengthen their position they wanted an economic policy related to business needs and an educational system open only to those with wealth and social status. Moreover, they were convinced that Upper Canada must have an established church and that its connection with the United Kingdom must be preserved unchanged; the former was to inculcate obedience and loyalty to the British connexion, the latter was to maintain the existing distribution of power in the province.[38]

The aggressiveness of the Family Compact and the upsurge of political radicalism in the United States and Great Britain had produced a reform group by 1825, but it was more amorphous in composition and beliefs than the oligarchy it opposed.[39] In a very broad sense the reformers comprised all those who were frustrated in their economic, social and political aspirations. They sought political institutions responsive to the wishes of the majority, equality of opportunity in the economy and in education, and the separation of church and state. Unfortunately the reformers did not agree on the manner in which these objectives should be secured. On one side stood the radicals who ultimately concluded that Upper Canada must climb aboard the North American "bandwagon," that is, accept the democratic philosophy and, if need be, sever the imperial connexion. On the other side were the Canadian or moderate reformers who were convinced that most Upper Canadians wished to be neither Englishmen nor Americans but Canadians, and sought to find ways of fostering this Canadian identity, a task made exceedingly difficult by the persistent intrusion of the loyalty issue. The tories claimed a monopoly on loyalty to the Empire and freely asserted that to differ with them was to accept the American side, which was by definition disloyal. Since anti-Americanism was a potent force in Upper Canada it was easy to smear the reformer as one who wished to destroy the Empire. Because of such pressures Upper Canadian liberalism acquired an elusive and ambiguous quality, rendering it almost indefinable.[40] Nevertheless, it probably expressed the feelings of the majority, and in its sensitiveness to diverse interests it had a potential affinity with Upper Canadian Methodism.

The conflict between tories and reformers did not emerge full-blown at any point but was intensified in a series of engagements on critical issues.[41] The dispute over church-state relations and the allied question of education was one of the earliest to arise and ultimately one of the most troublesome. As this conflict impinged directly upon the growth of Methodism, its leaders were drawn into it and eventually they were led into a much broader argument concerning the general development of Upper Canada.

The imperial government had planned, after 1763, to establish the Church of England in the province of Quebec, but the various instructions to that effect were never properly applied.[42] Nevertheless, the Constitutional Act of 1791 provided for the collection of tithes, the establishment and endowment of rectories, and the reservation of one-seventh of all the lands granted in Upper Canada for the support of a Protestant clergy, the responsibility of using this authority being left with the local government.[43] These provisions accorded nicely with Governor Simcoe's design for Upper Canada, yet he did not apply them effectively. Tithes were never collected and no rectories were founded until 1836.[44] In other respects, however, the Church of England was given privileges that the Church of Scotland shared to a limited degree. The right to marry and to hold property was confined to Anglican and Calvinist clergy, the reserves were set aside regularly, and public office was given largely to Anglicans or Presbyterians.[45] In addition the Church of England in Canada was subsidized by the Society for the Propagation of the Gospel, which was dependent financially upon the imperial government.[46] Considering these various circumstances the conviction grew among both supporters and opponents of the Church of England that it was in fact the established church in Upper Canada.

The clergy reserves question really precipitated a fundamental dispute concerning church-state relations in Upper Canada after 1815. In 1803 Bishop Mountain, whose diocese then included Upper Canada, had proposed that better methods of administering the reserves should be sought.[47] Sixteen years later the reserves in Upper Canada, which by this date comprised nearly two million acres, were placed under the jurisdiction of an ecclesiastical corporation, the product of energetic lobbying by John Strachan, Rector of York.[48] At this point certain members of the Church of Scotland pressed the government of Upper Canada for public assistance; their request was referred to the Crown Law Officers. The latter replied that the governor might properly divide the reserves revenue between the Churches of England and Scotland but they did not believe dissenters had any claim on the fund.[49]

The foundation of the Clergy Reserves Corporation and the Law Officers' opinion emphasized the critical nature of the reserves issue. The way was open for a bitter quarrel between the two state churches, and other communions wishing a share of the public bounty might join at any time. The crucial problem was that two churches representing a minority of Upper Canada's population were claiming the exclusive right to utilize a large portion of the province's principal resource—the land. If their claim were granted these lands not only would constitute an obstacle to settlers but would in time earn the established churches enough income to give them a considerable advantage over their competitors.[50] Upper Canadians with some knowledge of the separation of church and state in the United States and of the ineffectiveness of the Anglican and Scottish clergy, or those with a dissenting background in the United Kingdom, were bound to see this as an iniquitous arrangement. This opinion would be shared by many Anglicans and Presbyterians who were determined to adapt their churches to the North American environment or who felt that state assistance was morally harmful to any church.

Presumably such convictions led the Assembly of 1826 to urge the secularization of the reserves. The first bill to this end was passed the following year.[51] Doubtless his awareness of this rising antipathy to the Church of England led Dr. Strachan, the real head of that body in Upper Canada, to expound its policy in a sermon delivered on July 3, 1825, to commemorate the death of Bishop Mountain.[52] Once this statement became known the lines were fairly drawn between supporters and opponents of religious monopoly in the province.

As Strachan noted, the late bishop had had since his consecration in 1793 an exceedingly arduous task in furthering the growth of the Church in Canada, especially in finding clergy and the money to pay them. Strachan observed:

The religious benefits of the Ecclesiastical Establishment of England are little known or felt; . . . Sectaries . . . are increasing on every side. And when it is considered that the religious teachers of the other denominations, . . . a very few respectable Ministers of the Church of Scotland excepted, come almost universally from the Republican States of America . . . it is quite evident that, if the Imperial Government does not immediately step forward with efficient help, the mass of the population will be nurtured and instructed in hostility to our parent church, nor will it be long until they imbibe opinions anything but favourable to the political Institutions of England. . . . Even when churches are erected, the persons who give regular attendance are so few as greatly to discourage the Minister, and his influence is frequently broken or injured by numbers of uneducated itinerant preachers, who, leaving their steady employment, betake themselves to preaching the Gospel from idleness, or a zeal without knowledge, by which they are induced without any preparation to teach what they do not know and which . . . they disdain to learn.[53]

Dr. Strachan contended it was the primary duty of government to strengthen the Church's position in Upper Canada. "The Church establishment must be made efficient and commensurate with the wants of the people. . . ." "Can it be doubted that it is only through the Church and its Institutions, that a truly English character and feeling can be given to or preserved among the population of any Foreign possession? By adopting a uniform system of religious instruction for all her Colonies . . . [England] will establish an Empire more absolute than any."[54]

Strachan's statement seems remarkably archaic in spirit but in the light of English conditions at that time it was not. The real tragedy was that it had so little accord with the temper of the community. Yet in its snobbish dismissal of the Protestant denominations, its acute awareness of the close ties between Upper Canada and the neighbouring states, and in its concept of the Church as an instrument of imperial consolidation it expressed succinctly much of the tory position. Clearly, too, Strachan and those for whom he spoke were determined to retain the clergy reserves as an indispensable means of providing for the future growth of the Church in the province.

Whatever the views of Upper Canadians might be on the establishment and reserves questions, they were unlikely to respond sympathetically to an argument accompanied by what appeared to be gratuitous insults. The Methodists, assuming that they were one of the bodies of ignorant pro-American enthusiasts to whom the learned cleric referred, decided to make a public reply.[55] James Richardson and Egerton Ryerson, the preachers on the York circuit, were asked to prepare a statement but Ryerson alone responded with a "review" of Strachan's sermon that appeared in the reform *Colonial Advocate,* May 11, 1826.[56]

While he disclaimed any "reflection on the doctrines, liturgy or discipline of the church," Ryerson asserted that its exaggerated claims were founded upon the unscriptural doctrine of apostolic succession. "The Church of Christ as described in the scriptures is very distinct and different from such a religious establishment as that to which the Doctor alludes," and indeed the latter was the bane of Christianity. Likewise, he questioned Strachan's case against the Dissenters:

As to the Doctor's remarks on the qualifications, motives and conduct of the Methodist itinerant preachers, they are ungenerous, unfounded and false.... They are not republicans; neither are they infected with republican principles; nor have they come "almost universally from the Republican States of America." ... The hue and cry that "dissenters are disaffected to the Imperial Government," has stunned the ears of almost all Europe, for more than two centuries. It was first raised ... to give more unbounded sway to ecclesiastical domination ... and doubtless it is for the same purpose that it ... now continues its hideous shrieks through the "dreary wastes" of Canada.[57]

Although Ryerson's argument was not remarkable it caused great rejoicing in Methodist and reform circles and displeasure on the Anglican side.[58] Reformers began to accept the misleading idea that their interests were identical with those of the Methodists.

In this unsympathetic atmosphere Strachan turned to the imperial authorities for permission to sell some of the reserves, a course that merely emphasized the rigidity of the Anglican position.[59] To support his request he compiled from memory an ecclesiastical chart of Upper Canada in which he pointed out that there were thirty-seven Anglican and Presbyterian clergy in the province as compared with twenty to thirty Methodists, most of whom were disaffected persons from the United States. "The other denominations," he added, "have very few teachers and those seemingly very ignorant." Yet the people generally were sympathetic to the Church and if ministers and churches were provided they would gladly accept its ministrations. To this end Strachan urged that the reserves be utilized in an efficient manner.[60]

Anglican arrogance and the imputation of disloyalty to their opponents provoked a reaction in Upper Canada. A protest committee with William Ryerson as a prominent member was formed at York and was instrumental in presenting widely circulated petitions to the Assembly.[61] The investigating committee of the legislature promptly issued a report in which the reform position was stated precisely:

It would be unjust and impolitic to exalt [the Church of England] by exclusive and peculiar rights above all others of His Majesty's Subjects who are equally loyal, conscientious and deserving. A country in which there is an established church from which a vast majority of the subjects are dissenters must be in a lamentable state.... If the church is incorporated with the state, they are compelled by the obligations of Conscience to oppose one of the civil institutions of the country, a part of the government itself.

Therefore, it was desirable that the reserves should be sold for educational or other general purposes, an opinion which was

113

embodied in an address to the Crown.[62] A petition on the same subject bearing eight thousand signatures was presented by George Ryerson to the Colonial Office.[63]

No positive action was taken on this issue by the imperial authorities, although the select committee of the House of Commons, which in the spring of 1828 examined this question, condemned the clergy reserves system and questioned the exclusive Anglican claim on them.[64] In Upper Canada, meanwhile, Strachan impenitently defended his chart and his general policy in the congenial surroundings of the Legislative Council. This naturally induced William Ryerson to persuade Egerton to write an extended reply. "You had better endeavour," said William, "to write in a candid mild and sweet stile. It will have a much more powerfull effect on the mind of the public."[65] The letters, which were candid, if not sweet, appeared in the *Upper Canada Herald* during the summer of 1828.

Thus far the status of religion in the province had been examined from a legal and factual standpoint. In contrast, Ryerson's argument dealt with the implications of establishment for church and community. For him the lesson of history was that an established church is a divisive force in society, inimical to political freedom and harmful to true religion. This was confirmed by the recent experience of the Church in Canada; operating under privileged conditions it had not grown significantly. To give it additional advantages would encourage its ministers to become avaricious, proud and indolent, thereby endangering both Canada's welfare and its own. Ryerson concluded that the province would not flourish until all religious bodies were placed on an equal footing.[66]

Before the Canada Conference became independent some of its leading figures had taken steps which strongly suggested that the Methodists were prepared to support the reform side in Upper Canadian politics. But the position of the Conference itself had not been made clear, nor was it certain to what extent the Methodist laity would support their leaders. In any case the crux of the problem was that the church question and the associated education issue were related intimately with the existing system of government. The Methodists had to ask themselves if they wanted the kind of political reform that would make possible other social changes. The alternative was to agitate for specific adjustments that would improve the Methodist position in Upper Canada. Actually they took a stand that was ambiguous in a sense but reflected precisely the inner tension of the Methodist Societies.

Whatever course the Conference elected to pursue, a Methodist newspaper was required to make it known. Anson Green said the preachers felt "the need of a *Press* at our command, not only to explain our doctrines and polity, but more especially to fight the battles in which we were engaged for equal rights and for religious equality. We had so long been kept in the cold shades of what can scarcely be called religious toleration, that we had fully made up our minds to let our strength be known, while calmly, but firmly and persistently we demanded equal rights with any other and all other Churches."[67] As a result the Conference of 1829 decided to found the weekly *Christian Guardian* with Egerton Ryerson and Franklin Metcalf as editors.[68] Ryerson continued in this post until 1832, when he was succeeded by James Richardson.[69] Under his direction the *Guardian* speedily acquired an influential place in the life of the province.

During these early years the *Guardian* promoted a number of political ideas which were designed as the framework of Methodist policies and by which Methodist activities would be judged. Quite properly, one of the issues that was first raised was the origin and function of government. Civil authority, in the *Guardian's* view, had been created to meet certain human needs and as such deserved support. The Christian, however, who believes that government has been divinely established, has a higher obligation to accept its orders. Yet, the limits of obedience remain in question. Those who accept any extension of the state's power contribute only to the growth of religious and civil persecution. In fact, said Ryerson, echoing many greater writers, the constitution is a compact between ruler and ruled which should be observed so long as its terms are not infringed. If, for example, the constitution does not grant toleration, the Christian may resist passively, but if it guarantees tolerance, the Christian should defend his position actively. In these circumstances the opponents of the state may often be the defenders of its real interests.[70]

In actuality the *Guardian* had espoused two distinct concepts of government. If the Biblical philosophy of government were taken seriously, revolutionary or genuinely radical action was forbidden to the Christian. If the compact theory were to be his rule of action, he was likely to take a broad view of the limits of obedience. The *Guardian* really wanted the Methodist to pick his way carefully between two extremes, that is, to support a process of restoration not innovation, or to urge the acknowledgment in fact of those rights that he had in law. From the outset then, the *Guardian* sought to inculcate in its constituency a conservative variety of liberalism.

Although the Conference and its editor asserted the Christian's right to intervene in politics, he was at the same time encouraged to deal with such questions in a particular way. The Conference itself apparently felt that it and its members should take political action only when the welfare of Christianity or Methodism was at stake. In 1829 the Conference received a petition urging it to "take such means as will finally put a stop to our preachers connecting themselves with any political body or aiding in writing censorious pieces for publication against the constituted authorities of the country." The committee appointed to consider this plea reported: "While your committee entirely disapprove of connecting political questions with any vindication of our economy; while they say upon the authority of Divine Revelation, let no man speak evil of magistrates . . . Your committee will also add upon the same authority we ought to obey God rather than man."[71] Likewise, during the critical 1830 election the *Guardian* asserted that the Methodist Church was concerned about doctrines, not the claims of individuals. Its hope was that

Every elector should come free from the influence of party feelings. . . . He should come firmly united with the friends of his country . . . to do all that he lawfully can for his country's welfare—deeply revolving these thoughts in his mind: I am now about to give my name and influence towards entailing upon my posterity and country a dominant Priesthood—a partial system of education . . . or to confer upon the present and future generations of Canada . . . the tranquil and various advantages of equal religious freedom and privilege. . . . This important choice should in no instance be made under the guidance of sectarian feeling. A man's membership in any particular church is no test of his principles . . . on these vastly important questions.[72]

In effect, the Conference would not take sides but it was anxious that Methodists give their support to any candidate whose principles were sound, regardless of his political or religious affiliations. The real difficulty in all this was to convince outsiders that in trying to obey "God rather than man" the Methodists as a body were not throwing their weight behind the reformers.

Despite the narrowness of this path the *Guardian*, speaking for the Methodists, sought to stay within its limits. As the political temperature rose its attention was fastened on the consequent excesses of party welfare. The *Guardian* scored "the spirit which has been engendered in this Province by means of an abusive, slanderous and inflammatory press, supported by the wealth and influence of men in office and by the art and cunning of interested and evil-minded persons." If citizens were prevented from meeting and framing petitions Upper Canada would "soon be governed... by a mob-ocracy, alike fatal to Religion, good morals, order, peace and the happiness of society."[73] Discussing a reform petition, the

Guardian later stated bluntly: "If no item in this petition manifests hostility to British rule . . . what must be thought . . . of such anti-reformers as have written . . . so much about 'revolution, rebellion, republicanism' etc? On the other hand if there is any request or principle in this petition which savours of 'revolution, rebellion' etc., it is the duty of every loyal subject to use all lawful exertions to put it down."[74] Comment of this kind outwardly was sympathetic to reformers but in fact was actuated by concern for a reasoned examination of principles, a qualification that was frequently overlooked.

The editorial policy of James Richardson, Ryerson's successor in the *Guardian*, ought to have clarified the real Methodist position. Richardson's sympathies probably were more liberal than Ryerson's. He felt that his function was to guard religious interests, especially those of the Methodist Church. "With respect to questions purely political," he added, "we leave these to be discussed by those whose province it is to attend to them; we have more noble work before us. At the same time, we cannot but observe that civil and religious rights are often so blended together that it is scarcely possible to attend to the one without touching the other."[75] The *Guardian* would inculcate respect for authority, obedience to the laws and allegiance to the Crown. To this end it attacked critics of the Colonial Office and assured the public that the Methodists belonged to no political faction, least of all one of a radical character.[76]

Broadly speaking the Methodist attitude toward church-state relations and education must be examined against a background only moderately liberal. Methodists were persuaded to work for principles rather than factions. Specific words and deeds of the Conference and the Societies, however, tended to blur the lines that the *Guardian* especially had sought to draw.

During the first year of independence the reserves controversy subsided somewhat, a happy coincidence for the new Conference, already beset with the Ryanite secession.[77] But in the autumn of 1829 the Church of Scotland again demanded recognition as one of the established churches in Canada and requested a division of the reserves, a move promptly denounced by the *Guardian*:

The latitude of Canada never was designed to wear the shackles of an ecclesiastical or literary despotism; . . . if our government will be based upon the affections of an enlightened people . . . if the scourge of religious animosities is to be removed from our land . . . our Chief Magistrates must . . . deal alike with all . . . and be no respecters of persons.[78]

An anonymous contributor asserted that to fasten two establishments on the province would be reprehensible, for "liberty of conscience and worship is the unalienable birthright of every man as a member of the social body."[79] "The Methodists," the editor continued, "do not and never did desire any division of the spoils among themselves; ... they do not seek the slightest advantage over any other religious denomination." The dissenting ministers do not want "a farthing of the 'spoil'," for "they expect and receive their support on more apostolic and scriptural principles.... Can they ... trust in the arm of the flesh? Should they ever do so, we are persuaded that ... they will in respect to their simplicity, their innocence and their usefulness draw their last breath."[80]

Carrying forward the battle against ecclesiastical despotism the *Guardian* dwelt at length on the existing situation: "The executive obloquy and disabilities which ... still deprive the Methodists and others of privileges extended to another portion of the same compact is an infringement and absolute outrage upon the very first principle upon which every free government is founded." Governments, added the *Guardian*, should learn to respect their subjects: "Let them be admonished that the physical strength resides in the governed; ... that civil authority is founded in opinion; that general opinion ought therefore always to be treated with deference and managed with delicacy and circumspection." In Upper Canada general opinion was not being heeded, on the ground that to advocate the separation of church and state was treasonable; whereas "in identifying and unjustly exalting one sect with the government to the exclusion of all others is the fruitful source of all those jealousies, misrepresentations, religious animosities and disputes which have divided friends, exasperated enemies ... [and] spread dissatisfaction, contention and confusion in every part of the country."[81] It was therefore the duty of every Methodist to seek acceptance of the principle of religious liberty.

The election of 1830 returned a tory majority to the Assembly. The supporters of religious equality realized the need for action.[82] Since the imperial authorities seemed to be of a more open mind than their representatives and allies in Canada, their assistance was very properly sought.[83] A large meeting was held in York on December 10, 1830, at which Robert Baldwin presided and a committee of the Friends of Religious Liberty was appointed.[84] On motion of Dr. T. D. Morrison, a prominent Methodist and reformer, the audience agreed to petition the House of Commons "to take such steps ... that the Ministers of all denominations ... may be left to be supported by the people among whom they labour, ... that all political distinctions on account of religious faith be done away, ... that there be granted to the Clergy of all denominations ... equal rights and privileges ... and that the proceeds of the [clergy reserves] be appropriated to the purpose of general education and various internal improvements."[85] The petition subsequently drafted by Egerton Ryerson and Jesse Ketchum, another outstanding reformer, reviewed the religious history of Upper Canada, stressing the differences between Canadian and English conditions. At the moment the reserves were "a very serious obstacle to the improvement of the country" and were "not likely to be of any *religious* advantage to the Church of England." The petitioners continued: "The Ministers of other denominations have laboured more extensively to improve the moral condition of the Province than the Clergy of the Episcopal Church . . . and are equally deserving of the gracious consideration of His Majesty's Government." To maintain the Anglican monopoly of the reserves would mean the perpetuation of "unjust and impolitic political distinctions" prejudicial to "the happiness of the Province."[86]

While this petition was being circulated in Upper Canada the *Guardian* sought to keep the issue uppermost in the public mind. Readers were warned that "the projected system of church and state in this Province contains the seeds of greater evils" than the existing arrangements in Great Britain, and that the plausible scheme being put forward for a division of the reserves was merely a device to perpetuate controversy.[87] The Anglican counter-petition that was being carried about rather surreptitiously was assailed even more bitterly: "The Church of England or any other church with the pretensions . . . of a dominant or state church . . . will be viewed by the people of Upper Canada as an enemy to our liberties and a bribe to religious corruption." The people were reminded that citizens could not be robbed of rights and liberties without their own consent. They were urged to vote only for those candidates committed to equality of religious privilege. "Shall then this 'nightmare upon our constitution' . . . this . . . enemy to our liberties . . . this worthless and sinful prostitution of national property be tolerated and sanctioned in Upper Canada? The King expects every man to do his duty; and the King of Kings says 'be vigilant, be not weary in well doing.'"[88]

The Conference of 1831 affirmed in a memorial to the Crown that the Methodist preachers did not want any part of the proceeds from lands previously designated for the support of a Protestant clergy. No system of doctrine or form of worship "should be forced upon a province any more than upon an individual." Members of the Conference declared that they desired nothing for themselves beyond "equal and impartial protection."[89]

Meanwhile, George Ryerson was on his way to England with the petition of the Friends of Religious Liberty.[90] He had it presented to the House of Commons and met with Viscount Goderich, the Colonial Secretary. Ryerson impressed on him the necessity of giving the North American colonies "a liberal Government; free and popular institutions and full power to regulate and manage all their internal concerns, civil, literary and ecclesiastical."[91] Both Goderich and the House of Commons seemed impressed with these views of the Upper Canadian opposition; in November, 1831 the Colonial Secretary altered the imperial reserves policy significantly.

In his despatch of November 21 to Governor Colborne, Goderich advised him to seek from the legislature repeal of the reserves clauses of the Act of 1791 and the investment of existing reserves in the Crown. Nevertheless, Goderich did not intend to weaken the Church's position. Abolition of the reserves was not to be construed as acquiescence in the opinion of the petitioners that "any kind of church establishment" is "essentially anti-Christian and baneful to every interest of Humanity." On the contrary, in his view the reserves system was "a great obstacle to the improvement and settlement of the Province," and was "still more strongly to be condemned as a provision for the Ministers of Religion since it must have a direct tendency to render [their services] odious to the inhabitants."[92] A less objectionable way had to be found to provide for the needs of the Church of England.

Although Goderich's position was ambiguous, Upper Canada would have avoided many problems if his proposal had been carried out. A bill embodying his suggestions was placed before the Assembly and received its first reading but the legislature was prorogued before final consideration could be given.[93] It was not until seven years later that the imperial government seriously attempted to deal with the question.

In Upper Canada, however, during 1832 and 1833 the possibility of decision kept alive the conflict between supporters and opponents of the Church. The Church party sent Christopher Hagerman, the Solicitor-General, to England in the summer of 1832 to resist further insidious attacks on its privileges. To the *Guardian* this seemed a new move to maintain the Anglican monopoly. It admonished readers to make a final effort to prevent the reserves becoming a source of "contention and corruption" among the churches. Further, in the best interest of the province it urged that the reserves either be opened for regular settlement or appropriated to the promotion of education. The *Guardian* favoured education.[94]

When the Anglican authorities began to circulate petitions, the *Guardian* promptly called for a counter-agitation, for in its opinion "the crisis [was] now arrived for the decision of the important question, and all depended upon the voice of the people."[95] In response the association known as the Friends of Religious Liberty was reconstituted, petitions were prepared and were widely circulated. Egerton Ryerson, who was already in England, was asked to deliver them to the Colonial Secretary.[96]

3

As Ryerson's negotiations with the British government in the summer of 1833 marked the end of the first phase of Methodist participation in the reserves controversy, it would be proper at this stage to evaluate their contribution to it. To do this, however, would be to overlook the position taken by the Methodists on education, another highly significant facet of the political warfare in which the province was absorbed between 1828 and 1833.

By 1828 Upper Canada had acquired the rudiments of an educational system, but it had become the object of virulent public argument. At this time the province had 291 common schools partially supported by government funds, and ten district grammar schools that provided secondary education for those able to pay the fees and to maintain themselves away from home.[97] Since 1823 all these schools had been under the nominal control of the General Board of Education, whose president was John Strachan, Rector and Archdeacon of York.[98]

In addition to the common, grammar, and numerous private schools, the province had an embryo university. Its establishment was a cause close to Governor Simcoe's heart, but it was Strachan who gave the necessary impetus to the project.[99] At his instigation the question was raised by Maitland in 1818 and after protracted negotiations a royal charter was issued in 1827.[100] This instrument authorized the creation of King's College, York, of which the bishop of Quebec was to be the visitor, the lieutenant-governor of Upper Canada the chancellor and the rector of York the president. All members of the College Council were to subscribe to the Thirty-Nine Articles but there were to be no religious tests for students other than candidates in divinity.[101] The original endowment of the College was an allotment of 200,000 acres of crown reserves, exchanged for the same quantity of poorer land drawn from the school reserves originally set aside in 1797.[102]

Given the condition of education in England and the primitive state of Upper Canada in 1828, the educational facilities of the province were not without merit. The university charter itself, soon to be the subject of recrimination, was, in the opinion of influential Englishmen, impossibly liberal.[103] Nevertheless, the issuance of the charter coincided with the early stages of a controversy over education that in one form or another would continue for the rest of the century.

As the members of the Assembly pointed out, Upper Canada did not have enough schools and those that were in use were inefficient. The grammar schools especially were too widely separated and prohibitively expensive.[104] The simple answer was to provide more schools, but before this could be done certain fundamental questions about the rôle of education in provincial society had to be resolved. It was asserted that the government or compact party was determined to maintain an intimate association between the church and education and to provide adequate educational facilities only for the élite. Dr. Strachan certainly shared the former conviction but he wanted to provide education for those with ability rather than wealth or social position.[105] His colleagues in the Executive Council were "fully persuaded that the effects of the University, even on a moderate scale, but possessing sufficient recommendations to attract to it the Sons of the most opulent Families, would soon be visible in the greater intelligence and more confirmed principles of Loyalty of those who would be called to the various public duties." The university "in alliance with the Church would tend to establish a most affectionate connexion between this Colony and the Parent State."[106]

In marked contrast the Assembly contended that if the university was to be "of real service, the principles upon which it is established, must be in unison with the general sentiments of the people. It should not be a school of politics, or of sectarian views. . . . Its portals should be thrown open to all, and upon none who enter should any influence be exerted to attach them to a particular creed or church." In reality, however, the "principles of the charter" were "calculated to defeat its usefulness and to confine to a favoured few all its advantages."[107] The grammar schools, likewise, were said to be "converted into stepping-stones to the Episcopal Church." All of this was attributed to the baneful domination of Dr. Strachan, exercised through an office that the Assembly maintained had never been legally constituted.[108]

The Methodists initially were involved in this dispute through Ryerson's open letters to Strachan, published in the summer of 1828. In Ryerson's view Strachan's educational policy was based upon the inaccurate assumption that the Church was established in Canada and was in any case unsuited to Canadian conditions. "Considering the statements you have made," Ryerson asked, "would it not be generally thought paramount to establishing the Inquisition in Canada to tolerate your ill-founded University altogether under the control of the Church of England clergy, with you at its head?" Upper Canada needed "a system established by Acts of our Provincial Legislature—a system on an economical plan—a system conformable to the wishes of the great mass of the population—a system promoted by the united efforts of the laity and clergy—a system in . . . which the different bodies of clergy will not interfere—a system which will bring the blessings of education to every family."[109]

Unfair as Ryerson's statement probably was concerning Strachan's motives, it appeared to align the Methodists with the reformers on this issue, and was an accurate forecast of the educational policy that they would adopt. Between 1828 and 1833 the Methodist Church would take important steps toward bringing "the blessings of education to every family" in the province.

From its inception the *Christian Guardian* entered actively into the discussion about the kind of educational system that Upper Canada needed. In its view all classes required education in order to participate intelligently in public affairs, but in achieving this end it was imperative that certain principles be upheld. The advantages of education were said to be "but a sounding brass and a tinkling cymbal when not founded upon and sanctified by the undefiled and regenerating religion of Jesus Christ."[110] The *Guardian* felt as well that educational facilities must be adapted to local needs and circumstances. Schools must be located conveniently and operated efficiently.[111]

Above all the *Guardian* was concerned with the question of control over the means of education, to ensure that the legitimate needs of the majority were met. The editor felt that the best arrangement was to place "the direction of education in the hands of those who are personally interested" instead of leaving it to a "Lieutenant-Governor who depends upon the recommendation" of people "perhaps not as intelligent and probably in many . . . cases personally, politically or ecclesiastically interested."[112] This latter procedure would create "a powerful engine" for those who would "use it to promote their own favourite measures and give influence and currency to their peculiar sentiments and opinions, both political and religious."[113] "In an equitable and patriotic administration of Government, the more its agents and the people's agents are associated together in promoting the common weal . . . the less room there will be for Executive negligence or partiality or popular or local abuse."[114]

Both Methodists and reformers believed that the existing and proposed arrangements, especially in higher education, were designed to serve minority interests. Thus, Colborne's sensible decision to found Upper Canada College and to endow it with a portion of the school reserves drew the editorial fire of the *Guardian*, which objected to the use of public funds to train wealthy Anglicans along lines of dubious value to the province.[115]

It was the King's College charter that was subjected to the most bitter attack by the Methodists. Many signed the petitions presented to the Assembly in 1828 in which the exclusive provisions of the charter were criticized.[116] Two years later the Friends of Religious Liberty urged that all sectarian tests and preferences be excluded from it.[117] George Ryerson assured Goderich that

Constituted as the population of Upper Canada is, every independent man feels and acknowledges that it would be impolitic and unjust to confer upon any religious class such emoluments, power, and literary or other advantages as would virtually constitute that denomination the established religion. . . . I unite with my countrymen in resisting every encroachment upon our equal rights and liberties and the attempts of those who wish to . . . mingle with the fountains of knowledge the bitter waters of sectarian strife and jealousy.[118]

In reply Goderich requested the immediate surrender of the charter so that a new college might be established "upon a more enlarged basis," a step that was not taken for many years.[119]

Meanwhile the Methodists had made a much more constructive move on their own account. At the Conference of 1830 definite plans were made to establish a seminary in which "no system of Theology" was to be taught and all students were to be "free to embrace and pursue any religious creed."[120] The proposed academy was to be:

A place of learning, where the stream of educational instruction shall not be mingled with the polluted waters of corrupt example; where the pupils will be guarded against the infection of immoral principles and practices—where a good English and classical education may . . . be acquired—where the rudiments of the several Sciences will be taught— where scholars of every religious creed will meet with equal attention and encouragement—and where the terms will be as moderate . . . as the circumstances of the Province will admit.[121]

In effect Upper Canada Academy, as this new institution would be called, was to embody all those features that the Methodists found lacking in existing seminaries. Nevertheless, it was not "to compete with any college . . . but rather to be tributary to it, when one shall be established."[122]

In founding the Academy and in appealing to the public for financial support the Methodists were impelled, according to the *Guardian*, by the conviction that educated people are the "best security of a good government and constitutional liberty," whereas ignorant people are likely to become "the slaves of despots and the dupes of demagogues." Moreover, "sound learning is of great worth even in religion; the wisest and the best instructed Christians are the most steady and may be the most useful."[123] As Christians, Methodists had a moral responsibility to secure these advantages for their own children and for the community as a whole.[124]

4

The Methodist Episcopal Church and its organ the *Christian Guardian* followed a consistent and positive course in the political conflict of the years 1828 to 1833, but unfortunately the underlying purpose was frequently misunderstood. On the broad issue of the kind of government that Upper Canada ought to have the Methodist position was essentially conservative. In principle the provincial constitution embodied all the rights and privileges required by the people; the real problem was to ensure that its true spirit infused the actions of the legislature and the administration. This was more likely to obtain if persons and policies were judged on their merits rather than on their religious or political associations. Methodists therefore opposed the tyranny of bigotry, the excesses of radicalism and the competition for party advantage.

On the question of civil and religious liberty the Methodists' attitude was much more explicit. They insisted that every religious group in Upper Canada ought to be treated with equal consideration by the government and that all religious bodies ought to rely upon their members for support. Consequently they denounced the arrangements between the Church of England and the state and urged that the clergy reserves be used for educational or other general purposes.

The Methodists' educational policy was consistent with their views on the proper relationship between church, state and society. They were convinced that in a Christian and liberal community the educational system should be based on religious principles but ought not to be an instrument for sectarian indoctrination. Moreover, educational agencies should provide training along realistic lines, without discriminating in any way for religious, social or economic reasons. In effect the Methodists sought educational institutions that would do what Upper Canadians really appeared to want, rather than a restricted scheme to train Anglicans, aristocrats or loyalists.

The spirited manner in which the Methodists promoted their case for religious and educational reform made it appear much more radical than was intended. Richardson, when assessing their course between 1828 and 1833, contended that the Methodists "have had but one object in view, to the attainment of which all their efforts have been directed—Equal religious rights and privileges among all denominations of His Majesty's subjects."[125] They had pressed this principle to facilitate the growth of Methodism, but the manner in which their campaign was conducted indicated that Methodist leaders had a secondary objective, the development of Upper Canadian society along equitable lines. They believed that in attaining these ends it was neither necessary nor desirable for the Methodist Church to meddle in matters "purely political," nor for Methodists to align themselves with any political faction.

Actually the Methodist viewpoint was too subtle to be understood by tories and reformers, or indeed by the average Methodist. Many Upper Canadians regarded the Methodists as a formidable group among the reformers. Governor Colborne had been in the colony only a short time when he wrote home that "the Methodists are accused of being hostile to our government . . . and of undermining the loyalty of the people." "I believe however, their hostility is directed against the established church, and with the intention of strengthening their influence, they exert themselves to send as many Dissenters to the Provincial Parliament as they can."[126] Later he emphasized that "Mr. G. Ryerson and his brothers are at the head of a very numerous sect and with the assistance of a newspaper called the *Christian Guardian* possess much influence among the people of their persuasion. They take a very active political part in the province."[127] In so doing they had found "Mr. Mackenzie a useful partisan" and "had involved themselves in disputes which as ministers of the Methodist Episcopal Church they ought to have avoided."[128]

Dr. Strachan agreed with this judgment. To him it was clear that the object of the Methodists was "to pull down all establishments, undermine the loyalty of the people and constitute us a province of the United States." "The heads of the Methodists have formed themselves into a club or Society under the patronage of Mr. Hume and some other worldly members" of the House of Commons.[129] The Rev. A. H. Burwell felt it was essential to "open the eyes of some" to the "necessity of stemming the torrent of 'all denomination' mobocracy that is setting so rapidly in among us. I cannot help regarding it with fear and horror. . . . Egerton would carry the day . . . even in competition with the twelve Apostles themselves. It is thus that dissent from Episcopacy is made the parent of revolution and desolation."[130]

Although these outbursts probably reflected as much fear and prejudice as fact, it is noteworthy that the reformers themselves thought the Methodists were on their side—a belief whose depth was indicated by Mackenzie's anguished outcry against Ryerson's change of course in 1833.[131] John Ryerson asserted that "the *Christian Guardian* [took] a leading part against the exclusive claims of what was called the 'High Church party'. Indeed, the *Guardian*, and the Methodists, its supporters, formed the principal if not the only serious barrier to the success of the exclusive and monopolizing claims of the 'High Church party'."[132]

In all probability, the majority of the Methodist preachers did not meddle directly in political controversy. To claim the contrary would be to doubt repeated statements by Ryerson and others. Those who did participate in committees or who put forward petitions were careful to concern themselves only with the clergy reserves and education. Nevertheless, there appears to have been no real dissent in Conference from the line pursued by the *Guardian* and by its more active members. The fact was that none of the potential factions in the Conference could plausibly object to its political policy, for it could be justified either as a defensive measure or as a constructive contribution to the secular progress of Upper Canada.

There is no evidence that any significant number of Methodists or adherents disapproved of the line taken by Conference and *Guardian*. Objections would surely have been voiced in the *Guardian* or some other organ. This absence of complaint, coupled with the willingness of many Methodists to sign petitions against religious and educational monopoly, indicates that the spirit of the Methodist community was broadly liberal.

Yet it does not follow that the Methodists were solidly behind the reform leaders. Some of them doubtless regarded political activity as at best an unhealthy distraction from greater things; others possibly took the *Guardian* seriously when it urged that support be given to those with sound views, not those with specific party affiliations. Party lines were in fact so nebulous that tory candidates might well be more acceptable on occasion than reformers. Of course some Methodists were enthusiastic reformers. Mr. John Reynolds of Belleville was described by one observer as "an indefatigable agent in the sport of fishing for elections in behalf of his party. No farther gone than the last election I was met and accosted by him to part with my vote in aid of the views of the Ryersonian aristocracy."[133] Mr. Reynolds likely was not alone in his work. Yet the provincial election in which he was said to have campaigned so energetically produced a majority of tories, in a period when the Methodist Connexion displayed considerable influence and cohesion.

It may well be that the Methodists were not sufficiently numerous to swing any general election. Surely, though, the vital fact is that most of them stood, perhaps without wholly understanding why, in the centre of the Upper Canadian political spectrum. They sought a change in the operation of government rather than in its form; they fought for honest recognition of the principle of civil and religious equality; they were groping towards an order of things in which Canadian rather than other interests and needs would be given consideration.

The subtleties of the Methodist stand were regrettably lost on the self-appointed defenders of the Church and Empire in Upper Canada. To them it seemed imperative that a way be found to subvert and divide the Methodists. The latter, largely because they were poised so delicately in the structure of the Upper Canadian community, were unfortunately very subject to a flank attack. The offensive against them was begun in the spring of 1832.

REFERENCES TO CHAPTER FIVE

1. *MS Journal of Conference, 1828*, 1.
2. *Ibid., 1824*, 4-7.
3. *Ibid., 1827*. The delegates were W. Chamberlain, W. Slater, S. Belton, William and John Ryerson.
4. C. B. Sissons, *Egerton Ryerson: His Life and Letters* (Toronto, 1937), I, 77-78. Henceforth cited as *E.R.* See also Bangs's account in *History of the Methodist Episcopal Church*, III, 388-392. His opposition was largely based on a constitutional issue and apparently did not involve resentment against the Canadian stand.
5. *Journals of the General Conference*, I, 338, 346-347.
6. *The Doctrines and Discipline of the Methodist Epicopal Church in Canada* (York, 1829), 18-19.
7. *Ibid.*, 23.
8. J. Carroll, *Case and His Cotemporaries*, III, 215. Dr. Bangs was one of the candidates who declined election.
9. *Minutes of Conference, 1829*, 20.
10. *Discipline, 1829*, 6-16.
11. E. Ryerson, *Canadian Methodism: Its Epochs and Characteristics*, 129.
12. *Minutes of Conference, 1828*, 19-20; *Ibid., 1832*, 47-49.
13. See *E.R.*, I, 1-16.
14. *Ibid.*, I, 8; *Minutes of the Annual Conferences*, I, 394. Buck and Bright were the names usually given to oxen.
15. Carroll, *Case*, II, 441-442.
16. J. Carroll, *Past and Present* (Toronto, 1860), 271-272.

17. *Minutes of the Annual Conferences,* I, 354.
18. Carroll, *Case,* II, 350-351.
19. J. Carroll, *The School of the Prophets* (Toronto, 1876), 73.
20. *E.R.,* I, 2-3, 6-7, 9.
21. In 1828 Case was appointed superintendent of the Indian missions. That his influence was waning can be inferred from the Ryersons' attitude.
22. A. Green, *The Life and Times of Anson Green,* 1.
23. *Ibid.,* 5, 40-42.
24. Carroll, *Case,* III, 17. For Richardson's career as a whole, see T. Webster, *The Life of Bishop Richardson* (Toronto, 1876).
25. Franklin Metcalf, a New Yorker, was for a time assistant editor of the *Guardian.* He was one of the few who opposed the union with the Wesleyans in 1833. David Wright, a native of the Bay of Quinté region, became prominent in the forties.
26. He was put on trial in 1816. Carroll, *Case,* II, 64.
27. Victoria University Library, *The Journal of the Rev. George Ferguson* (Manuscript copy of the original), 193. For his career in general see the foregoing.
28. Carroll, *Case,* II, 399.
29. *Ibid.,* II, 441.
30. For a detailed study of Corson see John Carroll, *Father Corson; or the Old Style Canadian Itinerant* (Toronto, 1879).
31. The *Guardian* of January 1, 1831, stated that there were sixty-two itinerant preachers, of whom twelve were born in the United States, four in the British colonies, twenty-seven in Upper Canada, three in Nova Scotia, three in England and thirteen in Ireland. Only two or three were not British subjects. It is difficult to speak precisely about the educational attainments of the preachers. George Ryerson was the only college graduate in the group but obviously many others were well trained.
32. There were 8,753 white members in 1828. If one allows three adherents per member, thirty thousand is a reasonable figure.
33. Methodism was strongest in those areas which had a Loyalist or American background. It had little appeal for the Scots or for those areas settled by the better class of English immigrant.
34. There is no proper statistical evidence on this point. The Methodists appear to have had more difficulty gaining support in towns such as Kingston and York than in rural areas. The petitions sent to the Wesleyan leaders in 1816 and 1817 include signatures by justices of the peace and militia officers who were presumably adherents if not members of the Societies.
35. The continued and increasing flow of immigrants in combination with the poor system of communications kept the province in this condition. For an admirable description see G. W. Brown "The Durham Report and the Upper Canadian Scene," *Canadian Historical Review,* XX (1939), 136-140.

36. The term was first used by W. L. Mackenzie in his *Sketches of Upper Canada and the United States*, 409. It was consecrated by inclusion in the Durham Report.
37. See W. S. Wallace, *The Family Compact* (Toronto, 1915); A. Dunham, *Political Unrest in Upper Canada* (London, 1927), 30-36.
38. Dunham, *op. cit.*, 86.
39. For examples of the influence of American conditions see G. M. Craig, "The American Impact on the Upper Canadian Reform Movement Before 1837," *Canadian Historical Review*, XXIX (1948), 333-352.
40. This description is based on an analysis of the available literature.
41. In this connection the Gourlay agitation and trials, the alien controversy, and the Willis case were very important.
42. J. J. Talman, "The Position of the Church of England in Canada, 1791-1840," *Canadian Historical Review*, XV (1934), 361-366.
43. Kennedy, *Documents of the Canadian Constitution*, 215-217.
44. The tithe provision of the Constitutional Act was repealed in 1821. Talman, *Church of England*, 368. On the establishment of the rectories see T. R. Millman, *The Life of Charles James Stewart* (Huron College, 1953), 138-141.
45. On the marriage question see W. R. Riddell, "The Law of Marriage in Upper Canada," *Canadian Historical Review*, II (1921), 226-241. It was generally believed that in public appointments preference was given to Anglicans and Scots Presbyterians.
46. Talman, *Church of England*, 370; Millman, *op. cit.*, 116.
47. Millman, *Jacob Mountain, First Lord Bishop of Quebec*, 153-154.
48. *Ibid.*, 155-156. Eventually the reserves amounted to three and one-quarter million acres.
49. P. A. C., *Q325-1*, 192-199; *Q326*, 43-46.
50. The statistics on religious affiliation are unreliable, but contemporaries believed that members of the Churches of England and Scotland were in a minority in Upper Canada. The reserves could not be readily sold; thus they blocked communications and settlement.
51. A. G. Doughty and N. Story, eds., *Documents Relating to the Constitutional History of Canada* (Ottawa, 1935), 282-283. In 1827 the first of many reserves bills was passed by the Assembly and rejected by the Legislative Council. Dunham, *op. cit.*, 87.
52. For extracts of the sermon see *Claims of the Churchmen & Dissenters of Upper Canada Brought To The Test in a Controversy Between Several Members of the Church of England and a Methodist Preacher* (Kingston, 1828).
53. *Ibid.*, 19-20, 13.
54. *Ibid.*, 20-21, 23.
55. Ryerson, *op. cit.*, 140-142.
56. *Ibid.*, 142. The title of Ryerson's pamphlet was *A Review of a Sermon Preached by the Hon. & Rev. John Strachan, D.D. at York,*

U.C. 3rd of July, 1825 on the Death of the Late Bishop of Quebec. By a Methodist Preacher. Quotations here are from the reprint in Claims of Churchmen and Dissenters. . . .
57. Ibid., 27, 28, 32, 40, 50.
58. See Green, op. cit., 83; Ryerson, op. cit., 156-158.
59. Doughty and Story, op. cit., 373.
60. Ibid., 375-376.
61. *Claims of Churchmen and Dissenters* . . ., 170-172. Bulkley Waters, a Methodist, was the first to sign the petition.
62. Doughty and Story, op cit., 379-380, 382.
63. E.R., I, 71-73, William to George Ryerson, February 22, 1828.
64. Doughty and Story, op. cit., 472-475.
65. E.R., I, 76, W. to E. Ryerson, April 1, 1828. In his letters Ryerson referred particularly to Strachan's speech of March 7, 1828.
66. *Colonial Advocate,* July 10, 22, 31; Aug. 7, 1828.
67. Green, op. cit., 134-135.
68. *Minutes of Conference, 1829,* 27-28. Green preferred George Ryerson for the post but John backed Egerton. Green, op. cit., 135.
69. *Minutes of Conference, 1832,* 49.
70. C.G., October 8, 1831. See also his first editorial, November 21, 1829.
71. *Colonial Advocate,* September 17, 1829.
72. C.G., October 2, 1830.
73. Ibid., March 28, 1832.
74. Ibid., May 16, 1832.
75. Ibid., September 5, 1832.
76. Ibid., February 6; April 24, 1833.
77. Ryerson, op. cit., 263-269.
78. C.G., December 26, 1829.
79. Ibid.
80. Ibid., January 23, 1830.
81. Ibid., July 3, 1830.
82. Ibid., October 23, 1830.
83. Sir George Murray, the Colonial Secretary, apparently felt that Upper Canada did not require an established church. See C.G., September 18, 1830.
84. Ibid., December 18, 1830.
85. *Report on Canadian Archives, 1899* (Ottawa, 1900), 27.
86. C.G., December 18, 1830.
87. Ibid., March 5, 1831; April 2, 1831.
88. For the background of the Anglican petition, see Millman, *Stewart,* 105; C.G., May 7, 1831.
89. C.G., November 10, 1831. This statement elicited a rebuke from the Governor and a spirited rejoinder from Ryerson. Ibid., December 21, 1831.
90. E.R., I, 131.
91. C.G., January 25, 1832.

92. P.A.C., *G68*, Goderich to Colborne, November 21, 1831. Goderich's accompanying despatch (56) of the same date contained a draft bill for submission to the local legislature.
93. C. Lindsey, *The Clergy Reserves* (Toronto, 1851), 20. The vote on the first reading was twenty-nine to seven.
94. *C.G.*, September 26, 1832.
95. *Ibid.*, February 20, 1833.
96. *E.R.*, I, 172-175; *C.G.*, September 4, 1833.
97. On the common schools see J. G. Hodgins, ed., *Documentary History of Education in Upper Canada* (Toronto, 1894-1910), I, 102-104. Henceforth cited as *D.H.E.* See also G. W. Spragge, "John Strachan's Contribution to Education, 1800-1823," *Canadian Historical Review*, XXII (1941), 152-153. On the grammar schools see *D.H.E.*, I, 60-61, 270-271.
98. *Ibid.*, I, 203; Spragge, *op. cit.*, 155.
99. See S. R. Mealing, "The Enthusiasms of John Graves Simcoe," *Canadian Historical Association Report* (1958), 50.
100. See *D.H.E.*, IV, 280-286 and John Strachan, *The John Strachan Letter Book: 1812-1834*, ed. G. W. Spragge (Toronto, 1946), 184.
101. The charter is reproduced in *D.H.E.*, I, 221-225.
102. P.A.C., *G63*, Bathurst to Maitland, March 31, 1827. The school reserves of 500,000 acres were authorized by Portland in 1797. P.A.C., *G53*, Portland to Russell (6), November 4, 1797. The whole subject was reviewed in a supplement to the *Christian Guardian*, July 21, 1847.
103. The Archbishop of Canterbury strenuously resisted Strachan's ideas for the charter of King's College. See *D.H.E.*, IV, 280.
104. *Ibid.*, I, 270.
105. Spragge, "Strachan's Contribution," 156.
106. Doughty and Story, *op. cit.*, 304-305.
107. *D.H.E.*, I, 241.
108. *Ibid.*, I, 270-271.
109. *Colonial Advocate*, August 14, 1828.
110. *C.G.*, November 21, 1829.
111. *Ibid.*, January 16, 1830; February 12, 1831.
112. *Ibid.*, December 7, 1831.
113. *Ibid.*, December 5, 1832.
114. *Ibid.*, January 15, 1834.
115. *Ibid.*, October 1, 1833. On this subject see *D.H.E.*, I, 285-289.
116. Ryerson, *op. cit.*, 171-172.
117. *C.G.*, December 18, 1830.
118. *Ibid.*, January 25, 1832.
119. P.A.C., *G68* Goderich to Colborne (53), November 2, 1831. After much discussion the charter was amended in 1837, but this did not end the controversy. *D.H.E.*, II, 88-89.
120. The Conference of 1829 raised the subject but took no action. *MS Journal of Conference, 1829; Ibid., 1830.*
121. *C.G.*, November 6, 1830.

122. *Ibid.*
123. *Ibid.*, April 23, 1831.
124. *Ibid.*, March 20, 1833.
125. *Ibid.*, July 31, 1833.
126. P.A.C., *Q351-1*, 87, Colborne to R. W. Hay, March 31, 1829.
127. P.A.C., *Q356*, 88, Colborne to Hay, March 25, 1831.
128. P.A.C., *Q374-2*, 459, Colborne to Goderich, March 29, 1832. See also *Q374-4*, 783, Colborne to Goderich, June 18, 1832 in which he notes that Mackenzie had been allowed to hold political meetings in the Brockville Chapel.
129. *Department of Public Records and Archives of the Province of Ontario* (P.A.O.), Strachan Papers, Strachan to Hargreave, March 7, 1831.
130. P.A.O., Macaulay Papers, A. H. Burwell to J. Macaulay, August 13, 1831.
131. See Chapter 6, pp. 142-144.
132. Ryerson, *op. cit.*, 302-303.
133. *Kingston Chronicle*, September 24, 1831.

SIX

*"Altogether I fear
that the Wesleyan Conference is an obstacle
to the extension of civil and religious liberty."*

During the spring of 1832 John Ryerson received from Robert Alder the "astonishing" news that he and twelve missionaries were about to sail from England for Canada.[1] This was the prelude to negotiations between the English Conference and the Methodist Episcopal Church that resulted in a union of the two bodies in 1833. Although outwardly innocuous, this union led to momentous adjustments in the Methodist attitude towards the political struggle in Upper Canada—changes hopefully anticipated by some who helped precipitate the Wesleyan incursion into the province.

The Missionary Committee's decision to abrogate the treaty signed with the Methodist Episcopal Church in America in 1820 was the product of a complex set of circumstances. Although at the time the Committee had thought it proper to divide the work in the Canadas with the American Conference, it was probably aware that the government of Upper Canada regretted this step and it was certainly conscious of the outraged feelings of its adherents in the province.[2] Between 1821 and 1830 the outlook had not changed significantly. Dr. Strachan, ever vigilant for the loyalty of the province, urged the Committee in 1827 to send its preachers back to Upper Canada.[3] At the same time Governor Maitland indirectly offered assistance to the Lower Canada District to facilitate the expansion of its work into Upper Canada.[4] To Bathurst, too, Maitland expressed the hope that the imperial government might "be able by some means to afford such countenance and support to the establishment of these [Wesleyan] missionaries" as would induce the Society to resume its mission in Upper Canada, for "the Wesleyan Methodists have indeed never . . . manifested that jealousy of the Church of England which other sects have occasionally displayed."[5]

Apart from the evident interest of the colonial government and its own missionaries in Lower Canada, the Committee was stirred by requests from Napanee and York to rescue Wesleyan Methodist adherents from the care of unsuitable Canadian Methodist preachers.[6] Nothing would "calm the public mind," said John Fenton of York, more than the introduction of British Wesleyan missionaries into the province.[7] Although the Committee regarded it as "an object of great importance" to bring the societies in Upper Canada "into immediate communion with the British Conference," probably the decisive factor at this stage was its great interest in Indian missions.[8] These had proven remarkably successful in the United States and Canada, a fact that was brought home to the English Societies by a visit in 1831 from George Ryerson and Peter Jones, a native missionary.[9]

While the Canadians' fund-raising tour was in progress, the Committee informed Case that they had "decided upon commencing their long contemplated Mission to the Indians, convinced that where the field is so wide there need be no fear of any unpleasant or conflicting feelings among the Missionaries who may be employed."[10] The Rev. Thomas Turner, already a missionary in Lower Canada, was to be sent to Upper Canada to survey the situation.

In York, Turner met Hagerman, the Solicitor-General, the Governor and the Methodist Episcopal leaders. Colborne discussed the Indian problem at length, admitting that he preferred Anglican missionaries for the natives, but adding that because the Church of England was unable to supply the men he would assist the Wesleyans in every way. He also wanted the Wesleyans to send missionaries to the immigrants who probably would not join the Episcopal Methodists, "involved as they are in local political dissentions and in disputes with Methodist separatists. . . . Your [Wesleyan] . . . exertions are certainly required, as you must have perceived . . . from the large number of settlers that arrive from England every season."[11] Turner agreed with the Governor and emphasized that "the constant interference of our brethren in political matters has often given me pain and is, I fear, a hinderance to their usefulness and greatly lowers them in the estimation of sensible men"[12]

Against this grave threat the Canadian Methodists fought back vigorously. Their Missionary Board expressed willingness to assist in the establishment of Wesleyan missions in the Hudson's Bay area, but said an adequate job was being done in Upper Canada. "It may be proper here to observe that the progress of Wesleyan Methodism in Upper Canada has been far more rapid than in any other province of British North America. . . . You are perhaps not apprised that there are many persons in this province who would rejoice to witness party disputes among the Methodists, and would recommend any measure and do all in their power to create and foment them."[13] The committee felt, therefore, that the Wesleyan Missionary Society ought to reconsider its decision. This plea was reinforced by a lengthy letter from Egerton Ryerson to Richard

Watson, one of the leading Wesleyans.[14] To Ryerson it was clear that the contemplated mission was based upon a complete misunderstanding. The Methodist Episcopal Church was thoroughly Wesleyan and effective in dealing with all classes of people. As for political activity, this was something forced upon the Connexion by its enemies. In opposing the Church of England Ryerson continued: "I am persuaded that we are invading no man's legal or moral rights,—but are doing a necessary act of defence for ourselves, an important duty to the religious peace and interests of the country, and a valuable service to the British Throne." Those who were calling upon the Wesleyan Methodists to serve in Upper Canada were the least interested in its welfare; rather, they desired to raise themselves by promoting schism among the Methodists. "I . . . trust that [the Wesleyan Missionary Society] may never be induced to expend their funds . . . in carrying on a crusade against their brethren in Upper Canada."[15]

Unknown to the Canadian leaders Colborne's representations had been heeded at the Colonial Office. In the winter of 1832 Goderich asked "whether if Govt afford pecuniary aid, the Committee could consistently with their own special missionary [object] promote patriotic object by sending Wesleyan Miss. to Upper Canada."[16] With this tentative offer in mind the Missionary Committee drafted a report in February which was to serve as the official reply to the Canadian Missionary Board. According to the Committee the establishment of an independent Methodist Church in Upper Canada had nullified the agreement of 1820. In any event the understanding had never applied to the Indians and had been reached before the influx of English immigrants had so markedly altered the composition of the provincial population. Under these circumstances the Committee did not feel that to send missionaries to the Indians or to heavily populated areas could be regarded as an unbrotherly act on its part. The Committee also felt compelled to add "with affection but regret that the publication of a paper expressly by the Canadian Conference entering warmly and in the spirit of partizanship into the local politics of the province was not in the spirit or according to the practice of British Methodists, and contrary to that abstinence from such points which they enjoined upon their Missionaries, a circumstance which had created prejudice against the acceptableness of the Canadian Brethren with a part of the population of Canada."[17] To care for the Indians and, by inference, to provide a more acceptable kind of Methodism for the white population, the Committee was prepared to resume missionary work immediately in Upper Canada. Alder was to attend the

Lower Canada District Meeting, presumably to supervise this new enterprise.

Evidently, it was Alder's letter embodying "this announcement" and "the appointments" the Committee "had absolutely made" that struck the Canadian Methodist leaders "like thunderclaps."[18] In the light of the preceding negotiations it is difficult to understand why they should have been so stunned. Assuredly though, the Wesleyan plan posed a serious dilemma for the Methodist Conference. It had to choose between competition with the Wesleyans or amalgamation with them. For those who could remember the disturbances of 1816 to 1820 and for those who appreciated how rapidly the social complexion of Upper Canada was changing, the prospect of conflict had little appeal. There was no certainty that the use of the limited resources of the Connexion would produce a reasonable return in converts among a population drawn increasingly from the United Kingdom. Above all, to become rivals of the Wesleyans would effectively serve the interests of the enemies of Methodism and of the cause of religious liberty.

Nevertheless, the prospect of association with the Wesleyan Conference was in some ways equally unattractive. It would surely involve the surrender of Canadian Methodism's autonomy to a body whose attitude to secular issues was distinctly different from its own. On this point the experience of earlier years was reinforced by George Ryerson's striking testimony. He was certain that the governing views of the Wesleyans were "not suited to the meridian of America." He added: "I *detest* their politics . . . and their servile & time-serving clinging to the skirts of a corrupt, secularized and anti-Christian Church. They are very generally either anti-Reformers or half-hearted, lukewarm, hesitating reformers. . . . Altogether I fear that the Wesleyan Conference is an obstacle to the extension of civil & religious liberty."[19] With these opinions the Wesleyans would bring, although the Canadians did not yet know it, a government grant for missions that would inevitably be considered by objective observers as contrary to the voluntarist policy of Upper Canadian Methodism.

On the other hand, to those in the Conference and in the Societies who were concerned primarily with the survival of Methodism, some form of collaboration with the Wesleyans was bound to appear necessary. The burden of missionary work was becoming harder to bear; the Wesleyans with their greater resources might ease the strain.[20] A link with the Wesleyans would elevate the status of Methodism in Upper Canadian society and in particular it would help to remove the stigma of disloyalty associated with the American origins of the Canadian Conference. Those who felt that the

Methodists had become too deeply involved with the world probably anticipated that the Wesleyans would disengage the Canadian societies from such secular activities. Indeed, as those most involved in political controversy were ultimately concerned with religious rather than worldly considerations, they were themselves susceptible to this argument.

Still, it would doubtless be unfair and inaccurate to suggest that these alternatives were clearly formulated at this stage. Rather, those directly concerned, especially John Ryerson, cast about for "any possible way in which the evil could be averted." "It came into my mind suddenly," he wrote, "whether or not some arrangement could not be entered into by which the two Conferences could be united.... The more I thought of this, the brighter the streak in the cloud seemed to grow."[21] When Alder reached York in June, 1832, he was welcomed cordially and was asked to meet with the Canadian leaders to discuss the possibility of union.

The Canadians defended themselves energetically at the meeting of the Missionary Board held on June 29, insisting that they were perfectly justified in acting as they had in political matters. Alder made a firm reply but, as he observed later, the "little thunder & lightning that we had very much improved the state of the atmosphere, in consequence of which we breathed more freely and had a more distinct perception of things afterwards than before."[22] Stimulated by Alder's blunt speech and the persuasive eloquence of the Ryerson brothers the committee agreed that "the establishment of two distinct connexions of Methodists in this Province would ... be productive of ... party disputes to the discredit of Methodism ... but that the energies of the English and Canada Connexions, if combined, would ... close the door against all collision."[23] Alder was asked to attend the forthcoming Conference to discuss details of a possible union.

In the meantime he negotiated with Colborne and members of the local government. From Dr. Strachan he obtained letters of introduction for Mr. Turner, who was described as "almost one of ourselves."[24] The Governor was even more affable, keeping Alder for an hour and a half on his first visit. Colborne explained his policy toward the Episcopal Methodists, leading Alder to conclude that "his motives deserve the highest commendation." The Governor then discussed a grant to the Missionary Committee for the work it was about to begin in Upper Canada. Alder was to return again to find out how much money might be forthcoming.[25] Subsequently the amount was set at £900.[26]

Fortified by Colborne's moral support and the promise of financial assistance Alder hastened to the Upper Canada Conference to "improve the atmosphere" by the admixture of British oxygen with the noxious fumes of Yankeeism.[27] His Canadian brethren were ready to discuss a draft plan of union providing for the assimilation of Canadian into English Wesleyan practice. They were prepared to abolish the episcopate, to ordain their ministers according to the English form, and to place their missions under the Missionary Society.[28] The leading Americans in the Conference, Case and Metcalf, were strongly opposed to the scheme. The former left the chair and spoke forcibly about the rights of local preachers, the blessings of independence and the defects of foreign systems. Egerton Ryerson and his brothers took the lead on behalf of the plan. To Alder he confided, "We have given your Conference greater power than the opposition itself is at all aware of. . . . I framed all the resolutions with a view to this, so as not to destroy or weaken the effects of its operation. I therefore appeared very liberal and seemed to concede to the opposition a great deal when in fact I knew we were giving them nothing." Moreover, he realized that if the opposition had been as intelligent as its members were obstinate, the plan of union would not have been accepted.[29] Swayed by Ryerson's guileful presentation and perhaps by the promise of aid from the Missionary Society, the Conference reluctantly agreed to the plan.[30] Egerton Ryerson was appointed to carry out final negotiations with the English Conference.[31]

The striking feature of the union scheme was that no reference was made to the real points of difference between the two connexions. Whatever the original motives of the Missionary Committee may have been in deciding to resume its work in Upper Canada, there can be no doubt that in Alder's mind the primary consideration was the establishment of the right kind of Methodism in the province. Writing to Colborne after the Conference, he affirmed: "I have rigidly adhered to those great principles to which I had occasion to advert" in our discussions together. These "great principles" were, almost certainly, that it is proper for the state to assist religious bodies and that such groups, including the Methodists, should uphold and not interfere with constituted authority. He believed that his frankness in stating his principles helped him to gain the confidence of a large proportion of the Conference.[32] The Conference was sufficiently impressed, according to his account, to give its assurance that "the Christian Guardian shall for the future be an exclusively religious journal."[33] He did not claim, however, that any direct reference was made to the government grant, a move that would have been unwise for, as he wrote to his colleagues: "If we are to do anything with the Yankee we must be the Lords of the Treasury."[34]

Although Alder must have left little doubt about his objectives,[35] probably not all the Canadian preachers were aware of the implications of their actions. Some may have felt that in practice they could defend their interests effectively. Some were willing to see the *Guardian* curbed; others may honestly have thought that it could be an "exclusively religious journal" and still participate in the struggle for religious equality. Doubtless the majority were so appalled at the prospect of warfare with the Wesleyans that they were prepared not to look too closely at the dangers posed by union. Their suspicions lulled by the persuasive eloquence of its backers, they agreed to try the experiment.

In addition the Canadians may have anticipated that the Missionary Committee would take a more conciliatory line than Alder. Unfortunately for the future peace of Methodism in Upper Canada such an attitude did not prevail. In November, 1832, the Committee assured Goderich that its members had sought to determine "how we might best combine the views of your Lordship as to the diffusion of sound British principles in [Upper Canada] with our own objects of religious usefulness." At first they had thought simply of sending additional missionaries to the province, but the more attractive prospect of union with the Upper Canada Conference had emerged. If the union were effected the Methodist ministry would "in future be exclusively supplied either from England or from the college now building in Upper Canada under the control and direction of the British Conference. The influence of the United States will therefore be utterly shut out and the whole of the Methodists in Upper Canada become integral parts of our general body and subject to its general rules."[36] To Colborne, too, the Committee wrote that its operations would be "carefully watched over and as far as possible rendered efficient for all good public purposes," and that it would be "happy to receive" his suggestions.[37]

When Ryerson opened negotiations with the Committee in the spring of 1833 he found it willing to accept the union but insistent upon certain safeguards. The Committee stipulated that all its missionaries should be supervised by a general superintendent "representing the Parent Committee in such a sense as to possess a *veto* over the appointments of the missionaries ... if he judges that the ... principles of the union will be compromised by the appointments which may be proposed," a provision designed to assure that the right people would be put in proper places. The Committee then urged that "the *Christian Guardian* become strictly a religious newspaper like the *New York Christian Advocate* and that it shall not attack the principle of receiving aid from Government for the extension of religion."[38] It is clear from the terms of union that

Ryerson accepted the first stipulation, and it must be assumed that he gave some undertaking concerning the future course of the *Guardian*.[39] Otherwise the Committee would not have agreed to proceed with the union and to grant £1,000 toward missionary work in Upper Canada.

Ryerson reached York with the terms of union late in the summer of 1833, accompanied by the Rev. George Marsden who had been designated by the English Conference as the first president of the Conference in Upper Canada.[40] It was ironic that on his first appearance Marsden wore a round-breasted coat, short breeches, black silk stockings with silver knee and shoe buckles. His clothing may have been out of style in the new country but as for the man himself, in Green's words, there was "a vein of goodness, disinterested benevolence, and holy zeal visible in all his acts."[41] The consummation of union would owe much to his rather naïve eloquence.

When the Conference met in special session on October 2, 1833, Marsden assured the brethren that the union plan was a providential opportunity to bring together two great branches of Methodism. They were under one government and properly belonged in one body. When Metcalf observed that Alder had given "a kind of pledge" of financial assistance and that this was held up as "an inducement to the union," Marsden pointed out that if the English Conference had alluded to the matter it would have seemed that the Canadians were being bought. The latter simply had to outline their needs and they would be met. After discussion Egerton Ryerson and Green moved that the union be accepted; their resolution passed unanimously. At this point Case formally turned the session over to Marsden, with the assurance that he would continue to work in the interests of Methodism. At the same time Richardson gave up the editorship of the *Guardian* to Ryerson, but surprisingly he secured only a bare majority of three, an ominous indication of what might lie ahead. In all though, as one delegate observed, the union question had been settled in the Conference with much less difficulty than he expected.[42]

By the terms of union the Methodists in Upper Canada agreed that "the Discipline, Economy and Form of Church Government in General of the Wesleyan Methodists in England be introduced" into their Societies "and that in particular an annual Presidency be adopted."[43] The president was to be appointed by the parent Conference from its own members and was to exercise the same authority as the general superintendent. In the second place the English usage concerning admission and ordination of itinerants was accepted. This meant, among other things, that local preachers could no longer be ordained. Thirdly, missions to the Indians and destitute settlers then maintained by the Canadian Missionary Society became the responsibility of the Wesleyan Missionary Society. These were to be administered by a general superintendent selected by the English Conference and were to be assisted by an annual grant from the Society's funds.[44]

Outwardly these arrangements seemed innocuous and likely to serve the cause of religion generally and of Methodism in particular.[45] Perhaps without fully realizing it the Canadian Societies had committed themselves to a program of assimilation to the English form of Methodism led by Wesleyan missionaries. Of course there were many small points of adjustment to which few would object, but it was improbable in the first instance that the local preachers, an active and vocal element, would accept a change in their status. It was even less probable that either preachers or people willingly would accept direction on secular questions, but Ryerson's informal engagement with regard to the *Guardian* was certain to be used by the Wesleyans to justify their course. Above all, although the government grant was being made to the Missionary Society it would be difficult to argue that the Canadian Conference derived no benefit from it. As soon as the existence of the grant became known, suspicion of treachery among the Methodists and taunts of hypocrisy among their enemies would arise. There was every reason to expect that far from eliminating collision between the two conferences, the union, except under the most inspired leadership, would lead to strife between them. Indeed the Conference of 1833 had barely concluded its work when the storm broke.

2

In the *Guardian* of October 30, 1833, Egerton Ryerson published the first of a series entitled "Impressions Made By Our Late Visit to England," in which he dealt at some length with the party system in that country. The tory party was divided into two sections, ultras and moderates. An ultra was an unqualified tory, "a lordling in power, a tyrant in politics and a bigot in religion." Among the ultras, nevertheless, were "men of the highest Christian virtue and piety," representing a "major part of the talent and wealth and learning of the British nation." The moderates held the same opinions but acted "from *religious* principle." They contemplated "the good of the nation . . . without regard to party measures and uninfluenced by political sectarianism." To this group belonged many of the evangelical clergy, "a majority of the Wesleyan

Methodists" and such men as Colborne and Goderich. The whigs, in contrast, interpreted the consitution "upon the *principles of expedience.*" Finally, there were the radicals, "apparently headed by Messrs. Hume and Attwood; the former of whom . . . [had] never been known to promote any religious measure or object as such." Radicalism, Ryerson went on, "appeared to us to be but another word for Republicanism. . . . The notorious infidel character of the majority of the political leaders . . . of this party deters the virtuous part of the nation from associating with them." No Christian, he concluded, "could safely and wisely identify himself with either of them. . . . The most rational and effectual means for a true Christian to reform vice and to correct abuses is to know, enjoy and always abound in the work of Him who went about doing good."[46]

Ryerson's object in publishing these inflammatory statements is not wholly clear. In the *Guardian* he affirmed that his intention was "to correct an erroneous impression that had been industriously created that we are identified in our feelings and purposes with some one political party; [and] to furnish an instructive moral to the Christian reader not to be the passive or active tool . . . of any political party as such. . . . That our Christian brethren throughout the province . . . do not wish us to be an organized political party we are fully assured."[47] Less than a month later he stated that "our *object* and only object, in giving our impressions to the public was to *entertain* and *profit*."[48] To Alder he confided that after reading the *Advocate* and other radical papers he became convinced that "since the failure and disappointment of Mackenzie in his mission to England, the object and tendency of their [the reformers'] writings and proceedings was to unite with the French party in Lower Canada & make an effort to separate this Colony from the Parent Government. I felt it my duty to do what I could indirectly to neutralize their influence by adverting to Sir John Colborne in favourable terms, by showing the evils of party spirit & the dangerous character and tendency of radicalism in England."[49]

Examined in the light of circumstances and Ryerson's previous statements, the discrepancies between these accounts can be overcome. Mackenzie was disgruntled by the inconclusive result of his negotiations in England and he was beginning to move away from the more moderate reformers.[50] Sensing this, Ryerson naturally recoiled and began to stress that loyalty to the existing constitution that had infused all his earlier political pronouncements. At the same time, Ryerson's own experience in England had disillusioned him about the radicals. Neither he nor his brethren had previously realized that Hume and his associates were not notably religious men.[51] This discovery prompted him to judge individuals and issues on moral grounds, a tendency that had been most evident in earlier *Guardian* editorials, and one that many Methodists shared. Tactically Ryerson felt it necessary to demonstrate to the Wesleyans that the Canadian Methodists were not completely enmeshed in politics. The "Impressions" marked the first phase in a process of disengagement, one that the Methodists, with their peculiar outlook, might well have launched sooner or later.

Whatever the precise nature of Ryerson's motives, the publication of the "Impressions" produced a stunning uproar. This sharp reaction pointed up the prevalent misconception about the political objectives of the Methodists. W. L. Mackenzie greeted Ryerson's article with vituperation:

> The *Christian Guardian* . . . has gone over to the enemy, press, types & all, & hoisted the colours of a cruel, vindictive tory priesthood. . . . The Americans had their Arnold and the Canadians have their Ryerson; and oppression and injustice, and priestly hypocrisy may triumph for a time and wax fat and kick, but we yet anticipate the joyful day . . . in which the cause of civil and religious freedom shall win a great and lasting victory in this favoured land.[52]

The Methodist defection from the cause of freedom was seen by Mackenzie as the first fruit of the misguided union policy and particularly of the government grant to the Wesleyan Methodists. His conviction was shared by many.[53]

Ryerson was stirred rather than deterred by Mackenzie's denunciation. He admitted that "the decided part we have felt it our duty to take in obtaining and securing our rights in regard of the Clergy Reserve question has had a remote or indirect tendency to promote Mr. Mackenzie's measures. . . . But that we have ever supported a measure . . . on any other grounds than this, we totally deny." As for Mackenzie, Ryerson added: "However exceptionable much of his proceedings and writings were, their general tendency [had been] to secure rigid economy in the public expenditure, and to remove abuses which candour must admit have gradually grown up" in Upper Canada. Thus the Methodists had resolved "not to become umpire or partizan between Mr. Mackenzie and his opponents. . . . We regret that we have been compelled to do otherwise—desiring that all . . . of whatever merely political predilections might feel themselves equally at home in their church membership and equally profited by our editorial labours." "We may now," he concluded, "dismiss Mr. Mackenzie from our columns."[54]

Mackenzie could not be so easily dismissed, as Ryerson must

surely have been the first to realize. Despite many disclaimers the Methodists had become identified with the reformers. The *Guardian's* editorials did not put them above or outside the battle but seemed designed to transfer them to the tory camp. To John Ryerson and others of a conservative outlook this was a welcome reversal. Writing to Egerton from Hallowell in November, 1833, John admitted that the "Impressions" had created a stir; "the only good that can come from it is the breaking up of the union which has hithertofor existed between us & the Radicles." "We have reason," he continued, "to respect *Sir John Colburn* & it is our duty & interest to support the *Government*. . . . And as it respects the *Reformers* so called, take Bidwell and Rolph from them & there is not scarcely one man of *character,* Honour or even deacency among them, but with very few exceptions (I mean the leaders), they are a banditti of compleat vagabonds. . . . We have a host of Radicles in our Church—I am sorry to say it but it is so." For the present "the best way is to have nothing to say about Polliticks, but treat the government with great respect." "Have not we all leaned to much toward" the Radicals, and "will we not now smart for it a little, but one thing, the sooner the smarts come on the sooner they will be over."[55]

To William Ryerson, in contrast, his brother's statements were much more questionable. "As to the *Guardian,*" he wrote, "I am sorry to inform you that it has been much more popular than it is at present, and indeed if your *English impressions* are not more acceptable & useful in other parts than they are here, it will add little to your credit or to the usefullness of your paper to publish any more of them." Besides, "I cannot . . . but observe that it is rather unfortunate that if you did not intend to flatter or conciliate the Tory party in this country . . . you should express yourself in such a way as to be altogether misunderstood by both friends and foes."[56]

William Ryerson's apprehensions were shared by David Wright, superintendent of the Stamford circuit, and by other preachers in the Niagara peninsula. Finding it impossible "to stem the torrent of opposition" arising from "Ryerson's injudicious & uncalled for remarks," they called upon the *Guardian* to print their declaration that "the clergy of the Episcopal Church ought to be deprived of *every emolument derived from Governmental aid* and . . . the clergy Reserves," and that "our political views are decidedly the same which they were previous" to Ryerson's visit to England. These political views never were those of the moderate tory.[57] Similar sentiments were expressed in the York Society.[58]

Faced with such diverse reactions Ryerson admitted privately that his statements had "produced considerable excitement or rather pain in our Societies." But he believed that only a minority was alarmed and that the controversy would not last long. "It may blow off some of the chaff in *some* places."[59] The dispute over the *Guardian's* alleged change of front focused attention on the union with the Wesleyans, which was regarded by some as the source of this political shift. The Wesleyans, confronted by turmoil in the Canadian Societies, tried to strengthen their position. Indirectly they were abetted by men such as John Ryerson, who were determined to maintain Methodist unity. This movement stimulated agitation by those who disliked either the union or the *Guardian's* moderate course, or who considered the two to be opposite sides of the same coin.

Like most ecclesiastical marriages, the union of 1833 produced three parties where formerly only two had existed. From the outset the Wesleyans, especially those in the York and Kingston Societies and in the Lower Canada District, regarded the union negotiations most unfavourably.[60] In their view an energetic campaign by the Committee would undermine the Canadian Societies, whose political activities they regarded with horror. If there had to be a union, however, they held that the terms should be so rigorous as to deprive the latter of all freedom of action.[61] To the last moment men such as John Barry, the missionary in York, tried to enlighten the Committee about the condition of the Methodist Episcopal Church. "They now say," he wrote in August, 1833, "that in choosing a Union, they only choose the least of two evils, as were it not effected, the Missionaries would subvert their Societies."[62] The Conference had barely concluded its work when William Lunn, a prominent Montreal layman, urged that the union should be dissolved.[63] Meanwhile, in Kingston, where William Ryerson had been sent to consolidate the Societies, bitter controversy prevailed. "I do not believe a Union *ever will take place* unless we allow Mr. Barry, Hetherington, etc. to *reform* our discipline to suit their views & feelings and also dictate in what manner our press shall be conducted."[64] Indeed, Hetherington told John Ryerson that he was collecting "back no. of the *Guardian* to prove that [the Canadians] had been Political intermedlers."[65]

Much now depended on the Committee, its chief representative in Canada and the Canadian leaders. Confronted with so many complaints, the Committee became more firmly convinced that union was the lesser of two evils, and it removed some of the chief disturbers of the peace.[66] Alder was appointed to visit Canada again to clear up outstanding differences. But the policy that he eventually adopted owed much to the representations of Joseph Stinson, the new Wesleyan missions superintendent.

Stinson, a native of Leicestershire, was sent to Lower Canada in 1823. As a young man he was "as lovely in mind as in person. Although there was no cant or grimace about him, his was a pure, generous, courageous heart, full of good impulses." He was well educated, "naturally tasteful" and "a fearless horseman."[67] Stinson spent some time in Kingston and Lower Canada, returned to England in 1828 and was reappointed to Upper Canada in 1833. He had become a man of some tolerance and considerable prudence, but he held firmly to the same conservative political convictions as his Wesleyan brethren.

In his first report to the Committee Stinson noted the discontent in York and Kingston, which he attributed to minorities on both sides. The only genuine complaint the Wesleyans had was the *Guardian*: "I see no prospect of peace unless that paper is either discontinued or exclusively devoted to religious and scientific subjects & this is the opinion of a great number of the Canadian Preachers and a greater number still of the most respectable members of the Canadian Society."[68] Later he emphasized that "there is a strong party of *radicals,* radicals in politics and in religion who are sparing no pains to break up the union because they see that its existence will be a powerful check upon their levelling designs." The only way in which unparalleled confusion could be forestalled was "to secure the cooperation of all persons who are really attached to British Methodism and British Institutions in general."[69]

As the spring of 1834 advanced, agitation grew among the Upper Canadian Methodists. Stinson became increasingly alarmed and his prejudices more evident. The Kingston Wesleyans, he said, were being

lampooned in no very measured terms by these long faced, half starved Yankees [the Canadians] who publicly declare that all persons who do not join them are "destitute of all moral principle;" these very persons eat as much tobacco as would poison a pack of hounds & commit as many indecencies in the House of the Lord as would bring his exterminating judgment upon the whole Province were He not infinitely merciful.[70]

He was told that the union was designed to keep the Wesleyans out of Upper Canada and was now certain that most of the Canadian Methodists had no real interest in it. "Their political character as a body," he lamented, "is extremely objectionable, they delight in finding fault with the Government & the Governor—as to the

Church they hate her with all their hearts. There is not a radical meeting in the country at which some of the Methodist leaders and Local Preachers are not the most conspicuous characters." Hence it would require "most laborious and persevering efforts to check this antimethodistic, this unchristian spirit . . . nothing else will save the Province from rebellion & destruction."[71] Alder's presence was urgently required to effect a proper settlement.

While the Wesleyans were preparing to save the province by modifying the Canadian Societies to their taste, those who disliked the union were also gathering their forces, a move facilitated by the way the union was completed. Efforts were made to sound out lay opinion in 1832 and 1833, but the Conference foolishly neglected to seek a formal mandate from the Societies.[72] It was necessary, however, to submit alterations in the Discipline to the quarterly meetings, a step that was taken in the winter of 1833, providing a forum for those who objected to the trend of events.[73] Leadership amongst the opposition was taken by local preachers, who, as a result of the union, lost their district conference and the right of ordination.[74] Doubtless there were some local preachers with radical political sympathies who could readily appeal to the widespread discontent with the *Guardian's* course.

The first overt sign of rebellion was a meeting of local preachers at Saltfleet late in 1833 at which a decided stand was taken against the terms of union.[75] Meanwhile, a prominent local preacher in Napanee, P. J. Roblin, wrote:

I have been much . . . cast down and durst not tell my mind to any person, fearing the rod that is held over my head by certain individuals, and I need not say my head, but all the Locle preachers in Canada. The movements in regard to them [recently] are very strange. . . . Are we to be Disgrased, yea more anihilated. The movements making appear to thretin it. . . . Our rites are not to be wrested from us without our consent. . . . I do not believe our Societies will see us thrown to the Rats and snakes in this way.[76]

The agenda for a proposed meeting in Belleville included the union, previous pledges, the *Guardian,* its editor and local preachers' district meetings. What happened is not clear but in March of 1834 a provincial convention was held at Trafalgar. Sixteen persons attended, six of whom had been rejected for the itinerancy. A series of resolutions was passed wherein it was asserted that the Conference had broken its compact with the Societies and in consequence had forfeited its disciplinary rights over them. In the opinion of the delegates this action left the Methodist Episcopal Church intact in principle. Therefore plans were made to hold a subsequent meeting of all sympathetic local and travelling preachers to elect a bishop and to provide for the efficient operation of this communion. The scheme evoked derisive comment from the *Guardian*.[77] But it would take more than derision to end this anti-union agitation. The sixteen spoke for many who were not present and whose opposition must have been sensed by the Methodist leaders.

At this stage neither the Canadians nor the Wesleyans were ready to compromise. Despite his misgivings John Ryerson was still prepared to make the union work and to give short shrift to the agitators, a view seemingly shared by Egerton.[78] Stinson remained fully convinced of the wisdom of the union but stressed that "there are two parties in the U.C. Conference, one party strongly attached to the union and to Br. E. Ryerson—the others rather submit to it than desire it—these have the utmost confidence in Br. Richardson —if therefore it should be found necessary to make any little alterations it will be important to have the influence of both these Heads of Parties on our side."[79] Alder informed the Committee: "The famous radical Mackenzie of York has applied to the Conference to put [Ryerson] out. If they do it's all up with the union." With typical bluntness Alder added: "Mr. Grindrod and I will end it or mend it. . . . It must now be settled."[80]

The Conference that met in Kingston on June eleventh hardly convened in auspicious circumstances. The encircling gloom was deepened by the discovery that 1,109 members had been lost during the year, a shocking fact to the statistics-minded preachers.[81] But eventually the Conference accepted all the Wesleyan proposals. With the support of William Ryerson the Conference prevented the ordination of several local preachers and agreed that "in future the ordination of local preachers shall cease."[82] Alder successfully asserted the British Conference's right to send as many missionaries to Upper Canada as it liked, presumably in the hope of diluting the Canadian itinerancy.[83] The spirited discussion of this issue was followed by a "vehement debate" on the *Guardian,* an event whose immediate sequel was the election of Richardson as editor.[84] His refusal of the post cleared the way for Ryerson's re-election and the decision that the *Guardian* would become an "exclusively religious and literary journal."[85] Finally, and appropriately, the Conference adopted a friendly address to the Governor.[86]

The consequences of acquiescence by the Conference in the policies of the Wesleyans became evident almost immediately. On June 25 the Methodist Episcopal Church was organized at a convention held near York. Within a year it had twenty-one preachers and 1,243 members, many of whom must have been included in the members lost by the Wesleyan Conference in its first year of operation.[87] Probably some of those who joined the new church were moved by petty considerations or, as in the case of the local preachers, had selfish interests to protect. Many, however, felt that the union was unwise or that the Conference could no longer be trusted to take a liberal political position. In any case, the creation of this new body inevitably produced dissension and recrimination, not to mention litigation.[88] The Methodist Episcopal Church became a centre toward which discontented elements in the Wesleyan Conference gravitated for many years.

For the present, however, the decisions of the Conference ingratiated the Methodists with the government and the Missionary Committee. Egerton Ryerson promptly reported to Alder:

I understand His Excellency the Lt. Governor is much pleased with the proceedings of Conference. He was delighted with the *Address* and sent it off immediately to the Colonial Office. The *Conservative* press are unanimous in their commendation ... of the proceedings of conference. ... All the *reform* press acquiesce ... except three that advocate Mackenzie & Hume. The little agitator is going down apace. ... These circumstances leave no *political* ground for any local preacher or other party to oppose us, or agitate our societies.[89]

When Colborne received Alder and Stinson he admitted that the union "had already effected an amazing change for the better in the character of the people." He did not doubt that ultimately it would achieve "the great object" at which they aimed. His only fear was that "the British Conference had not obtained that power over the Canadian Preachers which was necessary to promote the dominancy of their own principles." Alder countered that the British Conference could "exercise as much control over the *Canadian* Methodists as was really necessary and desirable & that this great measure must be carried rather by influence than by legislative enactments." The only requirement was the continued financial assistance of the government, which Colborne agreed to provide.[90] Under these circumstances the prospect appeared reasonably hopeful.

Although the interval between the Conferences of 1834 and 1835 seemed more peaceful than the preceding year, it was marked by developments in the province and in the Connexion that intensified confusion within the Methodist camp. Out of this would come a temporary but critical association between the forces of Methodism and toryism.

Contrary to Ryerson's expectations, the reformers won a decisive victory in the election of October, 1834, an achievement that was immediately followed by the formation of "The Canadian

Alliance."[91] This body was designed to bring together all the forces of reform and thereby to force decisive alterations in the government of Upper Canada. In the legislature the reformers secured the appointment of a committee on grievances of which W. L. Mackenzie was chairman and Dr. T. D. Morrison a conspicuous member.[92] Vigorously prompted by the chairman, the committee investigated the grants to the churches from the casual and territorial revenues. Several Methodists could have testified concerning the grant to the Missionary Society but they were not asked to attend. The Seventh Report on Grievances indicted them, along with other denominations, for plundering the public revenue.[93]

The surge of reform activity, and this outspoken condemnation of the Methodists by leading reformers, widened the gap between the more conservative-minded Methodists and the reform politicians. Those Methodists who were dubious about the break with the reformers and who felt that the allegations of the Grievance Committee were justified, began either to avoid political commitments or to join the Methodist Episcopal Church. The rest, if they considered the position seriously, were likely undecided.

In addition to these external pressures the Conference and the Societies were seriously perturbed by internal dissension. The Wesleyans continued to be suspicious of their Canadian colleagues. When the *Guardian* again called for action on the reserves, Stinson reported: "I fear the way in which Br. R. is taking up the clergy reserve question will involve us in new disputes and difficulties," an opinion that presumably was put to Ryerson as well.[94] Doubtless, it was Stinson's concern about the condition of the Societies that brought the new president, William Lord, to Canada in November, 1834, far in advance of the next session of Conference.[95] Lord, a young, vigorous, sometimes indiscreet preacher, toured the province from east to west, trying to reconcile the Societies to the union and to widen the breach with the Episcopal Methodists. Privately he expressed the hope that those with episcopal sympathies would leave, thereby depriving the Wesleyan community of the "odium of Yankee politics."[96] After his speaking tour Lord was certain that he had soothed the people, and that if enough Wesleyan missionaries were sent out the full fruits of the union would soon be reaped.[97]

The ebullient Lord may have placated some Methodists, but the Canadian leaders were disturbed by other events. In the winter of 1834 there was a bitter quarrel between Richardson and Egerton Ryerson in which the former alleged that Ryerson had cast gross aspersions on his character and politics and had misled the local preachers about the consequences of union.[98] With the help of Richardson's close friend Case the dispute was resolved. Undoubtedly it strengthened Richardson's suspicion of the Ryersons, but it lowered him in the esteem of the Wesleyans. Moreover, it probably helped to confirm Ryerson's decision to leave his post with the *Guardian*.

When Ryerson first began to think of leaving the *Guardian* is not known, but in January, 1835, he was very troubled and believed that William Squire, a Wesleyan, should take his place.[99] John Ryerson and Lord objected to his decision but they shared William Ryerson's outspoken condemnation of Richardson: "Let the paper be given up an *hundred* times sooner than Richardson should be permitted to disgrace it *again*."[100] Subsequently Egerton Ryerson concluded that Ephraim Evans, a former Wesleyan who had begun to preach in 1827, should be his successor. Imposing him on the Conference, however, would cause a clash with Richardson's supporters and indirectly with all those edging toward the Methodist Episcopal Church.[101]

If disillusionment with the consequences of union lay behind Ryerson's decision to retire as editor, the union also created new problems for Upper Canada Academy, the educational venture taken up so hopefully in 1830 by the Canadian Conference. Adhering to its voluntarist policy, the Conference had originally solicited donations from Methodists and other sympathizers to make possible the establishment of the Academy. Apparently the preachers had pictured the new institution as the reform version of Upper Canada College; one paper reported that "from corner to top-stone [it] was built with the money of reformers."[102] The controversy between the Conference and the reformers inevitably led to the drying up of public support.

The Conference of 1834 had to take drastic measures to save the Academy. The means chosen owed much to the Wesleyans, who hoped that the Academy could be converted into a school for training preachers and others in the ways of British Methodism.[103] To this end the two leading liberals on the academy committee were replaced and the Conference decided to request financial assistance from the legislature, a definite departure from voluntarist principle.[104]

Although the financial difficulties of the Academy were acute the committee at first sought only incorporation from the Assembly.[105] The need for money was temporarily met by a loan, guaranteed by Egerton Ryerson and John Beatty, Richardson and Case having refused any aid.[106] Simultaneously Lord and Stinson urged the Missionary Committee to help the Conference and thereby prevent young Canadians from going to the United States for further training.[107] But no immediate reply was made and the Conference had to implement the decision of 1834, a step that would have decisive consequences for its political outlook.

Confronted by the shaky state of the Academy, differences among the principal members, Methodist Episcopal secession and reformers' abuse, the Conference of 1835 met in a sullen, uneasy mood. The atmosphere was hardly brightened with the news that membership had increased by a mere 176.[108] For nine days the preachers met in grave and sometimes bitter deliberation. Important decisions were reached concerning the *Guardian* and church-state relations. James Richardson, defeated by nine votes for the important office of secretary, led the attack on the *Guardian's* course of the past year.[109] His criticisms were not accepted; in consequence he and his ally Franklin Metcalf became more thoroughly alienated from the Conference.[110] Their vexation was not eased by the election of Ephraim Evans as Ryerson's successor, for the new editor's Wesleyan sympathies were well known.[111] In fact Evans' appointment made it certain the *Guardian* would adopt at least a neutral political course, possibly a conservative one.

If this step demonstrated the pervasive influence of the union, so too did the Conference's statement on government grants to religious bodies. Faced with critical resolutions on one side and the Wesleyan position on the other, the Conference adopted an equivocal position. In one resolution the preachers affirmed their belief in voluntary support for themselves: "No evil could be regarded by us with greater dread than the disturbance or weakening of that oneness of interest and feeling which has always existed and does exist unimpaired between us and the people over whom the Lord hath made us overseers." But they went on: "As this Conference has no interest in voluntary grants made by Government to religious bodies—none having been made to or received by it—and there being great diversity of opinion amongst our people on this subject —this Conference does not deem it a duty to pronounce any judgment on the matter."[112] At the same time the Conference decided to appeal to the imperial government for financial assistance for the Academy.[113] Lord might well assure the Committee that if the Canada Conference were pressed to accept a share of the clergy reserves it would "reluctantly submit."[114]

The subjection of the Canadian Conference to the Wesleyans and to the needs of the Academy, which was implicit in the decisions of 1835, could hardly have occurred at a less auspicious point in the history of Upper Canada. Responding to the growing reform agitation, in the fall of 1835 the Colonial Office appointed Sir

Francis Head to succeed Colborne as governor and urged a conciliatory course of action.[115] Welcomed as a "tried reformer," Head soon clashed with the leading reformers he appointed to the Executive Council.[116] Concluding that "the Republican Party are implacable; that no concession whatever would satisfy them; their self-interested object being to possess themselves of the Government of this Province for the Sake of Lucre and Emolument," he welcomed the resignation of his new Councillors.[117] On April 20 he prorogued the Assembly, reserving all money bills, and a month later the Assembly was dissolved.[118] The Governor then went to the country on the simple platform of loyalty to crown and empire against the designs of traitors and revolutionaries.[119]

In these crucial months when Head was taking the offensive against the reformers, the *Guardian* and its new editor moved towards the tory position. When Head published his instructions, their tone was commended by the *Guardian*. The editor believed that Upper Canada needed adjustments rather than fundamental reform in its constitution. In this situation the Christian should abstain from party politics and obey the laws.[120] The Seventh Report on Grievances was bitterly condemned as the product of an anti-Methodist plot by the radicals, whereas the sensational announcement that Colborne had created fifty-seven rectories was greeted with the feeble suggestion that the people must do something about this unwise action.[121]

The most blatantly partisan statements of the *Guardian*, the Conference and Ryerson were elicited by the dissolution of the Assembly and the ensuing election campaign. When the Governor began to smear the reformers as disloyal and seditious the *Guardian* asserted that despite their interest in changes the Methodists had always been loyal subjects. Although ministers had no right, said Evans, to meddle in politics, they must not allow their followers to be duped into supporting policies subversive of the constitution.[122] Voters were urged to declare "for the continuation of that unrivalled national blessing, the British constitution."[123] The Conference, meeting one week before the election, reminded the imperial government that "nothing could tend more directly to weaken the attachment of the people of this country to the parent state than the continuance of the system of exclusive patronage of any one church."[124] Yet in its message to the Governor, the Conference stressed its

undissembled admiration of the excellent constitution by which the rights and privileges of the inhabitants of this Province are so happily secured. . . . Deeply impressed with a due sense of the advantages derived from the connexion existing between this Province and the Mother Country it will be alike our duty and delight to inculcate, by precept and example, on the numerous people under our pastoral care and instruction those Scriptural principles of piety and loyalty which are essential to their peace and prosperity and to the perpetuation of that connexion. . . .[125]

This statement must have fostered the impression that the Conference was on Head's side.

These official pronouncements were supplemented by Ryerson's letters from England, published in the *Guardian*. In a letter written in March and printed on May 25, he commented favourably on Head and his instructions: "I rejoice to learn that His Excellency in his Government satisfies all parties but the party that wishes to subvert the existing Constitution of the Province." Reverting again to the compact theory he contended that "those vital parts of the Constitutional Act . . . which actually determine the respective prerogatives and rights of King and People . . . ought [not] to be changed at the bidding of the majority of the Assembly." So long as it was possible to make such changes, only injury would be done to the credit of the province.[126]

In addition to his advocacy of the constitutionalist position, Ryerson assailed Peter Perry, a leading reformer and member for Lennox and Addington, a strongly Methodist county. If, he said,

[Perry] will take his stand where he did once as a *Constitutional* Reformer—if he will defend the Methodists against the calumnies and destructive designs of the party now labouring to injure them . . . the Methodists in Lennox and Addington will not be Mr. Perry's enemies. . . . But if he should continue the course that he has pursued . . . in advocating changes in the Colonial Constitution destructive of its peace and connexion with the Parent State—can he expect that the Methodists are such traitors to the . . . interests of their own church and of their country as to support or countenance him?[127]

This criticism was motivated by Perry's outspoken attack on Ryerson in the legislature, but it was undoubtedly construed as an attack on the reformers generally.

This letter appeared as a pamphlet entitled *Peter Perry Picked to Pieces by Egerton Ryerson*. It was an ominous forewarning of the reform débâcle at the polls in June, 1836, an outcome that observers attributed largely to Methodist influence.[128] To Francis Hincks, then a young reformer, and later to W. P. M. Kennedy, "the controlling force in the elections was the Methodists under the direction of Egerton Ryerson."[129] This conclusion was easily reached, considering the sympathy of the *Guardian* and Ryerson for the government party, and the small majorities secured by many of its candidates among the restricted electorate of that period. Some leading Methodists did their utmost to ensure Head's victory. Writing to Egerton before the Assembly was dissolved, John Ryerson asserted that "the House of Assembly are a hissing & a by word." He expected that if there were an election there would be "a horrible thining among the Radicals—not one of them would be returned from the bounds of this district; every niggar of them would be kicked over the wall without doubt." Moreover, in a by-election recently concluded in Belleville, "every Wesleyan Methodist . . . was on the right side & so they were from the country with 8 or 10 exceptions."[130] After the June election, John exultantly confided to Egerton:

The present house of Parliament is decidudly superior in respectability & talent to any we have ever had in this province. . . . The Radicals met with a most tremendous overthrow. . . . Not one Radical was returned from the Bay of Quinty District. The preachers & I laboured to the utmost extent of our ability to keep every scamp of them out & we succeeded. And had the preachers of done their duty in every place, not a *ninny* of them would have been returned to this parliament.[131]

Egerton Ryerson assured Glenelg later that, in return for Head's promise that the clergy reserves would be settled satisfactorily, the Methodists had supported him.[132]

Despite this impressive testimony, however, the question remains: did the Methodists as Methodists support the government party in sufficient numbers to swing the election of 1836? It is doubtful that the ministers were as united in condemning reformers as Ryerson implied. The famous address to the Governor, for example, was pushed through the Conference of 1836 with the greatest difficulty. Some objected that it would involve the ministers in politics. Some were loyalists, while others were more concerned about a liberal settlement of the reserves. Probably only precedent and Wesleyan strength produced a reluctant unanimity. In any event this statement "greatly disturbed the minds" of liberal members of the Societies.[133]

Apart from the *Guardian* the most effective agents in moulding the outlook of ministers and Societies were the district chairmen or presiding elders. The election occurred when these people were taking up new appointments, but for the year 1835-1836 the chairmen were James Richardson, William Ryerson, David Wright, Anson Green and John Ryerson, for the Toronto, Niagara, London, Augusta and Bay of Quinté districts respectively. Richardson had great influence, which was almost certainly wielded on the reform side.[134] On the eve of the election William Ryerson assured Egerton: "We are anxious & willing to do all that we consistently can, but everywhere the *rectory question* meets us." In other words, he would reluctantly aid the forces of order.[135] In contrast, David Wright was one who had objected most strongly to the *Guardian's* course in 1833, and the tone of Green's diary suggests that he had little sympathy for the Head régime.[136] John Ryerson was the only chairman whose authority was unreservedly against the radicals. His district returned no reformers, but three were returned from York, five from Niagara, four from London and six from the Augusta district.[137]

Little direct evidence of the temper of Methodist Societies at this point has survived; what remains, however, indicates that they were not wholly sympathetic to the government side. George Ferguson, not a man to take sides, found that the people of the Augusta circuit were more interested in politics than in religion. They were particularly offended with the *Guardian*.[138] John Carroll, also a peaceable preacher, discovered among the Methodist people of Brockville great "dissatisfaction with the Conference on account of the Address to the Governor" which led them "to withhold all support except the simple penny a week and shilling a quarter."[139] Nearly six hundred members were lost between 1836 and 1837. There was, then, dissension and lack of sympathy with the Conference within the Societies.[140]

Nevertheless, any broad appraisal of the Methodist contribution in the 1836 election must give due weight to other factors. The Methodists as a body had every reason to take revenge on the reformers, who had so successfully pilloried their own leaders. The reformers had a case against the Methodists, but this was not likely to deter those who thought more of Methodism than of reform from defending the Conference. These same people no doubt were impressed by Head's assurance that he would settle the reserves question, for it was easy, although naïve, to believe that this problem could be adjusted independently of the general reform of Canadian institutions. The Wesleyans in the Canadian Societies were in the tory camp. Since they were concentrated in Kingston, Toronto, Hamilton and London they may well have contributed to the tory victories in those constituencies.

Given the complex cross currents in the Methodist Societies and their tradition of liberal sympathy, it would be incautious to say that theirs was the deciding voice in 1836. There is certainly no strong reason to believe that, at the behest of their leaders, they moved wholeheartedly to the side of church and state. Doubtless some did; others, perhaps the majority, may have been confused and hesitant; others may have believed that individual government candidates were more truly liberal than their opponents; some were probably unmoved by the current identification of reform and disaffection.

There is no need to look to the Methodists for the explanation of the government's victory in 1836; it can be accounted for adequately in secular terms. A host of influences affected Methodists and other electors. The reform majority of 1834, many of whose members were sufficiently moderate to be elected by middle-of-the-road voters, had done well by itself in the interval, and conceivably had begun to elicit a reaction among those who had little share in the bounty.[141] It was alleged, too, and apparently with some justification, that Head freely distributed favours on the eve of the election, a device of proven utility in other times and places.[142] Surely, though, the crucial factor at this point was the extent of the tory interest in Upper Canadian politics, an interest that had been growing steadily for fifteen years but which has been underrated because of the liberal bias of contemporary and later commentators.[143] In describing the choice for the electors as one between loyalty to the British connexion and republicanism, Head successfully appealed to this group, many of whom were moderate men. The result was that the Assembly gained a group of members who did little to remedy the condition of Upper Canada.

3

Two days before the election of 1836 Upper Canada Academy, whose principal was that staunch Wesleyan tory Matthew Richey, had been formally opened.[144] Unfortunately this new venture was overshadowed by its financial difficulties, which had been worsened by the improvident actions of William Lord.[145] To secure assistance, Egerton Ryerson began a siege of the Colonial Office in January, 1836, a siege that continued until the spring of 1837.[146] Ultimately, the imperial government sanctioned a grant to the Academy from the casual and territorial revenues, but the prolonged uncertainty on this score helped weaken the Methodist conviction that the clergy reserves should be secularized.

The first hint that the Methodists were considering the division of the reserves among the churches appeared in the *Guardian* for December 14, 1836.[147] Within a month John Ryerson wrote Egerton that "the Clergy lands will probably be divided between the Church, Catholicks, Presbyterians & Methodists." "We have said," to members of the Assembly, he continued, "that we believe our conference will accept of them, provided they are left free to appropriate them as they see fit for building chapels, parsonages & support of education, etc. . . . I conversed with the members & told them they should not mind what the *Guardian* said about giving them [to] education and nothing else. . . . He [Evans] mearly wrote that article to please the Radicals."[148] In April, 1837, Egerton discussed with James Stephen at the Colonial Office a division scheme that was considered by the Conference of 1837.[149]

The Conference of 1837 met in Toronto in June under the chairmanship of the Rev. W. M. Harvard, a veteran Wesleyan missionary, whose urbanity and piety concealed highly conservative political opinions.[150] The occasion's gravity and Harvard's caution stretched the session to ten days. Confronted as they were with the long-term needs of the Academy, the continuing but differently based suspicions of the Wesleyans and of many Canadian Methodists, indecision in the legislature, and a substantial decline in membership, the preachers decided to clarify their stand on government grants and the reserves.[151] The result was a series of ambiguous resolutions.

To begin with the Conference reaffirmed that it never had received any "public or Government grants" and "that it desired no other support for its members than the voluntary contributions of Christian liberality." True, grants had been made to the Missionary Committee, but these had been used "solely and entirely in the improvement of the long-neglected aboriginal Indian tribes and destitute settlers." Nevertheless, as these grants had "proved seriously prejudicial to the peace and tranquility of the Province" and as their continuance was being used "to embarrass the settlement of . . . the Clergy Reserves," the Conference disclaimed "any demand upon the Casual and Territorial Revenue" and left "it entirely to the unbiassed judgment of the authorities concerned to decide whether any public aid" should be given to the Indians and "if any, to what amount and through what agency."[152]

Having clarified its position on state aid the Conference restated its policy on clergy reserves:

It is the strong conviction and deliberate judgment of this Conference that the interests of religion . . . and the welfare of the Province require the earliest possible settlement of the long agitated Clergy Reserve Question, in accordance with the wishes and circumstances of the inhabitants. . . . While, as a body of Christian and Methodist ministers . . . we would conscientiously abstain from all needless intermeddling with secular politics, yet . . . this Conference has . . . expressed its decided conviction of the inexpediency of the establishment of one or more Churches in this Province.

The efforts of the Churches of England and Scotland to "secure an ascendancy over their Christian brethren of other denominations" would, "if successful, be in direct violation of those principles of civil and religious liberty for the maintenance of which this Conference still . . . contends."

Should any adjustment of the Clergy Reserve Question be proposed and determined on, which would not contravene the principles laid down in the foregoing resolutions, . . . the members of this Conference avow their determination not to receive or apply any legislative aid for their own pecuniary support; or for any other purposes than the religious and educational improvement of the Province in such way as may be in accordance with the views of a majority of two-thirds of the several quarterly meetings throughout the Province.[153]

The Methodist Conference, while continuing to subscribe formally to the voluntarist position, had deserted it in practice through force of circumstance. It was prepared to receive state assistance, knowing that although such grants would nullify the exclusive claims of the Churches of England and Scotland, they would place some churches in a more advantageous position than those who refused aid.

After the Conference the resolutions were submitted to a quarterly meeting in Belleville. Anson Green reported that "they were hailed with most cordial and *unanimous* approbation. Every brother present was much pleased with them and would . . . join in a petition to Parliament urging *our claims* for a share of the reserves."[154] Some of the ministers met in November, 1837, to devise a division scheme and settle upon a way to get it before the Assembly.[155] When the subject was brought before the leading members of that body no agreement could be reached, some being for division, others for reinvestment in the Crown. Ryerson urged "those members of the Assembly with whom we had most influence to vote for the reinvestment of the reserves in the Crown for religious purposes."[156] Subsequently he pressed Glenelg, the Colonial Secretary, to send out a draft bill covering reinvestment and distribution, for, he added: "Nothing but the influence of Her Majesty's Government will put an end to it."[157]

Fortunately, perhaps, these negotiations were obscured by the rising agitation which culminated in the rebellion of December, 1837. The *Guardian* exhorted every Methodist to "lift up your voice in prayer and exert all your energies to save your firesides and families from the untold horrors of civil war"; the paper was filled with exaltation when the rebels failed.[158] Ryerson produced a sternly conservative sermon on civil government, and Stinson wrote: "They [the rebels] will meet with a hot reception here [Kingston] &

many of them will bite the earth before the rascally rebel rag shall displace the glorious banner of Old England.... This is the most rascally unprincipled rebellion that ever disgraced a country."[159]

The high point of official Methodist opposition to the rebel cause was the publication in April, 1838, of President Harvard's pastoral letter. It was alleged that some Methodists were implicated in the rebellion; Harvard asserted that under a lawful government good Christians must be good subjects. "No man who is not disposed to be a good subject can be admissible to the sacraments of the church." He requested preachers to screen out all disloyal elements. "And should any person apply hereafter for admission into our church who may be ill-affected to the Crown under which we live ... tell him kindly but firmly that that is a commodity we do not deal in—that he has applied at the wrong door." Harvard's policy was supported by the *Guardian*.[160]

This ill-advised, typically Wesleyan statement was scorned by many Methodists.[161] Harvard reported: "Last night I was rather rudely arrested by one of our Leaders and a local preacher who termed my letter a bull—that I was acting like a Pope."[162] He was probably more surprised by Egerton Ryerson's counter-blast entitled "What is Christian Loyalty?" "Mr. Wesley," Ryerson recalled, "gives the right hand of fellowship to those who differ from him on many points ... nor can we with any reason or propriety allow less latitude and liberty of sentiment on doctrines and measures of government." He agreed that the rebels sought changes that would result in independence but they had to be shown their error by "the weapons of truth, not the sword of despotism or the brute force of mobocracy."

The discipline of the church does not authorize us to become the judge of another man's political opinions—the church is not a political association. Rebellion must be suppressed, but I believe one of the most effectual means of promoting all the evils of civil discord and commotion would be ... to rate [the] political orthodoxy [of others] by my own.... The most effectual means for Christian ministers to suppress the *spirit of sedition, privy conspiracy and rebellion* ... is to preach up the simple doctrine of "Fear God and honour the King."[163]

To Harvard he wrote that the "mode you recommend is unprecedented ... and will, I fear, produce the most disastrous results in the minds of preachers and people if the undoubted constitutional right of individual judgment and discussion on political matters be not fully understood and mutually acknowledged by all."[164]

At last, the Canadian Methodist worm had turned!

4

For those who thought of the Methodist Church as something more than a mutual salvation society, the interval between Ryerson's break with the radicals in October, 1833, and his resounding repudiation of Harvard's tory policy in the spring of 1838 was not a subject of rejoicing. The insidious attack launched by those who promoted the intrusion of the Wesleyans into Upper Canada had led in these years to a significant alteration in the balance of forces in the Methodist community, and in consequence to a different relationship between that group and the secular order. Those who put first the welfare of the Methodist Church as an institution, and those who thought that its function was to bolster the existing order, had come to the fore. Thus the Methodist Conference severed its informal association with the reformers and in 1836, particularly, supported the tories. Without formally giving up the voluntarist principle it accepted state aid to Indian missions and denominational education, and (in principle) the division of the clergy reserves. To many, therefore, it seemed that the Methodists had deserted the cause of civil and religious liberty.

This shift of emphasis at the official level was not the product of a corrupt bargain between the government and the Methodists. On the contrary, the powerful conservative influence of the Wesleyans, the determination of the preachers to carry out their spiritual duties, the financial requirements of the Academy, and the peculiar Upper Canadian identification of liberal political ideas with disloyalty, had strengthened those conservative and other-worldly forces that were always present within the Methodist community. Moreover, Ryerson and other perceptive Methodists had another positive reason for acting as they did at this point. For those who were more interested in principle than in partisanship and for those who sought genuinely acceptable solutions to Upper Canada's problems, there was much that was questionable in the reform agitation from 1835 to 1837. Although in trying to reconcile the traditions and needs of Methodism with what they conceived to be Upper Canada's real requirements the Methodists came very close to selfish self-defence, the complexity of their position should not be underestimated or misrepresented.

In any event, if one believes that the Methodists as a body had any influence on the course of politics before 1833, their activities between 1833 and 1838 presumably had some bearing on the outcome of the incessant political conflict of those years. Certainly, the whole question of church-state relations appeared to be no nearer to an acceptable solution in 1838 than it had been five years earlier. Firm adherence to the principle of separation of church and state by the Methodists might have forced its acceptance. Yet there is little evidence that the Methodists generally deserted the simple voluntarist position. In such ways as were open to them they doubtless continued to promote their ideas. At the same time it is apparent that only forceful action by the imperial government could have effected a solution to the church-state dispute. But the balance of political forces in that government made the likelihood of such action remote. The most that can be said is that Methodist hesitancy deprived the reformers of the opportunity to present a powerful united front on this issue to the governor and to the Colonial Office.

Despite the importance attached by many to the church and education questions at this stage, the critical element in the reform movement was a profound concern about the form of Upper Canada's government and the future economic development of the province. From 1834 to 1837 Mackenzie and his followers moved directly if perhaps unwittingly towards independence, a republican form of government, and an economic policy that would serve the pioneer farmer—objectives in no way compatible with the existing lines of economic and political growth. Again the query arises: did the policy pursued by the Methodist Conference and the *Guardian* have any significant effect on the growing radicalism of the reformers? Probably the outward turmoil was misleading. Mackenzie and his colleagues regretted the loss of official Methodist support, but, impelled as they were by powerful economic and social forces, the continuance of such support might well have given them greater confidence instead of inducing in them a greater degree of prudence. Only in so far as official Methodist assistance helped to produce the tory victory of 1836 did Methodism affect the course of reform policy. A different verdict then might have deterred the radicals from their violent course in 1837.

In reality, though, Upper Canada seems to have moved inexorably to the outwardly farcical crisis of December, 1837. Painful as its aftermath was, it was beneficial in that it focused attention on the urgency of Upper Canada's problems and the effective limits within which they could be resolved. The true significance of the part played by the Methodist Connexion in this situation was that in its vacillations and perplexities it dramatized the distinction between the tory, the radical and the liberal prescriptions for the province's needs. The Methodist leaders and probably the majority of their followers chose the liberal formula and became indirectly a powerful reinforcement for those others, such as the Baldwins, who sought similar broad ends. By refusing to commit themselves wholly to one side or the other they assisted toryism temporarily, but at length helped to keep Upper Canada within the British connexion, to clear the way for a constitutional system of government, and to maintain an individualist and capitalist social order in which the principle of civil and religious liberty would be upheld. It was not a glorious rôle—rather it was one for which Upper Canadian Methodism was best adapted.

REFERENCES TO CHAPTER SIX

1. E. Ryerson, *Canadian Methodism: Its Epochs and Characteristics*, 300.
2. See P.A.C., *Q329*, 273, Maitland to Bathurst, January 4, 1821. The Committee took the trouble to send a long letter to the Colonial Office. P.A.C., *Q330*, 99-105, Secretaries to Goulburn, July 3, 1821. See also *W.R.*, Reel 24, Resolutions of the Committee in reference to Upper and Lower Canada, 1821.
3. P.A.O., Strachan Papers, Letter Book, 1827-1839. Letter dated December 13, 1831, probably to Alder. *M.R.*, Reel 1, Committee Minutes, April 11, 1827.
4. *M.R.*, Reel 3, Minutes of Lower Canada District, 1827.
5. P.A.C., *Q344-2*, 327-328, Maitland to Bathurst, July 16, 1827. This letter was sent in connection with a petition from the Canada District Meeting requesting government assistance for Wesleyan missionary work in Upper Canada. *W.R.*, Reel 6, Petition of Canada District Meeting, May, 1827.
6. See *W.R.*, Reel 7, Petition from Members, Friends and Patrons of the British Wesleyan Connexion in the townships along the Napanee River, January 31, 1829.
7. *Ibid.*, John Fenton to the Committee, January 5, 1829. This request was countered by a statement from the Canadian leaders in York. *Ibid.*, Thomas Vaux *et al.* to the Committee, April 23, 1829.
8. See *W.R.*, Reel 24, Extract of Committee Minutes, June 18, 1828. The W.M.S. files contain many reports on Indian missions in the United States.
9. *E.R.*, I, 133; Peter Jones, *Life and Journals of Kah-Ke-Wa-Quo-Na-By* (Toronto, 1860), 295 ff; Findlay and Holdsworth, *History of the Wesleyan Methodist Missionary Society*, I, 423.
10. *M.R.*, Reel 1, Committee Minutes, May 11, 1831; *W.R.*, Reel 24, Townley to Case, June 13, 1831.
11. *W.R.*, Reel 8, Turner to Secretaries, October 26, 1831.
12. *Ibid.*, Turner to Townley, October 27, 1831.
13. *Ibid.*, Reel 24, John Ryerson *et al.* to Townley, October 14, 1831.
14. Watson became a missionary secretary for the second time in 1832.
15. *W.R.*, Reel 24, Egerton Ryerson to R. Watson, October 19, 1831.

16. *Ibid.*, J. James to R. Alder, February 6, 1832. As late as June, 1832, no decision had been taken on the form or amount of aid to be given by the government of Upper Canada.
17. *Ibid.*, Committee Minutes, February 15, 1832. The Committee stated that Mr. Turner had already been appointed to establish a mission at the St. Clair Reservation.
18. Ryerson, *op. cit.*, 307.
19. *E.R.*, I, 137-138, George to Egerton Ryerson, August 6, 1831.
20. *W.R.*, Reel 9, Stinson to Secretaries, November 13, 1833; *M.R.*, Reel 1, Committee Minutes, June 10, 1833.
21. Ryerson, *op. cit.*, 309.
22. *W.R.*, Reel 19, Alder to Watson, July 16, 1832.
23. *Ibid.*, Reel 24, Minutes of Missionary Board, June 29, 1832.
24. *Ibid.*, Reel 19, Alder to James, July 30, 1832.
25. *Ibid.*, Alder to James, July 16, 1832.
26. Although the Wesleyans thought of the grant as a special inducement to them to counteract the influence of the Episcopal Methodists, it was issued as part of a larger scheme. In 1831 Goderich directed that £5000 be taken from the casual and territorial fund to assist the Church of England, but because the reserves were becoming more profitable only £1000 was required. To sweeten the atmosphere generally, he then recommended that the remaining £4000 be used for grants to other churches. See P.A.C., *G69*, Goderich to Colborne (confidential), April 5, 1832. Colborne then recommended a grant of £900 to the Missionary Committee. Q374-4, 851-2, Colborne to Goderich, September 5, 1832. This was accepted by Goderich in November, 1832. G69, (103), Goderich to Colborne, November 22, 1832. Ironically, the Canadian Wesleyan Methodists or Ryanites were also given £600.
27. See *W.R.*, Reel 19, Alder to James, July 30, 1832. "I don't like Yankeeism. There will be no *oxygen* at the Conference but I mean to prepare a little to improve the atmosphere."
28. *Minutes of Conference, 1832,* 50-51.
29. See A. Green, *The Life and Times of Anson Green,* 160-161. Ryerson's account has recently been discovered in the Lower Canada records. M.R., Reel 3, Ryerson to Alder, August 17, 1832. Much later Methodist history is illuminated by Ryerson's reference to Case: "I expect he will never forgive me for my replies."
30. *Minutes of Conference,* 50-51. See *W.R.*, Reel 8, Alder to James, September 14, 1832. "You are to furnish certain pecuniary aid which you can do from the Governor's grant, etc."
31. *Minutes of Conference, 1832,* 49. See *M.R.*, Reel 3, Ryerson to Alder, August 17, 1832. "My instructions do not in letter go as far as you suggested but everything can be virtually accomplished that you desire."
32. P.A.C., *Q374-4,* 861-862, Alder to Colborne, August 27, 1832. He was also instrumental in the publication in the York Courier of an

address of loyalty from the Wesleyan Missionaries. See *W.R.*, Reel 19, Address of British Wesleyan Missionaries to Sir John Colborne.
33. *Ibid.*, Alder to Colborne, August 27, 1832.
34. *W.R.*, Reel 19, Alder to Watson, July 16, 1832.
35. *Ibid.*, Reel 8, Alder to Secretaries, September 14, 1832. In this Alder stated: "I have demanded for you more than has been conceded, but all will be granted." Alder left a memorandum with the Canadian Conference outlining the points on which their representative was to be ready to negotiate. Among these were proposals that the local preachers be put on the same footing as those in England, that Kingston should remain under British control and that camp meetings be considered. Also he was to be "instructed to assure the committee that the Christian Guardian shall assume a decidedly religious character for the future." *Ibid.*, Reel 19, August 15, 1832.
36. *Ibid.*, Reel 24, Watson to Goderich, November 22, 1832.
37. *Ibid.*, Committee Minutes, November 14, 1832.
38. *Ibid.*, Committee Minutes, June 10, 1833.
39. One should note in this connection the statement of Mr. William Lunn, a prominent lay Methodist of Montreal. "Mr. E. Ryerson is, I am happy to say, convinced of his errors in too great interference with politics and regrets the opposition he has made to the Lieut. Governor's views and wishes." *W.R.*, Reel 8, W. Lunn to the Secretaries, July 16, 1832.
40. *E.R.*, I, 186-187.
41. Green, *op. cit.*, 175.
42. This account is based on an anonymous document, dated October 2, 1833, in *W.R.*, Reel 24. The writer may have been Joseph Stinson, the incoming missionary superintendent. The vote for the editorship was: Ryerson—22, Richardson—19. Thomas Whitehead formally dissented from the vote for union; Joseph Gatchell, a superannuated preacher, was not present.
43. *Minutes of Conference, 1833*, 63.
44. *Ibid.*, 64-66.
45. *Ibid.*, 63.
46. *C.G.*, October 30, 1833.
47. *Ibid.*, November 6, 1833.
48. *Ibid.*, December 11, 1833.
49. *W.R.*, Reel 24, Ryerson to Alder, November 13, 1833.
50. Dunham, *op. cit.*, 139.
51. *C.G.*, November 6, 1833.
52. *Colonial Advocate*, October 30, 1833.
53. *C.G.*, November 20, 1833.
54. *C.G.*, November 6, 1833.
55. *E.R.*, I, 210-211, John to Egerton Ryerson, November 15, 1833.
56. *Ibid.*, 207-208, William to Egerton Ryerson, November [after the 8th], 1833.
57. *Ibid.*, 215, David Wright *et al* to Ryerson, November 21, 1833.

58. *Ibid.*, 221, Egerton Ryerson to D. Wright, December 6, 1833.
59. *W.R.*, Reel 24, Ryerson to Alder, November 13, 1833.
60. The Kingston Society had been maintained since 1820 in defiance of the settlement of that year. The York Society was apparently revived in 1832. See *M.R.*, Reel 3, Lower Canada District Minutes, 1832.
61. See the representations of the Lower Canada District Meeting. *W.R.*, Reel 24, Croscombe and Hick to the Secretaries, May 31, 1833.
62. *Ibid.*, Reel 19, Barry to the Secretaries, August 2, 1833.
63. *Ibid.*, Reel 24, W. Lunn to the Secretaries, October 17, 1833.
64. *E.R.*, I, 207, William to Egerton Ryerson, November [after the 8th] 1833.
65. *Ibid.*, 212, John to Egerton Ryerson, November 15, 1833.
66. *W.R.*, Reel 24, Committee Minutes, December 20, 1833.
67. J. Carroll, *Case and His Cotemporaries*, II, 488.
68. *W.R.*, Reel 24, Stinson to Alder, November 11, 1833.
69. *Ibid.*, Reel 9, Stinson to Alder, December, 1833.
70. *Ibid.*, Stinson to Alder. Received in London, April 21, 1834.
71. *Ibid.*
72. Constitutionally the Conference had no obligation to submit the union to the Societies, but this might have been a sound tactical action on its part.
73. The necessary majority was secured.
74. Carroll, *Case*, III, 408-409. See also *C.G.*, January 1, 1834. Local preachers had occasionally been ordained as local elders, i.e., preachers who did not itinerate and did not belong to the Conference.
75. T. Webster, *History of the Methodist Episcopal Church in Canada* (Hamilton, 1870), 299.
76. V.U.L., Roblin Papers, P. J. Roblin to J. Reynolds, December 21, 1833.
77. *C. G.*, March 26, 1834.
78. See *E.R.*, I, 212-214, John to Egerton Ryerson, November 20, 1833; 222-224, J. to E. Ryerson, January 8, 1834. Egerton's opinions may be inferred from the *Guardian's* attitude and his statements to the Lower Canada District Meeting of 1834. "He admitted that in . . . the discussion of the clergy reserves question they had been led into politics & had been identified with political parties to an extent which they did not intend & now regret. . . . There was a tendency to republicanism in the Province &, were it not for the union, in ten years this country would be lost to the Parent State." *W.R.*, Reel 24, Conversations at the District Meeting, May 18, 1834.
79. *W. R.*, Reel 9, Stinson to Alder, April 4, 1834.
80. *Ibid.*, Alder to the Committee, June 16, 1834.
81. *Minutes of Conference, 1834*, 75.
82. *MS Journal of Conference*, 1834.

83. *W.R.*, Reel 9, Minutes of Conference, 1834.
84. *Ibid.*, Carroll, *op. cit.*, III, 444.
85. *Minutes of Conference, 1834*, 84.
86. *Ibid.*, 86-87.
87. T. Webster, *op. cit.*, 323.
88. There was protracted litigation between the old and new bodies concerning ownership of church property.
89. *W.R.*, Reel 9, Ryerson to Alder, July 10, 1834.
90. *Ibid.*, Stinson to the Committee. Report on Indian Missions, 1834.
91. S. D. Clark, *Movements of Political Protest in Canada*, 362-366.
92. It is probable that the committee was appointed to divert Mackenzie's attention from schemes that interested other active members of the reform group. If so, this indicated that his position was growing weaker. See L. F. Gates, "The Decided Policy of William Lyon Mackenzie," *Canadian Historical Review*, XL (1959), 199.
93. *Seventh Report from the Committee on Grievances*, 1835, XIV-XVI.
94. See *C.G.*, November 19, 1834; *W.R.*, Reel 9, Stinson to Alder, November 1, 1834.
95. Carroll, *op. cit.*, III, 475.
96. *W.R.*, Reel 9, Enclosure in Stinson to Alder, February 8, 1835.
97. *Ibid.*, Reel 24, Lord to Alder, May 2, 1835.
98. *Ibid.*, Reel 9, Lord to Alder, January 16, 1835.
99. *Ibid.*
100. *E.R.*, I, 248, John to Egerton Ryerson, January 28, 1835; *E.R.*, 250, William to Egerton Ryerson, February 20, 1835.
101. *Ibid.*, William to Egerton Ryerson. *W.R.*, Reel 9, Stinson to Alder, April 21, 1835.
102. Quoted from the *British Colonial Argus* of Kingston in *E.R.*, I, 213n. See also *W.R.*, Reel 24, Lord to Alder, September 28, 1835.
103. *Ibid.*, Reel 10, Lord to Alder, August 19, 1835.
104. MS *Journal of Conference, 1834.* See *W.R.*, Reel 9, Ryerson to Alder, July 10, 1834. "We have got the Academy out of the hands of the building committee and got it legally settled for literary and other purposes. This will meet your views." For the proposed petitions see *C.G.*, July 9, 1834.
105. See *E.R.*, I, 252-254.
106. *W.R.*, Reel 9, Lord to Alder, January 16, 1835.
107. See *W.R.*, Reel 24, Lord to Alder, enclosure in Stinson to Alder, February 18, 1835; Reel 9, Stinson to Alder, April 21, 1835.
108. Carroll, *op. cit.*, IV, 2-3.
109. *W.R.*, Reel 10, Stinson to Alder, June 19, 1835; Carroll, *op. cit.*, IV, 3. Egerton Ryerson was the winning candidate.
110. Metcalf retired after the Conference; Richardson continued as chairman of the Toronto District.
111. For Evans' appointment see *Minutes of Conference, 1835*, 90. For his background see Carroll, *op. cit.*, III, 203.

112. *Minutes of Conference, 1835*, 96.
113. *MS Journal of Conference, 1835.*
114. *W.R.*, Reel 10, Lord to Alder, July 3, 1835.
115. A. Dunham, *Political Unrest in Upper Canada*, 175-176. H. T. Manning and J. S. Galbraith, "The Appointment of Francis Bond Head: A New Insight," *Canadian Historical Review*, XLII (1961), 50-51.
116. J. C. Dent, *The Story of the Upper Canadian Rebellion* (Toronto, 1885), I, 296, 306-311.
117. P.A.C., *Q389-2*, 356, Head to Secretary of State, February 5, 1836.
118. Clark, *Movements*, 370-371.
119. Dent, *op. cit.*, I, 328.
120. *C.G.*, February 10, 1836.
121. *Ibid.*, April 6, 1836. Actually only forty-four patents were signed; the remainder were held to be void. Millman, *The Life of Charles James Stewart*, 140.
122. *C.G.*, June 1, 1836.
123. *Ibid.*, June 8, 1836.
124. Quoted in *E.R.*, I, 348.
125. *Minutes of Conference, 1836*, 135-136.
126. *C.G.*, May 25, 1836.
127. *Ibid.*, June 1, 1836.
128. The reformers secured eighteen out of sixty-two seats. *C.G.*, July 13, 1836.
129. Kennedy, *The Constitution of Canada*, 152. See also F. Hincks, *Reminiscences* (Toronto, 1884), 18.
130. *E.R.*, I, 332-333, John to Egerton Ryerson, May 4, 1836.
131. *Ibid.*, I, 361, same to same, September 25, 1836.
132. P.A.C., *Q412-3*, 624, Ryerson to Glenelg, April 9, 1838.
133. Carroll, *op. cit.*, IV, 120-121.
134. Immediately after this Conference Richardson rejoined the Methodist Episcopal Church in the United States.
135. *E.R.*, I, 338, William to Egerton Ryerson, June 14, 1836.
136. See Green, *op. cit.*, 203-204, where he speaks of "many good friends and valuable members having been blown out of their seats in the storm."
137. For the election returns see *C.G.*, July 13, 1836.
138. Ferguson, *MS Journal*, 151.
139. Carroll, *op. cit.*, IV, 124.
140. *Minutes of Conference, 1837*, 150.
141. Gates, "The Decided Policy of William Lyon Mackenzie," 198-199.
142. Dent, *op. cit.*, I, 329-332.
143. G. Arthur, *The Arthur Papers*, ed. C. R. Sanderson (Toronto, 1957), part III, 135-142. Clark, *op. cit.*, 464-478.
144. *C.G.*, June 29, 1836.
145. Evidently Lord had spent unwisely for the Academy and had then drawn on the Missionary Society to meet the obligations incurred. See *W.R.*, Reel 10, Lord to the Secretaries, July 3, 1835.

  E.R., I, 366, John to Egerton Ryerson, January 2, 1837; *Ibid.*, 362-363, Lord to E. Ryerson, October 13, 1836; 390-391, E. Ryerson to Alder, November 25, 1837.
146. For these negotiations see *E.R.*, I, chapters 8 and 9.
147. *C.G.*, December 14, 1836.
148. *E.R.*, I, 368, John to Egerton Ryerson, January, 1837. See also *W.R.*, Reel 19, W. Harvard to Alder, January 24, 1837.
149. P.A.C., *Q412-3*, 592, Ryerson to Glenelg, April 9, 1838. See *MS Journal of Conference*, 1837.
150. Carroll, *op. cit.*, IV, 130-131.
151. 591 members had been lost. *Minutes of Conference, 1837*, 150.
152. *Minutes of Conference, 1837*, 164-166.
153. *Ibid.*, 166-168.
154. *E.R.*, I, 382, A. Green to Ryerson, July 26, 1837.
155. P.A.C., *Q412-3*, 593-594, Ryerson to Glenelg, April 9, 1838. For the Methodist plan see *C.G.*, January 17, 1838.
156. *Ibid.*, 596-697, Ryerson to Glenelg. In January, 1838, however, Ryerson had strongly opposed reinvestment. See *E.R.*, I, 403-404, Ryerson to Stinson, January 13, 1838.
157. P.A.C., *Q412-3*, 600-601, Ryerson to Glenelg, April 9, 1838.
158. *C.G.*, December 6, 1837; December 13, 1837.
159. *E.R.*, I, 400. *W.R.*, Reel 19, Stinson to Alder, December 8, 1837.
160. *C.G.*, April 8, 1838.
161. Carroll, *op. cit.*, IV, 178, 179. Green, *op. cit.*, 220.
162. *W.R.*, Reel 19, Harvard to Alder, April 28, 1838. He noted that he had been invited to dinner by Strachan. He realized, though, that Evans' support had "signed the death warrant of his editorialism."
163. *C.G.*, May 9, 1838.
164. *W.R.*, Reel 19, Harvard to Alder, April 28, 1838 (Enclosure)

SEVEN

"From whatever part ... a man may emigrate, when he settles in Canada are not all his interests Canadian?"

Egerton Ryerson's vigorous criticism of President Harvard and his related defence of M. S. Bidwell were approved heartily by his Methodist brethren. They saw that these steps, like the "English Impressions," signalled a decisive shift in the Methodist outlook.[1] At this point the Conference dropped its policy of collaboration with the tories and partially realigned itself with the reformers, a move that resulted in the dissolution of the union.

For all those concerned with the future of Upper Canadian Methodism, its position in the spring of 1838 was not a happy one. In 1833 the Connexion had boasted 16,039 members; in 1838 the total stood at 15,328, a shocking figure when compared with the general growth of the population.[2] True, the loss could be explained by the Episcopal secession, but to many this must have been cold consolation. Rather, there was a widespread conviction that the Methodist community had lost much of its spiritual vitality—a condition that could readily be traced to the dissension marking its history since 1833.

Despair over the religious feebleness of the Societies was coupled with disillusionment about the public posture of the Connexion and the development of Upper Canada. Association with the local government and the tories in the Assembly had brought no lasting benefits. The reserves question was unsolved; the position of the Academy was still uncertain. Governor Head in fact had done his best to thwart the imperial authorities' desire to assist this new venture.[3] This action, and his curious behaviour in the rebellion, must have led many Methodists to conclude with John Ryerson that Head was a "frolicking little cur."[4]

But it was clear in the spring of 1838 that more was out of joint in Upper Canada than could be attributed to the idiosyncrasies of the retiring Governor. The rebellion, far from indicating to the tories the necessity of conciliation, had become the pretext for ruthless intimidation of reformers.[5] The execution of Lount and Matthews and the disgraceful treatment of other political prisoners were shattering experiences for the Methodists.[6] To Egerton Ryerson "punishments for *political* offences were never beneficial." "The fact however is," he added, "Sir Francis deserves *impeachment,* just as much as Saml. Lount deserves *execution*. Morally speaking, I cannot but regard him as the more guilty culprit of the two."[7] John Ryerson had an interview with the new Governor, Sir George Arthur, on behalf of the culprits, but came away "much cast down & affected."[8] William wrote: "My Dr. Br. my own spirit is almost entirely broken down. I feel . . . like leaving Canada too & I am not alone in these feelings."[9]

There was no immediate remedy for the disgraceful conduct of the forces of reaction, but in their plight the Canadian leaders became increasingly critical of the union that had contributed to it. As early as May, 1837, William Ryerson had written: "The less we have to do with the English Conference and their Preachers the better it will be both for our conference and the church at large. . . . The Union works *badly*, very *badly*, for us, and I am sick, in my very soul sick of it."[10] In March, 1838, John confided to Egerton:

Never did high Churchism take such rapid strides towards undisputed *domination* in this country as it is now taking, & never were the prospects of the friends of Civil & Religious liberty so gloomy & desperate as they now are; & Harvard & Evans love to have it so. Mr. H. is a *weak* high church *despot* & Evans is his *intire tool*.

On vital questions such as the reserves, the *Guardian* was "basely & survily *silent*," while it printed "war stories true, false & . . . every species of ribaldry against the American Government . . . for the purpose of pleasing some 2 or 3 dosen high church Aristochrats."[11] "It is truly laughable as well as disgusting," wrote John Ryerson, "to see how he [Harvard] & Evans soft soap & lick each other. They concoct & write their articles together & then praise & eulogize each other for their wonderful productions. O! if you were here it would *absolutely* make you sick."[12] "Under the blessing of Providence," he concluded, "I see only one remedy & only one & that is for you to take the Editorship of the *Guardian* again."[13]

Although Egerton realized that this course would antagonize some of the Wesleyans he agreed that "the *complaints* . . . mentioned" were "almost if not quite universal." He felt "there was never such a time" as this for the Methodists "to stamp upon the public mind," their "Constitutional & Scriptural political & religious doctrines & to give the tone to the future government and legislation of the province." Although reluctant to leave the itinerancy Egerton was resolved "to go back to the old truly Methodistic ground," that is, to do what his brethren wanted.[14]

Ryerson's determination to accept the *Guardian* editorship if it were offered was strengthened by the sympathy of Stinson and the comments of Anson Green and John Ryerson.[15] Green had resolved to resist Harvard's instructions on loyalty but his heart was sickened by the "storm gathering in every quarter." Ryerson's reply was "a balm to the afflicted heart. . . . The lowering skie began to clear up and we are . . . enabled once more to hope for a clear sun."[16]

For John the political situation demonstrated "the detestible & wicked character" of the "*unprincipled*, melicious, cruel & unjust [tory] party; indeed they never appeared so odious, so hateful, so black to me before." But he asked cautiously: "Will it be well for *us* to stem the vipery nests at the present time?" Yet the thought of the *Guardian*, in which Evans "costickly" sneered at those who were leaving the province in despair, filled him with shame.[17] The course had to be changed.

The Conference at Kingston in June, 1838, needed no urging to mend its ways. Preachers and people were appalled at the state of the province and at the realization that both Conference and *Guardian* had contributed to it. Ryerson's stand against Harvard and for Bidwell was approved, and he was elected both as secretary and editor.[18] The members were gratified to hear that Harvard was being sent to Quebec, there to impress Lord Durham with his talents. The Committee was asked to appoint the familiar and well-liked Stinson in his place.[19] Regrettably, the belief that in any conflict Stinson would side with his Canadian brethren was unsound.

The peaceful deliberations of the Conference in 1838 were the prelude to one of the most embattled phases of Canadian Methodist history. In the background throughout the ensuing months were the Durham mission, the publication of his report and the determination of Durham's successor Charles P. Thomson to implement some of his recommendations.[20] The actions and statements of Durham and Thomson provided a massive foundation for the renewal of the reform onslaught on the existing social and political order in Upper Canada. But the forces that had won so handsomely in 1836 and 1837 fought back with equal vigour, abetted by the extreme radicals who, with the connivance of their sympathizers in the United States, sought in the fall of 1838 to liberate the province from British rule.[21] Despite the prestige of Lord Durham it was appallingly difficult for reformers to avoid the imputation of disloyalty. The critical point in the settlement of Upper Canada's destiny had indeed been reached.

In this perplexing situation the Methodist Conference and its journal sought the middle ground. The first objective naturally was to advance Methodism as a spiritual agency, but in addition the Conference was anxious to help solve Upper Canada's political and social problems. Inevitably these ends were not kept separate; what seemed good for Methodism seemed desirable for Upper Canada as well. Consequently the Methodists avoided the most vocal tory and reform elements and they supported Lord Durham and his successor. Those who insisted that reform and disloyalty were identical were firmly repulsed, as were those who still believed that Upper Canada needed a system of privileged churches and educational institutions.

Unfortunately it was not easy for the Methodists to live down their public support for the Head régime and their vacillation on the reserves question. It was equally difficult to be liberal yet not to join the reform forces, to be loyal and yet not be classed with the tories. Moreover, this conflict was not external to the Methodist community. Every liberal article in the *Guardian* further separated the Canadians and the Wesleyans, so that in short order the Conference had to choose between total humiliation and the loss of its native support, or a breach with the latter. The course taken by the Connexion in the hectic months between the summer of 1838 and the summer of 1840, and its denouement, must be seen in the light of this paradoxical situation.

Although their position was dangerous, the Methodist leaders were in no mood to hesitate. In his first editorial of July 11, 1838, Ryerson stated his views on public affairs and the church question: "I am opposed to the introduction of any new and untried theories of government. . . . I assume that this Country is to remain a part of the British Empire and view every measure . . . in reference to the well-being of the country in connexion with Great Britain. . . . I repudiate party spirit . . . the bane and curse of this country for many years past. It has neither eyes, nor ears, nor principles nor reason." Nothing more was needed than the acceptance of the political views of Durham and Arthur. As for the reserves, Ryerson advised secularizing them for educational purposes, but if necessary they might be divided.[22]

By October, 1838, it was clear that the Assembly favoured reinvesting the reserves in the Crown, hoping the Lords would support the Anglican claim.[23] To prevent this move the Conference circulated a petition pleading again for secularization.[24] Ryerson published a series of open letters to W. H. Draper, the Solicitor-General, the most outspoken of which appeared in the early months of 1839.

In these letters Ryerson suggested three ways of disposing of the reserves: reinvestment, division, or secularization. The first was unjustified as it was contrary to majority opinion in Upper Canada. Also, it involved referring the question from a competent body to one less competent. If the imperial parliament, having inadequate and partisan information, dealt with the issue unwisely, this would weaken the imperial relationship. Ryerson concluded that any man "who will not submit to the constitutionally collected sentiments of the country of which he is a subject or citizen . . . is an enemy to the chartered rights of his fellow men and a traitor to the principles of the constitutional compact."[25]

Division was equally unsuitable for it would alienate all who believed in the voluntary principle. In any case it was an arrangement of expediency in that Upper Canada was neither morally destitute nor poor enough to require a subsidized ministry. "As no one church embraces a sufficiently large portion of the population to justify the exclusive endowment of its clergy—as the endowment of more than one class of clergy . . . is clearly invidious, anti-British, unprincipled and impracticable, the Reserves should not be appropriated to the endowment of any priesthood but for purposes beneficial to the whole population."[26]

As for secularization, Ryerson affirmed that church establishment and the reserves were not related questions; one was within the imperial jurisdiction, the other was a purely local concern. Thus, secularization would not violate the constitution. In any event the history of Canada indicated that the cause of religion would progress more effectively under the voluntary system than any subsidy scheme. Upper Canada required a good educational system; the reserves could be devoted to that purpose. It was time to decide whether Upper Canadians wished to confer great benefit or great harm upon themselves.[27]

When the legislature moved toward investment the *Guardian* became more incisive than it had been for years. The Methodists had been willing to accept any reasonable compromise but the Church party had prevented solution and aroused public controversy. The people had lost confidence in the provincial and imperial governments' ability to settle the question. A *Guardian* editorial stated:

The proposition of reinvestment under such circumstances but proclaim[s] in peals of thunder to the ears of the inhabitants . . . 'You will not submit for us to apply the proceeds of one-seventh of your labour to the support of one or more hierarchies; we will therefore place those proceeds in the hands of the Incapables of Downing Street and the Capable Bishops will compel . . . the incapable ministers to do what we dare not do; and your loyalty and intelligence will of course induce you to bow in humble submission to the decision of the Incapables.'

Turning to Governor Arthur, Ryerson asserted: "He is not a statesman ... and is not a friend of civil and religious liberty," for had he not described provincial opinion on this issue as mere local excitement? In any case, reinvestment would be "a breach of faith" because the Assembly had been elected on the understanding that the reserves would be devoted to education. Finally:

The moment this recommended act of spoliation ... is committed—committed under vice-regal dictation on the one hand and legislative subserviency on the other—that moment the inhabitants will know their future doom ... —that executive intimidation, clerical patronage and political bribery are to be the order of the day—that the resources of the country are to be absorbed in the payment of debts and the enrichment and elevation of certain families and parties ... with no other hope ... than increased expense to England, progressive diminution in credit, in trade, in the value of property and in the enjoyment of public safety and social happiness.[28]

Although the *Guardian* expressed the feeling of a more extensive constituency than its own communion, the Assembly which it had helped to elect finally accepted a reinvestment bill in the spring of 1839.[29] To counter this measure three strong letters by Egerton Ryerson were sent to Lord Normanby, the acting Colonial Secretary. For the moment the matter rested there.[30]

This vigorous campaign over the reserves question was the major Methodist effort to secure "the free and impartial administration" of the provincial constitution "for the benefit of all classes."[31] It was conducted against a background of rising animosity and fear, stimulated by the extreme tories and by the clandestine schemes of the liberation forces on both sides of the border.

In the fall of 1838 invasion threatened and many hesitated to sign the reserves petition for fear of tory reprisals. The *Guardian*, however, insisted that the real danger facing Upper Canada was not rebellion or invasion but dissatisfaction over partisan appointments, the deliberate linking of reform and disloyal opinions, and the seditious abuse of the imperial authorities by tory newspapers. The tories were purposely raising an uproar in order to obscure their unwillingness to satisfy the wishes of the people and the Colonial Office. At this juncture it was the duty of every man to uphold lawful authority, but it was equally his duty to enforce the social contract.[32]

The invasion came, nevertheless, first at Prescott on November 11, and at Windsor on December 4.[33] Fortunately the invaders were easily foiled, even though the Upper Canadians were notably reluctant to help the authorities.[34] In this crisis the *Guardian* printed a shrewd address from Stinson and Ryerson as president and secretary of the Conference. In their view the proscription of all religious denominations but one was the principal source of friction in Upper Canada and the reason for the evident unwillingness of its people to defend it. The Methodists in particular had been abused for their part in trying to resolve the church question, but they did not seek independence in order to secure redress. Besides, the Methodist Church had always been loyal in the spirit of its founder. The address concluded:

> Let us then brethren regardless of past injuries or present grounds of complaint rally round the standard of our country in obedience to the authorities whom Almighty God in his providence placed over us, and when peace and safety in the land are again re-established we will one and all renew with redoubled ardour our exertions to obtain those rights and privileges and advantages which belong to us as men, as Christians and as Canadian British Subjects.[35]

But this call for loyalty and reform, especially in church-state relations, did not satisfy the tories and some of their Methodist sympathizers. The *Guardian* for December 5 contained an address to Governor Arthur from several prominent Toronto Methodists who hoped that no Methodists would give anyone cause to doubt their loyalty.[36] This statement was hailed by the *Toronto Patriot* as representative of the real views of Wesleyans, in contrast with Ryerson's Yankee opinions.

This move was designed to subvert the Conference's political policy. Ryerson replied that the Methodists had tried for years to halt the strife engendered by factious religious minorities but their proposals had never been judged on their merits. Instead, ferocious abuse had been heaped on him; the government was trying to stifle discussion; others, such as the Toronto Wesleyans, were seeking to divide the Methodist Societies. On general political issues Methodists had shown their loyalty and the *Guardian* had frequently supported government policies that were inherently bad. Now, when the whole weight of the government was thrown on the side of reaction, Ryerson was told to keep silent, but this he would not do. Constituted authority must be upheld, but civil rights and Christian principles would be surrendered to no one.[37]

Unfortunately, efforts to ensure that the majority would rule in the reserves issue helped stir up the latent conflict with the Wesleyans, evident in Evans' ouster in 1838. Before Ryerson's brush with Arthur, Stinson wrote: "You are . . . in great danger of exciting a feeling against the Government so hostile that its entire subversion will be attempted. . . . There is a strong, a very strong feeling against a dominant church, but a majority of the Province would rather have that and connexion with Great Britain than republicanism—I would!"[38] In a subsequent report to Alder on the Methodist troubles in Toronto, Stinson said: "I agree with Mr. Ryerson and the Canadian brethren in opposing a dominant church and in desiring an equitable division of the clergy reserves but am opposed to any sentiment in the Guardian which militates against the principle of an establishment and which . . . recommends the alienation of church property from religious purposes." He continued: "I decidedly disapprove of much which Mr. Ryerson writes & dread the ultimate effect of the mode which he adopts in discussing the Church Question." Hence, both Arthur and Stinson wished advice and assistance from the Committee. "I greatly fear that things are going on towards that point at which we must either split with the Government or with the Canadian Conference—to me this is an awful prospect."[39]

The Committee was equally alarmed at events in Upper Canada; it disapproved of the principles espoused in the *Guardian* and feared that the Canadian agitation would lead the Governor to revoke the Society's grant. Meeting on January 30 it decided to send Alder to Upper Canada, for, as he wrote to Stinson: "There is a difference of principle between us & others which must be settled if the union is to be maintained."[40] This difference was defined in an earlier letter received by Stinson in March, 1839, and in a statement composed by the Secretaries in February.[14]

Alder asserted that one of the most important duties of government was to provide for the religious instruction of its people. The principle of church establishment should not be conceded nor abandoned. If there were no alternative in Upper Canada but to choose between the voluntary principle of religious instruction and the endowment of "that branch of the Reformed English Church which is established in the province it would be the duty of the government to adopt the latter course." In contrast, the Canadian Methodists were opposed "not to any particular application of a great principle but to the principle itself . . . which we maintain to be reasonable, Scriptural and Wesleyan." Naturally all Canadian Methodists had the right to express their opinions on all public questions, but as citizens, not as Methodists. In particular, Alder continued: "The official organ of the Connexion should not be identified with such proceedings." He urged Stinson to persuade Ryerson to change his ways:

If you should fail . . . it will be for you to consider whether you are not as President of the Conference impowered to interfere officially and authoritatively with the management of the Conference Journal. . . .

According to one of the articles of union between the British and Canadian Conferences it is agreed that the Guardian shall be a religious newspaper and although the editor . . . doubtless does believe that the article in question is not . . . affected by such communications . . . we are of a different opinion.[42]

To Normanby, Alder announced his impending visit to Canada. His aim was "to allay the unhappy feeling which exists among . . . the members of the Wesleyan Methodist Church . . . in reference to the Clergy Reserves and Rectory questions and to put an end to discussion of these questions, calculated I fear to increase the difficulties with which the local government has to contend and to retard the settlement of affairs in that province."[43]

These pronouncements were probably bewildering to a Colonial Office that relied upon the accuracy of Ryerson's statements, and encouraging to Arthur, who had strong tory sympathies.[44] The Upper Canadian Methodists were in no way deterred. As Ryerson's attack intensified in the last of the Draper letters and the Normanby letters, the Wesleyans' attitude became increasingly hostile, a fact well known to the Canadians.

When he heard of Alder's impending visit, Richey, still principal of the Academy, exclaimed: "Should your efforts to purify Methodism from the pollution of politics, the science of the streets—to elevate its grovelling character—to stamp it with the resplendent signet of true British loyalty be successful, you will rank among the most honoured instruments of a beneficent providence."[45] To him it was evident that Ryerson and his brethren sought to smash the union, an action eminently desirable, for nothing would be lost and much might be gained. Commiserating with Stinson he wrote: "Little does he [Alder] conceive in what a *bed of nettles* you lie. However I suppose you will take off your nightcap when he comes and allow him to take a nap on the same voluptuous mattress."[46] Stinson had thus far taken a moderate position but was now convinced that the Canadians would not be deflected from their course. It made him "sick" to think that the British Conference was identified with such an agitation. A year earlier, he lamented, Ryerson "assured me that he would not write against the Government or against the Church of England. . . . I now declare that I have lost all confidence in his attachment to the British Government & to the British Conference." Actually, "the only motive which influenced the Ryersons to form the union was to exclude British influence & at the same time use the good name of the British Conference to accomplish their own ambitious & selfish purposes."[47]

It was no surprise when in May the *Toronto Patriot* printed the

Secretaries' letter to Arthur, dated February 8, 1839, in which they strongly deprecated the *Guardian's* political course. To Ryerson this suggested collusion between the government and "that most vulgar and profligate journal." It was the kind of step never taken by any Canadian Methodist against the English Conference. Ryerson affirmed "that the affairs of the Wesleyan Methodist Church in Canada . . . are under the sole direction of the Canadian Conference. . . . The 'sentiments' expressed at the present time and for months past in the *Guardian* are those which have been avowed by the Methodist Conference in this province from the beginning."[48]

With sounds of battle in the background the Conference met in Hamilton on June 12.[49] Ryerson was given a handsome vote as secretary.[50] Nevertheless, Alder was determined to have his way. Many wished to dissolve the union but his intention was to preserve it, for he believed that dissolution would be "the precursor to an immediate severance of the Colony from the parent state."[51] But the union could not be continued unless the policies of the Canadian Conference could be brought into line with those of the Missionary Society. In effect the Conference would have to accept alteration of the *Guardian,* and the Wesleyan concept of church-state relations.

Before the Conference Alder had reminded the Canadians of their informal agreement to keep politics out of the *Guardian*. But, "the Ryersons were inexorable. . . . They stood on the printed Articles of Union."[52] At the Conference he renewed the controversy but the preachers merely resolved that "the Christian Guardian shall be properly a religious and literary Journal to explain our doctrines and institutions; to defend them when necessary; to vindicate our character if expedient; . . . together with a summary of civil and general intelligence."[53] Past experience had demonstrated that this kind of injunction would not seriously inhibit the editor.

On the second question, church-state relations, Alder fared somewhat better. He objected strenuously to the resolutions of 1837 and especially to those in which the Canadian Conference disclaimed interest in government aid. Since these clashed with views of the British Conference they were rescinded.[54] In dealing with the reserves the Conference stressed that it had been obliged to speak out on the question of ecclesiastical establishment in the province and on its determination to maintain constitutional and religious rights and privileges. But the Conference had no desire "to interfere with the merely secular party politics of the day."[55]

An open clash had been averted but the real differences between the two conferences remained. The *Guardian* and the Conference were certain to defend Methodist interests in a way that the Secretaries would not like; ultimately the Canadians had a different conception of their interests. They were not interested in secular politics as such, but they had little sympathy for the Church of England and less for the principle of establishment; they wanted a settlement of the reserves in accordance with Canadian and not English conditions. Realizing this, Alder concluded rather pathetically, "the Canadian Conference was almost too much for me."[56]

Before Alder left Canada he was warned that post-conference optimism was being dissipated. Wesleyan sympathizers, particularly those in Toronto, assured Stinson that they would not be associated with a church that honoured the great sinner Ryerson while it disciplined lesser figures. The beliefs of Ryerson and his supporters could not be changed; the only solution was severance of the union.[57] These dissenters would have been ignored but for the persistently liberal tone of the *Guardian,* a quality that promptly aroused the ire of the Missionary Committee.

In a long letter to the Book Committee, the supervisory board of the *Guardian,* Alder warned that at his insistence the British Conference had appointed a Canada Committee, and that his report to it would depend upon the way in which the June resolutions concerning the *Guardian* were implemented. "In my judgment," he wrote, "the Guardian has not been uniformly conducted since the Conference in accordance with the spirit of the Resolution in question." "I beg ... to inquire," he continued, "whether the Xtian Guardian is to be bona fide a Religious Journal & whether all party Politics are to be excluded from its pages," for after all "our business as Methodist Missionaries is to save souls."[58] Stinson was told to urge his brethren to ask for a share of the reserves: "If the Guardian oppose Government endowments, call a special meeting of the Book Committee & call the Editor to order. If a majority encourage him, protest against it & let us know.... The obnoxious Resolutions of 1837 were rescinded because if all endowments for Religious Purposes are to be opposed in the Guardian we cannot maintain the Union."[59]

Faced with this near-edict Stinson summoned the committee. Agreement was easily reached to exclude secular politics from the *Guardian,* but the Wesleyans led by Ephraim Evans and Richey were not satisfied. The former regretted that the spirit of the Conference resolution had not been fulfilled, whereupon Egerton Ryerson secured assent to a statement "that the committee ... expresses its determination ... to maintain the resolution ... in reference to the religious & general character of the Guardian." Matthew Richey then proposed and the committee agreed that "all political discussions not directly bearing on our religious and educational rights and privileges be excluded from ... the

Guardian.... Nonetheless it is distinctly understood that the above resolutions are not designed to prevent the advocacy of an equitable settlement of the clergy reserves question." Stinson's motion that all political material be excluded was rejected; instead, Ryerson's proposal to print selected contemporary opinions was accepted.[60]

Although an open clash had been averted, the persistent controversy between the Wesleyans and the Canadian Methodists was unfortunate for it coincided with a most critical phase of the province's history. While the Book Committee was papering over the cracks in the Methodist wall, Charles P. Thomson, the new Governor General, was establishing his administration.[61] Thomson brought instructions not to grant responsible government, but to govern the Canadas in accordance with the wishes of the people.[62] The very ambiguity of this new policy left it open to various interpretations. Such groups as the Methodists could do much to thwart or to promote the Governor's scheme for popular, but not responsible, government, not to mention his plans for settling the clergy reserves.

Considering their reform sympathies perhaps most Methodists would have welcomed full support for the Durham Report—an attitude that would have involved them in direct association with the new leaders, Baldwin and Hincks, and in incipient opposition to the new Governor. The *Guardian* had given strong backing to Lord Durham; to have done much more would have meant bringing "mere party politics" into the paper, a step that in the interest of Methodist unity the Canadian leaders were loth to take. It is evident, though, that Egerton Ryerson was naturally drawn to Thomson's side. Although a more scrupulous man than the new Governor General, Ryerson was like Thomson in that he too was a manager rather than an innovator, a liberal conservative, not a real reformer. In the winter of 1839 the *Guardian* firmly backed the Thomson régime.[63]

The Methodists were especially drawn to the Governor by his evident determination to settle the reserves question. The reinvestment bill, whose passage the Methodists had fought so bitterly, was disallowed in the summer of 1839. In explanation Russell wrote: "I cannot admit that there exist in this country greater facilities than in Upper Canada for the adjustment of this controversy. On the contrary the provincial legislature will bring to the decision of it an extent of accurate information as to the wants and general opinions of Society in that country in which Parliament is unavoidably deficient."[64] With this vindication of reform opinion Thomson fully sympathized. He was convinced that until this matter was settled no political change would be effective in Upper Canada.[65]

The scheme that the Governor devised was a variant of the earlier division proposals. He decided to consolidate existing obligations to the Churches of England and Scotland as a first charge on the reserves fund. The remainder of the potential revenue was to be divided among the recognized churches in the province, no restrictions being placed on the way that such grants might be spent.[66] Here was a settlement indeed, but of a kind that the Methodists had never supported wholeheartedly. Would they accept such a compromise?

Speaking at least for the Book Committee, the *Guardian* supported Thomson's proposal. Secularization was still preferable but it was not politically practicable. Those being paid from the fund could not be legally deprived of such support. Most significant, in the *Guardian's* view, was the acknowledgment that the reserves were a religious trust, belonging to the entire Upper Canadian community rather than to one or more churches. Under Thomson's scheme the revenue was to be distributed in a way that would eliminate executive patronage and permit each religious group to use its share in its own fashion. This elimination of distinctions would contribute greatly to harmonious development of the province.[67]

Whatever the merits of Thomson's bill, the *Guardian's* case for it was a far cry from its position of 1832. The new scheme undermined the pretensions of the religious monopolists for the first time, but it did not follow that Methodists should accept a share of its benefits. Still, in spite of previous hesitations promoted largely by the Wesleyans, acquiescence came rather easily. Determination to maintain the union, as well as the serious needs of the Academy, helped to remove the doubts of Methodist leaders. More positively, they recognized that the Governor General's plan was sensible and that if it were not supported, worse consequences might follow. It had been a long fight and the Methodists were resigned to an imperfect outcome. "It has been said that the Editor of the Guardian and his friends desired to keep the question open for agitation to promote sinister objects: our present endeavours furnish the appropriate reply."[68]

In 1840 the Methodists found themselves in a three-front war, with the Anglicans, the ardent reformers and the Wesleyans. Bishop Strachan's campaign for better terms was resisted as unpatriotic and disloyal, the product of ambition and selfishness.[69] The reformers, led by Francis Hincks, whose own genius for compromise was not yet revealed, denounced the Methodists as traitors to the cause. The *Guardian* asserted that secularization of the reserves was utterly impracticable. The new bill at least recognized the rights of all denominations, the principle Methodists had always upheld. By attempting to raise a party of "no compromise" Hincks was merely emulating Mackenzie at his worst; he was not acting in the spirit of a true reformer or of the original reformers.[70]

Conflict with the right and the left of course was not new to the Methodists. They might have undertaken a more formidable campaign on behalf of the new reserves bill and the Thomson régime but for the dissension within their own ranks. In adopting a course that took the Wesleyan attitude into account, the Canadians precipitated a struggle leading directly to the severance of the union.

While Alder was in Canada in 1839 he had persuaded Governor Arthur to renew the grant to the Society out of the casual and territorial fund.[71] Stinson and Richey were also instructed to confer with the Governor General about continuing the grant. The latter, concerned with the reserves bill, discussed the question with them. Subsequently Stinson and Richey wrote to him in their official Canadian capacities, not as representatives of the British Conference. They urged that the original religious objectives of the reserves be upheld in any disposal of the properties:

The Church of England being in our estimation *The Established Church* of all the British Colonies, we entertain no objection to the distinct recognition of her as such, and had the reserves been exclusively appropriated to her according to the original intention . . . we should not have interfered with this matter.

But, since the reserves had become a subject of legislation the two men were "at a loss to conceive any . . . reason why the Wesleyan Methodist Church should be placed in a position in any degree inferior to the Church of Scotland." After all, had not the British government urged the Wesleyans to extend their work in Upper Canada and had they not given loyal support? Thus, "we regard it of vital importance to the permanent peace and prosperity of the Province, as a British Colony, that the sum to be appropriated to us be given to the Wesleyan Methodists . . . connected with the British Wesleyan Conference."[72] Knowing the union was in a precarious condition, the Wesleyan representatives in effect had not simply asked that the government recognize its financial obligation to the Society, but that the Wesleyan Methodists should receive the Methodist share of the reserves. In addition, by accepting the Church of England as the "established" church, they had committed their Canadian brethren to a principle that the latter abhorred.

The Governor General called upon Egerton Ryerson to analyse the financial relationship between the two conferences. Ryerson's reply outlined the history of the union and clarified the distinction between the circuit work, for which the Conference was wholly responsible, and the missions that the Society supported. He declared "that a Government grant to the British Wesleyan Conference and a grant to the [Canadian] Conference are two very different things." A grant to the Society would not benefit the Conference. Nevertheless:

Should a dissolution of the Union take place ... as intimated ... by Messrs. Stinson and Richey, the Conference in England would claim the missions in this Province—nothwithstanding their original establishment by the Canadian Conference and the annual collections made to support them. But I apprehend no disposition on the part of the British Conference to dissolve the union unless they can get Government aid independent of the Canadian Conference. ... I conceive therefore that any grants intended to benefit the Wesleyan Methodist Church in Canada, ought undoubtedly to be placed at the disposal of the Conference of that church.[73]

One disingenuous statement had been matched by another; it could be made to appear that Ryerson was advocating the transference of the Wesleyan grant to the Canadian Conference.

This letter, in conjunction with the *Guardian's* defence of Thomson's measures, brought to a head the smouldering conflict between the Canadians and Wesleyans. As usual their exasperation was expressed by Richey:

As ... to the indispensable necessity of closing partnership with men who speculate on our capital without sharing the profits, whose intrigue and selfishness is manifest to all men—who are not properly a church of God but a ... political faction, never, never, can pure Wesleyanism coalesce with such *abominable stuff,* till streams return to their fountains —till sparks fly downward and the earth begins to revolve on its axis from east to west.[74]

Stinson, already "sick" of the union, because of "the undisguised avowal of the Canadian Brethren that they *will never* abandon the advocacy of their own views," presumably urged Richey to inform the Committee of the Canadian designs.[75] Richey asserted that Ryerson and his colleagues had connived with the Governor to deprive the Wesleyans of their rights. He hoped that "the death warrant of the union" was on its way.[76]

Stung by this evidence of Canadian intractability and even perfidy, the Society pressed its case at the Colonial Office. Alder requested "that in any settlement ... of the clergy reserves or of the casual and territorial revenue ... the continued annual payment of £700 may be secured to the Wesleyan Methodist Conference in London." "We have reason to believe," he went on, "that there are influential individuals in Upper Canada" who desire "either to dissolve the union or to adopt measures which would render the connexion nominal" because it has helped to check "dangerous political designs and tendencies. ... It is hoped ... that the operation of the clergy reserves bill will forward ... the diminution of that wholesome influence which British Methodism ... now exercises there." At the moment too, the same individuals wished "to remove a part or the whole of the annual sum now secured to the ... Society ... from under [its] control and to appropriate it to other parties who have not the least claim [to it]." He therefore inquired whether the clergy reserve bill affected the Society's claim to the annual grant and whether any request for a new appropriation of the grant had been received.[77]

In fact Thomson had already recommended that any aid to the Methodists should go to the Conference in Upper Canada—a recommendation "founded upon ... statements and public documents submitted ... not only by Mr. Ryerson but by various parties connected with the Wesleyan community in Upper Canada."[78] He added: "No one the least acquainted with the subject is ignorant of the great benefit conferred upon the cause of religion & morality by the exertions of the [Canada Conference] at a time too when neither the London Society nor the missionary societies of other provinces had entered upon the important task of affording religious instruction to the people."[79] Unfortunately, in conveying this decision to the Society, the Colonial Office left the impression that the Governor General had accepted Ryerson's alleged claim that the Canada Conference should have "the exclusive management of the yearly grant."[80]

This regrettable statement brought to a peak the resentment of the Missionary Committee against its wayward charges in Upper Canada. Another forceful plea that the imperial government should honour its obligations to the band of faithful Wesleyan workers in Upper Canada was sent to the Colonial Secretary.[81] On the same day, April 29, the special Canada Committee of the British Conference resolved that in the grant negotiations Ryerson had acted with "great and culpable irregularity" and that he had "discovered an utter want of ingenuousness and integrity by ... attempting to gain the possession ... of the Grant made by the Crown to the Wesleyan Missionary Society." In addition he had broken his promise to Alder and defied his conference by making the *Guardian* "a political and party organ." Even so the committee did not wish to implicate the Upper Canada Conference, which, it was hoped, would repudiate Ryerson's dishonest actions and make the *Guardian* a truly religious newspaper. If the Canada Conference did not take these steps, the committee agreed that its "painful duty" would be to recommend the dissolution of the union. In that event the Society should retain the Indian missions in Upper Canada that it had saved from ruin at great cost.[82]

Richey naturally received the committee's resolutions happily. "Your dispatches," he wrote, "will summarily and most effectively test the spirit of Canadian Methodism." They would afford the Conference "a fair opportunity either to throw off or rivet the chain of Ryersonian tyranny. May they know the day of their visitation! .... We have to do with a very wily and ambitious triumvirate; but we are not without proof that the Lord *taketh the wise* in their *own craftiness*."[83] If uncharitable, this exclamation was not without justice, in the light of the sly way in which Ryerson sold the union to his brethren in 1832.

With this bitter antagonism in the background the Upper Canada Conference met in Belleville on June 10 and continued in session until June 30. Anson Green recalled that "we had not gone far in our business before the dark cloud which for some time we had seen approaching began to settle down upon us with fearful portent."[84] The Conference waited two days before allowing Richey to bring forward the charges against Ryerson, who by that time had been elected secretary by a considerable majority.[85] In reply to the contentions of the British Conference, Ryerson delivered what one observer called "a seven hours mystification."[86] He and others rejected the claim of the British representatives to act on behalf of the Canada Conference without consulting it.

Turning to the financial issue Ryerson argued that in his letter to the Governor General he was not trying to secure the Wesleyan grant as long as it was a charge on the casual and territorial revenue. But he anticipated that, if the reserves bill passed, such charges would be transferred to the latter fund, on which the British Conference had no claim. Any grants paid out of it ought to go to the Methodists in Canada.[87] By a vote of fifty-nine to eight this view was accepted by the Conference.[88] That body also rejected Ephraim Evans' motion that members repudiate any move to affect the British Connexion's monetary claim upon the government, a claim that had existed before the union was formed.[89]

The Wesleyans, having lost the financial struggle, directed their fire at Ryerson's editorial policy. Case and Evans urged the preachers to condemn the editor for not upholding the decision of the last conference. Neutralization of the *Guardian,* they held, had been a condition of union, but failure to observe this rule had been a major source of unrest in the Connexion.[90] This resolution also was lost. The Conference did agree, however, that "the [*Guardian*] be confined to purely religious and literary subjects and items of general intelligence—the Clergy Reserve question being considered a religious question as a matter of course."⁹¹

The Conference then took the offensive with a series of resolutions to be carried to the English Conference by William and Egerton Ryerson. The Wesleyans were to be told that "we cannot recognize any right on the part of the Committee to interfere with the Canada Conference in the management of our own internal affairs . . . and especially with our own views and proceedings on the Question of the Clergy Reserves." As for the president, he was not to consider himself "the organ or representative of the Wesleyan Body in Upper Canada," particularly in political negotiations. Although the preachers concurred with Ryerson's views on the financial issue, they said they had no interest in the Society's claims on the government. But, as they were anxious to dispel erroneous impressions held by the Wesleyans and to preserve the union, they were sending a delegation to resolve the points at issue.⁹²

The two Ryersons left for England on July 1. Stinson and Richey sailed the same day but in another ship. At the suggestion of Elijah Hoole, one of the secretaries, the Ryersons were treated with scant courtesy by their English brethren.⁹³ The British Conference decided to dissolve the union because it could not be identified with "any body however respected, over whose public proceedings it [was] denied the right and power of exerting any official influence."⁹⁴ Hearing this verdict the Canadian delegates hastened back to Upper Canada to reconstitute an independent Methodist church.

As the statement of the British Conference indicated, this unfortunate outcome to the prolonged Methodist controversy of 1839 and 1840 was not simply the result of misunderstanding or of individual mistakes in judgment. The British Conference was willing to be associated with other Methodist bodies only if it held the power to veto their decisions, a right it claimed as the senior branch of Methodism in the empire. To the parent conference this principle was essential because submission "to Ecclesiastical Authority resident in the parent state . . . [could not] fail to strengthen the political and civil ties by which the Colonies are united to the Mother Country, and to secure loyal and constitutional obedience to the Imperial Government in all the Colonial Dependencies of the Crown."⁹⁵

The Canada Conference was determined to oppose the principle of church establishment and to effect a reserves settlement beneficial to Canadians alone. As for the proper relationship between imperial and Canadian interests, Ryerson told the Special Conference of 1840 that Upper Canada consisted of a population . . . from various parts of the British Empire, and to a limited extent . . . of natives of the United States. . . . The use of the word *British* in a local and restricted sense as applying almost exclusively to natives of Great Britain is as untrue and anti-patriotic as it is unchristian to attempt to excite the sectional feelings which such an illegitimate use of the term is intended and calculated to create. Can any Christian English settler in this Province be a party to . . . the inculcation of a feeling which will brand his own Canadian-born children? Is not a person born in Canada as much a British-born subject as a person born in any other part of the British Empire? And is not a conference of British subjects assembled in Canada as much a British conference as one assembled in England? From whatever part . . . a man may emigrate, when he settles in Canada are not all his interests Canadian? . . . CANADA is . . . HOME . . . and any attempt to excite feelings from the *place of their birth* against those who have been born in the *place of their adopted residence* is unpatriotic, unchristian and unnatural.[96]

2

In the years between the Rebellion of 1837 and the death of Sydenham the people of Upper Canada decided where their "home" was to be. They had the opportunity, in principle at least, to become independent or to become partners in that great democratic experiment—the United States. Equally they had the option of remaining subservient to Britain, and accepting the views of those self-appointed guardians of empire who considered Durham and Russell traitors and who spoke of the Durham Report "as a deliberate and sweeping denunciation against every man in the country."[97] The Upper Canadians had a third choice. They could accept the offer extended by Durham and Sydenham on behalf of a reluctant government, an offer of partnership with Britain in the progressive and systematic advance toward self-government, to establish a "home" in which the various Canadian traditions and interests would be reconciled.

In the struggle to decide which of these options would be taken up there was no question about the Methodist position. Canada was indeed their "home"—their objective was to secure recognition of the fact. Despite the American ties of many Methodists, the Connexion was essentially British in outlook, but it was not prepared to equate loyalty with subservience. To be British in spirit implied, as Ryerson indicated, recognition of the rights of Canadians to provide for their own needs in their own ways—ways that would take into account not only local conditions but the distinctive backgrounds that Canadians shared.

It is in this general context that the Methodist attitude toward the Durham Report and the political and social policies of Sydenham must be assessed. Doubtless Ryerson did not fully understand the concept of responsible government, but in this he had much company. Yet he proclaimed: "[The Report] will form a new era in British Colonial government.... It is all that the most enthusiastic friend of the Canadas could desire and more than we had ventured to anticipate."[98] It would become

A rallying point for hitherto differing parties—a centre of attraction for . . . otherwise uncongenial particles. . . . Lord Durham's report presents a British constitutional monarchy . . . in an aspect so inviting as to captivate the affections of the dissatisfied republican—to revive the desponding hopes of the Loyalist . . . and humble the pretensions of the haughty aristocrat, and restore confidence to the community at large.[99]

Moreover, the *Guardian* emphasized that, apart from the union, Durham did not propose "the alteration of a single letter of the established Constitution"; rather he recommended that the people of Upper Canada "should be governed as in England, by the *men*, as well as the *institutions* of their choice." This was a concept vastly different from the "responsible government" of Mackenzie and Papineau.[100] Sydenham, the exponent of popular government within the limits of the imperial connexion, was strongly supported by Methodists generally, and was helped in pushing through a settlement of the church question that served as a guide-post to a definitive solution.

Ryerson and others realized that the urgent task was to promote understanding of the alternatives facing Upper Canada and to muster support for the policy most likely to benefit the majority. In stating precisely the implications of Durham's report and of Sydenham's system, Methodist leaders helped to rally a large section of the people around the Durham-Sydenham position. When argument seemed necessary, to point up defects and dangers of the ultra-tory or ultra-reform views, the *Guardian* helped to supply it.

To say this is not to claim that Methodist support was indispensable to Upper Canada's new leaders, nor does it answer the protest that Methodists could have done much more. One political figure asserted at the time that "the dissatisfied Scotch & Methodists . . . united with the Radicals in support of any measure which Mr. Thomson may propose form an overwhelming majority and you may expect to see great changes."[101] If Methodist influence had been lacking in this combination it would have been seriously weakened; on the other hand it probably would have taken a stronger tory group than Upper Canada had to resist Sydenham effectively. It could be argued that if Methodists had formed intimate ties with the reform leadership, considerably more might have been accomplished. The clergy reserves might have been secularized, and the position of the reform party might have been improved.

These suppositions, none the less, have tenuous bases. It is too easy to suppose that the Toronto *Examiner* spoke for reformers in condemning the reserves legislation and the Methodist attitude towards it.[102] The Methodists were not alone in their weariness and willingness to compromise. Had they been intransigent there might have been no settlement, or a less satisfactory arrangement than the one effected—a conclusion that does not in any way excuse the Methodist willingness to claim a share in the proceeds. In a very real sense the Methodist Church's policy was that of the reformers. To have drawn closer to men such as Hincks would have constituted a tacit admission that they were the authentic spokesmen of reform, an assumption that many would have questioned at this stage. To have gone beyond the forceful support given to Durham and Sydenham would have added one more element of disunity to a religious community already sorely beset with internal troubles.

Judged in the light of its general position in the years 1838 to 1840, the public statements and acts of the Methodist Church were as positive and effective as they could be. Whatever the reasons for its actions (and they were not wholly altruistic), that body contributed measurably to the development of circumstances in which the people of Upper Canada could for the first time devise their own solutions for their own problems. In the creation of the new climate of opinion, which was the vital element in the new situation, the overt acts of the Methodist Conference were possibly less significant than the inner experience of the Methodist community. As a body of people directly involved in the reconciliation of local and English influences, and in the search for a viable form of self-government, they developed an intuitive awareness of the complexity of Canadian existence and a determination to be Canadians. In this struggle the Methodists were not alone; rather, their distinctive feature was the intensity of their experience and of their desire to profit by it. Without this kind of preparation the growth of the Upper Canadian community would have been immeasurably more difficult.

REFERENCES TO CHAPTER SEVEN

1. *E.R.*, I, 464-466.
2. *Minutes of Conference, 1833, 1838*, 46, 192.
3. *E.R.*, I, 405-408, E. Ryerson to John Joseph, January 25, 1838.
4. *Ibid.*, I, 361, J. to E. Ryerson, September 25, 1836.
5. See J. C. Dent, *The Story of the Upper Canadian Rebellion*, II, 155-156, 195.
6. The trial is described in Dent, II, 247-250. William Ryerson's description of conditions in the Toronto jail is in *E.R.*, I, 460-461.
7. *Ibid.*, I, 440, E. to J. Ryerson, April 4, 1838.
8. *Ibid.*, I, 445, J. to E. Ryerson, April 12, 1838.
9. *Ibid.*, I, 461, W. to E. Ryerson, May 4, 1838.
10. *Ibid.*, I, 375, 376, W. to E. Ryerson, May 18, 1837.
11. *Ibid.*, I, 433, J. to E. Ryerson, March 17, 1838. See also, Egerton's sharp letter to Stinson, January 13, 1838, I, 403-405.
12. *Ibid.*, I, 453, J. to E. Ryerson, April 26, 1838.
13. *Ibid.*, I, 434, same to same, March 17, 1838.
14. *Ibid.*, I, 439-441, E. to J. Ryerson (Private), April 4, 1838.
15. *Ibid.*, I, 467-468, J. Stinson to E. Ryerson, May 17, 1838.
16. *Ibid.*, I, 469, A. Green to E. Ryerson, May 21, 1838.
17. *Ibid.*, I, 470-472, J. to E. Ryerson, May 22, 1838.
18. J. Carroll, *Case and His Cotemporaries*, IV, 184-185; *Minutes of Conference, 1838*, 185, 188.
19. *Minutes of Conference, 1838*, 202-203; *W.R.*, Reel 19, Stinson to Alder, July 4, 1838.
20. Lord Durham's report was presented to the imperial government in February, 1839. Thomson was appointed Governor General in August.
21. S. D. Clark, *Movements of Political Protest in Canada*, 394 ff.
22. *C.G.*, July 11, 1838.
23. C. Lindsey, *The Clergy Reserves*, 40.
24. *C.G.*, October 10, 24, 1838.
25. *Ibid.*, January 30, 1839.
26. *Ibid.*, February 20, 1839.
27. *Ibid.*, February 27, 1839.
28. *Ibid.*, March 6, 1839.
29. *Ibid.*, May 15, 1839. The reinvestment bill passed the lower house by a vote of 22-21.
30. The Normanby letters were also published in the *Guardian*, on May 15, 22, and 29.
31. *C.G.*, May 29, 1839.
32. *Ibid.*, November 7, 1838.
33. For a detailed examination of these events see A. B. Corey, *The Crisis of 1830-1842 in Canadian-American Relations* (New Haven, 1941), 77-81.
34. Clark, *op. cit.*, 407.
35. *C.G.*, November 21, 1838.

36. *Ibid.*, December 5, 1838. Those who prepared this address refused to subscribe to the official Methodist statement.
37. *C.G.*, December 12, 1838; January 9, 16, 1839.
38. *E.R.*, I, 491-492, Stinson to Ryerson, November 2, 1838.
39. *W.R.*, Reel 11, Stinson to Alder, January 1, 1839. See also M. Richey to Stinson, January 1, 1839. He reported that Messrs. Lunn and Ferrier, prominent Montreal laymen, were trying to secure the cancellation of the *Guardian's* subscriptions in that city. "Mr. Ryerson's course appears to me too inflammatory."
40. *M.R.*, Reel 1, Committee Minutes, January 30, 1839; *W.R.*, Reel 11, Alder to Stinson, January 30, 1839. In a letter from T. Jackson to the secretary of Conference, March 23, 1839, the Canadian views were sharply condemned. *C.G.*, September 30, 1840.
41. *W.R.*, Reel 19, Stinson to Alder, February 25, 1839; *C.G.*, May 22, 1839. Stinson was authorized to show Alder's letter to Governor Arthur.
42. P.A.C., *Q416-2*, 308-315, Arthur to Glenelg, May 14, 1839. (Enclosure, Alder to Stinson, January 14, 1839).
43. P.A.C., *Q423*, 150-151, Alder to Normanby, March 11, 1839.
44. Arthur Papers, II, 161-166, Arthur to Normanby, June 8, 1839.
45. *W.R.*, Reel 11, Richey to Alder, May 17, 1839.
46. *Ibid.*, Richey to Stinson, May 17, 1839.
47. *Ibid.*, Stinson to Alder, May 23, 1839.
48. *C.G.*, May 22, 1839.
49. The Conference was preceded by an exchange of letters in the *Guardian* between Alder and Ryerson. See *C.G.*, May 29, June 12, 1839.
50. *MS Journal of Conference, 1839.*
51. *W.R.*, Reel 11, Alder to the Secretaries, July 1, 1839.
52. Carroll, Case, IV, 238.
53. He wanted to convert the *Guardian* into a religious monthly. A motion to this effect was lost, but he asserted that at the end of 1839 the change would take place. *W.R.*, Reel 11, Alder to the Secretaries, July 1, 1839; *MS Journal of Conference, 1839.* For the resolutions see *Minutes of Conference, 1839*, 215.
54. *Minutes of Conference*, 1839, 215-216. See also Alder to the Secretaries, July 1, 1839.
55. *Ibid.*, 214.
56. *W.R.*, Reel 11, Alder to the Secretaries, July 1, 1839.
57. *Ibid.*, Stinson to Alder, July 1, 1839.
58. *Ibid.*, Alder to the Book Committee, October 9, 1839.
59. *Ibid.*, Alder to Stinson, October 8, 1839.
60. *Ibid.*, Stinson to Alder, November 1, 1839.
61. Thomson, later Lord Sydenham, was appointed in August, 1839. P. Knaplund, ed., *Letters from Lord Sydenham to Lord John Russell* (London, 1931), 26. He paid his first official visit to Toronto in November, 1839. *C.G.*, November 27, 1839.

62. For Russell's instructions and the vital dispatch concerning tenure of office see Kennedy, *Documents of the Canadian Constitution*, 516-525.
63. See, for example, the *Guardian* of November 27, December 11, 1839, and April 15, 1840.
64. Kennedy, *op. cit.*, 521. The bill was disallowed on technical grounds.
65. Knaplund, *op. cit.*, 61.
66. *C.G.*, January 8, 1840.
67. *Ibid.*, January 15, 1840.
68. *Ibid.*
69. *Ibid.*, January 29, 1840.
70. *Ibid.*, February 5, 1840.
71. *M.R.*, Reel 1, Committee Minutes, December 11, 1839.
72. *W.R.*, Reel 12, Stinson and Richey to Thomson, January 3, 1840.
73. *C.G.*, September 30, 1840, E. Ryerson to Thomson, January 17, 1840.
74. *W.R.*, Reel 11, Richey to Stinson, February 14, 1840.
75. *Ibid.*, Reel 19, Stinson to T. Jackson, December 9, 1839. There are no available letters from Stinson on this point.
76. *Ibid.*, Reel 19, Richey to Alder, March 13, 1840.
77. P.A.C., Q429-2, 273-276, Alder to Russell, February 12, 1840.
78. P.A.C., Q270-2, 463-465, Thomson to Russell, February 12, 1840. Q273-1, Thomson to Russell (135), July 18, 1840. See also Knaplund, *op. cit.*, 48. "I attach the *greatest* importance to this."
79. *Ibid.*, Thomson to Russell.
80. P.A.C., Q429-2, 280, R. V. Smith to Alder, April 15, 1840.
81. *W.R.*, Reel 12, Alder to Russell, April 29, 1840.
82. *Ibid.*, Resolutions of a Committee appointed by the British Conference of 1839 . . . , April 29, 1840.
83. *Ibid.*, Reel 19, Richey to Alder, May 22, 1840.
84. Green, *op. cit.*, 235.
85. *W.R.*, Reel 12, Minutes of Conference, 1840 (Rough draft). *MS Journal of Conference, 1840*. The vote was forty-three for Ryerson out of a possible sixty-four.
86. *W.R.*, Reel 12, W. Scott to Alder, July 10, 1840.
87. *Ibid.*, Draft Minutes of 1840.
88. Richey's censure motion was defeated. The eight dissenters were Andrew Prindle, John Douse, Benjamin Slight, James Norris, William Scott, Ephraim Evans, Matthew Richey, and Matthew Lang. *MS Journal of Conference, 1840*.
89. *W.R.*, Reel 12, Draft Minutes. This motion was lost by a vote of forty-four to eighteen.
90. *Ibid.*
91. *Ibid.*; *Minutes of Conference, 1840*, 233-234. The original motion was lost by a vote of nineteen to forty-six.

92. *Minutes of Conference, 1840*, 241. The resolutions were passed as a group by forty to eleven votes. *MS Journal of Conference, 1840.*
93. *W.R.*, Reel 12, Hoole to Alder, n.d.
94. *C.G.*, October 7, 1840. For this whole episode, the issues of the *Guardian* for September 30 and October 7, 1840, provide the essential documents.
95. *W.R.*, Reel 12, Alder to Russell, April 29, 1840.
96. *C.G.*, November 11, 1840.
97. *Ibid.*, May 15, 1839. This is taken from one of Attorney-General Hagerman's speeches in the Assembly.
98. *Ibid.*, April 6, 1839.
99. *Ibid.*, July 17, 1839.
100. *Ibid.*, June 5, 1839.
101. P.A.O., Macaulay Papers, J. Macaulay to A. Macaulay, December 24, 1839.
102. Knaplund, *op. cit.*, 53-54. Sydenham claimed that prominent reformers were outraged at Hincks's attack on the reserve legislation.

EIGHT

"You are building a new church in a country possessing all the elements of a mighty empire."

For the Methodists of British North America the decade of the eighteen-forties was a time of crisis. October, 1840, witnessed the dismal collapse of the union between the English and Upper Canadian Conferences, inaugurated so hopefully in October, 1833. Another seven years would pass before the warring Conferences could compose their differences and renew their former association. In marked contrast, during this same interval the Missionary Committee, while manfully resisting its former Canadian brethren, sought vainly to persuade the Methodists of the eastern districts to establish an autonomous conference and to accept a greater degree of responsibility for their own welfare. During and after 1847 the latter began to move steadily toward the goal of self-government, which was attained in 1855. Their reluctant and hesitant progress in this new direction provided a kind of framework for the rôle that they played in the life of the Maritime Provinces.

Despite its unsympathetic attitude to the Canada Conference and its minute supervision of the Societies in the eastern provinces the Missionary Committee had apparently never envisaged the permanent dependency of the British North American districts. As early as 1821 Richard Watson had written: "You must all exert yourselves to excite the people to support their own ministry.... You must not let the spirit of *pauperism* and dependence on the Committee get ascendency among them."[1] When Robert Alder made his historic visit to Upper Canada in 1832 he may have had in mind the formation of a general conference in America. Six years later, faced with a widening gap between revenue and expenses, the Committee was convinced that the North American districts must assume a greater share of responsibility for their own maintenance.[2] Wiser heads in that body were also beginning to see that if the missionary districts were to support themselves they must be allowed more freedom of action. As the Society's financial difficulties grew in the ensuing decade, its willingness to loosen the ties binding the overseas brethren was stimulated.

The first step in this new direction was taken by Alder. In 1839 he asked the preachers of Nova Scotia and New Brunswick to consider the reunion of the two districts.[3] To some this was apparently an unwelcome proposal for they merely agreed to consider the question, but to others it was an attractive idea presented at the wrong time. Four years earlier Enoch Wood had written:

The plan of independence is not new to my mind; it has been plain enough from the Committee's own communications that they have been aiming at this for a long time. . . . I like the idea of being free mighty well! Some of the Committee's own regulations retard rather than advance the work. . . . If [a plan] can be adjusted . . . our people would be more interested in the work and we should generally increase.[4]

Now, however, Wood realized that the Methodists in this region still lacked the confidence that would be engendered by an increasing number of adherents and by the development of their own institutions. Without this confidence they would be unlikely to accept self-government.

During the eighteen-forties and early eighteen-fifties the economic and social development of the Maritime Provinces proceeded rapidly, but was marked by many vicissitudes. With the tide of immigrants at its height, the two mainland provinces registered an absolute increase in population. Yet from 1849 to 1852 especially, emigration was almost as striking and unsettling as immigration.[5] The principal economic enterprises of the area advanced perceptibly but their progress was marred by the recessions of 1842 and 1849.[6] So difficult were conditions in the latter year that Richard Knight said he saw a multitude of beggars in the streets of Saint John and Fredericton.[7]

Despite the fluctuations of the economy the people of this area were conscious of living in more settled, although more demanding, conditions. In Nova Scotia the spirit of local nationalism flourished, and in New Brunswick the crust of loyalist conservatism was further undermined. In both provinces the incipient political and social conflicts of the eighteen-thirties gathered strength and brought about substantial alterations in political and educational policy.

For the Methodist Societies these changing circumstances presented both stimulation and tribulation. Working in a more prosperous community they could have expected greater contributions from their followers, but the fluctuations in the economy and in the flow of emigrants brought a feeling of instability and despair. They were conscious, too, of the growing cohesiveness of the provincial societies to which they belonged, an awareness that led them to re-examine their own relationship with the Missionary Society. Above all, the fervent political and educational controversies of these years suggested to some withdrawal from the world but to others, probably the majority, it was clear that the Methodists must prepare their own defences.

In these difficult conditions much depended upon the calibre of the missionaries themselves. Fortunately for the New Brunswick District William Temple, growing old and careless, was replaced as chairman by Enoch Wood in 1843.[8] From that date until he went to Canada West in 1847 Wood brought his initiative and administrative ability to bear in strengthening and consolidating the Societies in New Brunswick.[9] Regrettably his talents were not matched by those of the honest, obedient Knight who sought valiantly but unimaginatively to persuade the Nova Scotia District to give up its traditional ways. Such vigorous figures as Humphrey Pickard and Alexander McLeod were oriented toward the local cause. The older preachers, however, retained English sympathies. This helps to explain the ambivalent reactions of the itinerants to the Committee's proposals.

The Committee was in no way deterred by the casual reception given to its conference scheme in 1839. In a circular to the chairmen of all the North American districts four years later, it stressed its deepening financial difficulty. With one eye on the continuing schism in Canada West it recommended the consolidation of the work in British North America, an arrangement that could easily be expanded to take in the erring brethren to the west.[10] Once again the Committee was rebuffed; only the New Brunswick District recommended a quadrennial conference to deal with major questions.[11]

Wood found that the reasons for this tepid response and the remedy for it were not difficult to uncover. "The great secret of aversion to a separate conference," he suggested, was "dependence upon 'home', an unwillingness to bend to circumstances for the more rapid progress of the cause among the scattered and destitute populations of this wilderness." The preachers must adapt themselves to the country and the chairmen must put men in places where they would do the most good. In thirteen years the membership had risen from seven hundred to four thousand and there were eighteen thousand in the congregations.[12] If the proper steps were taken the Methodists would grow rapidly in numbers and influence. For him as for Knight the "day of opportunity" had come.[13]

Between 1843 and 1847 the two chairmen laboured energetically to get their respective districts to stand on their own feet and thereby to stimulate opinion favourable to self-government. In this cause they were unwittingly helped by the Committee when it imposed further financial restrictions in 1844 and dealt casually with personnel matters.[14] As their incomes became more precarious and their exasperation more intense, the preachers became more receptive to new ideas. When Alder's grand tour of the American districts was announced early in 1847, Wood assured him that the preachers generally, and the influential Pickard and Rice particularly, anticipated a new departure.[15]

Alder arrived in Halifax on May 4, 1847, and proposed to the leading figures that on his return from Canada a joint session should be held to examine a conference plan.[16] As he was delayed in Canada West the preachers considered the general scheme at Sackville early in July.[17] In these "conversations" the opposition to any change was led by McLeod and Dewolfe, two of the more powerful native missionaries: "McLeod became suddenly reconciled to the plan when nominated to be Editor of the paper proposed ... and Dewolfe played off a good deal of sophistry, but was ably handled by Bro. Pickard."[18]

With the dissenters disarmed, Richey, acting for Alder, was cordially received by the brethren later in the same month.[19] The ministers who gathered in Halifax on this occasion declared that

The proposal made ... in 1843 to form a convention or conference by blending the Lower Districts into one Ecclesiastical Body, maintaining a relationship to the English Conference equally as fraternal and beneficial as that which now exists, has the cordial approbation of this meeting and whensoever the basis of such organization shall be laid before the Brethren ... such proposal shall have our most serious and practical attention.[20]

To this end they decided to call a provincial conference to meet at Saint John in July, 1848.

In private letters Temple and Wood gave strong support to this positive step. The veteran Temple admitted that many of the missionaries had long sought a greater degree of independence, but he warned: "We are British Methodists and we want only British Methodism established among us."[21] Enoch Wood felt it was time for a change. All the elements of an independent and successful church were available, and required only "to be thrown into form" to have a powerful effect upon the educational and religious welfare of the colonies.[22] If the districts were left alone he thought they would become "the prey of little factions, fomented by a few of the older men who cling to the old ways for the sake of their supposed goodness and safety, lacking the enterprise necessary to take a commanding influential position."[23]

Characteristically, however, the Committee did not take advantage of the favourable situation in the Maritime Provinces until 1852. In this interval certain changes occurred that strengthened the hand of those who thought the eastern districts could govern themselves. The first of these was the belated foundation of a weekly Methodist newspaper. After protracted negotiations the monthly *British North American Wesleyan Methodist Magazine* had begun publication in 1841, but had never been wholly satisfactory.[24] A weekly newspaper was felt to be essential to provide a regular flow of information about the Methodist community and to defend its interests in an often hostile environment. The Magazine was suspended by the joint district meeting of 1847 and a weekly, *The Wesleyan,* was proposed in its place.[25] After further urgent appeals to the Committee the first issue appeared in April, 1849.[26] Almost at once the morale of the Societies was strengthened by this new and effective defender of their position.

The vitalizing effect of *The Wesleyan* was intensified by changes in leadership that took place after the 1847 discussions. In the late summer of that year Enoch Wood was moved to Canada West to become missions superintendent and unofficial manager of the reunited Wesleyan Methodist Church.[27] To fill his place Knight left the Nova Scotia District and was soon replaced by Ephraim Evans, late editor of the *Guardian* and more recently a bitter opponent of the principal Methodists in Canada West.[28] Although he was markedly Wesleyan in sympathy, Evans had unconsciously absorbed the working principles of Upper Canadian Methodism and he soon realized how tradition-encrusted were the habits of his ancient district. Evans began to shake up preachers and laity in the hope of recruiting enough itinerants to staff the field, and of raising money in the province to finance Methodist operations.[29]

Evans was not content simply to revive the work in his district. In 1851 he assured the Committee that action on the conference plan "ought not to be much longer delayed."[30] Without its "somewhat authoritative interference" there were some who would not give "the subject the consideration it deserve[d]." A conference backed by smaller district meetings in which, as in England, laymen were represented, would rouse the people "who are *now too willing to plead ignorance of our financial economy and to receive the bread of life at the cost* of the Missionary Society."[31]

While Evans sought to impart a new spirit to his district the Committee procrastinated, partly because of Alder's retirement in 1851 and more importantly because the Conference was warding off the violent assault that led to the great Wesleyan disruption of 1851-1852.[32] Early in 1852, however, John Beecham, the senior secretary, announced the division of the Nova Scotia District and the Committee's decision to put its older missions on an independent footing.[33] The district meetings were to examine the whole question carefully so that they might contribute constructively to the great work of forming "a new church in a country possessing all the elements of a mighty empire." The Society hoped that the foundations would be so laid that the church to be built upon them might "grow with the growth of the empire itself."[34]

Encouraged by Richey and Evans the two Nova Scotia districts received the Committee's proposal with enthusiasm.[35] The New Brunswick District was prepared to act, but without alacrity. It would not be easy, the members asserted, to maintain their work in a community where barter was still common and ready money scarce. For them financial assistance would long be necessary.[36] Moreover, both districts shared the view expressed in Nova Scotia: "We would from our inmost souls, deprecate any change in our position from which danger to the great doctrinal and disciplinary principles of genuine Wesleyan Methodism might justly be apprehended.... It is our firm and united resolve by the grace of God to maintain them inviolate."[37]

With this qualified acceptance the Committee was content. Giving up its long standing desire to amalgamate all the Methodist Societies in British North America, it appointed Dr. Beecham in December, 1854, as its delegate to found the Conference of Eastern British America.[38] The venerable secretary arrived in Halifax on his historic mission on May 24, 1855.[39]

After a quick tour of the Maritime Provinces and a visit to the Canada Conference, Beecham, John Ryerson and Enoch Wood met the missionaries in the first session of the new Conference.[40] In the future the president would be provided by the British Conference, which in turn retained a veto over the acts of the Conference.[41] The Missionary Society was to give some financial assistance in the difficult period of transition.[42] The funds of the Conference were to be managed by joint committees of ministers and laity and the circuit stewards were to take part in the financial district meetings. Seventy-nine ministers were charter members of this new agency; they were responsible for 13,136 members.[43] Methodism in the eastern provinces had indeed come far since the days of William Black and the brothers Mann.

This transformation of the Wesleyan missionaries in the Maritime Provinces into ministers of the Wesleyan Methodist Connexion of Eastern British America marked the beginning of a new and fruitful relationship with the parent conference. But the event and the protracted negotiations preceding it are equally noteworthy in that they were such important factors in the total history of this branch of Methodism in the eighteen-forties. Throughout the period between 1840 and 1855 the ministers, and to a lesser extent the Societies, were both inhibited and stimulated by the prospect of self-government and by the tantalizing way in which the prospect receded and then came into view again. No doubt some came to feel that commitments should be avoided so that the achievement of self-government would not be impeded; others were anxious to assume new functions as a prelude to a new status. On the whole this situation gradually created a new feeling of confidence within the Methodist community—an attitude indicated by the alacrity with which the new arrangements were accepted.

Important as was the emergence of this new awareness of the potentialities of the Methodist Societies, no examination of the context in which they viewed public responsibilities would be complete without some account of their religious attitudes. It has been suggested elsewhere that the Methodists of the eastern provinces, in sharp contrast to their fellow Methodists in Upper Canada, were decorous and respectable evangelicals. Their most interesting feature in the eighteen-forties is that they became more respectable and yet more evangelical. Much attention was paid to erecting handsome church buildings and to raising funds by devices that an older generation would have regarded as questionable.[44] Of these the most popular was the tea meeting—a church supper followed by a series of lengthy and improving addresses. In the same vein the New Brunswick District Meeting of 1847 found time to discuss the wearing of gowns, a practice that it deemed inexpedient at the time.[45]

Yet outwardly respectable as these Methodists were, the circuits and the congregations continued to be swept by revivals. In 1841 William Leggett, soon to leave the itinerancy for the Church of England, declared that "one evening in Fredericton the work surpassed anything ever known in the Province. When I invited the penitents to come forward, seventy at once flocked around the altar, thirty of whom in a short time obtained a remission of sin."[46] Three years later Sampson Busby described the protracted meeting at Cape Tormentine as "one of the most powerful and successful I ever witnessed."[47] Even in Halifax, long a stony field, Evans stated that the doctrine of entire sanctification had been "prominently presented in pulpit ministrations and in classes. Several now professed to enjoy perfect love."[48] Similarly, when the new chapel was opened in Fredericton, Richard Knight expressed the fervent hope that it would soon be the scene of a revival. It came quickly. Judge L. A. Wilmot, reformer and class leader, assured him that "showers of blessings could scarcely convey a correct idea of our visitation. I should say *stream, no, rivers, nay,* a *torrent* every day increasing in *depth* and *length* and breadth.... I am striving after an entire consecration. I am ready to part with all for Christ."[49] Most striking of all was the belated introduction of the camp meeting. The first was held in September, 1850.[50] Several years later three thousand attended a meeting near Woodstock where, despite the rival attractions of the "morals-polluting, self-degrading and swindling heroes of the circus . . . a hallowing influence rested on the assembled multitude, and all must have felt the place to be solemn and sacredly awful."[51]

At this point in their history the Methodists in these provinces had brought their religious practices more nearly into line with those of the evangelical section of the community, an adjustment that presumably broadened the Methodist appeal. This factor, along with a growing stability in the congregational structure and a continuing concern for respectability, increased Methodists' interest in the welfare of their church. But it did not effectively broaden their understanding of the rôle their group might play in the social order. Rather, the religious atmosphere within the Methodist Societies, and their hesitant progress toward independence, led them to assume a more aggressive public posture whose objectives were more defensively Methodist than altruistic.

2

In the eighteen-forties the great interest of the Methodists was education, a cause that frequently led them into interesting political by-ways. The uncomfortable decade of the thirties had closed with Charles F. Allison's splendid offer to construct a Methodist academy at Sackville. Shortly after Allison's initial letter had been received, Wood informed the Committee that the donor was willing to provide £4,000 and seven acres of land as a site. In the proposed academy eighty students would be given "a sound Christian and an honest English education" in an environment "Wesleyan throughout."[52]

The Committee's cordial approval was secured and the project went ahead rapidly. The main difficulties were the acquisition of funds and teachers.[53] For the first the planners naturally looked to the local legislatures; for the second they considered their former associate, Matthew Richey, late principal of Upper Canada Academy and Charles Dewolfe, a native Nova Scotian with influential connections.[54] "Surrounded as we are by a religious democracy," Wood exclaimed, "we nevertheless are determined to be thoroughly Wesleyan."[55] He agreed, however, with Temple who felt the principal should be a man who would bend to circumstances, for the manners and habits of the new world were not those of the old.[56]

As Richey was unable to become principal, Wood belatedly

realized that his younger colleague, Humphrey Pickard, had the requisite qualifications—a view that he imposed in spite of much opposition.[57] With Pickard was associated as governor and chaplain Albert Desbrisay, the saintly "Islander," now too unwell for circuit preaching.[58] Secure in the knowledge that grants had been made by the legislatures of Nova Scotia and New Brunswick, the Academy was formally opened on June 29, 1843.[59]

In his inaugural address, Principal Pickard defined education as "that instruction and discipline which are necessary to prepare men for the duties and enjoyments of existence." This instruction would be "thorough—designed to teach the student to think not less than remember . . . to prize moral excellence even more highly than intellectual acquisitions." It would include the wisdom of the past and the insights of philosophy and science but "the volume of inspiration" would be the "most valuable textbook," to be studied "with the anxiety which the importance of its truths should excite and with the deference due to a message from Heaven." Pickard's hope was that

Each mind will be itself a living volume of incalculable value, to be here filled with chapters of this [school's] history, and which being well bound with good moral habits and principles may issue self-circulated through society to be profitably read by many in this world and afterwards elevated to the library of Heaven.[60]

The training that the Academy gave in mathematics, science and languages was thus never an end in itself. From the outset it was thought of as a place in which religious, moral and intellectual discipline would be fruitfully combined in a thoroughly Wesleyan atmosphere. This combination proved to be exceptionally attractive to the sons of Methodists and those in other communions.[61]

Sackville (later Mount Allison) Academy was the principal but not the only Wesleyan educational institution. Working as they did in an area poorly provided with primary and secondary schools and one in which denominational rivalries were still powerful, the preachers sought to establish Wesleyan day schools.[62] The joint district meeting of 1847 appointed a committee for this purpose and recommended the establishment of a girls' school at Sackville.[63] The Ladies' Academy, the first of its kind in the eastern provinces, was opened on August 17, 1854.[64] In the same year the Varley Wesleyan day school, the chief product of the committee's work, began instruction in Saint John.[65]

As New Brunswick and Nova Scotia made serious efforts after 1850 to build up their elementary school systems, religious primary schools became less important.[66] In contrast, the Sackville Academy was considered from the outset as another entrant in the controversy over the form of higher education in the two provinces. It was in defence of this institution specifically that the Methodists became involved in the political disputes of this period.

The chief bone of contention in New Brunswick was King's College, Fredericton, formally opened on January 1, 1829.[67] As an Anglican institution receiving an annual grant of £2,200 from the limited provincial revenue, it was naturally resented by other religious groups and by supporters of secular education. This denominational jealousy was helpful in securing the Assembly's support for a grant to the Methodist Academy, and the predominantly Anglican Council reluctantly concurred.[68]

The Methodists were naturally gratified when in April, 1843, L. A. Wilmot, the most influential Methodist layman in Fredericton, became an executive councillor.[69] He had shown marked interest in education since 1835 and it was anticipated that he would be an effective opponent of Governor Colebrooke, who was thought to have high church proclivities.[70] But Wood stressed: "While our interest is increasing in the Upper Branches, and we still maintain our hold on the Assembly it matters very little what opinions of a religious nature His Exy. may entertain."[71]

In reality Governor Colebrooke's views on the subject of King's College and its relationship with other provincial institutions did matter. Following earlier abortive attempts, in 1845 Wilmot secured passage of a bill that significantly reduced the Anglican control of the College. Reserved by the Governor, it was eventually approved by the imperial government.[72] In the negotiations that preceded and followed its acceptance the Methodist leaders provided some insight into their own educational opinions.

Enoch Wood, the agent and reporter in this affair, admitted that King's College was considered "an incubus, more than a blessing to the province" and that the Anglicans could retain the original charter only by supporting the claims of other groups for state support.[73] He found, moreover, that Colebrooke wished to establish an institution resembling the University of London, including King's and other colleges, and that the Governor wanted him to act as an intermediary with the Baptists and Presbyterians. Wood avoided any commitment but he was evidently much taken by the plan. To Alder he wrote that it exactly met their views; but, the proposed relationship with "Literary Institutions of Evangelical Bodies" differing from the Episcopalians would have to be defined fairly and honestly.[74]

When the revised charter finally passed, the university plan had to be put aside, but the Methodists took advantage of the new conditions. As King's was still partially Anglican, the Methodists continued to seek grants for the Academy. At the same time they worked with the Governor in implementing college legislation, urging in particular that the college examining board should include the heads of other academies. Colebrooke, according to Wood, seemed very much taken with the idea and felt strongly that the College should be popular and useful. The Governor stated distinctly that he had appointed Wilmot and Hill to be members of the College council because they were Wesleyans.[75]

King's College languished until in 1859 it was transformed into the University of New Brunswick, so these manoeuvres had no great immediate consequence.[76] It is clear, though, that in so far as Wood and his associates spoke for the Methodists of New Brunswick they were most anxious to keep higher education under religious control. They had no complaint about King's College as such, provided equitable arrangements were made for non-Anglican students. In trying to secure their objective of state-supported and religiously oriented higher education they were prepared to negotiate behind the political scenes. They did not apparently realize that the best way to challenge monopoly was to work toward a new system of government in New Brunswick. On this question the New Brunswick records are silent.

Although the Methodists of Nova Scotia had no school of their own to protect, they were led to comment on the political warfare of that province, partly in defence of the Academy, partly on behalf of their educational principles. In February, 1843, William Annand, friend and colleague of Joseph Howe, moved a series of resolutions in the Nova Scotia Assembly condemning the policy of chartering and endowing denominational schools and colleges, and urging the establishment of one good college free from sectarian control. This was a revival of the abortive Dalhousie scheme of the thirties.[77] The resolutions were accepted by the Assembly and a fierce public controversy ensued in which Howe, the chief exponent of the central non-sectarian university, faced his cabinet colleague, the Baptist champion J. W. Johnston.[78] Throughout 1843 there was increased agitation, culminating in a dissolution and general election, in which Johnston secured a minute majority.[79]

The Methodists, who stood to lose if Howe's side won the verdict, were doubtless expected to align themselves with the tories. Conceivably many individual Methodists did so, but Charles Dewolfe asserted that many Methodists supported the reformers, "owing to the great contempt with which the Church Party have treated them." The ministers, on the other hand, "kept completely aloof from the party politick of the day," a tactic that perhaps induced the Methodist laity not to participate actively in the campaign.[80]

The tory victory of course halted the onslaught on denominational education, but there was little abatement in the political uproar.[81] For the Methodist preachers at any rate this was a sore trial. Richard Knight noted in 1844 that there were political meetings everywhere: "Withering indeed is their influence upon religion." The Baptists, he believed, were grasping for power: "I do not say that they will try every man's work by *fire,* but I am sure they will by *water.* And I know not that there is so much difference between burning and drowning." For him the only solution was to abstain from politics, especially the colonial variety, for "they are a storm in a teapot."[82] A year later he reiterated: "As a body we have resolvedly and advisedly kept ourselves aloof from this political strife, but in some cases we have not been able to restrain our members and more especially our congregations."[83]

At this stage the battle for party government was being joined in Nova Scotia. In December, 1846, the province was in the decisive phase of the contest. Yet Knight complained that it was "cursed with political madness." All was hypocrisy among the conservatives; the Anglicans and Baptists were using each other. He felt the reformers were, if anything, worse—a party "embracing the Papists to a man.... Responsible government ... is the bane of this once harmonious province. The awful injury inflicted on religion by the last elections has not been remedied, and I fear will not [be] ere the new elections shall produce renewed and still more fatal excitement." "However," he concluded, "the Lord omnipotent reigneth and in Him alone is our trust."[84]

Fortunately, deliverance was at hand. The general election of 1847 was followed by the accession of a reform ministry in which Howe was provincial secretary, and by the relaxation of political tension.[85] If the supporters of church-oriented education expected a renewal of the onslaught of 1843 they were disappointed. Howe in responsible office admitted that a large portion of the people favoured the denominational principle of education and that it would not be wise to revive sectarian bitterness again. Rather he proposed that all institutions which maintained certain standards should be helped by the state.[86]

In taking this stand Howe perhaps had one eye on the Methodists. Petitions on behalf of the Academy were being circulated and Evans saw Howe privately. He frankly informed him that Methodist principles on the subject were strongly fixed and that it would be dangerous for a provincial ministry to array itself against the religious feeling of the country in attempting to establish a godless system of public instruction.[87] In addition the 1849 District Meeting urged all Methodists to support their educational enterprises and not to countenance any system not based on scriptural principles.[88]

Two months earlier in the first number of *The Wesleyan* the editor had assured his readers that the paper would be guarded against sectarianism. Mere party politics would be excluded but anything which involved the intellectual, moral or religious well-being of the provincial population would be discussed.[89] Among these subjects was education and it received much editorial space in the spring of 1850.

In February when the question of education grants was again before the Assembly *The Wesleyan* contended that the kind of education given would determine the respectability and influence of any people, and that the whole question should not be made a party issue.[90] The problem in Nova Scotia was whether the province should have a purely secular or a religiously controlled system. *The Wesleyan* stated that if the secular plan were chosen its opponents would array themselves "openly, palpably, vigorously and perseveringly against this scheme, and we are confident no Institution can succeed or prosper in opposition to the religious sense of the people." The supporters of denominational schools, the editor emphasized, claimed equal rights and would not be satisfied with less. They would object to being taxed for the support of one college, wherever situated, to which they could not conscientiously send their children, unless some assistance were given to those seminaries to which they could adhere.[91]

The Assembly decided to continue the existing arrangements but *The Wesleyan* did not drop the subject. Evidence was brought forward that religious institutions supported by the state were common in the United States. Much attention was devoted to weak spots in the position of the secularists[92] and an able letter from a "Wesleyan" reviewing the whole educational question was printed approvingly. To this contributor the community was a partnership whose qualities would be determined by the kind of education its members received. The state's duty was to see that every child received an education. The issue was how much education and what kind of education should be provided. The writer of the letter felt that an adequate primary system and a comprehensive system of secondary education were required. Especially the poor, he thought, should feel deeply anxious for public support of schools; the wealthy always could get what they required. The writer concluded: "Those who talk about education for the poor and education for the rich, assuming that everything which is done to maintain academies and colleges is . . . exclusively for the benefit of the rich and strive by so awakening class prejudices to secure the sanction of the majority for the crusade against existing institutions, are endeavouring either ignorantly or wickedly to mislead the public mind."[93]

Apparently the Secretaries felt that *The Wesleyan* was providing too much stimulus for the public mind, for its supervisors were called to account. Evans assured Alder that *The Wesleyan* would heed his suggestions. But he added that in the face of the crisis it would be of permanent benefit to the country if the paper could help "ward off the blow aimed by non-religionist and popish scheming at the religious instruction of our youth."[94] His colleague, the editor of *The Wesleyan*, promptly reacted to the accusation of political meddling and recalled that education had been specifically mentioned in his original statement of policy as a proper subject of discussion. The editor maintained that the subject of education did not come under the category of party politics for it pertained to the whole life of the people. *The Wesleyan's* purpose was to defend denominational institutions and "to keep the educational issue from becoming a party football."[95]

Another letter from a "Wesleyan" promptly appeared, urging the establishment of an adequate number of residential secondary schools in which religious influences would be strong. Any system of secular education, it was said, would be

> infidel and atheistic in its tendency ... and as such it should be earnestly protested against by every Christian in the province, notwithstanding the gross inconsistency of a few who brand ... as sectarian and vicious the system of higher education which renders respectable denominations of Christians responsible to the parents and public for carrying on the work of education, not upon sectarian but upon truly catholic principles.

The writer believed that a secular system could never receive the sanction of an enlightened Christian people, nor would its supporters be permitted by the people of the province to proceed as far as their brethren in Canada West. He pleaded with the editor to defeat any godless university proposal before it could be implemented, for no such arrangement would ever work in Nova Scotia.[96]

Clearly the Methodists of Nova Scotia were as devoted to the principle of secondary and higher education under denominational auspices as were their brethren in New Brunswick. They regarded the Academy as their institution and were prepared to defend it and the ideal which it represented, whatever the political risks involved. As Nova Scotia politicians were less given to "log-rolling" than their New Brunswick counterparts, the Methodists were obliged to come out publicly and vigorously on the side of denominational education. Yet it is equally evident that their stand on this question was no indication of their general political position.

If any further proof were needed of the political neutralism of the ministers, it was provided by a special district meeting in 1852. This session was called to examine allegations that one of the younger preachers, Mr. W. C. Beals, had engaged in political activity. His colleagues expressed their "unfeigned regret that Mr. Beals should by his appearance at the hustings and by unguarded conversation ... have departed from that strict neutrality imperative on all our ministers in such cases." They admitted that among the Methodists, "as among all other Christian denominations there are those ... who entertain radically different views on political questions and they have an indisputable right so to do." But for ministers to identify themselves with either party would be to foster schism within their own communion.[97] In so acting the Nova Scotia ministers were taking the expedient and perhaps the only practicable step. Their statement nevertheless reflected the Committee's long standing prohibition on political activity, the conservatism of many, and their general unwillingness to relate Christian principles to broad political issues.

While the preachers were either tory sympathizers or uninterested in politics, the Methodist laity apparently continued to be of diverse political persuasions. Some doubtless were influenced by the outlook of their spiritual guides; others were certainly on the reform side. Charles Fisher and L. A. Wilmot were not alone in New Brunswick; in 1843, at least, many Nova Scotia Methodists were thought to be on Howe's side. Although the latter were said to have joined the reformers because of the unfriendly attitude of Anglican tories, it is conceivable that many of them were genuine reformers. On the other hand, little more than a decade later some Methodists in Nova Scotia were alleged to have left the liberal party because it included many Roman Catholics.[98] One cannot say that the Methodists of the Maritime Provinces were attached to any one political group.

3

The place of the Wesleyan Methodists in the life of the eastern provinces can be more easily grasped during the years from 1840 to 1855 than in earlier periods. The picture is that of a religious community moving rather hesitantly toward independence from the English Conference and the Missionary Society, adapting its spiritual outlook more closely to local needs, and building up institutions to defend its interests. On the whole this should have been a stimulating process, but because of past inhibitions and present leadership the secular potential of the Methodist economy was not fully exploited.

Politically, the Methodist Societies continued to exert a minor and elusive influence. Their religious leaders were not above political activity; some of their lay leaders were active reformers, but in general the Methodists did not stand out as a significant group in the political warfare of this era. It may well be that many of them sensed the liberal implications of their beliefs and of their polity, but if so this liberalism did not emerge in practice. One could maintain that the Methodists acted as political Methodists only when they were concerned about their interests or were moved by religious prejudice. Nevertheless, as a body of people who were consistently taught to place principle above partisanship and to take responsibility for others, they may well have acted as a mediating force in the politics of Nova Scotia and New Brunswick.

If the Methodists do not stand out as a major force in the political sphere, it must be said that their educational principles were put forward concisely and with some effect. Like their compatriots in Upper Canada they were convinced that in education all sections of the population must be treated equally by the state. They were entirely willing to look to the state for support for their educational efforts; indeed, they assumed that it was the duty of government to aid religious bodies in this field. Moreover, they held that in higher education the proper combination of religious and intellectual nourishment could only be effected under denominational auspices, a principle embodied in Mount Allison Academy and subsequently in Mount Allison University. Although the educational views of the Methodists were clear it could hardly be said that theirs was the determining voice in the educational struggle of this period. Being one of the smaller religious bodies they were effective only when joined with the powerful Anglican, Presbyterian and Baptist groups.

Apart from their political and educational activity the Wesleyan Methodists made another contribution to the social development of the Maritime Provinces, albeit a less tangible one. As a group who quietly worked out an accommodation between local and English interests, they may have been a factor of some significance in supporting the peaceful way in which these provinces progressed from dependence to self-government. At the same time they had kept alive, and would continue to maintain, a sense of kinship with England that would help delay the emergence of self-conscious societies in the eastern provinces.

But despite their various achievements one still might feel that the Methodists did not play a remarkable part in the life of their times. Their justification would have been that the things of this world were not of great importance in the face of eternity. To prepare men for entrance into the "library of Heaven" was to them of vital importance, and it was in the light of this purpose that they assessed the secular tasks of Methodism.

REFERENCES TO CHAPTER EIGHT

1. T. W. Smith, *History of the Methodist Church* . . ., II, 435.
2. *M.R.*, Reel 1, Committee Minutes, January 30, 1839. In 1840 the Society was £20,000 in debt. *Ibid.*, Reel 2, Alder to R. Knight, April 2, 1840. Doubtless this problem helped to harden the Committee's stand on government grants in Upper Canada.
3. *M.R.*, Reel 5, Minutes of Joint District Meeting, 1839.
4. Findlay and Holdsworth, *History of the Wesleyan Methodist Missionary Society*, I, 347-348. Wood was speaking of a North American union but his basic assumptions are made clear here.
5. Easterbrook and Aitken, *Canadian Economic History*, 239; *W.R.*, Reel 16, Knight to the Secretaries, January 8, 1849.
6. Easterbrook and Aitken, *op. cit.*, 244-245.
7. *W.R.*, Reel 16, Knight to the Secretaries, January 8, 1849. For conditions in 1842 see *ibid.*, Reel 13, Temple to Alder, March 29, 1842.
8. Temple had thoroughly jumbled the District accounts. See *W.R.*, Reel 14, Wood to Alder, June 13, 1843.
9. In 1847 Wood was appointed missions superintendent in the reunited church of Canada West. See below, page 255.
10. *M.R.*, Reel 2, E. Hoole to the chairmen of the North American Districts, April 17, 1843. For the negotiations with the Canada Conference see below, pages 225-228.
11. *M.R.*, Reel 5, Nova Scotia Minutes, 1843; Reel 6, New Brunswick Minutes. The Newfoundland District, which was equally short of money, resisted the Committee's plan. Smith, *op. cit.*, II, 443.
12. *W.R.*, Reel 13, Wood to Alder, July 30, 1842.
13. *Ibid.*, Knight to the Secretaries, February 28, 1842.
14. *Ibid.*, Reel 14, Wood to Alder, March 30, 1844.
15. Alder's primary objective was of course the reunion of the Canada Conference and the Canada Western District. See below, page 251. For views of Wood, Pickard and Rice see *W.R.*, Reel 15, Wood to Alder, March 30, 1847.
16. *Ibid.*, Wood to Hoole, May 6, 1847.
17. *Ibid.*, Minutes of Several Conversations Held . . . at Sackville, July 3, 1847.
18. *Ibid.*, Reel 19, Wood to Alder, November 9, 1847.
19. Overcome by his toils in Canada, Alder was unable to meet the representative group of missionaries gathered in Halifax. *W.R.*, Reel 15, Minutes of a Meeting of Wesleyan Ministers . . . in Halifax, July 19-20, 1847.

20. *Ibid.*
21. *Ibid.*, Temple to Alder, July 26, 1847.
22. *Ibid.*, Wood to Secretaries, July 29, 1847.
23. *Ibid.*, Reel 19, Wood to Alder, September 8, 1847.
24. See above, pages 92-93, for the background. *The B.N.A. Wesleyan Methodist Magazine* was published from 1841 to 1844, suspended temporarily in 1845 and finally in 1847.
25. *W.R.*, Reel 15, Minutes of Several Conversations . . . 1847.
26. *Ibid.*, Knight *et al.* to the Secretaries, April 4, 1848; Knight to the Secretaries, August 18, 1848; Reel 16, E. Evans to Alder, February 7, 1849; *M.R.*, Reel 1, Committee Minutes, September 27, 1848. Alexander McLeod was the editor.
27. *W.R.*, Reel 15, Wood to the Secretaries, July 29, 1847.
28. He refers to his appointment in *W.R.*, Reel 15, Evans to Alder, September 1, 1848.
29. *W.R.*, Reel 16, Evans to the Secretaries, June 24, 1850, in which he announced the establishment of contingency and supernumerary funds. He found that the preachers disliked selecting new missionaries as these would share in the grant from the Society. In 1849-50, the District deficit was reduced from £244 to £70.
30. *W.R.*, Reel 16, Evans to the Secretaries, December 11, 1851.
31. *Ibid.*, February 4, 1852.
32. *M.R.*, Reel 1, Committee Minutes, July 11, 1851. Appropriately, Alder retired to orders in the Church of England. For the controversy in the English Conference see E. R. Taylor, *Methodism and Politics,* 165-180.
33. The Conference of 1851 decided to divide the district. One reason for the division was to find a place for Richey who had retired as president of the Canada Conference. See below, page 255.
34. *M.R.*, Reel 2, Beecham to Evans, April 10, 1852. Identical letters were sent to the chairmen of the Nova Scotia West, New Brunswick, Newfoundland and Canada East Districts.
35. See *W.R.*, Reel 17, Richey to Beecham, July 7, 1852. A joint meeting was held and a series of resolutions passed. Reel 16, Resolutions . . . adopted . . . by a united meeting of the Nova Scotia Western and Eastern Districts . . . 1852.
36. *M.R.*, Reel 6, New Brunswick Minutes, 1852; *W.R.*, Reel 17, Knight to the Secretaries, June 26, 1852.
37. *W.R.*, Reel 16, Nova Scotia Resolutions, 1852.
38. The Committee held on to the federal plan as the only available means of incorporating the Canada Eastern District in a larger body. This obstacle was overcome by the union of this district with the Canada Conference in 1854. See *M.R.*, Reel 2, Beecham *et al.* to Richey, April 9, 1853. For the Canadian union see below, pages 255-256. For Beecham's appointment see *ibid.*, Committee Minutes, August 29, 1853; December 13, 1854. The long delay was caused by the negotiations preceding the establishment of the Australian Conference.

39. Smith, *op. cit.*, II, 446.
40. *Minutes of Several Conversations between the Ministers of the Wesleyan Methodist Connexion or Church of Eastern British America* (Halifax, 1855), 5.
41. Beecham was the first president, Matthew Richey the co-delegate or vice-president. The veto had a limit of one year.
42. Newfoundland was a particular problem in this respect.
43. *E.B.A. Minutes*, 5-19. It should be noted that the Wesleyan Methodist Connexion or Church of Eastern British America included Nova Scotia, New Brunswick, Prince Edward Island, Newfoundland and Bermuda.
44. The new chapel opened in Fredericton in 1853 was expected to cost £3,050, a large sum in those days. *W.R.*, Reel 16, Knight to Hoole, October 13, 1851.
45. The matter was raised by the Fredericton Society. It is of interest that in the voting the native ministers were all on the negative side. *M.R.*, Reel 6, New Brunswick Minutes, 1847.
46. *W.R.*, Reel 13, Leggett to Alder, March 1, 1841.
47. Quoted in Reel 14, Wood to Alder, April 27, 1844.
48. *Ibid.*, Reel 16, Evans to Alder, March 22, 1850.
49. Quoted in Reel 17, Knight to Hoole, April 11, 1853.
50. For the rules see *The Wesleyan*, August 5, 1850.
51. *Provincial Wesleyan*, October 15, 1857.
52. *W.R.*, Reel 11, Wood to the Committee, January 24, 1840.
53. The Committee of course refused to assume any financial responsibility. *M.R.*, Reel 2, Committee Minutes, February 12, 1840.
54. *W.R.*, Reel 13, Temple to the Secretaries, December 15, 1841.
55. *Ibid.*, Wood to Alder, June 30, 1841.
56. *Ibid.*, Temple to the Secretaries.
57. Wood was not greatly attracted by the idea of Richey's appointment. In any case he was needed in Canada West. See *W.R.*, Reel 13, Wood to Alder, June 30, 1841, and March 30, 1842; Richey to Wood, February 7, 1842 (copy).
58. Smith, *op. cit.*, II, 394-395.
59. The New Brunswick legislature gave a capital grant of £500. *W.R.*, Reel 13, Wood to Alder, March 30, 1842. Both legislatures gave operating grants of £200 each. *Ibid.*, Reel 14, Temple to Alder, March 29, 1843.
60. *B.N.A. Wesleyan Methodist Magazine*, III, 1843, 284-292.
61. The average attendance was more than one hundred, including among others the son of the Governor of Prince Edward Island. There was some criticism of the Academy by Anglicans but in 1846 the New Brunswick legislature eulogized its operations. *W.R.*, Reel 14, Wood to Alder, May 31, 1845, and October 12, 1844; Reel 15, Wood to Alder, January 31, 1846.
62. See K.F.C. McNaughton, *The Development of the Theory and Practice of Education in New Brunswick, 1784-1900* (Fredericton,

1947), chap. 6. See also *W.R.*, Reel 13, Wood to Alder, July 15, 1843. He alleged that the government was giving clandestine help to the Roman Catholics. "Swarms of young ones rally out of their premises, where they are fed by the public funds."
63. *W.R.*, Reel 15, Minutes of Conversations ... at Sackville, 1847.
64. Charles Allison offered £1,000 for this venture, and his offer was matched by the people of Sackville. *Ibid.*, Knight to the Secretaries, August 18, 1848. *M.R.*, Reel 1, Committee Minutes, September 27, 1848. *W.R.*, Reel 17, Pickard to Osborn, October 12, 1852; Smith, *op. cit.*, II, 396.
65. *W.R.*, Reel 17, Knight to Hoole, November 8, 1852; Knight to the Secretaries, July 29, 1853; Smith, *op. cit.*, II, 390. The initial sum for this school came from the bequest of half a ship to the Society. Other schools were opened but remained in operation only briefly.
66. For this question see C.B. Sissons, *Church and State in Canadian Education* (Toronto, 1959), chapters 4 and 6.
67. A. W. Trueman, *Canada's University of New Brunswick* (New York, 1952), 12-13.
68. Hannay, *History of New Brunswick*, II, 100; *W.R.*, Reel 13, Wood to Alder, June 30, 1841. In 1843 all but two members of the Legislative Council were Anglicans.
69. J. Hannay, *Wilmot and Tilley* (Toronto, 1907), 72.
70. *Ibid.*, 51-56.
71. *W.R.*, Reel 13, Wood to Alder, July 15, 1843.
72. Hannay, *Wilmot*, 55-56. For the terms of the bill see Hannay, *History*, II, 100-101.
73. *W.R.*, Reel 15, Wood to Alder, February 2, 1846.
74. *Ibid.*, March 27, 1846. See also Reel 19, Wood to Hoole, May 18, 1849, where he states that he worked for one university with affiliated denominational colleges.
75. *Ibid.*, Reel 15, Wood to Alder, February 26, 1847.
76. Sissons, *op. cit.*, 221.
77. J. Howe, *The Speeches and Public Letters of Joseph Howe*, ed. J. A. Chisholm (Halifax, 1909), I, 417-418.
78. C. Martin, *Empire and Commonwealth* (Oxford, 1929), 206-207.
79. J. W. Longley, *Joseph Howe* (Toronto, 1906), 86.
80. *W.R.*, Reel 14, Dewolfe to Alder, January 2, 1844.
81. In 1845 grants were given or renewed to all the colleges and academies except Dalhousie. Harvey, *An Introduction to the History of Dalhousie University*, 58.
82. *W.R.*, Reel 14, Knight to the Secretaries, December 16, 1844.
83. *Ibid.*, October 11, 1845.
84. *Ibid.*, December 12, 1846.
85. Martin, *op. cit.*, 234-235.
86. Chisholm, *op. cit.*, II, 15, 19.

87. *W.R.*, Reel 16, Evans to Alder, February 7, 1849.
88. *W.R.*, Reel 5, Nova Scotia Minutes, 1849.
89. *The Wesleyan,* April 7, 1849.
90. *Ibid.,* February 9, 1850.
91. *Ibid.,* February 23, 1850.
92. *Ibid.,* March 2, 9, 1850.
93. *Ibid.,* March 23, 1850.
94. *W.R.*, Reel 16, Evans to Alder, May 16, 1850.
95. *The Wesleyan,* May 18, 1850.
96. *Ibid.,* June 1, 1850.
97. *Provincial Wesleyan,* July 22, 1852.
98. *Ibid.,* April 28, 1859.

NINE

"With secular parties or politics we have nothing to do.... In secular affairs ... Christians should agree to differ."

While the Methodist Societies in the Maritime Provinces, in common with the people of those provinces, moved slowly, and in some cases reluctantly, towards self-government in matters political and religious, the Societies of Upper Canada finally attained that status after years of acrimonious controversy.[1] For the Canadian Methodists the involved wrangle with the Wesleyans in 1840 was their "1837," but their rebellion, unlike Upper Canada's was temporarily and outwardly successful. They and the Wesleyans sampled a kind of independence, but in the end it proved unsatisfactory for both. Almost at the same time as the province itself, the Canadian and Wesleyan Methodists reached a settlement through which the diverse claims of local and metropolitan interests could be reconciled.

If the first action in the Canadian Methodist rebellion was the fierce debate of the Conference of 1840, the second was the special conference summoned by the Ryerson brothers for October 22 of that year.[2] In Carroll's words: "The call was almost universally responded to. Never had the ministers of the body assembled under such peculiar feelings. On both sides, we have reason to believe there was much prayer to God. It was like two contending armies appealing to the God of battles on the eve of an engagement, which was to decide their quarrel. A pitiful scene it was, but nevertheless exciting."[3]

On the appointed day about eighty preachers met at nine o'clock in the Newgate Street Church. The aged veteran, Thomas Whitehead, who was asked to conduct the opening worship service, gave out the hymn "Jesus Great Shepherd.... For oh! the wolf is nigh."[4] The Conference was then formed with Case as president and J. C. Davidson, a British sympathizer, as secretary.[5] By a majority of three votes the doors were opened to the public, a move designed to publicize the Canadian case and forestall charges of "railroading," such as had been made in 1832 and 1833.[6] Someone suggested that Stinson be invited to attend. Egerton Ryerson remarked that Stinson had no more business there "than a Ryanite preacher."[7]

The delegates spoke at length and, so Stinson alleged, in an abusive manner. William supported Egerton, "in his most extravagant style,"

217

charging that the British Conference was not sound on temperance and that the British preachers were of poor calibre.[8] Most of the preachers felt their representatives had a good case; they accepted resolutions highly critical of the behaviour of the English Conference. The Conference held that the latter's actions were based upon "defective and partial" information and that its allegations about the grant had been "expressly contradicted by His Excellency, the Governor General of Canada." British assumption "of the right and power of an 'official influence' and 'efficient direction' over the 'public proceedings' of this Conference" was said to be "repugnant to the express provisions of the Articles of Union . . . ," whereas "the avowed dissolution of the Union by the English Conference . . . is a plain and lamentable violation of . . . obligations to this Conference and to the Wesleyan-Methodist Church in Canada." Its members were nevertheless willing to resume good relations with the British Conference whenever that body began to practise Methodist principles.[9]

But at the time there was no hope of reconciling the two bodies, a fact emphasized by the withdrawal of several members of Conference, including William Case and Ephraim Evans, and the organization of the Canada Western District under the Wesleyan Missionary Society.[10] The Canada Conference reduced the number of districts from six to five, under the chairmanship of Green, William Ryerson, Davidson, Henry Wilkinson and Richard Jones.[11] Egerton Ryerson was appointed superintendent of the Toronto circuit; John Ryerson became Book Steward and unofficial supervisor of the *Guardian,* whose editor was the young Wesleyan, Jonathan Scott. Whitehead was pressed into the presidency. The Conference pledged itself to prohibit political discussion; the *Guardian* was to take a neutral course, except when Methodist principles were attacked. The Societies were urged to unite with the preachers in "promoting glory to God in the highest, peace on earth and goodwill amongst men."[12]

The Canadian Methodists thus set out upon the road of independence and travelled it for seven years. In this interval the three Ryerson brothers, Anson Green, Richard Jones, Henry Wilkinson, John Carroll, and the successive editors of the *Guardian*—Scott, George Playter and George Sanderson—were perhaps the leading influences in the Connexion.

William Ryerson, elected president of the Conference in 1841 and missionary agent in 1842, was at the height of his powers as a preacher, evangelist and defender of Canadian Methodist interests. In contrast, Egerton Ryerson's influence was less noticeable, whereas John Ryerson's position probably was stronger than in the previous decade. John's primary concerns were institutional development and respectability, interests shared by Anson Green, which induced the two to consider compromise with the Wesleyans. Of the three lesser figures, Jones, Wilkinson and Carroll, the latter was the most charitable and tolerant. All were greatly concerned with the spread of Methodism as a religious rather than a political or social force, but they were unwilling to admit that their task could be accomplished in other than Canadian terms.

The Methodist cause could be helped or hindered by the *Guardian's* editorial page. In the years of separation three editors held office, but their achievements were not remarkable. Jonathan Scott, Ryerson's successor, was better fitted to be an evangelist than an editor, and Sanderson was a mediocre journalist. George Playter took over the editor's chair with a considerable reputation as an apologist for the Canadian point of view, but his earlier promise was not fulfilled. He did, however, have Ryerson's ability to insinuate where positive statements were forbidden. The *Guardian* continued to be a vehicle of Methodist policy, although not an entirely effective one.

Behind the Ryersons and their associates stood a body of preachers no more easily described in 1840 than in earlier years. Despite the secession of the Wesleyan sympathizers, the itinerants were far more numerous than in 1828, and the majority had been taken into the work since that date.[13] Their leaders were principally of Canadian or American origin but they themselves came from England and Ireland, as well as Upper Canada.[14] Their reactions on this account, however, were not always predictable. At the Conference of 1840 Wesleyans such as Scott and Playter sided with the Canadians; others such as Case and Evans joined the Wesleyans. Their educational attainments were similarly diverse. Some, such as Alexander McNab and James Spencer, were graduates of Cazenovia Seminary or Upper Canada Academy; there were others, such as Principal Hurlburt of the Academy, who had university degrees. Perhaps a declining number of them had limitations similar to those of the aging veteran George Ferguson. These were men from humble homes and of modest literary capacity, whose fundamental impulse was religious. But the very diversity of their backgrounds and their experience of denominational controversy made them less interested than their predecessors in other than the needs of the Methodist Church as a corporate body.

Societies to which circuit preachers ministered were scattered among sixty-five circuits.[15] Their members were largely rural dwellers, a distinction emphasized by the loss of many urban Methodists to the Wesleyans.[16] They were moved by the evangelical spirit and were absorbed in revivals, and in camp and class meetings. Still there was a certain shift of interest, especially in urban societies, made obvious by the construction of bigger and better churches.[17] Methodism remained the religion taught in schoolroom and barn but these kinds of environment were becoming unsatisfactory. For the average Methodist, as for the itinerant, the institution was perhaps beginning to mean more than the faith itself. It might become harder to make Methodists see the social implications of their belief.

External conditions were equally challenging. On October 28, 1840, while the special conference was still in session, the dissident Wesleyan missionaries met in a district meeting with Stinson and Richey as chairman and secretary respectively.[18] They stationed themselves in accordance with decisions of the British Conference and recommended that the war be carried into the enemy camp in Hamilton and London.[19] This action raised awkward questions for the Canada Conference. Ministers who had been lost could be replaced, but the funds that had maintained the expanding mission field were now sadly depleted. Unless the missionary spirit were aroused the Methodist advance would recede. But in the long run the Wesleyan stand raised the more difficult issue of competition versus reunion. Competition was not likely to promote either the spiritual or social welfare of the societies. Yet if reunion were sought, could it be effected without humiliating concessions? The Wesleyan secession proved to be one of the most distracting problems of the Canadian Methodists, until it was ended by reunion in 1847.

Schism in the body ecclesiastic was accompanied by important changes in the body politic. In the Sydenham administration Upper Canada at last had a government that met the standards so long proclaimed in the *Guardian,* an administration that seemed to heed public opinion and sought to treat all sectors of the population equitably. The forces of privilege had felt the breath of what was to them a powerful and evil wind. Above all, the question of church-state relations had been resolved, after a fashion. The Clergy Reserves Bill, finally passed by the imperial parliament, had left the Churches of England and Scotland in a special position, but their exclusive claims were rejected.[20] Although this settlement might be unjust, the conditions of revision were altered by Lord Sydenham's success in securing the union of the provinces.[21] Henceforth the presence of the French representatives would greatly affect any effort to make adjustments.

The winter and spring of 1840-1841 were marked by a strenuous attempt to revive the morale and missionary spirit of the Canadian

Societies. Two teams of missionaries were despatched—Egerton Ryerson and Anson Green to the west, John Ryerson and Peter Jones to the east. During the winter Green travelled thirteen hundred miles on horseback, in carriages and sleighs to participate in sixty missionary gatherings.[22] Ryerson and he were cordially received everywhere, not only by Methodists but by prominent people in other communions.[23] In Toronto and London Green noted that they obtained £1,300 in cash and subscriptions, "a much larger amount than we ever received before on this ground; and yet we pledged ourselves to no particular course, nor to any political party."[24] Similar news came from eastern districts of the province.

The constructive efforts of the missioners were matched by a vigorous anti-Wesleyan campaign in the *Guardian*. Its high point was the publication of two letters from George Playter entitled "A Voice From Canada" and "A Second Voice From Canada." He pleaded with the Wesleyans to stop their schismatic endeavours because they were mean, wasteful of men and money, and not of a missionary character. "The English Conference is the rich man having 'exceeding many flocks and herds.' The Canada Conference is the poor man having 'nothing save one little ewe lamb which he had brought and nourished up.' Now the rich man is labouring to take away the poor man's little ewe lamb." Playter insisted that the Wesleyans had no monopoly on Britishness or on loyalty and that no real differences between the two bodies existed with respect to government grants, or in the quality of their newspapers. Dissolution of the union was illegal and would bring an accumulation of evils.[25] One of these was indicated in the *Guardian's* earlier comment on Ephraim Evans' work in Hamilton: "He must be told his work is an abomination, his use of the name of the Head of the Church a desecration, and the prayers put up to God from a schismatic heart are, in his own language, a stench in his nostrils."[26]

In spite of such vigorous opposition in the pulpit, on the platform, and in the press, the Wesleyans went their way, fortified by the Missionary Society and the conviction that thousands of Canadians were eager for their ministrations. Stinson still believed that the best men in the Canada Conference would desert it and that the Ryersons would go to the United States. He predicted that "British North America will be favoured with a system of Methodism upon which our Fathers can look with satisfaction and delight . . . and which will form one of the strongest links in that chain which binds this colony to the Parent State."[27] This prediction was not to be fulfilled but Stinson's judgment was not entirely at fault. It was possible that many of the recent immigrants might want to return to the jurisdiction of the Wesleyan Conference or that they might be led to believe that the Canadian Methodists were politically dangerous. In urban communities some might prefer the rather more decorous ideas and behaviour of such men as Richey. Everywhere, too, much might be accomplished by exploiting local prejudices against leading members of the Canadian body. That in June, 1841, the Canada Western District had a membership of 1,627 was considered an indication of the effectiveness of these inducements.[28]

In the midst of the conflict, voices on both sides were occasionally raised in behalf of accommodation between the two bodies. It was always Stinson's intention to fight back only when necessary, and Slight and Evans professed to be unhappy at the prospect of collision.[29] Matthew Richey alone insisted that no compromise be made, for the Ryersons would use any agreement to "cramp and neutralize our energies." The Wesleyans, he felt, were in a magnificent position, and one that could only be maintained if the Ryersons were completely disregarded.[30] Then, in an obvious bid for authority, he insinuated that Stinson's "truckling" to the Canadians had forfeited the respect and confidence of the friends of Wesleyan Methodism in Canada.[31]

Although it could hardly be called "truckling," Stinson did more than deprecate the schism. He suggested to Alder that reunion might be possible on the basis of a wholesale apology by Ryerson and the admission of Canadian preachers to the Wesleyan Conference. "I think I hear you say—Tush Stinson! What are you raving about."[32] In any event he had two meetings with John Ryerson in which he emphasized that "it would be a noble object to get the whole of Methodism in the British Empire *really under the control of the British Conference & one with it in spirit & in interest*," for this alone would save Canada from ruin.[33]

Richey, however, believed that no progress was possible unless the Canadians publicly retracted their slanderous statements and placed themselves and their property entirely under the jurisdiction of the British Conference, a prospect as unlikely as a moderation in the Canadian winter.[34] But in later conversations John Ryerson was said to have offered major concessions. "*He was willing and desirous*," according to Stinson, "*for the entire work in this Province to become missionary—& that if the British Conference would make it so—they would place all their church property—their chapels—their Academy—their Book Room . . . under the control of the British Conference—& make everything theirs—and that Egerton would go and join the New York Conference.*" Richey and Stinson agreed that this was a feasible arrangement; it would ensure continuance of the grant and acquisition of a share of the reserves. Stinson concluded: "I really think after all there is something honourable & good about [John Ryerson]."[35]

When the Canada Conference met at Toronto in June, 1841, its temper was indicated by the election of the eminently Canadian William Ryerson as president, with Anson Green as secretary.[36] The preachers were cheered by the addition of six hundred members and ten candidates for the itinerant ranks, but they were equally aware of disquieting factors.[37] Bitterness was sharp in many places, the grant question was still unsettled, and the reserves bill had not become operative. Many may have secretly sympathized with John Ryerson's willingness to make great sacrifices for an arrangement with the Wesleyans; however, the forces of appeasement did not prevail.[38]

The Conference accepted a series of resolutions asserting that "there is no sufficient or justifiable ground of hostility, division or disunion between the English and Canada conferences: that for the honour of christianity and the character of Methodism, a speedy end should be put to these unnatural scenes of schism and contention."[39] The Conference was willing "to submit the matters at issue . . . to the decision of any tribunal which may be equally selected by committees" of the two conferences.[40]

An equally reasonable position was adopted concerning the reserves. The preachers were "deeply aggrieved that unmerited injustice [had] been done to the Wesleyan Methodist Church in Canada . . . by the unequal and unjust provisions of [the Reserves Act]." Nevertheless, they recommended "an abstinence from any re-agitation of the question. We submit to it as a law, for conscience sake, whilst our representatives properly remonstrated against it as a bill."[41] The Societies were urged instead "not only [to] preserve the unity but promote the efficiency of the body. 'Adorn the doctrine of God our Saviour in all things.' Still 'be subject to principalities and powers' and 'pray for kings and for all that are in authority'. . . . Let us be faithful to God and to one another and what can harm us?"[42]

Six years passed before the conciliatory temper of the Canada Conference was reciprocated by the Wesleyan Conference. In the interval certain important developments occurred which led both sides seriously to reconsider their positions. If government support were forthcoming and if they secured a large number of adherents, the Wesleyans were prepared to continue their operations. If they found that their position was deteriorating and if they found the Wesleyans in a reasonable mood, the Canadians were prepared to sacrifice much. The partial fulfilment of the expectations of each side had produced by 1847 a climate favourable to negotiation.

One of the features which distinguished Canadian from English Methodism was the higher cost of maintaining the latter. This disparity arose from the English missionary's assumption that he should have an assured stipend, the necessity of maintaining Indian missions, and the unfavourable conditions under which the missionaries worked in the older settlements.[43] Consequently government support was important to the Wesleyans, while their conviction that they ought to receive such support was fortified by the argument that they were doing a real service to the government.[44] But this was an extremely thorny problem.

Despite the unsettled state of the question, Governor Arthur paid Stinson the grant for 1840, whereupon both Alder and Ryerson pressed for its continued payment to their respective organizations.[45] Sydenham, who cared not "a fig for Mr. Alder and the English Conference," did not resolve the issue before his untimely death.[46] As his departure coincided with the formation of the Peel ministry, the chances of the Wesleyans seemed greatly improved. They immediately laid siege to the Colonial Office and to Sir Charles Bagot, who succeeded Sydenham in October, 1841.[47]

In the usual lengthy letter to Stanley, the new Colonial Secretary, Alder emphasized that Sydenham's attitude was contrary to the wishes of the Wesleyan Connexion and of all conservative people in Canada West.[48] Subsequently, in February, 1842, Stinson, Evans and Richey took up the matter with the Governor General, on which occasion his diplomatic talents were fully revealed. When he informed his visitors that his opinion had already been sent home, Richey assured him that, if the decision were unfavourable, no opposition would be forthcoming, for "loyalty with us ... is ... an integral and essential part of religion." The conversation then turned to the subject of reunion, giving Richey an opportunity to expose Ryerson's preposterous claims. Bagot appeared to agree with these strictures, remarking incidentally that he was related to Wesley. His callers departed in a cheerful frame of mind.[49]

The hopes of both parties, however, were soon dashed. In December, 1842, the Colonial Office informed them that the law officers reported that "neither Society is exclusively entitled to the Grant and that the payment of it should not at all be made," but if the Societies "should be re-united the difficulty which has arisen would reach the most convenient and effectual close."[50]

This negative answer had been anticipated by the Wesleyans and probably by the Canada Conference.[51] The imperial government's policy seemed to favour the elimination of differences, but neither side was likely to give way on financial grounds alone.[52] Each party was optimistic about its prospects for gaining adherents. The

Canada Conference of 1842, for example, received ten preachers on trial and was delighted to find that 2,461 new members had been added during the year.[53] Replying to the English Conference's union resolutions of 1841, the Conference insisted that "the schisms and divisions which the Agents of the London Wesleyan Committee have been, and are still making in our societies and congregations in Upper Canada, are . . . causeless, unmethodistic and unjustifiable."[54] Nevertheless, the Conference again proposed to submit points of difference "to the decision of any disinterested tribunal."[55]

The Missionary Committee's attitude toward such overtures was determined by the advice of its Canadian agents, who sent optimistic reports. One missionary admitted that the political sympathies of the Canada Conference made it in some respects more adaptable to Canadian circumstances, but British Wesleyanism was more acceptable to the loyal and respectable classes. Many people, he claimed, were disgusted with Ryerson's "devious, inconsistent and unchristian course."[56] Ephraim Evans wrote in the same vein, emphasizing that his circuit swarmed with Wesleyan sympathizers and that many other areas had potential Wesleyans. Four chapels had been built since 1840 and several others were under construction. Evans hoped that any suggestions made by Ryerson would be disregarded, for "you know his restless, intriguing, mischievous temperament."[57]

Stinson regarded the question more dispassionately. He liked the Canadian arbitration proposal. Roman Catholic power in Canada was "fearful" and the Church of England was becoming more exclusive: "If they could sweep us all out of the province they would do it with a good will."[58] Alder thereupon wrote unofficially to Green and John Ryerson but left no doubt that the conditions of reunion were the removal of Egerton Ryerson and the muzzling of the *Guardian*.[59]

The Canada Conference elected John Ryerson president at its 1843 session.[60] Later in the year the Victoria College Board again considered the conflict with the Wesleyans. "An unanimous desire [was] expressed that some arrangement might take place by which the painful collision between the Connexions should be terminated." To this end the Board proposed the establishment of a British North American Conference under the general supervision of the British Conference, or the withdrawal of the Wesleyan missionaries with the exception of those stationed in Kingston and Toronto. Ryerson of course preferred the first alternative which he felt was "Methodistic & honourable." Writing to Stinson, he pleaded for at least an informal reply to be used in private negotiations among the Canadian ministers.[61]

That the Canadian leaders were sincere in making this proposal is beyond question, but their motives were not precisely outlined. Clearly Ryerson himself and Anson Green were not as antagonistic to the Wesleyans as were Ryerson's brothers and colleagues. Why, they argued, should the growth of Methodism be impeded by controversy, now that many of the points of difference between the two Methodist bodies had become less significant? Egerton had apologized and could be made to humiliate himself further. The *Guardian* was no longer a political journal; the church and education questions soon would be settled.[62] No time should be wasted in taking advantage of these favourable conditions.

Although the Canada Conference was making progress, Ryerson and his associates realized that time was not on their side. As the origins of the conflict with the Wesleyans faded into the past its continuance was likely to drive away possible adherents. There was always a chance, too, that the voices of tolerance and charity might make themselves heard. In any event new perils were arising. The Church of England was already beginning to reflect the spirit of the Tractarian movement, and with this its self-righteousness increased.[63] At the other extreme, Millerism was gaining converts, especially in the Toronto area.[64] The *Guardian's* concern for the old Methodist ways indicated that its editor felt that the Methodist cause was slipping spiritually.[65] Confronted with these manifest difficulties at a time when the Committee was again thinking in federal terms, the Canadian Conference decided to seek a rapprochement with it.

Aware of the Committee's plans and realizing that some overture might come from the Canadians, the Canada Western District had already stated its views. The missionaries admitted that intolerance was as "rancorous and rampant" in Canada West as it was in England, but they were determined to maintain their "authority as ministers of Christ," and their "Constitutional privileges as *British Christians.*" They deprecated "any measure which would involve *even the least* approximation of the Districts of British North America towards their *independence* of the British Conference."[66]

As the awful prospect of agreement between the Committee and the Canada Conference loomed closer Richey and his brethren spoke in stinging terms. In a characteristic tirade Richey wrote:

I confess I am amazed that our Body after the painful experience they have repeatedly had of the faithless character of the leading men of the Canada Conference and of their disguised or avowed radical hostility to British influence both ecclesiastical and political should meditate any species of arrangement with [them].

He would rather join the Church of England than associate with men "who . . . sigh for the day when the *Union Jack* should cease to float over this land and every particle of the influence of the British Conference be annihilated."[67]

Deprived of Stinson's steadying influence, the missionaries in special session at Hamilton reflected Richey's prejudices. They felt bound to put their brethren on guard against measures that would "operate most disastrously upon the interests of that form of scriptural christianity" that they were disseminating in Canada West. In their view the Canada Conference had perpetuated false impressions. If the *Guardian* were less bitter, this was part of an "insidious plan" of deception. The political crisis raised "the collateral claims of patriotism and christian loyalty."[68] A noble governor was

Now anxiously engaged in a contest for the maintenance of principles rightly deemed by him as absolutely essential to the preservation of the Province to the British Crown. . . . In all ordinary cases of political party disputes we would stand aloof. . . . But we cannot regard any measure by which the influence of British Wesleyanism in the Province would be shorn of its strength or its universal diffusion be prevented otherwise than as a national calamity, inevitably involving the Executive Government . . . in inextricable embarrassment and hastening onward such a triumph of democracy, as by the blessing of God on the extension of the Scriptural influence of our body may be for ages, perhaps for ever averted."[69]

"We are eminently set," Richey added later, "for the defence of the Gospel against Popery and Puseyism and for the maintenance . . . of the British Constitution in this agitated . . . colony."[70]

At the very moment when the missionaries were airing their views a conciliatory letter from the Missionary Committee was on its way. While the British brethren still felt the Canadians were in error, they were not "less sensible of the evils which spring from divisions amongst Christians, especially those who professedly maintain common views of Christian truth and order. . . ."[71] The English leaders were conscious of the Church's hostility and realized that they could be accused of mixing politics with religion.[72] Thus the Canadians were offered a settlement, but not the federal one they preferred. Rather, "will Mr. Ryerson and his Friends place themselves under the exclusive direction of the British Conference? What is to prevent them from doing so and thus in very deed become one with us?"[73] Alder nevertheless added that "the present state of separation with all its disadvantages is to be preferred to a formal, cold, and heartless union. . . . We can neither surrender nor compromise any great Christian and Wesleyan principle. We must, however, not allow merely political principles and predilections to assume that character in our estimation, which, however important, are very secondary and subordinate to the office of our mission."[74]

Although the Secretaries were willing to extend a hand to the Canada Conference, they were not prepared to concede the vital point, the right of the latter to manage its own affairs. For its part the Canada Conference still believed that it could drive the Wesleyans to the wall. Until each side was prepared to settle for rather less than it wanted, offers to negotiate were bound to be unproductive.

2

While this complex ecclesiastical battle was in progress Canada West was not standing still. The early eighteen-forties witnessed the emergence of critical political and educational conflicts within the framework established by the Sydenham régime. The Canadian Methodists' response to the challenge posed by this new situation was conditioned by their preoccupation with denominational warfare, and also by the compromises that had already been made to maintain the semblance of Methodist unity.

For most Upper Canadians the two great issues of this period were the achievement of responsible government and the establishment of an acceptable system of primary and higher education.[75] In the first of these the Methodist Conference was reluctantly involved, in the second it played an active and presumably influential part.

When Lord Sydenham died unexpectedly in September, 1841, the *Guardian* printed Ryerson's eulogy. The Governor General "found a country divided; he left it united; ... he found it mantled with despair, he left it blooming with hope.... His Lordship ... solved the difficult problem, that a people may be colonists and yet be free." All this Sydenham accomplished in the face of most formidable obstacles—the "hitherto defective theory and worse than defective system of Colonial Government ... a system which was despotic from its weakness, and arbitrary from its pretences to representation," and "worst of all, the conflicting claims of ecclesiastical pretensions." Many would say, Ryerson concluded, "in the death of this ... distinguished Governor—I have lost a Friend."[76]

Ryerson indeed had lost a would-be benefactor whose ideas of public policy were the closest to his own of any governor he had known.[77] The Methodist community, likewise, had supported Sydenham because he had dealt fairly with the religious issue and had governed in that impartial, responsible way that had long been advocated by the *Guardian*. Great as the Governor General's achievement was, however, it was evident before his death that he had merely laid the foundations for a new phase in the struggle for self-government, a development in which his successor Sir Charles Bagot found himself entangled.

In these circumstances the Methodist Connexion could do something either to help or hinder the advocates of further constitutional and political change. Since the Methodist ranks probably included a considerable number of reform sympathizers, the church at large might well have responded to the vigorous espousal of the emerging Reform Party. But repeated pledges had been given that party politics would not be mentioned in the *Guardian;* any serious breach in the rule would, it was felt, endanger the Canadian Methodist cause. The Conference therefore stood out against the identification of Methodism with any political organization; instead, it reminded its adherents of the need to achieve Christian perfection.

Even so the Conference could not entirely avoid political involvement, and it could not hide the political sympathies of some of its members. The *Guardian* printed with approval Ryerson's estimate of Bagot as a man noted for his impartiality, and his unwillingness to introduce English problems into Canada.[78] Upon Bagot's untimely death it paid tribute to him as a Christian gentleman who promoted all Wesleyan Methodist institutions.[79] Nothing was said, however, about the late Governor's assiduous and skilful efforts to rule realistically, or of the great crisis of 1843 in which Sir Charles Metcalfe was so deeply involved.

The Baldwin-Lafontaine ministry, constructed with such care by Bagot, fell by its own hand in November, 1843. It was the end of a promising experiment in responsible government, but more than the government's opponents rejoiced at its termination.[80] Concerning the point at issue, the Governor's refusal to accept the advice of his ministers on certain patronage questions, the initial reaction of John Ryerson, Anson Green and probably Egerton as well was opposed to the Governor General and favourable toward the ministers. Green wrote: "The President [John] thinks with you that the *Council* are on the safe side of the question. . . . I think they should have waited until His Excellency *refused to ask their advice*. . . . In my opinion both parties have acted indiscretely and awkwardly."[81]

To Egerton the crisis took on a different character.[82] A disciple of Sydenham rather than Durham, one who believed that colonial government needed a change in outlook rather than in structure, a man devoted to the imperial connexion and with great respect for the Crown, Ryerson was naturally drawn to the Governor's side. Moreover, when he accepted Metcalfe's offer of the superintendency of education in Canada West he felt bound to demonstrate that "His Excellency is entitled to the verdict of the country on every count of the indictment got up against him."[83] The vindication took the form of a series of letters first printed in the *British Colonist*, a moderate Toronto tory newspaper.[84]

Ryerson contended that the late reform ministers had acted unconstitutionally in their dealings with the Governor General, and that they had really been more concerned with partisanship than responsible government. In organizing and promoting the Reform Association of Canada, they might lead the province into a worse situation than 1837.[85] When it became clear that his argument was having some effect, the Association put up R. B. Sullivan, who as "Legion" controverted Ryerson's views in the pages of an old enemy, the Toronto *Examiner*.[86] From these two points the storm of controversy widened to create a climate of opinion within Canada West that was reminiscent of the inglorious days of 1836 and 1837.[87]

When the general election began in October, 1844, there was much uncertainty about the outcome. As in 1836, however, the result was a bitter defeat for the Reform Party. Out of forty-two members for Canada West, only eight to twelve reformers were returned, in contrast to the strong reform lead in Canada East.[88] What had happened? Had the Methodists listened sheepishly to the voice of Ryerson and had they turned the tide, as they were said to have turned it in 1836 under somewhat similar conditions?

A simple answer to this query would be as misleading and inaccurate as in the case of the 1836 election. Certainly, the Methodists had reason to dislike the old reform government, composed of men such as Hincks, who in 1840 had attacked its members as turncoats, and Sullivan, the erstwhile servant of the Arthur régime. The educational legislation sponsored by Baldwin was not entirely attractive either.

When the Conference met in 1844 it was faced with a strong protest from the Toronto circuit about Ryerson's activities, evidence of concern felt by many preachers and laymen.[89] The Conference reacted ambiguously, electing reform sympathizers Richard Jones and Henry Wilkinson as president and secretary respectively. To meet the Toronto protest the preachers resolved, apparently at Ryerson's suggestion, that

While we disclaim all intention of controlling the political sentiments of any of our ministers, so long as those sentiments do not contravene the Discipline of the Church nor contradict the Word of God,—we will not as a Body be responsible for the political doctrines of any member or members of our Conference or Church or party in our Country, but leave our people perfectly free to exercise their own judgments in political and civil affairs.[90]

In its address to the Societies the Conference urged its people to devote themselves to the "two-fold work of promoting growth of grace in the members of the church and the conversion of souls to it." They were to

Guard against the indulgence of a secular party spirit and duly respect the constituted authorities and established laws of the land. With secular parties or politics we have nothing to do. . . . In secular affairs as well as in the more important affairs of religion, Christians should agree to differ, where they cannot think alike; should cherish a spirit of kindness, moderation and liberality; . . . and obey them that rule over us . . . that we may lead a quiet and peaceable life in all godliness and honesty.[91]

In effect the Conference sought a neutral position, a tactic that reflected a natural concern for the spiritual task of Methodism and also, one may suppose, a delicate balance of political interests within the church. Certainly it was not prepared to provide the kind of support for the existing régime that it gave in 1836.

A similar combination of neutrality and covert leaning toward the reform side was evident in the *Guardian* during the Metcalfe controversy. One of Ryerson's confidants alleged that in the spring of 1844 Jonathan Scott was active on the reform side, but if so, this was not reflected in the *Guardian*.[92] At the Conference Scott was replaced by George Playter, who hastened to explain the political resolutions. In his view Scott was not relieved because he had excluded politics from the paper; the Conference did not wish to inhibit public political discussion. Rather, its "intention was to dry up the erroneous belief that the Conference was a party or would be a party in the [Metcalfe] case."[93] No mention of Ryerson was made in the *Guardian*.

Nevertheless, Playter provided some strong hints about his own position and possibly about the views of many Methodists. Frequent references were made to Baldwin's campaign. When the *Guardian's* subscribers surreptitiously received copies of the *British Colonist* containing Ryerson's last Metcalfe letter, the editor's response was irate.[94] He thought this crude device was designed to suggest that the Methodists were really unsympathetic to the late government. But Playter said this was not so: "If others have reasons for stirring up the minds of the people against the late councillors, the *Christian Guardian* has none." The Methodists had received many favours from the former government and had criticized it only when it acted against its own principles. Moreover,

The Methodist people have not to look to the side arrayed against the late Council for countenance, much less friendship. . . . The Methodists and all other non-Episcopalian bodies have no favour to expect but everything to fear from *that* intolerant party of which 'John Bishop of Toronto' is the head. . . . Woe be to Canada, if the misrule prior to the Union of the Provinces should ever return.[95]

At the same time, "the paper is not and will not be a party political paper. . . . The religious and moral interests of the community are our chief objects."[96] As for the Methodists:

We hope to find [them] no longer disregarding their own civil rights and privileges; for they may be well assured that if Methodists do not attend to their own interests in the Province neither men in office nor any others will perform for them what they should and must do for themselves. Whilst we have no wish to exalt the Methodists politically above, we have certainly no desire to see them below their fellow-subjects and fellow-christians in the Province of Canada.[97]

All Christians, Playter wrote later, should vote responsibly and seek to elevate men of character and religious principle: "Only let your politics be as it becometh the Gospel of Christ."[98] Once more there is a strong suggestion of sympathy for the reformers, coupled with a characteristic plea that Methodists not be swayed by partisan considerations.

John Carroll, in close touch with Methodist opinion, believed that by Ryerson's course "a large proportion of the people of the Province and a vast many members of the Church were highly offended." He was certain that "this circumstance gave a check to the ingathering into the Societies which was going on . . . a proof by the way, that however defensible as a natural right, interference with political questions by ministers and Churches is highly impolitic and productive of embarrassment."[99] Similarly, George Ferguson wrote: "I am sorry to see so many of our people running into low radicalism, and I am afraid the Methodist Ministry is two deep in the charge (quite a number in our beloved Conference); I have know doubt but the Governor will loose the election in Canada West."[100]

From the Wesleyans significant evidence was forthcoming. At their special February session in 1844 the Wesleyan missionaries promised not to meddle with political parties. But they averred that "we should be criminally deficient in an important branch of practical religion did we not in such a crisis recognize it as a part of our duty, as Ministers, to enforce by precept and example, a cheerful obedience to lawful authority." For them it was a matter of rejoicing that "our members and hearers with scarcely an individual exception are arranged on the side of constitutional maintenance of the Royal prerogative."[101]

In contrast, so they alleged, the Canadian Methodists "with equal unanimity [and] true to the principles in which they have been assiduously trained are found sustaining those political leaders whose theories would reduce [Metcalfe's] authority to a nullity." In by-elections at Belleville and London they had been conspicuous in opposition to the tory candidates.[102] To these words, written before Ryerson's intervention on the tory side, Richey added after the election: "Truth, loyalty and justice have triumphed over misrepresentation, faction and republican selfishness! Canada is not to be severed from the greatest Empire on which the Sun ever looked in his ample circuit." In his view this "auspicious" triumph owed nothing to Ryerson:

Through the influence of a delusion which time will soon dissipate [it] ... will doubtless be attributed in no small degree to the shield thrown over his Excellency by the compassionate Dr. Ryerson. ... As a body the Canadian Methodists remain however as *they were,* opposed to His Excellency and exasperated by Mr. Ryerson's advocacy of His cause, little knowing the depths of his artifice.[103]

There is good reason to believe that the Methodist vote was not tossed wholesale to the tories in the election of 1844. Doubtless some Methodists were already of that persuasion, and it would be strange if some were not induced by Ryerson's prestige and his argument to vote for conservative candidates. In some constituencies these, perhaps in combination with Wesleyan voters, may have been sufficient to produce a conservative verdict.[104] It would be equally plausible, though, to argue that dissension among reform supporters, the confused situation between the Governor and his opponents, and the powerful effect of the loyalty cry could together account for the reform débâcle in 1844.

In any event, during these years of independence one does not get a clear picture of the political posture of the Canadian Methodists. In contrast to the conservative Wesleyans, the Canadians appear to have been broadly reformist in sympathy, although their public position was largely non-committal.[105] On the subject of education, however, the Methodist outlook emerges much more definitely. Here their principles eventually would lead them into as difficult a course as the great political controversy of 1844.

3

Although the subject had been examined at length and considerable legislation had been passed, in 1840 Canada West did not have an effective, comprehensive system of primary education. The university question was still open, too, with the Anglicans clinging to the modified King's College charter and other denominations looking on suspiciously. In both areas of education the eighteen-forties would bring substantial adjustments.

During its first session the united legislature, perhaps debilitated by the summer heat of Kingston, passed an act to provide a general system of elementary education for the province. The bill stipulated that no specific type of religious instruction would be given, but separate schools might be established.[106]

Passage of this act was greeted sympathetically by the *Christian Guardian*. The editor hoped that the need for competent, well paid teachers would be kept in the foreground. They should be selected on tolerant, liberal lines, excluding only those professing atheism or deism. Furthermore: "The instructions given should be founded on a moral and religious basis. . . . Knowledge without Religion is vain; and there is no true 'wisdom' till we begin to 'fear' the Lord."[107] Obviously, at this stage the *Guardian* had little interest in separate schools for Protestants or Catholics, feeling rather that the proper religious atmosphere might be secured by intelligent screening of the teachers themselves.

The Act of 1841, having been passed for the whole province of Canada, soon proved useless, but it was not until 1846 that a satisfactory educational bill was drafted by Egerton Ryerson, the new Superintendent of Education for Canada West.[108] His appointment elicited from the *Guardian* a statement of principle that foreshadowed its later remarks about elementary schools. In 1844, when the rumour of his appointment was greeted with vituperative dismay by the *Church*, the *Guardian* felt bound to combat this "proscriptive" attitude. The Methodists stood firmly for civil and religious liberty, and regarded "the policy announced by the *Church* with unmitigated abhorrence." Other churches had done more for the country than the Church of England. Why then should it have a monopoly of the places to be filled by government?[109] When the government finally appointed Ryerson, the *Guardian* reminded Canada West that for years the Methodists had laboured to establish civil and religious equality and that this was one of the first occasions on which the principle had been upheld: "We ardently desire that the proscription on account of religious belief may no longer have place in the Province."[110]

When the Act of 1846, the first fruit of Ryerson's work, appeared it was printed in its entirety in the *Guardian* as a testimony to Methodist approval of its principles.[111] In his preliminary report Ryerson had said education was

That instruction and discipline which qualify and dispose the subjects of it for their appropriate duties and employments of life, as Christians, as persons of business and also as members of the civil community in which they live. The basis of an Educational structure adapted to this end should be as broad as the population of the country ... the whole based upon the principles of Christianity, and uniting the combined influence and support of the Government and the people. The branches of knowledge which it is essential that all should understand, should be provided for all, and taught to all; should be brought within the reach of the most needy, and forced upon the attention of the most careless.[112]

Turning to religious instruction Ryerson had insisted that he did not want "sectarianism in any form but, the general system of truth and morals taught in the Holy Scriptures. ... To inculcate the peculiarities of a Sect, and to teach the fundamental principles of Religion and Morality are equally different." The latter could be taught without infringing the rights of any student. He had continued:

In these remarks I mean no objection to schools in connection with a particular Religious Community. ... I refer ... to a kind of teaching ... which unchristianizes four-fifths, if not nine-tenths of Christiandom, —a teaching which substitutes the form for the reality ... the symbol for the substance ... the dogma for the doctrine—the passion for Sect, for the love of God and our neighbours: —a teaching which as history can attest, is productive of ecclesiastical corruptions, superstition, infidelity, social disputes and civil contentions and is inimical alike to good government and public tranquillity.[113]

It is evident in the bill that Ryerson thought these results would follow if extensive provision were made for dissent. As in earlier legislation provision was simply made for a Protestant school where the majority teacher was a Roman Catholic and a Catholic where the majority teacher was a Protestant. Ryerson regarded the separate school as an exceptional device to be used very sparingly in meeting special needs. He had no desire at any time to encourage denominational schools as such.[114] Likewise, Canadian Methodists in the main were unsympathetic to those who wanted schools under ecclesiastical control.

The more pressing Methodist concern was not the common schools but the provincial system of higher education. Despite the amendment of the King's College charter in 1837, its supporters continued to regard it as the exclusive preserve of the Church of England and they were most reluctant to surrender any portion of the endowment. When the College finally opened in June, 1843, Bishop Strachan was still president. The major addresses were given by the Bishop, Chief Justice Robinson and Mr. Justice Hagerman. They left no doubt that King's would continue to be an Anglican college, albeit open to students and staff from other churches.[115]

Spurred by Anglican obstinacy, Canada West had acquired two other Protestant colleges. Queen's College in Kingston was opened in March, 1842, under the auspices of the Church of Scotland, as a training school for Presbyterian clergy. Queen's charter was more exclusive than the amended charter of King's College in that its trustees had to be either clergy or laity of the Church of Scotland, and its staff had to subscribe to the Westminster Confession.[116] In contrast, the Methodists opened the University of Victoria College in June, 1842. Its charter was an amended version of the liberal document under which Upper Canada Academy had been constituted in 1836.[117] Its founders wished to impose no tests on trustees, staff or students, their design being to provide a liberal education firmly grounded on Christian principles for all who desired it, and to raise the educational level of the Methodist ministry.[118]

These three institutions, and to a lesser extent Regiopolis, the Roman Catholic college, were at the centre of the educational controversy of the eighteen-forties. Their directors were in agreement on the necessity of basing their teaching on Christian foundations but they believed that this could best be done under denominational auspices. All of them were prepared to accept state assistance. On the other hand some believed that it was desirable to establish a secular university system, whereas others felt the state should support secular institutions alone. There was general insistence that King's College must either be deprived of its substantial endowment or transformed into a real provincial university.

Largely at the instigation of Queen's College, the Baldwin administration, in October of 1843, introduced a university bill that envisaged creation of the University of Toronto, with all the university functions of the existing colleges, especially the right to examine and to confer degrees, except in divinity. Control of the university was to be vested in a large board, principally composed of non-university personnel. All the colleges were to be included in the university and were to be represented on the Caput, or executive council. The university was to acquire the total endowment and for the present was to pay annual grants of £500 to Queen's, Victoria and Regiopolis. It was to be a secular institution, but the colleges were to retain such tests as they had already established.[119]

The government's proposal was considered by the Victoria College Board at meetings on October 24 and 25, 1843. In a series of resolutions drafted by Egerton Ryerson the Board expressed qualified approval.[120] To begin with the bill provided "effectively against the abuses which have been practised under the general and indefinite provisions of the Amended Charter of King's College and for the future management of the University upon principles of justice and fairness to all parties." At the same time, however, "from circumstances peculiar to ourselves, [it] deprives us of important rights and privileges that we now enjoy, without conferring upon us any corresponding advantages." Consequently the Board appealed to the government "to grant us such assistance as our peculiar circumstances suggest." Objection was also made to the extensive authority of the University Convocation over the colleges, to the vague recognition of Christian doctrine in the proposed charter, to the suggestion that the proper function of the colleges was the teaching of divinity, and to the inadequate financial provisions of the proposed legislation.[121]

The Board's reasoning was outlined by Ryerson in a letter to the *Guardian*. For some time, he emphasized, the university question had been discussed but Victoria had not participated, not because its directors had no opinion on the matter but because it stood to lose by the plan proposed to meet existing abuses. Its Board would have liked to see Victoria omitted from the new bill, but as this would have undermined its effectiveness it had "consented to resign certain . . . rights and privileges for the accomplishment of general objects so comprehensive and important," especially, as John Ryerson put it, the effectual destruction "of the dominancy of the high church party in matters of education."[122]

When Strachan protested vigorously against the bill, his statements were firmly countered by the *Guardian*. The Bishop's plea was described as "a palpable specimen of Diocesan pride and haughtiness, a tissue of self-evident error, and a dark, hateful Puseyite libel on all the non-Episcopalian churches in Canada." The editor wanted to know why the bill should be described as atheistical when every college would have the right to teach theology. Indeed, the best way to create anti-clerical sentiment was to insist on the validity of one form of religious doctrine! In any case, the editor asked: "Who invested Bishop Strachan with the prerogatives of Chief Judge over the churches of Canada?" The real source of the Church's objections was that in its original form King's College "was to be a massive lever, heaving pusillanimous men by multitudes into The *Church,* or if sturdy non-conformists, heaving them elsewhere," a process that would be inhibited in future. All the abuses that had made King's College "a grand Error" would be eliminated by Baldwin's bill—"a Grand Corrector."[123] The point was driven home by Ryerson in his analysis of W. H. Draper's defence of King's College in the Assembly:

> I argue for no particular University Bill; but I contend, upon the grounds of right and humanity, that Presbyterians, Methodists and all others, ought to participate equally with the Episcopalians in the Educational Advantages and Endowments that have been derived from the sale of Lands . . . set apart . . . for the support of Education in Upper Canada.[124]

Although the Baldwin bill came to nothing because of the ministry's resignation in November, 1843, the controversy attending it illuminated the university question. Apparently the Methodists were prepared to sacrifice a good deal in the interests of amalgamation but they were determined that the Anglican monopoly of the endowment should be broken and that the various groups should be treated equitably by the government. Unfortunately, Strachan's attack on the other denominations obscured their mutual suspicion of the secular implications of Baldwin's proposal. It was likely that, if opportunity offered, the Methodists and others would adopt a somewhat different policy.

In the spring of 1845 this question was taken up again by the new Draper ministry, a body whose head was on amiable terms with the Methodists, and some of whose members were rabid supporters of King's College.[125] Apart from its own disunity the government had to contend with changed circumstances, especially the fact that the disruption of the Church of Scotland had greatly weakened Queen's and had led to the foundation of Knox College, a divinity school designed to function on the voluntary principle.[126] In effect the government had to juggle not only the diverse claims of Anglicans, Presbyterians and Methodists, but also the secessionist Presbyterian argument that state support and denominational control should not be combined. The Methodists, too, were in a weakened position; Victoria, deprived of Ryerson's energetic leadership, had begun to decline.[127] Here was an opportunity for the government to reach a final settlement, but one that could only be utilized if its own inner divisions could be kept within bounds.

Draper's first university bill, introduced on March 4, 1845, provided for the establishment of a University of Upper Canada whose original constituent colleges would be King's, Queen's and Victoria.

Each of the colleges was to surrender its university privileges except in divinity. The endowment was to be vested in the university but the income was to be distributed more liberally than by the earlier bill, whereas the university was to be administered by a Caput, so constituted as to ensure an Anglican majority.[128] In other respects, such as the definition of the respective functions of the colleges and the university, the bill was vague in the extreme. Outwardly it was not an unreasonable measure.

Before the terms of the proposal were generally known the *Guardian* noted that Methodists had not been consulted about the new legislation and thus were not committed to it. They were resolved only to uphold the general principle "that our privileges are not Inferior To Others," but were open to argument as to the means to be used.[129] Subsequently, the editor stressed that no denomination liked the idea of amalgamation, as expressed in Draper's scheme: "To speak the honest truth, we as Methodists have no more desire to unite with other bodies in the education of our youth than other bodies have to unite with us." The proposed arrangement left the Anglicans in a preferred position, yet no bar was raised against extravagant sects: "Considering what man is and what christian sects have been to each other, we shrink from the responsibility of advocating a measure which we are strongly apprehensive of failing."[130]

On the contrary the *Guardian*, for once in agreement with Strachan, favoured division of the endowment since it would facilitate diffusion of university institutions and prevent denominational collisions. Naturally, though, it rejected the Bishop's proposal that the endowment should be divided on the same basis as the clergy reserves. Rather, the editor suggested that each church with more than 10,000 adherents be given one-fifth of the fund, which division would leave two-fifths for the Roman Catholics and the smaller churches.[131] Nevertheless, the *Guardian*, John Ryerson and Anson Green felt that it would be better to accept the general principles of Draper's bill than to prevent its passage altogether.[132]

Opposed by the Church of England and leading members of government and opposition, the Draper bill was dropped after scraping through on the second reading.[133] While the ministry was trying to consolidate its forces the Methodists and reformers sounded discordant notes on the college issue. The *Guardian* bluntly asserted that

Denominational education for colleges is the order of the day in England, and in the United States. It is the order of the day in Canada . . . and yet some persons, —from, we fear, very selfish and sectarian motives, —wish to break up the established order of things, and to substitute some new and untried theory, under the cover of liberality and unsectarianism. . . . The amalgamating, irreligious college would soon become more unpopular than the present one is. Finally, it would become merely a richly endowed school for the people of Toronto.[134]

Holding these views, the Wesleyan Methodists were appalled when early in February, 1846, some of the people of Toronto raised their voices to another tune. At a meeting in the Congregational Chapel clerical representatives of the smaller denominations, along with Methodist, Anglican and Presbyterian laity, urged the transformation of King's College into a secular, provincial university, retaining the whole endowment.[135] In an unfriendly account of the event the *Guardian* insisted that it wished to see all parties fairly treated but would oppose the selfish views of Presbyterians as well as those of Anglicans. "Are the *smaller* and *younger* bodies," the editor asked, "to have their opinion embodied in statutes in opposition to the will and desire of the *oldest* and *largest* churches of the Province?"[136] Two weeks later Egerton Ryerson again emphasized that Victoria had been willing to accept amalgamation in 1843 and that it had waited three years under great financial strain for a settlement of the university issue. Nevertheless, the Methodists would rather have no university than tolerate the godless institution envisaged by the Toronto meeting.[137] They now sought a division of the endowment or permanent financial assistance that would enable Victoria to grow in accordance with its founders' principles.[138]

The Draper legislation was revived in 1846 despite the views of Methodists, Free Churchmen and others, but again it was pushed aside in the Assembly.[139] Before the tories could bring forward a new plan the Methodists were to pass through a great internal crisis, affecting their course in matters political and educational.

4

When the Canada Conference reassessed its position and moved toward union with the Wesleyan Conference in 1846 many Methodists, and especially the "low radical" party in the Conference, must have looked back with concern at the course followed by the Connexion since 1840.[140] The Canadian body had survived but in the process had adopted a neutral political position. In the great battle over the political development of Canada, the Conference and the *Guardian* had taken almost no part; indeed neither support nor criticism had been accorded to Egerton Ryerson when he came to Metcalfe's defence. Moreover, while continuing to pay lip-service to the principle of religious equality the Methodists had acquiesced, albeit reluctantly, in an inequitable settlement of the clergy reserves.

In contrast, the Canadian Methodists had taken a considerable interest in educational disputes of the early eighteen-forties. The *Guardian* at least had strongly supported the establishment of a comprehensive, efficient system of elementary education in which denominational interests would be heeded as little as possible. At the same time the Conference had clarified its position on higher education. Here too its primary concern was to secure equitable treatment for all members of the community, but it also sought a close relationship between religion and university education. Somewhat hesitantly the Methodist leaders had concluded by 1846 that this latter objective could best be attained in denominational colleges supported by the state.

Such were the official attitudes and policies of the Methodist Connexion between 1840 and 1846. The question is—were they a significant factor in the political and social evolution of Canada West? Certainly the virtual silence of the *Guardian* on political issues deprived the province of a distinctive point of view and one that could have been of some value in the stormy days of 1844. Similarly, if the *Guardian* had seriously agitated the clergy reserves question, it would very possibly have been taken up at an earlier date than it was. Above all though, the Methodist Conference's political inaction must have led many Methodists to conclude that there was no real difference between the contending groups, a conclusion that may well have worked to the tories' advantage.

If the direct political influence of the Conference was essentially negative, its educational activities were surely of greater import. Although the Methodists did not initiate action on the university question, their strong adherence to the principle of equality of treatment was not easily disregarded. They showed willingness to sacrifice much in the interest of definitive settlement, but circumstances they could not control prevented any agreement at this juncture. On the other hand, it is perhaps regrettable that the Methodists' suspicion of the secular sympathies of some reformers led them to oppose the stand taken by the voluntarist leaders of the smaller churches in 1846. If the Methodists were committed, as they repeatedly said they were, to principles of civil equality and majority rule, there was a real question as to whether their educational policy was more likely to implement these principles than the policies of voluntarists and reformers. It would have been well for the Methodists to explore the deeper implications of these differences of opinion.

As in earlier periods, the Methodist community counted for something in the life of Canada West. The limited evidence suggests that as a body the Methodists were perhaps becoming more self-centred, but on the whole they continued to be a liberal-minded group. Moreover, as a Connexion struggling with the complexities of ecclesiastical independence, they doubtless contributed a heightened awareness and understanding of the difficulties to the province's search for a viable form of political existence.

REFERENCES TO CHAPTER NINE

1. New Brunswick, for example, was pushed toward responsible government. See W. S. MacNutt "Responsible Government in New Brunswick," *Canadian Historical Review*, XXXIII (1952), 111-128.
2. Egerton and William Ryerson reached Toronto on September 22, 1840. *E.R.*, I, 558. They began to publish their report in the *Guardian* of September 30.
3. J. Carroll, *Case and His Cotemporaries*, IV, 309.
4. *W.R.*, Reel 19, Stinson to Alder, November 2, 1840. Whitehead, who was born in New York State in 1762, warned the Conference of 1832 against taking British gold.
5. Carroll, *op. cit.*, IV, 309. Egerton Ryerson declined election as secretary. *W.R.*, Reel 19, Stinson to Alder, November 2, 1840.
6. *Ibid.*; Carroll, *op. cit.*, IV, 310.
7. *W.R.*, Reel 19, Stinson to Alder, November 2, 1840.
8. *Ibid.* For Egerton's speech, see the *Guardian* for November 4, 1840.
9. *Minutes of Special Conference, 1840*, 249-252.
10. *Ibid.*, 245. Those who withdrew were either very close to English Methodism or had, as Case did, a special interest in Indian missions.
11. *Special Conference Minutes*, 246-248.
12. *Ibid.*, 260.
13. There were 107 preachers stationed by the Conference of 1841; in 1828 there were forty-eight itinerants.
14. Out of a group of sixty-nine preachers, nineteen were Irish, twenty-two English and twenty-eight Canadian. Carroll, *op. cit.*, IV, 319.
15. In 1828 there were thirty-two circuits. *Minutes of Conference, 1828*, 19-20.
16. In 1841, Toronto, London, St. Catharines and Kingston had 1,716 Canadian Methodists out of 17,017. For losses to the Wesleyans, see Carroll, *Case*, IV, 325-326.
17. The *Guardian* refers frequently to matters of this kind.

18. *M.R.*, Reel 4, Canada Western District Minutes, 1840.
19. The Missionary Committee had decided to retain those missions or stations established before union or that had been maintained largely by the Society. These included Toronto, Kingston, Alderville, St. Clair, Goderich, Barrie, Guelph, Warwick and Adelaide, Amherstburg. *M.R.*, Reel 1, Committee Minutes, September 9, 1840. To this list, the District Meeting recommended the addition of Brantford, Cornwall, Stratford, Saugeen, London and Hamilton. *Ibid.*, Reel 4, District Minutes, 1840.
20. For the background of this settlement see J. S. Moir, *Church and State in Canada West, 1841-1867* (Toronto, 1959), 36-38. The bill is printed in the *Revised Statutes of Upper Canada* (Toronto, 1842), II, ch. 78.
21. The Union Act was passed in July, 1840, and proclaimed in February, 1841.
22. A. Green, *The Life and Times of Anson Green*, 243.
23. *C.G.*, December 2, 1840. Among those present were J. H. Dunn, the Baldwins, James Richardson, Jesse Ketchum and J. H. Price.
24. Green, *op. cit.*, 243.
25. *C.G.*, February 10, 1841.
26. *Ibid.*, January 6, 1841.
27. *W.R.*, Reel 19, Stinson to Alder, November 2, 1840.
28. *M.R.*, Reel 4, District Minutes, 1841. Most of the members were in Toronto, Kingston, Hamilton, London and Guelph.
29. *W.R.*, Reel 19, Stinson to Alder, November 24, 1840.
30. *Ibid.*, Richey to Alder, February 3, 1841.
31. *Ibid.*, Richey to Alder, February 20, 1841.
32. *Ibid.*, Stinson to Alder, January 20, 1841.
33. *Ibid.*, April 16, 1841.
34. *Ibid.*, Richey to Alder, April 20, 1841.
35. *Ibid.*, Stinson to Alder, May 3, 1841. For Egerton's mood at this time see *E.R.*, I, 575-577, Ryerson to Bangs, May 10, 1841.
36. *Minutes of Conference, 1841*, 260. According to Stinson, John Ryerson would have been elected, but for the opposition of one of his relatives. *W.R.*, Reel 19, Stinson to Alder, June 16, 1841.
37. *Ibid.*, 261, 266.
38. Again Stinson asserted that the best men in the Conference were with John Ryerson. *W.R.*, Reel 19, Stinson to Alder, June 16, 1841.
39. *Minutes of Conference, 1841*, 295.
40. *Ibid.*, 285.
41. *Ibid.*, 270-271.
42. *Ibid.*, 273.
43. For example, the grant for Canada West in 1841-42 was £2600. *M.R.*, Reel 1, Extract of Minutes of Sub-Committee of Reference, September 22, 1841. In the early years costs were unusually high because congregational contributions were allocated for new buildings.

44. The Society was financially embarrassed during the forties.
45. *W.R.*, Reel 13, Alder to Russell, June 14, 1841; *E.R.*, I, 567-569, E. Ryerson to Sydenham, March 17, 1841.
46. Knaplund, *Letters from Lord Sydenham ... to Russell*, 92. See also *W.R.*, Reel 13, R. V. Smith to Alder, June 23, 1841.
47. Letters were written to Lord Ashley, Arthur, Bagot and Stanley, the new Colonial Secretary.
48. *W.R.*, Reel 13, Alder to Stanley, September 19, 1841 (Copy). See *ibid.*, Bagot to Alder, October 12, 1841.
49. *Ibid.*, Reel 19, Richey to Alder, February 28, 1842.
50. United Church Archives, Richey Papers, G. W. Hope to Alder, December 9, 1842. The Canada Conference sent a further appeal in June, 1843. This was again rejected. *W.R.*, Reel 14, Colonial Secretary to John Ryerson, November 21, 1843.
51. *W.R.*, Reel 13, Alder to Stinson, April 18, 1842.
52. The Society allocated £2100 to Canada West for 1842-43. *M.R.*, Reel 1, Minutes of Sub-Committee of Reference, September 22, 1841.
53. *Minutes of Conference 1842*, 304, 310. The missionary receipts were £3000. *C.G.*, March 2, 1842.
54. *Minutes of Conference, 1842*, 327.
55. *Ibid.*, 328. The tribunal envisaged was the American Methodist episcopate and specifically Bishop Joshua Soule. Green and Ryerson had already raised the question with him. Green, *op. cit.*, 250. *W.R.*, Reel 19, Stinson to Alder, May 9, 1842.
56. *Ibid.*, Reel 13, J. G. Manly to Alder, June 21, 1841. See also *M.R.*, Reel 4, Stinson and Richey to the Secretaries, June 11, 1841, in which they contended that many Canadians would be British Methodists or nothing.
57. *W.R.*, Reel 19, E. Evans to Alder, March 22, 1842.
58. *Ibid.*, Reel 19, Stinson to Alder, May 9, 1842.
59. *Ibid.*, Reel 13, Alder to J. Ryerson and A. Green, July 4, 1842. The English Conference of 1842 rejected the arbitration plan. See *MS Journal of Conference, 1843*.
60. *Minutes of Conference, 1843*, 329. The arbitration plan was again discussed at this session. *Ibid.*, 352-354.
61. U.C.A., Richey Papers, John Ryerson to Stinson, November 7, 1843. This overture was backed by William Ryerson, Henry Wilkinson, Richard Jones, and other influential itinerants. Egerton had also been induced to write apologetic letters to the Secretaries. See *C.G.*, December 21, 1842; November 1, 1843.
62. *Ibid.*, Ryerson to Stinson.
63. The *Guardian* carried on a running battle with the *Church*, the implacable organ of the Church of England in Canada West.
64. *C.G.*, March 15, 1844; April 10, 1844.
65. *Ibid.*, September 7, 1842; February 8, 15; June 7, 1843.
66. *M.R.*, Reel 4, Canada Western District Minutes, 1843; Richey and Evans to Alder, May, 1843.

67. *W.R.*, Reel 14, Richey to E. Hoole, February 24, 1844.
68. The reference here is to the Baldwin-Metcalfe crisis.
69. *M.R.*, Reel 4, Minutes of a special district meeting, February 12, 1844.
70. *W.R.*, Reel 19, Richey to Alder, March 18, 1844.
71. U.C.A., Richey Papers, Alder to Richey, February 3, 1844.
72. *Ibid.*, Alder to Richey, March 25, 1844.
73. *Ibid.*, February 3, 1844.
74. *Ibid.*, March 25, 1844.
75. The development of the economy and the establishment of an efficient public service were of great importance but they did not attract so much public attention. The clergy reserves question was largely in abeyance until 1849.
76. *C.G.*, September 29, 1841.
77. *E.R.*, I, 537, 543.
78. *C.G.*, February 23, 1842.
79. *Ibid.*, May 24, 1843.
80. Professor Sissons is of this opinion. *E.R.*, II, 45-46. Certainly the political situation was very unstable.
81. *E.R.*, II, 49, A. Green to E. Ryerson, December 27, 1843.
82. Merritt thought the Governor had a case, but also thought it essential to keep Canadian affairs under Canadian control. *E.R.*, II, 47, 50.
83. *Ibid.*, II, 60.
84. The letters were republished in a pamphlet entitled: *Sir Charles Metcalfe defended against the attacks of his late counsellors* (Toronto, 1844).
85. The Association held its first great general meeting on March 25, 1844 in Toronto. J. M. S. Careless, *Brown of the Globe* (Toronto, 1959), I, 49-52.
86. *Ibid.*, 55.
87. J. C. Dent, *The Last Forty Years: Canada Since the Union of 1841* (Toronto, 1881), I, 359-361.
88. *E.R.*, II, 73; Careless, *op. cit.*, 57.
89. *MS Journal of Conference, 1844*.
90. *Minutes of Conference, 1844*, 366-367. The resolution was presented by Anson Green.
91. *Ibid.*, 371-373.
92. *E.R.*, II, 56, McNab to Ryerson, March 1, 1844.
93. *C.G.*, July 3, 1844.
94. There is some evidence that Ryerson was involved in this affair. C. B. Sissons, ed., "Letters of 1844 and 1846 from Scobie to Ryerson," *Canadian Historical Review* (XXIX), 1948, 402.
95. *C.G.*, September 4, 1844.
96. *Ibid*.
97. *Ibid.*, August 28, 1844.
98. *Ibid.*, October 9, 2, 1844.
99. Carroll, *op. cit.*, IV, 398.

100. *E.R.*, II, 71, G. Ferguson to E. Ryerson, September 21, 1844.
101. *M.R.*, Reel 4, Minutes of special district meeting, February, 1844.
102. *Ibid.*
103. *W.R.*, Reel 19, Richey to Alder, October 29, 1844. See also Mahlon Burwell's comment: "I have been greatly amused by the tremendous flogging that Scamp Egerton Ryerson has given to those other Scamps of the Reform Association. . . . Egerton having sailed at all points of the Political Compass carries no weight of character with him & . . . I do not believe his voluminous letters have changed the minds of as many as *three* of the freeholders of Upper Canada." P.A.C., Merritt Papers, M. Burwell to W. H. Merritt, November 11, 1844.
104. The Wesleyan missionaries asserted that, in some constituencies, their supporters would hold the balance in an election.
105. There is little contrary evidence on this point.
106. *D.H.E.*, IV, 48-55. See also Sissons, *Church and State in Canadian Education*, 14-16.
107. *C.G.*, November 24, 1841.
108. Ryerson's report on which the bill was based is printed in *D.H.E.*, IV, 140-211.
109. *C.G.*, March 27, 1844.
110. *Ibid.*, October 30, 1844.
111. *Ibid.*, July 8, 15, 22, 1846.
112. *D.H.E.*, VI, 142.
113. *Ibid.*, VI, 147.
114. *D.H.E.*, VI, 158; *E.R.*, II, 254.
115. The opening is described in *D.H.E.*, IV, 277-292.
116. *Ibid.*, IV, 215, 84-88.
117. *C.G.*, July 6, 1842. The royal charter was amended by the united legislature in the summer of 1841. *D.H.E.*, IV, 57-61.
118. N. Burwash, *A History of Victoria College* (Toronto, 1927), 489, 504.
119. For the bill see *D.H.E.*, V, 61-86. For the background negotiations see Moir, *op. cit.*, 85-88.
120. *C.G.*, February 25, 1846.
121. *Ibid.*, November 1, 1843. The other denominations already received reserves money, whereas Victoria had a heavy investment in buildings which the others did not have.
122. *Ibid.*; Richey Papers, Ryerson to Stinson, November 7, 1843.
123. *C.G.*, November 22, 1843. Strachan's petition is reprinted in *D.H.E.*, V, 27-31.
124. For Draper's speech see *D.H.E.*, V, 36-47. Ryerson's letter is in *C.G.*, January 3, 1844.
125. Although they differed on occasion, Draper and Ryerson respected each other and worked well together. Henry Sherwood, leading light of the extreme tories, was the Solicitor-General.
126. Moir, *op. cit.*, 90; Careless, *op. cit.*, 59-60.

127. Ryerson's new appointment took him away from the college and out of the country. *E.R.*, II, 76-93; Sissons, *A History of Victoria University*, 67, 69-70.
128. *D.H.E.*, V, 159-166. Draper's plan was embodied in one major and two supplementary bills.
129. *C.G.*, March 5, 1845.
130. *Ibid.*, March 12, 1845.
131. *Ibid.*
132. *Ibid.*, March 19, 1845.
133. On the second reading in March there was a majority of eleven for the bill. *C.G.*, March 26, 1845. The *Guardian* printed Baldwin's speech against the motion to proceed to the third reading. *Ibid.*, August 6, 1845. The editor thought the Methodists would settle for something like the University of London. *Ibid.*, September 17, 1845.
134. *Ibid.*, January 28, 1846.
135. *Ibid.*, February 11, 1846. Dr. Burns, the Free Church leader, was one of the active organizers of the affair.
136. *Ibid.*
137. *Ibid.*, February 25, 1846.
138. *Ibid.*, March 25, 1846.
139. Moir, *op. cit.*, 95-96.
140. This is John Ryerson's phrase. *E.R.*, II, 91, John to Egerton Ryerson, June 24, 1845.

TEN

"Only by union can Methodism be great and powerful."

Although the Canada Conference and the Wesleyan Conference were in a conciliatory mood in the spring of 1844, it was not until 1846 that definitive steps were taken to heal the breach between them. In the interval each side had been persuaded that the perils of unity were fewer than those of disunity. Once this stage was reached it was possible to effect a durable understanding that had important consequences for the evolution of Canadian Methodism.

Despite the dangerous implications of the Metcalfe crisis, the *Guardian's* new editor George Playter took a strong line against the Wesleyans in the months following his appointment.[1] But the optimism reflected in Playter's tactics was soon belied by the appearance of the *Toronto Periodical Journal,* published by anonymous influential members on the Toronto circuit.[2] Its ostensible object was to secure an unequivocal declaration of political neutrality from the Conference, or as John Ryerson put it, "by agitation among our people to drive the Conference to censure you [Egerton] & your political writings."[3] In addition the *Journal* advocated lay representation in Conference, doubtless with a view to creating the right kind of political atmosphere in that body.[4] If its backers were "an infamous cleek," their activity was symptomatic of discontent that might easily prove dangerous to the Conference.[5]

The reality of lay unhappiness became evident when the Conference of 1845 tabulated the membership. For the first time since 1840 members had been lost on important circuits in all parts of the province.[6] Some may have gone to the Wesleyans, others to the Methodist Episcopal Church or the New Connexion Methodists.[7] In any event the preachers tacitly agreed that one way to halt decay was to end the war with the Wesleyans. A large committee was appointed "to decide on all matters of difference between the British Conference and the Canadian Conference."[8] The *Guardian* too urged all Methodists to work for unity in the face of the allied dangers of Popery and Puseyism.[9]

In the months between the conferences of 1845 and 1847 the attention of both sides was concentrated on steps to effect the 1847 reunion. Although the Canada Conference was willing to compromise it was not prepared to become simply a missionary district of the British Conference, whereas some such as John Carroll realized that in any settlement the laity must be consulted and their co-operation enlisted.[10] The Conference of 1846, confronted by continuing decline in membership, appointed John Ryerson and Anson Green as delegates to the British Conference "with a view of having all the Wesleyan Societies in British North America associated in one great Christian community under the direction of several Annual Conferences, in connection with one general Representative Legislative Conference."[11] The loss of members was attributed to "the want of more of the life of God in the soul, —that well-spring of all personal enjoyment, activity, and success."[12]

The selection of Green and Ryerson was in itself significant since, as Green later admitted, "from the beginning we lamented the disruption, and did our best in a quiet way to heal the breach." As for obstructions, "we knew but too well that mountainous difficulties lay in our path, but these difficulties were increasing instead of diminishing by delay. Their people and ours were getting further apart all the while and more estranged from each other."[13] That these convictions were shared by many in the Conference was indicated by the dismissal of the unfortunate Playter, because of the *Guardian's* tone and because "they felt it necessary to sacrifice the author of the 'voice from Canada,' to appease the anger of the British Conference."[14]

As in the past, the Canadian preachers' desire for a settlement was countered by outright opposition in Canada and by hesitant acquiescence in London. The British missionaries were still convinced that given time and financial support they would wrest the initiative from their Canadian opponents. This was vital to them because, as one put it: "Since the dissolution of the Union we have had a considerable approximation towards British Wesleyanism in Spirit & Character—so that now it is not that mongrel—medly—mixture which it was previously—we are raising now a select Class of Methodists in this colony."[15] Thinking in this vein they hastily gathered in a special district meeting.

The Secretaries were warned that "we cannot now think that any importance is to be attached to an alleged desire that an end should be put to strifes and contentions which really only exist among themselves, [the Canadian Methodists] and to which we solemnly declare we are in no wise contributory." Those who urged reunion were the same preachers who had sanctioned the violent course of the *Guardian*. True, Playter had been dropped. "It now suits that Conference apparently to blame the late Editor for doing what he was authorized to do, not because they seriously disapprove of his course but because they can hardly expect a hearing from the British Conference, unless some show of a desire to cease hostilities be made." In any case the Canadian proposals were "unsound and ill-digested, impracticable and suspicious"—the creation of men with "sad tendencies" to diverge "from the straightforward path of Christian simplicity and truth, to the crooked ways of worldly diplomatists." Therefore they pressed the British Conference to wait until they had strengthened their position.[16]

While the Committee sympathized with its agents in Canada, it was beginning to realize that a compromise must be reached. Some had discovered that Egerton Ryerson was not the rogue he was alleged to be. The Conference as a whole was concerned about internal unrest, the weak financial position of the Society and the need for Protestant unity in the face of Catholic revival.[17] Hence, when Stinson suggested to Alder that they had "been too thin skinned about Canadian Wigism," the latter replied: "If these people really do desire to be one with us, as I believe such men as John Ryerson does, let them at once . . . move towards their object . . . and they will find no lack of willingness in any quarter to consider any well digested scheme for promoting peace and union."[18]

Although the Canadian delegates were convinced that failure "would be injurious to a very great extent if not absolutely ruinous," their mission proved to be "a critical and difficult one."[19] They were rudely received by Alder in London and again at the Conference in Bristol, but eventually they secured the recognition of Alder's colleagues.[20] On September 9, 1846, the two Canadians met with the British committee, supplemented by Richey as representative of the Canada Western District.[21] Then "a most full, frank & undisguised exposition of all the matters of misunderstanding etc. was entered into. After this full unbosoming of ourselves . . . a total different fealing seemed to come over Drs. Bunting, Alder & the whole committee."[22] Ryerson added: "More kindness, more nobleness of sentiment & fealing I never witnessed than was manifested towards us after we had succeeded in removing suspicion, fears, etc."[23] In this changed atmosphere agreement was quickly reached to eliminate the Canada Western District and to unite the Canadian and English Conferences on a basis similar to the existing union with the Irish Conference. The vexed question of the grant was settled by allowing the Society to retain it for Canadian purposes.[24]

On their return to Canada Green and Ryerson presented this plan to the executive committee of the Canada Conference and a number of leading laymen at a meeting in Cobourg on November 19, 1846.[25] The substance of the scheme had already been outlined by the *Guardian* and had been received "with mingled feelings. A portion of [the Canadians] and the more pious and consistent among the missionary party were much pleased; but others, on both sides of the house, were displeased, disappointed and warlike."[26] Apparently these sentiments were not strong in the committee for the actions of the delegates were unanimously approved and the articles of settlement were then put before the quarterly meetings.[27] The latter were told *"the truth, the whole truth* & nothing but the truth!" But "in explaining the basis to [them] & especially those of a certain cast everything was made to appear" so as "to meet their prejudices & quiet their fears as much as possible."[28] Presented in this manner the plan proved to be very acceptable.[29]

As was expected the Wesleyan missionaries and their adherents were much more intransigent in their opposition. Condemnatory resolutions were passed by most of the circuits and at a special district meeting in February, 1847, the preachers urged delay until the proposals could be modified.[30] Richey added that he was hindered by lack of information and by Canadian propaganda designed to show that "the British Conference repents of the destructive course it has pursued since the dissolution of the Union." He felt, however, that union on sound principles was still possible, and thus exhorted Alder: "In the name of the Lord then *come and at least make an honest & vigorous effort.*"[31]

Armed with this contradictory advice, the blessing of the British Conference, and his own conceit, Dr. Alder arrived in Toronto in May, 1847. His first step was to meet with the Wesleyan missionaries and induce them to accept the reunion plan. Alder prefaced his remarks with this statement: "With regard to the printing of resolutions and exciting the people to disaffection by conversation it was much to be deplored; they [the preachers] would have done better to have been praying." Ephraim Evans replied that the preachers were not there to have their way but "to be guided aright according to the will of God." A confused and rambling discussion ensued in which the leading of the spirit was not evident. William Case proclaimed that he would not be handed over to the Canada Conference "without some guarantee he would be free from agitation.... He never wish[ed] to see or hear a repetition of what he ha[d] seen and heard in that Conference.... We ought not to conceal from ourselves the fact we have to deal with talented men, and men who are not over-nice about conscience.... Before there was any 'hugging and kissing' there should be some 'confession'." Alder agreed that "unless men can be obtained to guide and to lead and ... to control and direct all would be in vain," but he felt that under an able administration the proposed arrangements would "accomplish all that anyone can reasonably desire in respect to the efficient control of the British Conference." He concluded: "We are now about to *act*: we have had plenty of time for deliberation: are we to scratch each other's faces for three years longer and then think we should embrace? We cannot resume our former position. . . . Only by union can Methodism be great and powerful."[32]

While this animated discussion was still in progress the Canada Conference assembled on June 3 in the Adelaide Street Church, Toronto.[33] William Ryerson was elected president but the two managers, John Ryerson and Anson Green, seized the initiative at once, especially in the cordial attitude they displayed to the Wesleyans. The two went to meet Alder and Richey at their hotel. "The Doctor took my arm," Green recalled, "and Mr. R. took that of Dr. Richey, and in this friendly way we walked through the streets to the Adelaide-street Church, when we conducted them to the platform and introduced them to the Conference."[34] The members of the Canada Western District were also invited to be present, "for it was important that all our ministers should thoroughly understand the negotiations."[35]

John Ryerson rose to explain the reunion scheme, using as his text a pamphlet opposing it produced by Playter and three others.[36] The Conference then took up the articles in turn. Each was accepted by a large majority and the whole scheme was passed with a vote of 82 to 8.[37] "This second union, although not carried in the Canada Conference with the same apparent unanimity as the first one, really proved vastly more harmonious and complete."[38]

On the first Saturday evening of the Conference the Wesleyan preachers resumed their consideration of the question. Reviewing the events of the past week Alder confessed that he was "amazed at the result of the deliberations: God was in it and God alone would accomplish it." William Case, too, felt that it was time to forgive and forget: "Their hands and eyes and voice all testify that they are changed! We should meet them. The country have confidence in us."[39] In their last address to the British Conference the missionaries submitted to the inevitable: "Influenced by the magnanimity and forbearance of our President we are convinced that our own minds have been graciously directed to salutary conclusions."[40]

Amiable social relations between the two bodies were renewed. The sessions of Conference were distinguished by many tears and prayerful meetings between Wesleyan and Canadian preachers. Towards the end there was a joint meeting of the two Toronto congregations and the Conference in the Richmond Street Church. Alder took the chair and addressed the throng in a "lofty and apostolic" fashion. John Ryerson spoke "under the influence of hallowed emotions." Richey, "imbued with the spirit of a seraph, carried the audience with him in his feelings of charity and love while delivering his impromptu but unequalled address. . . . Love, the atmosphere of heaven, was the atmosphere here; joy leaped from the eyes of the assembled."[41] Once again union had been launched in typical Methodist fashion.

To what was the Canada Conference now committed? The preamble to the articles of union emphasized that

> it is extremely desirable that the unseemly differences which for some time have unhappily existed between the two branches of the Wesleyan Methodists in Western Canada, who agree in doctrine, and substantially in matters of discipline, should terminate; and that a plan be adopted for securing their cordial ecclesiastical oneness and the concentration of their associated efforts in spreading the 'Common Salvation' in Upper Canada.[42]

Hence it was agreed that the two Conferences be reunited as nearly as possible on the basis of the relationship between the English and Irish Conferences. The property of the Canadian church was to remain in its hands, except for chapels whose deeds required that their pulpits be filled by the British Conference. The English Conference was to appoint annually a president and a co-delegate (vice-president), the latter to be either an English or Canadian preacher. Moreover, "all . . . the acts, admissions, expulsions and appointments . . . of the Canadian Conference" were to be "laid before the ensuing English Conference, and when confirmed by their vote," were to be considered "valid and obligatory."[43] The discipline was to stand unchanged, except that the district chairmen were to be stationed on circuits and the advisory committee that helped to select them was to be elected by the district meetings. The English Conference was to appoint a general superintendent of missions and all the Canadian missions were to be under the jurisdiction of the Wesleyan Missionary Society, to whose funds the auxiliary Canadian society would contribute, and which would annually allocate the sum to be spent in Canada West. This money was to be distributed by a standing Canadian committee including the president, the co-delegate, the general superintendent and the district chairmen. All missionaries were to be full members of the Canada Conference, but if they were members of the English Conference they were to retain their rights and privileges in that body.[44] To make the arrangement more palatable the English Conference agreed to contribute £1,000 annually to missions and £600 to the Conference Contingent Fund to assist in building up circuits in "new and destitute settlements."[45] In return the Canadian Conference was to join in requesting that the government grant be paid to the Society.

On the surface these arrangements seemed innocuous, but their implications and the issues not mentioned were of considerable significance. The way was open in principle for an even greater infusion of Wesleyan influence than under the previous union. Not only would the president and general superintendent normally be from the English Conference, but there was no guarantee that the co-delegate would not be a Wesleyan as well. There was nothing to prevent the Society from sending out additional men to augment the strength of these officials and of the preachers who returned to the fold in 1847. Through these men it might be possible to shape the Methodist outlook along Wesleyan lines. The English Conference, however, had unwittingly given away one of the major devices for making its influence effective, by urging the adoption of its own system of district chairmen.

After a trial period from 1842 to 1844 the Canada Conference had reverted to the customary practice of leaving the district chairman without a circuit so that he might carry out general supervision over the district as had the presiding elder. This was a provision that John Ryerson saw would help greatly in making "British influence effective, (a thing I devoutly desire)."[46] The chairmen were to have circuits and thus would be precluded from exercising much control over their districts. In addition, the committee that would assist the president in choosing chairmen was to be selected by the districts, a device that would restrict the president's authority.

Apart from this potentially weakening situation the British Conference had secured a veto over the acts of the Canada Conference, and in the financial settlement had tied the latter to the parent body more closely than before. Of the two matters the financial understanding was more vital. For assistance that was less generous than it appeared the Canada Conference was pledged to help the Society secure the government grant and the arrears accumulated since 1840.[47] As it was anticipated that all grants of this kind would be transferred to the clergy reserves fund, the Canadian Methodists would not be in a position to press for outright secularization when the question was revived. In effect the English party had won the reluctant acquiescence of the Canadians in the principle of state assistance for religious purposes.

Ostensibly the English Conference was in a better position than formerly to mould the Canadian Methodist Church in its own likeness, to raise its level of religious sophistication, to make its system of church government less liberal, to keep it out of politics except for tacit support of conservative principles, and to lead it into closer co-operation with the state. Actually these consequences did not follow to the extent that was perhaps anticipated, for the working of the reunited church was conditioned by internal problems of the Wesleyan Conference, the calibre of its representatives in Canada, the reactions of the Canadian Methodists, and the provincial environment.

The kind and degree of pressure which the English Conference could exert upon its Canadian brethren was greatly affected by its own difficulties. The years 1850 and 1851 were marked by continuous controversy in the English Conference, which diverted its attention from Canadian affairs at the time when growing pains might have been expected. Moreover, though the forces of conservatism won in England, traditional tory and Anglican associations of the Conference were seriously weakened.[48] In consequence the British Conference found it increasingly difficult to object either to the ecclesiastical or the political views of its Canadian brethren.

Aside from this domestic turmoil the British Conference was fortunate in its representatives in Canada. Matthew Richey served as co-delegate in 1847 and 1848, as president in 1849 and 1850, and then left for Nova Scotia where he was to remain for the rest of his career.[49] In his new rôle he overcame earlier antipathies and worked faithfully with the Canadian preachers. He was succeeded by Enoch Wood, appointed as missions superintendent in 1847, an office he continued to occupy as president from 1850 to 1858.[50] Those who had known his work in the eastern districts would have anticipated the effective and skilful way in which he reconciled the needs and interests of the two Conferences. Living in New Brunswick had not altered in any way Wood's natural predisposition toward conservatism in ecclesiastical and political matters, but, as Carroll noted, he was "a Colonist by adoption and feeling. He [was] conservative yet progressive."[51] Unlike most of his predecessors, with the exception of Joseph Stinson, Wood had an ability to understand and defend what he regarded as legitimate Canadian concerns. His prudence, caution and discernment enabled him to deal fairly with both sides and thereby to promote harmonious operation of the union.

The balance of forces among the Canadian leaders was a fortunate one for Wood. The appointment of John Ryerson and Anson Green as delegates to England in 1846 and their success in bringing off the reunion project, confirmed the ascendancy in the Conference of two men as shrewd and prudent as Wood himself. Their influence was emphasized and enhanced by the positions they held, John Ryerson being chairman of the Hamilton and Toronto districts and co-delegate from 1850 to 1858, whereas from 1847 to 1853 Green continued to be the Book Steward, an appointment that placed him at the very heart of connexional activity. In contrast, Egerton Ryerson was increasingly preoccupied with educational work and William seemed to have little influence.[52] The triumvirate of Green, Wood and John Ryerson, whose interests were so much alike, was in a good position to impose its views on the church as a whole.

The band that effectively united these men was their determination to make the union work and through it to promote the steady expansion of Methodism in membership and spiritual influence. They were successful partly because of their own policies and conditions within the Wesleyan Methodist Church as a whole.

From the outset both sides did not wish to revive controversies of the past. For a time after the Conference of 1847 the *Guardian* was filled with complimentary remarks from secular newspapers and with favourable reports from the circuits.[53] Its optimism was confirmed by Wood, who described joint services in Toronto at which "brethren long estranged were again united in holy exercises; the sight and feeling were heavenly."[54] He saw no reason to doubt the sincerity of the Canadians; he believed they were heartily sick of dissension and conflict. In any case, no alternative policy was available to the Wesleyans. They might win in the towns but "to compete with the [the Canadians] in the country parts of the Province where their influence is so pervading and established could not be done without an enormous outlay. . . . Their system is one of adaptation, often carried out with much personal sacrifice and loss."[55]

The disgust at agitation that Wood found among Canadian preachers and people did not derive simply from recognition of the sinfulness of religious dissension; it was symptomatic of the growing self-awareness of the Wesleyan Methodist body, one consequence of its long struggle for survival. Inevitably, to many Methodists the task of building up Wesleyan Methodism for its own sake seemed more important than any other project. They became less willing to participate in disputes or crusades that might endanger their primary objective, and this attitude was encouraged by Wood and Ryerson.

There was considerable concern for the institutional growth of Wesleyan Methodism, indicated by the construction of new churches and the interest in prompt payment of ministerial salaries. Some also sought to liberalize the Methodist system.[56] To begin with, the union scheme provided that district chairmen should also have circuits, thereby reducing their authority and effectiveness. This adjustment was not made in 1847 and if Enoch Wood had had his way, would not have been made later. He thought it unwise.

Looking at the large number of young and inexperienced men composing the Conference and at the great gatherings of all kinds of mere officials ... who crowd around the Quarterly Board ... with the tendencies to democracy peculiar to some portions of the country, blighted by the worst of English and Scotch radicals and these carried into their religious thinkings and actings, something more than a mere novice is required to preside at their councils.[57]

If the plan were adopted Wood felt that the number of districts should be increased to give the chairman a greater opportunity to exercise his influence, and that the co-delegate should reside in Canada West. The change was made, none the less, but it is significant that the number of districts was raised and that the Conference soon acquired a semi-permanent executive in the persons of Wood and John Ryerson, men who thought alike on questions of democracy in church and state.

Some of the preachers remained dissatisfied. In 1853 George Playter brought in resolutions proposing the annual election of district chairmen, payment of all deficiencies of salary each year, and a veto of prospective stations for those with fifteen years' experience. In Wood's opinion Playter's speech "was a tissue of conglomerated nonsense, the main design of which was an attack upon the Executive of the Conference, attempting to show that every evil, personal or connexional which had been endured for the last 20 years was to be attributed to the corruptions and imbecility of the men who had filled office."[58] There was a brisk fight in which many expressed confidence in the president, although indicating that they would prefer a weak successor. Then Egerton Ryerson was induced to put forward a compromise solution binding the president to accept advice in the appointment of chairmen.[59] Once again conservative forces in the itinerancy held their own, but they were on the defensive.

Equally noteworthy alterations in the relationship between clergy and laity were made, or at least attempted, at this point. Recognizing the growing importance of the laity, the Conference of 1848 instituted the financial district meeting, composed of the circuit superintendents and one steward from each circuit.[60] A more interesting development was the controversy that ensued over a proposal to incorporate the various Methodist societies and institutions. A bill for the purpose was introduced in the legislature by Billa Flint, a prominent Methodist layman, and was immediately attacked by some secular newspapers.[61] Eventually it was amended to incorporate only those funds maintained and shared by the ministers alone, perhaps because the original bill might have put lay members in Conference.[62] John Carroll commented: "The history of this matter proves that ministers may be stupidly opposed to reasonable lay co-operation and laymen may be unreasonably suspicious of their ministers."[63] Ostensibly some Methodists wished a larger share in the management of their church; some of their ministers, led by the president, were not ready to concede such claims in full.

To what extent these attempts to alter the balance of power in the Methodist organization were accompanied by changes in the spiritual climate of the church is a difficult question. Outwardly the situation was unchanged. The *Guardian* frequently printed accounts of revivals and camp meetings; each year the Conference admonished members to attend to the means of grace that they might advance toward holiness. But subtle adjustments were taking place. The Methodist Connexion was no longer simply a community of seekers after holiness; it was a church with continuing responsibilities towards the children of its members. The Conference referred frequently to family worship and promoted Sunday Schools, the *Sunday School Guardian* and the Tract Society.[64]

This change in the character of the Connexion was intimately connected with a decline in evangelical fervour, more marked than in the early eighteen-forties. The Conference of 1854, for example, saw a strenuous battle, precipitated by Egerton Ryerson's suggestion that attendance at class meeting should not be a condition of membership in the Methodist Church.[65] Ryerson was supported by a few young men but was strongly opposed by Richard Jones, Henry Wilkinson, and John Carroll. Unwilling to compromise, Ryerson resigned, to the evident pleasure of some.[66] The fact remained that many did not attend class regularly and when they did, took part perfunctorily. To them traditional Methodist piety was unacceptable.

The appearance of professional evangelists and attempts to make camp meetings respectable were equally indicative of changing attitudes. In the early eighteen-fifties the *Guardian* first began to describe the visits of the Rev. James Caughey, the noted American preacher.[67] To many it must have seemed strange that the Methodist Church would use the services of a professional evangelist. At the same time the *Guardian* was printing letters urging that camp meetings be provided with permanent sites to make them respectable. Preachers were being told to avoid spiritual hilarity, hair-splitting, and talk of damnation, and to content themselves with sober, sincere, revival preaching. Prayer meetings too should be carefully controlled so that the most vociferous would not be mistaken for the most pious.[68] To a later generation, professional evangelism and religious decorum are not out of the ordinary, but at this period in the development of Methodism such emphases indicated a less spontaneous form of worship.

Anyone seeking to understand the Wesleyan Methodist attitude to the secular realm in the years immediately following 1847, must take into account not only these subtle alterations in the spiritual quality of Methodism, but also the whole complex of forces affecting the life of the Connexion. The Wesleyans' influence, the desire for peace, the denominational concern of the principal Canadian preachers, all pointed to a cautious course. Conversely, increasing lay interest in the government of the church and the restiveness of some preachers in the face of a kind of oligarchy, were suggestive of liberal sentiments. The weakening of the old evangelical spirit could have brought a broader and less self-centred piety, but at this stage the effect seems to have been the opposite. As a respectable denomination moving out of the pioneer stage, the Wesleyan Methodist Church inclined toward a narrower view of its social responsibilities than it held in earlier years. It had not changed fundamentally; rather, it allowed greater scope for those inward-looking forces, ever present in Methodist life and never wholly submerged.

2

The society in which the Wesleyan Methodist Church functioned after 1847 was turbulent and swiftly changing. Between 1850 and 1853 the province entered the railway age, whose opportunities would eventually divert the attention of its people from old issues and alignments.[69] But rapid emergence of new economic and social conditions was obscured at this juncture by the last important skirmishes between the remnants of the Family Compact and the Reform Party. While proponents of the new order sought to accelerate the material development of Canada West, prominence once more was given to responsible government, clergy reserves, and education.

While Wesleyan and Canadian Methodists were in the midst of reunion negotiations the province became embroiled in bitter controversy, culminating in the general election of 1847-1848. Lord Elgin reached Montreal in January, 1847, and soon made known his adherence to the concept of responsible government, a move that stimulated political interest, particularly in the fate of the shaky Sherwood-Daly ministry.[70] The latter, pushed by John A. Macdonald, the Receiver-General and a moderate Presbyterian tory, decided to make one last effort to settle the university question, doubtless with an eye to the general election that was soon to come.[71]

Macdonald's two university bills, introduced on July 9, 1847, were remarkably simple and yet were calculated to meet the needs of Anglicans, Presbyterians, and Methodists. The first bill restored King's College to the direct control of the Church of England, and the second established a board composed of representatives of the four colleges and the state to administer the university endowment. From the endowment revenue King's was to receive £3,000 per year, Queen's, Victoria and Regiopolis, £1,500 each. The remainder, apart from £2,500 for the grammar schools, was to be set aside for colleges subsequently established.[72]

The proposed legislation was hailed by the *Christian Guardian*. The editor contended that this was the most satisfactory proposal yet put forward, by reason of its "comparative equality and liberality" and its recognition of the connection between "Science and Religion." "We believe no reader of the Guardian would wish to have the secular education of his son severed from instruction in the principles and morals of the Christian Religion." In preserving this relationship the bill conformed to the examples of America and Europe where no one seriously thought of separating religion and university education. "Such a monstrous conception was reserved for certain wise-acres in Canada." The editor admitted that this was apparently a different line than that taken by the Methodists in 1843 and 1844 but he argued: "There is a wide difference between the Provincial university talked of in 1844 and that which is now advocated by the opponents of the present measure. The same phraseology is used, but a very different thing is meant; and thus a gross sophism is played off upon the public." Victoria College was still prepared to become part of a larger institution but would not participate in "a marble-hearted system of ungodly education." But because the Macdonald bills would "confer upon Upper Canada the benefits of liberal education . . . upon Christian principles to a fourfold greater extent than the novel and unprecedented scheme of one non-Christian National University," this legislation deserved "the most cordial support" of all Methodists.[73]

With strong opposition from King's College Council and dissension in the Assembly, the government decided to postpone the university bills. Dissenting parties had time to agitate the question.[74] The Methodist Conference's special committee met with the Victoria Board on October 27. Evans and Richey opposed any action because they objected to proposed recognition of Regiopolis, but they were brought around by that skilful veteran of New Brunswick politics, Enoch Wood. In the end the committee decided to publish an address to the Wesleyan Methodist Church and circulate a petition on behalf of the Macdonald plan.[75]

This address to members and friends of the Wesleyan Methodist Church stressed that the Conference sought a Christian settlement of the university question and had no interest in its political aspects. Its concern was with "the Christian character of the . . . education of youth and therefore the Christian principles and religious and general interests of the country." In his accompanying editorial Sanderson argued that the country was now faced with a choice between one great, inaccessible, secular university and accessible religious colleges. He agreed that in taking a stand for the latter and for the government's legislation the Methodists would be accused of political partisanship, but he concluded: "Let it be published, then, to every politician in the land . . . that *it is a question in which we have no interest or concern whatever in any of its possible aspects to political parties.*"[76]

Reformers and secularists were not to be put off with quaint assertions. The tide of criticism continued to rise, especially when election rumours began to circulate, but the *Guardian* held its ground. The editor thought it a new idea to assert that the university question was a purely political one. The *Guardian* had no interest in parties as such for they were unprincipled organizations. "Had we even the power to do so, we would never for a moment think of committing the Church on a political question to a political party."[77] The forthcoming election was similarly greeted with a blunt editorial. Why, Sanderson asked, was the university legislation not opposed on its own merits, rather than as a measure supported by Methodists and Catholics? The Methodist Church was solely concerned with the fate of a just and liberal proposal, the effective alternative to a godless university scheme.[78] The *Guardian* added: "We . . . suggest to our members and friends who approve of the University Bill supported by the Connexion to understand . . . the position of the candidates . . . on this great question."[79] The implication was that Methodists should vote for tories.

In taking this position the Methodist Church was really doing more crudely for the tories what it had done for the reformers before 1833, but this line of policy was markedly different from that of recent years. It was said that "tho' the other members of the [committee] *might* not have known an election was at hand, Dr. Ryerson *did*," and that "he worked upon the feelings of the Committee . . . to arouse the antipathy and opposition of the Wesleyans against the Baldwin & Lafontaine party and secure Messrs. Sherwood & Coy in power."[80] In reality, Ryerson did not play a conspicuous part in the October discussions and his own correspondence does not indicate that he had advance warning of the election. The Methodist leaders and the *Guardian* thought the Macdonald bill was the best available. With that narrowness of outlook that was beginning to typify Methodist decisions, they pushed ahead in support of the bill without regard for consequences.

Whatever the background of the *Guardian's* position, the Methodists were asked to vote in a particular way in an election with broad implications for development of the province. According to Wood the Methodists at Long Point were led astray by a Presbyterian minister in a manner that might have led one to "suppose that the whole of the laity of the Wesleyan Church of Canada had arisen in their might against the ministry of the Connexion."[81] John Carroll, in contrast, believed that the Conference's policy produced much "complaining and agitation," reflected in the loss of nine hundred members during 1847-1848.[82] Perhaps many other Methodists shared John Ryerson's view that "in trying to get fixed in their seats for four years," the tories had executed a "contemptible manoover."[83] The election returns cannot be interpreted precisely. The western part of the province returned reformers, the eastern section tories. Areas with large concentrations of Methodists returned tory and reform candidates indiscriminately.[84] It is not certain that the Methodist vote was really significant on this occasion.

In any event Enoch Wood and probably some of his colleagues were "more than ever convinced of the necessity of the Church of God standing aloof from all political movements; there is little pure honesty in any of them."[85] The fact remained, though, that the formation of the great reform ministry of 1848 cleared the way for decisive action on the clergy reserves and university questions. In their solution, the Methodists' rôle reflected the new balance of forces in the Connexion.

Despite the long history of the clergy reserves and the known antipathy of the Reform Party to the 1840 settlement, the issue was scarcely discussed in the 1848 election. Before the new ministry was installed it was announced that at last a surplus had accumulated in the reserves fund, which might be shared by other denominations than the Churches of England and Scotland.[86] Almost at once public interest in the matter revived, especially among groups determined not to accept a share in the fund and those such as the Wesleyans who were undecided.[87] When the Clear Grit movement emerged a year later, committed in principle to secularizing the reserves and rectories, the agitation gathered powerful momentum.[88]

Only three courses of action were open—acceptance of the 1840 settlement, secularization with provision for those already dependent on the fund, or outright secularization for educational and general purposes. By treating the matter as a constitutional question after

1840, the Methodists had avoided any definite commitment, but there is good evidence that most Methodists disliked the existing order.[89] Some may have felt that proceeds of the reserves should be equitably divided; probably the majority wanted secularization.[90] The union of 1847, however, put them in a difficult position. Wesleyans who returned to the fold were very willing to accept state assistance. Moreover, the Conference was committed to support the Missionary Society's application for renewal of its grant. Since any such claims would have to be paid from the reserves fund, the Conference would find it most awkward to promote complete secularization.

When the union was completed steps were taken immediately to secure payment of the current grant, and of the sum that had accumulated since 1840.[91] At first the government appeared willing to proceed rapidly, but then decided to place the Wesleyans on the same footing as the Churches of England and Scotland, that is to calculate the amount on the basis of stipends to specific individuals.[92] At first Richey, supported by Green and Egerton Ryerson, resisted this proposal. But later Richey gave the provincial secretary a list of the Canadian and Wesleyan missionary stations for the years 1840 to 1846, and emphasized that to withhold the grant would embarrass the Society and endanger the union.[93] Fortified by calculations based on Richey's letter, by which it appeared that the Society was in debt to the Canadian treasury, the government temporized. Finally it was prodded into paying by Wood, Dr. Dixon (the Conference president for 1848), John Ryerson and Elgin.[94]

Wood induced Green and the two Ryersons to gain the approval of Conference in 1848 for an arrangement whereby the deficiency in subsequent grants would be supplied from its share in the reserves.[95] The same combination of forces likely led the Conference to petition for a share in the reserves surplus to be used for education and "distressed parsonages."[96] The Canada Conference was becoming very closely tied to Wesleyan views and interests.

It is not surprising that the Conference of 1849 took no notice of the rising agitation about the reserves.[97] In May, 1850, the *Guardian*, angered by taunts and allegations of the reform press, at last reviewed the history of the reserves question and indicated the attitude of the Methodists to the subject.

The *Guardian* recalled that in 1840 the Methodist Conference had protested vigorously against the amendment of Sydenham's bill in the Lords. When it became law, nevertheless, it was changed for the Methodists into a constitutional question, not subject to denominational agitation. The Church as such now could not participate in the argument because of the interests of certain groups connected with it. This was its real reason for hesitation, not the expectation of sharing in the reserves. The Society's grant had been secured before the reserves bill was passed and would have been paid in any case. The Conference would not take anything for its members, but, the editor emphasized: "The Wesleyan Body has always maintained the right of each Denomination to receive legislative aid for Educational purposes.... It has ever been distinguished by the advocacy of common justice to all denominations and classes of the population. We apprehend it will not give up the rights of common justice and common sense in respect to itself."[98] In other words the *Guardian* was not unwilling to see the reserves question reopened, but for the peace of the Connexion it did not want to participate in the controversy. It was apparent that the editor had no objection to a settlement based on an equitable division of the fund.

A month later J. H. Price, a member of the government, introduced a series of resolutions calling for the repeal of the Clergy Reserves Act and the passage of a new bill to distribute the fund in such ways as the Assembly desired.[99] The lengthy but temperate debate on these proposals was concluded by acceptance of an address to the Crown.[100] Although Elgin and Grey were not anxious to respond to this pressure Grey agreed in January, 1851, to ask parliament to reinvest the reserves in the Canadian legislature, subject to protection of existing rights in the settlement.[101]

Outwardly the Methodist Church was unperturbed, but the Conference of 1851 unanimously agreed that the act of 1840 was "at variance with the sentiments and feelings of the Canadian People, and most unjust to the Wesleyan and several other religious denominations." As this was an imperial act, however, the Conference "regarded the Clergy Reserve question as one between Canada and Great Britain . . . and therefore as requiring provincial action rather than denominational agitation." It was a matter of regret that the Churches of England and Scotland were again trying to secure advantages for themselves "against their brethren of other Protestant Churches." Hence the Conference concurred in the legislature's efforts to regain "its constitutional rights of legislation," and expressed its "warmest gratitude for the decision of the Imperial Government to take the necessary steps to restore to the Canadian Legislature the power of disposing of the Clergy Reserves . . . according to the wishes of the people." Moreover, the preachers protested against "any measure for any endowment or grant in perpetuity to the Church of England or of Scotland not secured upon equal conditions to every other Protestant denomination in

Upper Canada." For their own support they would continue to rely "upon the voluntary contributions of our congregations ... being determined ever to maintain inviolate those holy bonds of unity and oneness which have characterized the rise, progress and wide extension of our labours as a religious body in Upper Canada."[102]

Once again the Conference had affirmed its faith in the voluntary principle for the maintenance of the ministry itself, but it would not reject such assistance as might be given to all denominations for educational purposes. In expressing appreciation of the action of the Canadian and British governments, the ministers tacitly accepted the principle of secularization; as the *Guardian* remarked, it was not hard to guess what the wishes of the people would be.[103] Anson Green summarized the Methodist position: "Help to all or help to none, is our motto, and we have, at least, nine-tenths of the country with us in this opinion. We are indifferent as to which way the question is decided, provided equal justice be meted out to all. ... We desire an open field, equal advantages and fair play."[104]

The Methodists seemed closer to this objective when in November, 1851, the new Hincks-Morin ministry, pledged to a solution of the reserves question, called a general election.[105] The *Guardian* seized the occasion to issue a typical but blunt pronouncement. The Methodists were reminded that no political system would work effectively unless it was based on religious and moral principles and that a poor system would work better with moral men in control than a perfect system operated by immoral men. The *Guardian* urged its readers to consider the character of the candidates "rather than attach too high an importance to a mere political profession." Above all, "there is the need of constant watchfulness, intense solicitude and earnest prayer that the churches, while contending for important objects, do not let down the tone of their spirituality." Turning to civil rights the editor stressed that

We yield the palm to none in the advocacy of equal civil and religious rights; and we express our ardent desire that the question which has so long agitated the country should be settled in a form different from that which now exists and that the whole proceeds of the Clergy Reserves be applied to promote the educational interests of the country in a way that will afford all classes of the community an equal advantage or the opportunity of participating in the advantages for which they might be applied.[106]

When the election returns were completed it was clear that the supporters of a new and equitable settlement had improved their position. Some doughty supporters of the Church of England were gone; some moderate tories had replaced them.[107] Unfortunately this auspicious situation was balanced by the accession of the conservative Derby ministry, which promptly indicated its determination not to proceed with repeal of the Clergy Reserves Act.

The Derby government fell in December, 1852, and was replaced by an administration headed by Aberdeen, with Newcastle as Colonial Secretary.[108] The latter promptly took up Grey's policy and in April, 1853, secured passage of a bill reinvesting the reserves in the hands of the provincial legislature.[109] The bill, so smoothly delivered from Westminster, was not taken up in Canada for another year and in the interval there was a confused, acrimonious controversy.[110]

While the argument raged, the Wesleyan Conference met in Belleville on June 7, 1854. As it was confidently expected that the ministry would soon act on the reserves, this seemed to be the last chance for a Methodist stand. The tone of the Conference was set by the *Guardian* of June 7 in which the editor wrote: "It is beyond the power of any body of men to effect any material change in the minds of the people of Upper Canada." Moreover, in his view the Conference had "no authority to say that the people shall not receive aid from that source [the reserves] in supporting their religious institutions."[111] When William Ryerson moved that the Conference press for secularization, the brethren, whom Wood had "endeavoured to inoculate . . . with the doctrine of Abstractedness from political strife," rejected his proposal.[112]

The mute Conference of 1854 had barely concluded when the Assembly was dissolved and a general election was called.[113] Its sequel was the formation of the MacNab-Morin ministry which finally disposed of that aged bone of contention—the clergy reserves. The plan, concocted by the Attorney-General West, John A. Macdonald, provided that proceeds of the reserves would be used for municipal purposes; existing stipends and allowances would be paid for life or might be commuted to form individual or denominational funds.[114]

In company with many tories and reformers, some Methodists indicated their dissatisfaction with the government's bill. At a meeting in Kingston they pressed their clerical brethren to join them in one last expression of dissent, but unable to secure their help, they proposed "a complete, entire and final scheme of secularization to embrace all proceeds of Clergy lands, funded or otherwise."[115] Their protest was unavailing. The Methodist Church was not excepted from the reserves settlement for its president was "in correspondence with those on whose moderation and fidelity" he could depend.[116]

In the end the bill passed in its original form.[117] The Wesleyan Methodist Church received £9,768/11/0 (currency). The Society transferred the whole sum to the church in Canada on the understanding that it be used for missionary work.[118] In similar transactions the great clergy reserves conflict drifted ingloriously into history.

3

While Canada West was moving haltingly to a definitive settlement of the clergy reserves question, the university issue moved into a new phase that made serious difficulties for the Methodists. At the middle of the decade the problem had not been resolved, but the Wesleyan Methodists had helped to solidify the basic lines of contention.

Supporters of denominational education, who had played such a conspicuous part in the great election of 1848, were naturally disheartened by the accession of the Baldwin-Lafontaine Ministry. Their fears were confirmed in April, 1849, when Baldwin brought down an "Act to Amend the Charter of the University Established at Toronto." This provided for the creation of the University of Toronto in which no religious tests would be required and no divinity taught, but which would assume direct teaching responsibilities. Colleges affiliating with the University would become divinity schools with minimal representation in the senate. The endowment was reserved for the exclusive use of the University and was to be administered by a three-man board.[119] The government intended to create one secular provincial university with a monopoly of available funds and of the right to teach. No reference was made to existing grants to colleges, but termination of such grants was implied, as was the disappearance of the institutions themselves. They were to be forced to the wall in an unequal struggle.

To the *Guardian* the new plan was "the most objectionable one ever submitted to the country" for its leading feature was "Infidelity."[120] In Wood's private view "the design [was] to swell up the power and patronage of the Colonial government" by getting hold of the endowment. "Religious denominations," said Wood, "must be corrupt and inefficient indeed if they cannot employ public means for Educational purposes with as much honesty and success as any class of politicians."[121] Curiously, though, the Methodists took no official steps against the government scheme, perhaps because Wood really preferred one provincial university and had no strong attachment to Victoria College.[122]

The university bill became effective in January, 1850, posing the alternatives of affiliation or opposition for the denominational colleges. Early in March, John and Egerton Ryerson, Richey and Wood met to consider Victoria's case.[123] Egerton reported that the ministry planned to bring in a bill to clarify the position of religion in the University. He had been working on a plan to have Richey appointed Professor of Rhetoric and English in the University, presumably in return for Victoria's capitulation. "It was plain" to Wood that *the subject had been presented to Dr. Richey* before [the] *meeting* and equally apparent that he approved of the proposition." There was therefore some feeling that affiliation might be feasible, or at least that Victoria should be moved to Toronto.[124]

Before the Conference met in June this scheme had been partially upset by Richey's abrupt departure for Nova Scotia. Although he returned to preside in the Conference of 1850 he was now convinced that the suggested professorship was part of a plot against him and that the "university [was] an anomalous semi-infidel affair in which religion, while ostensibly recognized is virtually proscribed." "Such an institution," he concluded, was "no place for a Methodist Minister," a view that had some justification.[125]

The Conference, however, was not decidedly of Richey's opinion. An "animated and exciting debate" was held on the future course of Victoria. A party led by William Ryerson strongly advocated affiliation. "His speech," according to Wood, "was the most amusing exhibition of sarcastic drollery I ever listened into. To keep up a university or a pretence to do so that one student a year may graduate under Wesleyan Literati is too much to bear."[126] Faced with the prospect of no state assistance and the languishing condition of the College, the Conference reluctantly agreed to move it to Toronto.[127]

The decision of 1850 was not implemented, apparently because the valuable college property could not be sold advantageously.[128] In the end Victoria was saved by two things—efficient leadership and a hopeful change in government policy. As Richey was unwilling to become principal, S. S. Nelles, a young Canadian minister, was appointed in his place.[129] Reluctant to take the post, Nelles soon assumed a leading place in what was to be a dynasty of able Canadian heads of the College. To him "study without prayer" was "arrogance, prayer without study" was "fanaticism." His students were expected to "scorn everything low, everything dishonourable," everything that was "unworthy" of them "as gentlemen and as Christians."[130] As principal he scorned defeat; it was a quality that stood Victoria in good stead.

While Nelles was restoring a sense of vigour and purpose to the

College, the university question was tackled by the new and agile chief minister, Francis Hincks. Once an inveterate foe of the Methodists, Hincks was now one of Ryerson's principal supporters and he turned to him for advice on university policy. In his reply Ryerson asserted that the University of Toronto was an affront to the religious convictions of Upper Canada, and would not become an effective institution. The remedy was to provide adequate support for the denominational colleges and maintain University College for those who wished a secular education. The university as such could confine its teaching to subjects such as philosophy and history and undertake general supervision of the colleges.[131]

Under Hincks' skilful direction, a bill embodying what appeared to be the substance of Ryerson's plan passed the legislature in April, 1853. By this act the Baldwin Act of 1849 was repealed and the University became, like the University of London, an examining body. Teaching in arts subjects was to be given by University College and those denominational colleges which affiliated with the University. Unfortunately the financial provisions were a characteristic Hincks compromise. Instead of providing a reasonable grant for denominational institutions the bill stipulated that the surplus income from the university endowment should be appropriated annually for academic education.[132] A surplus never materialized.[133]

The way in which the reconstituted university would function was not clear. For the moment it appeared that the Methodist objective in higher education was on the verge of achievement.

4

In retrospect it can readily be seen that between 1847 and 1855 the Wesleyan Methodist Church did not play a remarkable part in solving the complex problems that bedevilled politicians in Canada West. Neither Conference nor *Guardian* was specific on the question of a working system of self-government. In the most crucial phase of the struggle, the *Guardian* was allowed to intervene indirectly on behalf of those least willing to accept the province's new situation. There were no further lapses of this kind; apart from occasional admonitions, the *Guardian* showed no interest in the burgeoning party conflict of the early eighteen-fifties.

The Methodist position on the clergy reserves was similarly hesitant and ambiguous. The Conference continued to subscribe vaguely to the principle of religious equality, and its members refused to undermine the voluntary principle as it applied to themselves. No serious protest was made, however, against the compromise settlement that the ministry effected, nor did the Canadian leaders attempt to dissuade their English brethren from taking a slice in the final division. The fact was that the Conference no longer really cared about details of this question; Methodists and others had thwarted the Anglicans and Presbyterians and that was enough.

In a sense the Methodist Church was equally uncertain on the question of university policy. Some members of the Conference, led by Egerton Ryerson, were convinced that the only sound solution of this question lay in state support for secular and denominational institutions alike, such assistance to be given on an equitable basis. Yet they were also anxious to collaborate with the government, provided that in some way a genuine link could be maintained between Christian principles and higher education. This attitude was in turn related to the difficulties of operating a college, and to the lack of interest in Victoria's future among some members of Conference and doubtless of the Church at large. Methodists had protested against Baldwin's university legislation. They had come very close to giving up Victoria College and finally had given enthusiastic backing to the Hincks scheme, in hopes that it would be a workable compromise for all.

On the whole the Methodist performance in the last days of the clergy reserves battle was a sorry spectacle. Those who sought complete secularization, preferably for educational purposes, lost a valuable ally in the *Christian Guardian*. The Conference lowered its own prestige by its acceptance of a share in the settlement. Still there were extenuating circumstances. A substantial body of Methodists, lay and clerical, disagreed with the Church's official policy. Their influence was probably felt on the secularization side. It should also be said that a solution different from Macdonald's was not likely feasible. The imperial government was unwilling to overlook vested rights, whereas in Upper Canada there was no more agreement on details of reserves policy than there had ever been. The most one can argue is that a concerted effort might have eliminated the commutation scheme and made possible assignment of the reserves surplus to education alone.

In much the same way, evaluation of the Methodist rôle in the university question depends upon assessment of the general situation. Methodist opposition to the new University of Toronto is understandable in the light of the apparently deliberate design to exclude religious influences from it. Yet Baldwin was surely not as anticlerical as his actions suggested. A vigorous and constructive effort by the Methodists to make the University a more palatable institution might well have evoked a favourable response from the government. Even so there is no certainty that Queen's or Trinity would have been willing to forego their claims as independent universities.[134]

From the aspect of provincial opinion one sees the Methodist position differently. Their assumption, shared by the other denominational colleges, was that most people wanted church-controlled universities. If the Methodists were correct, their support for the reshaping of the University of Toronto into a federation of church and secular colleges was a sensible move. It was not their fault that the bill was so vaguely worded at certain points, nor was it their doing that University College continued to display the same selfish spirit that had marked King's College. For the present the Conference and Victoria College felt with some justification that they had helped to lay down a sound policy.

Finally, it is apparent that the direct contribution of the Methodist Church to the development of party government after 1847 was insignificant, notwithstanding the notorious intervention of Conference and *Guardian* in the election campaign of 1847. The establishment of the Wesleyan Methodist Church was nevertheless of some importance in the broad political evolution of Canada West. In its new form the Methodist Church had lost little of its Canadian spirit; rather, it had achieved a compromise between colonial and imperial claims that freed it from concern about metropolitan influences. Gradually a more vigorous nationalist impulse emerged within the Methodist community. As an expanding Canadian denomination the Wesleyan Methodist Church became an example and inspiration to the secular nationalist forces that were stirring within the province of Canada.

REFERENCES TO CHAPTER TEN

1. George Playter became editor in 1844. For his views see *C.G.*, October 9; December 11, 1844.
2. The agitators were named by John Ryerson in a letter to Egerton. *E.R.*, II, 92, John to Egerton Ryerson, June 24, 1845. They were long-standing opponents of the Conference. Carroll, *Case and His Cotemporaries*, IV, 434.
3. *E.R.*, II, 92.
4. *Toronto Periodical Journal*, January, 1845.
5. The words are John Ryerson's.
6. The net loss was 803 members. *Minutes of Conference, 1845*, 383. Woodstock, Brantford, Dundas, Nelson, Albion, Belleville, Hallowell and Augusta were among those circuits with fewer members.
7. The New Connexion Church was particularly attractive to aggressive laymen.

8. *Minutes of Conference, 1845,* 386. Technically this step was taken in reply to a similar move by the British Conference in 1843. See Anson Green: "After the proposition we made them [in 1843], we are scarcely prepared at this Conference to meet their committee; but some of us hope to take a step in that direction next year." *The Life and Times of Anson Green,* 287. John Ryerson, too, was "anxious to do most anything to effect an adjustment of our misunderstandings."
9. *C.G.,* September 10, 1845.
10. Carroll hoped for the creation of a British North American Conference. *C.G.,* December 17, 1845.
11. *Minutes of Conference, 1846,* 20-21. A net loss of 1,389 members was incurred.
12. *Ibid.,* 19.
13. Green, *op. cit.,* 290-291.
14. Carroll, *op. cit.,* IV, 462.
15. *W.R.,* Reel 19, John Douse to the Secretaries, November 21, 1845.
16. *M.R.,* Reel 4, Minutes of a Special District Meeting, June 20, 1846. Harvard, too, hoped that the Committee would not agree to "leaving us in *any* sort or *degree identified* with a body of brethren who are *essentially diverse* from us; and who have taken the utmost pains to lead the people of Canada to *distrust* us and to *dislike* us." *W.R.,* Reel 19, Harvard to Alder, June 13, 1846.
17. According to Stinson, Egerton Ryerson had strongly impressed some members of the English Conference. *Ibid.,* Reel 15, Stinson to Alder, March 2, 1846. Ryerson made an extended visit to England and the continent in 1845.
18. *Ibid.,* Stinson to Alder; Alder to Stinson, March 4, 1846.
19. *E.R.,* II, 119, J. to E. Ryerson, August 7, 1846. Carroll, *op. cit.,* IV, 478.
20. Green, *op. cit.,* 295-296; *E.R.,* II, 120-121, J. to E. Ryerson, September 15, 1846; E. Ryerson, *Canadian Methodism: Its Epochs and Characteristics,* 438.
21. The committee members are listed in *W.R.,* Reel 15, Extracts from Journal of Conference, Bristol, 1846.
22. *E.R.,* II, 120-121, J. to E. Ryerson, September 15, 1846.
23. *Ibid.,* 121.
24. *Ibid.* This involved the appointment of the president and missions superintendent by the English Conference and placing the missions under the Society. The parent conference was to have a veto on the decisions of the Canada Conference and also was to contribute to its funds.
25. United Church Archives, Richey Papers, J. Ryerson to Richey, November 20, 1846.
26. Green, *op. cit.,* 306; *C.G.,* October 14, 1846.
27. U.C.A., Richey Papers, Ryerson to Richey, November 20, 1846. According to Green the committee agreed "to co-operate" in making the plan "palatable to our people."

28. *Ibid.*, Ryerson to Richey, December 2, 1846.
29. *W.R.*, Reel 15, Green to Alder, February 18, 1847. The Wesleyan preachers regarded the Canadian version of the proposed union as "inadequate, erroneous and injurious." When the chairman of one district was shown an accurate copy of the plan, the result, so they said, was its rejection by most of his circuits. *M.R.*, Reel 4, Minutes of a Special District Meeting, February 17, 1847.
30. The Hamilton circuit called the reunion scheme "inexpedient" and "utterley repugnant to the feelings" of the members. *W.R.*, Reel 15, Minutes of a Special General Meeting, December 7, 1846; *M.R.*, Reel 4, Minutes of a Special District Meeting, February 13-17, 1847.
31. *W.R.*, Reel 19, Richey to Alder, February 22, 1847. Stinson also pointed out that it would be foolish not to act. Thousands of Methodists were emigrating to Canada. "Are they," he asked, "to pitch their tents in the midst of a divided Methodist Church?" *Ibid.*, Reel 15, Stinson to Alder, March 25, 1847.
32. *M.R.*, Reel 4, Summary of discussions between Alder and the members of the Canada Western District.
33. *Minutes of Conference, 1847,* 25.
34. Green, *op. cit.*, 297.
35. *Ibid.*, 309.
36. *Ibid.*, 309. The pamphlet was: David Wright and others, *Considerations on the Proposed Reunion of the Canadian and English Wesleyan Conferences* (Picton, 1847). The others were Cyrus Allison, Asahel Hurlburt and G. F. Playter.
37. *C.G.*, June 9, 1847. The circuit vote was: 59 for, 22 against, 5 not reported. *E.R.*, II, 138.
38. Carroll, *op. cit.*, V, 3.
39. *M.R.*, Reel 4, Summary of discussion . . . 1847.
40. *W.R.*, Reel 19, Address of Canada Western District, 1847.
41. *C.G.*, June 16, 1847.
42. *Minutes of Conference, 1847,* 35.
43. *Ibid.*, 36.
44. *Ibid.*, 36-38.
45. *Ibid.*, 38.
46. *Minutes of Conference, 1842,* 311-312; *1844,* 359; U.C.A., Richey Papers, J. Ryerson to Richey, December 2, 1846.
47. The annual grant of £1600 promised by the English Conference and the Society was not in addition to the provincial grant, the latter being included in it.
48. M. Edwards, *After Wesley* (London, 1935), 163.
49. Richey suffered a severe accident in October, 1849. On this account and probably because of differences with the Ryersons he resigned in 1850. *W.R.*, Reel 19, Wood to Hoole, October 19, 1849; *ibid.*, Wood to Alder, September 24, 1850. Harvard returned to England; Ephraim Evans went to Nova Scotia for a time.

50. *W.R.*, Reel 15, Wood to the Secretaries, July 29, 1847; *ibid.*, Reel 19, Wood to Alder, September 24, 1850.
51. J. Carroll, *Past and Present* (Toronto, 1860), 246.
52. Ryerson was also dropped from the minutes for one year because he would not submit to the Conference's policy on class meetings. *E.R.*, II, Chapter 9.
53. *C.G.*, June 23, July 7, 1847. There was a dispute in London and of course the Kingston circuit showed uneasiness.
54. *W.R.*, Reel 19, Wood to Alder, August 27, 1847.
55. *Ibid.*, November 9, 1847.
56. *C.G.*, October 25, 1854.
57. *W.R.*, Reel 19, Wood to Alder, January 26, 1848.
58. *Ibid.*, Reel 17, Wood to Beecham, June 24, 1853.
59. *Ibid.*
60. *Minutes of Conference, 1848,* 69. This was in line with Wesleyan practice.
61. *C.G.*, September 3, 1851.
62. *W.R.*, Reel 19, Wood to Alder, September 26, 1851.
63. Carroll, *op. cit.*, V, 110.
64. *Minutes of Conference, 1848,* 71; *1851,* 162-163.
65. Carroll, *op. cit.*, V, 170; *W.R.*, Reel 20, Wood to the Secretaries, June 18, 1854.
66. *Ibid.*, Wood to Osborn, June 24, 1854; *E.R.*, II, 286-295. In Wood's view, Ryerson's withdrawal was "not calculated to do us any harm."
67. *C.G.*, February 9, 1853.
68. *C.G.*, November 29, 1854.
69. For a discussion of the influence of railways on provincial opinion see J. J. Talman, "The Impact of the Railway on a Pioneer Community," *CHAR* (1955), 1-12.
70. Draper took refuge on the bench in the spring of 1847. For Elgin's actions see Martin, *Empire and Commonwealth,* 304-308.
71. J. S. Moir, *Church and State in Canada West,* 96. For Macdonald's appointment see D. G. Creighton, *John A. Macdonald: The Young Politician* (Toronto, 1952), 120.
72. *D.H.E.*, VII, 4-7.
73. *C.G.* July 21, 1847.
74. *D.H.E.*, VII, 40-41; Creighton, *op. cit.*, I, 123-124; Moir, *op. cit.*, 98-99.
75. *W.R.*, Reel 19, Wood to Alder, November 9, 1847.
76. *C.G.*, November 10, 1847.
77. *Ibid.*, November 24, 1847.
78. *Ibid.*, December 8, 1847.
79. *Ibid.*, December 15, 1847.
80. *W.R.*, Reel 19, Wood to Alder, January 26, 1848.
81. *Ibid.*
82. Carroll, *op. cit.*, V, 18-20. Doubtless some who left disliked the union.

83. *E.R.*, II, 165, J. to E. Ryerson, March 10, 1848.
84. For example, Frontenac, Cornwall, Niagara, Hamilton and Toronto elected tories, whereas in the Yorks, Halton, Hastings, Lincoln, Norfolk, Oxford and Wentworth, reformers were elected.
85. *W.R.*, Reel 19, Wood to Alder, December 21, 1847.
86. Lindsey, *Clergy Reserves*, 50.
87. The Free Church was the other likely applicant.
88. J. C. Dent, *The Last Forty Years*, II, 186.
89. *C.G.*, December 25, 1844.
90. Elgin, for example, reported subsequently: [Ryerson] "is much more decided against the present settlement than I expected to find him and declares that no man who desires to be elected even for a municipality in U. Canada dare commit himself to the support of it." A.G. Doughty, ed., *Elgin-Grey Papers, 1846-1852* (Ottawa, 1937), II, 724.
91. The amount withheld had been invested in Canadian funds. Cathcart, the administrator, was ordered to pay it to appropriate Methodist officials. P.A.C., *G450*, 273, Grey to Cathcart, September 30, 1846.
92. U.C.A. Richey Papers, Memoranda Relative to the Annual Grant from the Reserves of Canada to the W.M.S. n.d.; *W.R.*, Reel 19, Wood to Alder, December 21, 1847. Evidently the government's design was to reduce the fixed charges on the reserves fund as incumbents retired or died. *Ibid.*, Reel 20, Richey to Alder, January 5, 1848.
93. *Ibid.*, Reel 19, Wood to Alder, December 21, 1847; Wood to Hoole, January 4, 1848; Richey to Daly, January 20, 1848.
94. *Ibid.*, Wood to Hoole, February 4, 1848; Wood to the Secretaries, July 10, 1848. Wood remarked: "Had not the papers [Richey's lists] been in the way we should have obtained between four and five hundred pounds more than we did besides settling the Annual claims on a basis much more favourable to the Society." Wood to Alder, March 20, 1849.
95. *W.R.*, Reel 20, Wood to the Secretaries, June 26, 1848. The motion is in the *MS Journal of Conference, 1848*.
96. *Journals of the Legislative Assembly, 1849*, Appendix JJJJ.
97. Wood thought the reserves and university questions were both designed "to swell up the power and patronage of the Colonial Government." *W.R.*, Reel 19, Wood to Alder, March 20, 1849.
98. *C.G.*, May 22, 1850.
99. Dent, *op. cit.*, II, 216.
100. *Elgin-Grey Papers*, IV, 1504-1510.
101. *Ibid.*, II, 697-698; P.A.C., *G138*, 50, Grey to Elgin, January 27, 1851.
102. *Minutes of Conference, 1851*, 158-160. The resolutions were drafted by E. Ryerson, G. R. Sanderson and James Spencer. Ryerson had recently returned from England where he had advised the ministry on the matter. *E.R.*, II, 210-231.

103. *C.G.*, July 2, 1851.
104. Green, *op. cit.*, 335.
105. Dent, *op. cit.*, II, 246-249, 252. The British Government, meanwhile, had not acted on its earlier promise. *Elgin-Grey Papers*, II, 815-832.
106. *C.G.*, November 26; December 3, 1851.
107. For example, J. H. Cameron and G. Sherwood were defeated. See Dent, *op. cit.*, II, 253; Moir, *op. cit.*, 64.
108. The Hincks-Morin government blamed the British government for its inability to act, but there is reason to believe that it was more interested in other matters.
109. P.A.C., *G453*, Newcastle to Elgin (2), January 15, 1853; *Globe*, May 12, 1853.
110. Dent, *op. cit.*, II, 224; R. S. Longley, *Sir Francis Hincks* (Toronto, 1943), 299-300.
111. *C.G.*, June 7, 1854.
112. *W.R.*, Reel 20, Wood to the Secretaries, June 18, 1854. *MS Journal of Conference, 1854*. See also Wood's comment: "As a church we are happily free from all parties, attending to our proper work as ministers of Christ." *W.R.*, Reel 21, Wood to Beecham, July 22, 1854.
113. Dent, *op. cit.*, II, 292.
114. *Statutes of Canada, 1854-55*, I, Cap. 2.
115. *C.G.*, October 25, 1854.
116. *W.R.*, Reel 20, Wood to Hoole, November 20, 1854.
117. Creighton, *op. cit.*, I, 215.
118. *W.R.*, Reel 20, Beecham and Wood to G. E. Cartier, July 5, 1855; Beecham to Wood, July 6, 1855; Wood to Beecham, August 10, 1855.
119. *D.H.E.*, VIII, 119-121.
120. *C.G.*, April 18, 25, 1849.
121. *W.R.*, Reel 19, Wood to Alder, March 20, 1849.
122. It should be recalled that Wood sympathized with the promoters of centralized university education in New Brunswick. See *W.R.*, Reel 19, Wood to Hoole, May 18, 1849.
123. Anson Green, who should have been present, was excluded because of "the active feelings he [had] lately shown in some political movements in which his father-in-law was concerned." Green's father-in-law was Caleb Hopkins, a leading Clear Grit. *W.R.*, Reel 19, Wood to Alder, April 4, 1850.
124. *Ibid.*
125. *W.R.*, Reel 16, Richey to Alder, September 19, 1850. For an assessment of Baldwin's declaratory act concerning the status of religion see Moir, *op. cit.*, 107.
126. *W.R.*, Reel 19, Wood to Hoole, June 20, 1850.
127. *Ibid.; D.H.E.*, IX, 20; *C.G.*, September 25, 1850.
128. For Wood's efforts see *W.R.*, Reel 20, Wood to Hoole, January 7, 1851.

129. Sissons, *A History of Victoria University*, 86-87. He was acting principal until 1852.
130. *Ibid.*, 95, 97.
131. *E.R.*, II, 260-261.
132. *D.H.E.*, X, 117-129.
133. W. S. Wallace, *A History of the University of Toronto* (Toronto, 1927), 65.
134. The charter of Trinity College passed the legislature in August, 1851. T. A. Reed, ed., *A History of the University of Trinity College, Toronto, 1852-1952* (Toronto, 1952), 49. Trinity became what King's College was intended to be.

ELEVEN

"Methodism: disinterested and selfish, liberal and conservative."

In many ways the decade of the eighteen-fifties was a decisive turning point in the history of British North America and of its flourishing Wesleyan Methodist community. Throughout the scattered provinces the age of the pioneer was passing; the first faint tremors of industrial revolution were being felt. On the land the period of settlement was drawing to a close; elsewhere the railway and the steamship symbolized a new era of speedy communications, busy speculation, and material progress. The growing towns and cities, though still outranked by rural areas, imparted a new air of sophistication to provincial society and epitomized the increasing complexity of its needs and aspirations.

More striking still was the great transformation in the world of politics. In Upper Canada, in Halifax, and in Fredericton only the remnants of oligarchic rule remained. A citizen of Kingston and a fearsome Scottish immigrant were the principal political figures in Canada West; that equally formidable Scot, Bishop Strachan, was now confined largely to his ecclesiastical duties. Joseph Howe was the dominant personality in Nova Scotia; New Brunswick was about to hide its cherished engine of corruption behind the façade of responsible government. With this political revolution, accompanied as it was by a reluctant recognition that the development of British North America would be determined by North American and British influences, there had come the easing of old tensions and the healing of old sores.

In Upper Canada as in the Maritime Provinces the separation of church and state had been largely effected, except in the realm of education. It was no longer seriously asserted that there was a correlation between evangelical Protestantism and disloyalty to the British connexion; on the contrary, such prominent Methodists as L. A. Wilmot and Egerton Ryerson held important public positions. The forces of Protestantism, stimulated by bigotry and the gradual emergence of Canadian nationalism, now were drawing together for a long battle with a traditional enemy, the Roman Catholic Church.

Within the Methodist churches, as in British North America generally, it was clear that one generation was giving way rapidly to another. The establishment of the Conference of Eastern British America marked the coming of age of the mission inaugurated so hopefully three-quarters of a century earlier by William Black. In Canada West, too, by 1855 the English and Canadian Conferences had reached a satisfactory understanding with each other. Old rancours and suspicions had lost their force; each side was determined to live with the other in a Christian spirit. In the two conferences older preachers were being pushed aside by younger and more sophisticated men. In October, 1855, "Father" Case, the apostle to the Indians, slipped quietly into eternity. A year earlier his close friend Anson Green had been dismissed from his influential position as Book Steward. The old order was going and with it would go something of that spirit of sacrifice and simplicity that had characterized these Methodist bodies.

As the generation of Case and William Ryerson, of Alder and Richey became the substance of fading memory, the more thoughtful among preachers and people may well have paused to consider what Wesleyan Methodism had meant to the political and educational development of British North America. Doubtless some were convinced that much had been accomplished; others probably felt that through compromise and hesitancy many fruitful opportunities had been lost. In broader retrospect, what verdict can be given? What ends did the Methodists seek? What was their real contribution to the emerging Canadian society?

Throughout this essay the general contention has been that no simple label can be attached to the social and political ideals of the Wesleyan Methodists and to the policies by which they sought to attain their objectives. Their position was in fact many-sided and was certainly not fixed. Moreover, differences of outlook persisted between the Methodists in the eastern provinces and in Upper Canada, and between ministers and members of the Societies.

In any attempt to assess the Methodists' political outlook the starting point must surely be the recognition of their fundamental aversion to involvement in this sphere. For them politics was a "dirty" business that could only contaminate the Christian. This was generally coupled with an admission that, since evasion of responsibility was really impossible, the believer should apply moral criteria to politicians and their actions. Above all, the Methodist was expected to judge men and issues on their merits and not in the light of partisan considerations.

Unfortunately, the formative years of Wesleyan Methodism in British North America were a critical period in the evolution of our secular institutions. Within this general context the establishment of responsible government was of decisive importance. In this area the Methodists' attitude and objective was, for many, maddeningly elusive, but in actuality it was reasonably intelligible.

The official policy of the Methodists in the Maritime Provinces was to ignore the fierce conflict that occurred in Nova Scotia particularly, over local self-government. Colonial politics was "a tempest in a teapot" in which preachers and people were to meddle as little as possible. It was recognized of course that individual Methodists had a right to advocate or reject political reform, but the general emphasis on stability and loyalty suggested that those who resisted change were better Christians than those who worked for it.

In contrast, the stand taken on this issue by the Upper Canadian Methodists was very susceptible to misinterpretation. From the outset they contended that the province's government was based upon a contractual understanding, and that, if its terms were observed properly, existing sources of discontent would be eliminated. Any attempt to alter the form of the contract was in their view unjustifiable and would imperil the imperial connexion, to whose continuance they were firmly attached. But—and this was an important qualification—they believed that the constitution must be interpreted in the light of Canadians' real concerns, not to suit the interests of radical or conservative minorities.

Holding these views, the Methodist Conference applied them in what appeared to be an inconsistent and vacillating fashion. Between 1829 and 1833 its sympathies were ostensibly with the rising reform politicians, whereas from 1833 to 1837 it moved steadily toward the tories. The trend was abruptly reversed in 1838 and strong suport was given to Lord Durham and his successor. But, if the cordial reception of the Durham Report indicated a return to the Methodist stance of before 1833, the qualifications suggested for its implementation, and the close association that developed between Sydenham and the Methodists, apparently pointed in another direction. Ryerson's appearance in the lists on behalf of Metcalfe in 1844, and the subsequent efforts of the Methodist Conference to ignore the crucial question at issue in 1847, completed the process of disillusionment with the Methodists as a political force.

That as a result many should have regarded the Methodist Conference as a cynical and self-seeking body was not surprising, but their criticism was not wholly justified. Assuredly the Methodist leaders leaned on occasion too far to the right or to the left; assuredly they were actuated in part by selfish interests. Nevertheless, their course was in keeping with their determination not to commit their church as such to a party-political stand, and their conviction that Upper Canada needed a change in outlook rather than in institutions. In its twists and turns, however, there was implicit a steady drift away from political activity and towards acceptance of the existing order.

For most Methodists, of course, the general problem of secular self-government was less important than the specific issues of civil and religious liberty and education, tied though these ultimately were to the resolution of the first question. Here again the position of the Methodists in the eastern provinces was less clear-cut than in Upper Canada.

Evidently the former Societies believed that they should be permitted to practise their faith without hindrance or discrimination. Doubtless, too, if they had found themselves in an extremely invidious position they would have reacted firmly and strongly in defence of their rights. But their behaviour in this field was conditioned and moderated by their official friendliness toward the Church of England. It would almost appear that they were prepared to countenance political favours to the Church, provided that these did not interfere with their own freedom of action. They were unwilling to say, publicly at least, that there should be help for all or help for none, or that no denomination should be assisted in any way by the state. In effect, they were not strongly committed to the principle of separation of church and state.

At first glance, the standpoint of the Upper Canadian Methodists on this matter was diametrically opposite to that of their Maritimes brethren. Initially they clamoured ferociously for full acceptance of civil and religious liberty and equality. Access to public office and educational opportunity ought to be solely according to merit. The Church of England, they argued, should be entirely deprived of public assistance, in particular of the clergy reserves, and as a corollary every religious body should be treated in the same way by government. As this statement was associated with fervent assertions that each church should be wholly maintained by its own people, it was accepted that the Methodist Church was a firm advocate of the voluntarist principle and of the complete divorce of church and state.

Originally this widespread opinion was entirely sound. In this area, however, as in others, the Conference's position was subsequently modified. While they upheld the voluntary ideal in the normal operations of the church and resisted church establishment, the Methodist leaders reconciled themselves to the co-operation of church and government in some fields. Their original motto "help for none" was gradually replaced by the slogan "help for all," although they were fully aware that, since some churches would refuse aid of any kind, this meant "help for some." That this could have been implicit in their original pronouncements on this subject is evident, but it would be more accurate to say that the Methodist community altered its principles without wholly acknowledging it.

The Methodists' strong interest in civil and religious liberty was accompanied by, and in part the product of, an early and sincere concern about the problem of education. On this point the policy of the Methodists in the eastern provinces was precise, if limited. Confronted with a society in which sectarian rivalries were strong and facilities inadequate, they conceived it their duty to establish schools in which Methodist children could be properly trained in Christian and secular knowledge. They thought it fitting that the state should assist such ventures and that in so doing it should give no significant advantage to one group. To secure their objective they intervened in politics, seeking support where it might be found, regardless of other considerations.

In Upper Canada the nature of the educational challenge was much the same as in Nova Scotia and New Brunswick, but the Methodists' response was rather different. On the one hand they urged the establishment of a national system of elementary schools in which ample provision would be made for the needs of the majority and for the inculcation of Christian morality in a non-sectarian form. Conversely they were distinctly unsympathetic to the establishment of separate schools for Anglicans and Roman Catholics. On the other hand their initial stand on the university question was to advocate the elimination of the Anglican monopoly and the creation of generally useful institutions of higher education. At the same time they founded Upper Canada Academy, a secondary school with minimal ecclesiastical controls, to be supported by fees and public generosity. But before the Academy was transformed into Victoria University it had ceased to be a voluntarist agency. Because of Victoria's needs and their continuing interest in the development of a genuinely popular university system, they took an active part in the furious disputes over this issue. Eventually they called for equitable state support for a group of denominationally controlled colleges, a proposition that was seemingly popular but which was bound to work hardship on those who would not accept it. In this as in the case of the clergy reserves the Methodist Conference appeared to have compromised its original principles.

Considered as a whole the formal positions taken up by these two Methodist bodies reflect the underlying motives that determined their actions. Their primary intention was to establish and maintain the most effective conditions for preaching and practising Christianity as they understood it. Nevertheless, as men and women who sought to attain holiness in this life, they had a deep sense of responsibility for their fellows, which led them to examine the rôle of the church and the Christian in society. The Methodists in the eastern provinces differed from their Upper Canadian brethren in the relative weight they gave to each of these fundamental considerations and in the range of their secular activity.

To the former, living under the restraining hand of the Wesleyan Conference and functioning in a community only moderately unfriendly, it seemed natural to emphasize Methodist needs as such. Similarly both internal and external pressures induced them to adopt a detached and mildly critical attitude toward the reshaping of their social environment. To the latter, however, imbued with an independent spirit, and constantly harassed by the Wesleyans and by other hostile forces, it appeared imperative to stress the altruistic side of Methodism. Moreover, they drew upon the implications of their faith and their polity in formulating a sharp critique of the Upper Canadian political and social order. It was the genius or the misfortune of Methodism that in acting as it did each branch of the Connexion could claim to be a legitimate embodiment of the Wesleyan tradition.

While there were these very real differences between the attitudes of the Maritimes districts and the Canada Conference, at the midcentury they were evidently becoming less obtrusive. Thrown increasingly on their own resources, the former were adopting a more assertive and self-confident, if not broad-minded, approach to their problems. In Canada West, however, the persistent criticism of the Wesleyans and the elimination of many obstacles to Methodist growth brought to the surface that anxiety about the welfare of the Methodist Church that had been for many the real justification of Methodist political action. For them it was no longer the case that what was good for Canada was good for Methodism; rather, they were beginning to feel that what was good for Methodism was good for Canada.

Whatever the nature of the forces that shaped the reactions of the Methodists, their presence and the various alterations in their stand were clearly of some importance in the evolution of British North America. But the quality and the extent of their contribution cannot be assessed simply in the light of their overt activities. Rather, the intangible influences that emanated from the Methodist Societies and the limit set by their numbers should not be overlooked. Furthermore, in this final reckoning, clarification of those much abused terms *liberal* and *conservative* must be sought, if only to establish an objective context within which Methodism can be placed.

During the first half of the nineteenth century there were so many strands of opinion and interest in British North America that to separate them into meaningful categories is extraordinarily difficult. But it is not really straining the evidence to suggest that, after 1840 especially, two distinct types of political and social orientation were emerging in the provincial societies. On the one side were those who were hesitant about the advance toward self-government, who, if they did not hanker after church establishment, had no objection to the collaboration of church and state, who were prepared to envisage a wide range of government action and who were rather loath to admit that they were living in North America. They were indeed more willing to interpret Canadian problems in English than in local terms. Here were at least some of the ingredients of the conservative tradition. On the other side were those who sought to establish autonomous parliamentary institutions, who were committed to the principle of a secular social order, who wished to limit the rôle of the state, and who had an acute awareness of the reality of Canadian needs as against the powerful pull of the United States and Britain. Unwilling to reject either, they attempted to define solutions to Canadian problems in which elements drawn from each would be fruitfully combined. Such was the substance of the liberal outlook.

Assuming that this analysis has some validity, to what camp did the Methodists really belong and in what ways did they contribute to the growth of these admittedly ill-defined political groupings? At first glance the Maritimes Methodists would appear to fit neatly into the conservative category. To be fair to them, however, it should be recalled that some Methodist laymen in Nova Scotia and New Brunswick were certainly reformers, and that all lived within the context of a democratic gospel and a constitutional system of church government. Yet lacking better concrete evidence one must conclude that in the first instance they stimulated an aloofness from politics that could only have been detrimental to the development of party government. They strengthened the hands of those who desired co-operation between church and state, at least in education, and who were attached firmly to the British connexion. They may well have contributed to the undue perpetuation of a colonial attitude in this region; or more positively, they may have helped to ease the transition from colony to nation.

But, if the Methodist rôle was essentially conservative, it was also a minor one in the eastern provinces. Numerically, the Methodists counted for much less than the Anglicans, Baptists and Presbyterians. Their inability to secure converts in large numbers, which was assuredly the consequence of their imperfect and reluctant adaptation to local conditions, left the field to their rivals. In Nova Scotia this was perhaps of little importance, but in New Brunswick, where Anglican influence was particularly strong, a more powerful Methodist contingent might conceivably have given greater substance and vigour to the factional politics of the Province. The historian, however, must content himself with what was, rather than what might have been. The relative insignificance of Methodism merely emphasizes the necessity of examining the parts played by its competitors.

If it is relatively easy to categorize the Methodists in the eastern districts, the same cannot be said of their Upper Canadian colleagues. Exception can be taken to almost any positive statement about their political affiliation and the results of their actions. Obviously some, especially among the preachers, were apolitical and others were unquestionably conservative. Furthermore, some Methodists may have been fervent radicals or reformers for reasons entirely unrelated to their religious background. Even so, the evidence strongly suggests that the sympathies of the Canadian Methodist community were essentially liberal—more liberal in reality than the Conference's behaviour would indicate. Undoubtedly, though, they were liberals with a difference. They were prone to adopt a detached attitude, often at the very time when others felt that partisanship was imperative; they submitted eventually to church-state collaboration in some areas. Certainly, too, with the passing years their ardour for liberal causes diminished significantly.

To argue that the Canada Conference was a liberally-oriented body is not, of course, to evaluate the extent of its influence on the transformation of Upper Canada. The intense and intricate wrangle over civil and religious liberty doubtless would have occurred without Methodist intervention and possibly would have been settled much as it was without their help. But the fervour with which they tackled this issue and the skill with which the *Guardian* defended the reform position gave this struggle a form and substance that it might not have had otherwise. Conversely, their hesitant course after 1835 may well have delayed the final disposition of the clergy reserves, and probably contributed to the unsatisfactory compromise at the end.

Similarly, the need for educational reform was evident to many in Upper Canada during the thirties and forties. The Methodists deserve to be remembered, none the less, for their vigorous espousal of legislation that would provide a comprehensive and popular system of primary education. To say that their ideas were unique would be erroneous; rather, they assisted in bringing the province into the orbit of North American educational development.

For contemporaries, however, the crucial issue was the shaping of the university system. Most of those concerned, including many Anglicans, were dubious from the outset about the monopolistic features of King's College. The critical point was to devise a policy that would do justice to the religious convictions of the people and also provide colleges where and when they were needed. Given the diversity of opinion on this subject, the chances of making a wholly satisfactory arrangement were always minimal. Realizing this, the Methodist leaders sought a solution that would secure substantial justice for all. In so doing they could have displayed more vision and insight, but their relative moderation was possibly a decisive factor in keeping open the path to a settlement by which ultimately the various parties were satisfied.

The Methodist impact in the broader realm of politics is much more difficult to assess than their work in education. That they exercised a powerful influence on the outcome of certain general elections is at least an open question. It could hardly be said either that their critique of political partisanship helped to curb the fury of party warfare in Upper Canada. Conceivably this led some Methodists to adopt an aloof attitude towards political issues, which was in itself unhealthy. Their refusal to adopt an incisive stand on responsible government is open to criticism. But considering the immense complexity of the circumstances within which this matter had to be resolved, it was improbable that a group such as the Methodists could have played a decisive part in bringing it to a head. By emphasizing frequently that in politics right attitudes were as important as institutions, the *Guardian* drew attention to a vital aspect of the evolution of parliamentary government.

Surely, though, the Methodists' principal contribution to the political and social growth of Upper Canada was the least tangible. In their pronouncements on the clergy reserves, on education, on the constitution and on government, there is a consistent preoccupation with the working out of genuinely Canadian answers to Canadian questions—that is, answers based on a realistic assessment of Canadian conditions and the wishes of the Canadian people. This viewpoint was peculiarly important because it reflected not only a shrewd analysis of the Canadian situation but also the experience of the Methodist community itself. It was because the Conference was constantly involved in the arduous task of adapting a complex creed to a new environment that its adherents gained a heightened awareness of what was really feasible and desirable in Upper Canada. That one of the largest and most cohesive religious bodies in the province should have been so intimately concerned with the definition of what was in the national interest greatly strengthened the hands of those similarly actuated and was a powerful stimulus to the emergence of Canadian nationalism.

2

Even so, when all this has been recounted, some readers may well ask—why thresh this old straw again? Whether we like it or not, and many evidently do not, religious forces have been an influential factor in the history of Canada. To estimate their true significance requires a sympathetic analysis of each denomination's evolution, and particularly of its conception of the relationship between church and society. It is in this context and in the hope of stimulating further studies that this book has been written.

More particularly, the history of the principal forms of Wesleyan Methodism in British North America casts much light on the potentialities of evangelical churches. In Upper Canada adroit leadership produced much more striking results than in the Maritime Provinces. Ultimately, however, both bodies drew back from that close identification with secular causes that was frequently urged upon them, and in the process incurred odium for what seemed to be either hypocrisy or vacillation. Clearly the Methodists, like other human beings, were not above sharp practice, cowardice, or inconsistency, but generally they were moved by other considerations. They were keenly aware that in their own tradition there was no support for a thoroughly radical social philosophy. For them, too, the priority of man's salvation was inescapable and in the end all their commitments were judged in the light of this principle.

At the mid-century, moreover, the pressures that in future would shape the Wesleyan Methodists' response to the world already were becoming evident. The Methodist churches, soon to be united, and already major institutions, inevitably would hesitate to adopt causes dangerous to their own security. But as the evangelical impulse declined and as Methodists became more concerned with the Christian life, the theological eclecticism of their communion would assume a new importance. This, in combination with the old imperative of holiness, would leave Methodism open to new and powerful insights into the social relevance of the Gospel. Thus the inner life of the Connexion would be characterized by a creative tension that would be productive of an independent, if often crossgrained and intolerant, attitude toward the temporal order.

NOTE ON SOURCES

The student of British North American Methodism is fortunate in the wealth of manuscript and printed material available. First in importance in the manuscript category are the Egerton Ryerson Papers located in Victoria University Library. The substance of this large body of correspondence, an indispensable source for the history of Upper Canadian Methodism, has been published by C. B. Sissons in *Egerton Ryerson: His Life and Letters* (2 vols.; Toronto: Clarke, Irwin, 1937-1947). The Archives of The United Church of Canada, now housed in the Victoria University Library, has microfilm copies of the Wesleyan Methodist Missionary Society's records pertaining to its work in British North America. These films, made for Victoria University and the Public Archives of Canada from originals in the Society's London headquarters, include an immense body of letters from Wesleyan missionaries in America, instructions sent to its missionaries by the Society, and the minutes of missionary district meetings. This collection is basic to an understanding of the growth of Wesleyan Methodism in the Maritime Provinces and the relations between Wesleyan and Upper Canadian Methodism.

In addition to these large accumulations the United Church Archives has a number of small but useful sets of papers including the Nathan Bangs and Matthew Richey Papers, as well as journals of William Case, George Ferguson, and Benjamin Slight. Mount Allison University Library has a similar assortment of manuscripts relating to William Black, Duncan McColl, and Matthew Richey. The Canada Conference's journals and the appendices to its minutes, also held by the Archives, provide many tantalizing glimpses of that conference's operations, not revealed in the austere language of the printed minutes.

For unvarnished and sometimes prejudiced opinions of Methodism and its leaders, the Colonial Office records, especially C.O. 42, Series Q and G in the Public Archives of Canada, are of considerable value. Use may be made of the Bidwell, Macaulay, Robinson, and Strachan papers in the Ontario Archives. The diary of Simeon Perkins, held in typescript by the Public Archives, casts much light on the early history of Nova Scotia and the development of Methodism there. The section for the years 1780 and 1789 has been edited by D. C. Harvey and C. B. Fergusson (Toronto: The Champlain Society, 1958).

In the considerable body of published primary material certain items are noteworthy. *The Life of Mr. William Black: Written by Himself* is in volume five of Thomas Jackson's *Lives of Early Methodist Preachers* (London: Wesleyan Conference Office, 1866). This interesting sketch unfortunately terminates in 1788. In contrast, the *Life and Times of Anson Green* (Toronto: Methodist Book Room, 1877) is a reminiscent account of the entire career of this prominent Canadian Methodist. It tells much about the author and the inner life of the Methodist Church. No one should neglect the journals of the Rev. William Proudfoot, a minister of the United Associate Synod. Mr. Proudfoot considered the Methodists and his American Presbyterian brethren equally repulsive. His papers were published serially in the *Transactions of the London and Middlesex Historical Society* (1915, 1917, 1922) and in the *Papers and Records of the Ontario Historical Society* (1930, 1932, 1933, 1934).

For the early history of Methodism in the United States Bishop Asbury's *Journals* (3 vols.; New York: Lane and Scott, 1852) is a fundamental source. Similarly Wesley's *Works*, of which I have used the third edition (14 vols.; London: John Mason, 1829-1831), his *Journal* (8 vols.; London: Epworth, 1910-1916), and his *Letters* (8 vols.; London: Epworth, 1931) are indispensable for the formative years of Wesleyan Methodism.

The published records of the various Methodist conferences are very extensive but of limited usefulness. The Canada Conference minutes, for example, do not always include important decisions and generally make no reference to the background of decisions taken. Yet for information about the numbers and locations of Methodists, lay and clerical, and for authentic texts of major pronouncements these volumes are essential. The consolidated minutes of the Canada Conference and of the Annual Conferences in the United States, the journals of the American General Conference, and the minutes of the English Conference are in the United Church Archives; the minutes of the Conference of Eastern British America are in the Mount Allison University Library. The missionary reports of the English Conference that appeared under various titles from 1805 to 1817, and as the *Annual Reports* of the General Wesleyan Methodist Missionary Society from 1818 forward, are helpful in tracing the expansion of that Conference's missionary domain. These can be consulted in the United Church Archives.

Fortunately these dry records have been greatly and carefully amplified by the early Methodist historians. For Upper Canada two works are pre-eminent: G. F. Playter's *History of Methodism in Canada* (Toronto: Wesleyan Printing Establishment, 1862) and John Carroll's *Case and His Cotemporaries* (5 vols.; Toronto: Wesleyan Conference Office, 1867-1877). The former carries the story only until 1828, but is judiciously phrased, generally accurate, and enriched by much original material. The latter is really a history of Upper Canadian Methodism from 1805 until Case's death in 1855, and includes much of Case's correspondence as well. Carefully composed, with a large measure of tolerance and good sense, Carroll's work is rightly cherished by all students of Methodism.

The comparable account of Methodism in the eastern provinces is T. W. Smith's *History of the Methodist Church of Eastern British America* (2 vols.; Halifax: S. F. Huestis, 1877-1890). This is not so well ordered or informative but again it provides material and impressions not otherwise available. One should not overlook Matthew Richey's *Memoir of the Late Rev. William Black, Wesleyan Minister* (Halifax: W. Cunnabell, 1839) in which among many flights of pious rhetoric the main outlines of Black's career are given.

The Methodist Episcopal Church in the United States produced several able historians in the nineteenth century, among whom were

Nathan Bangs and Abel Stevens. The former's *History of the Methodist Episcopal Church* (4 vols.; New York: Mason and Lane, 1838-1841) incorporates many original documents and reveals much about the temper of early American Methodism. In contrast, Abel Stevens' *History of the Methodist Episcopal Church in the United States of America* (4 vols.; New York: Nelson and Phillips, 1864-1867) is one of the first efforts to put American Methodist history in a broader perspective.

In the vast body of contemporary newspapers certain items are of particular importance. The *Christian Guardian,* founded in 1829 and now on file in the United Church Archives, is without doubt one of the greatest repositories of information concerning the development of Upper Canadian Methodism and the secular history of the province. The *British North American Wesleyan Methodist Magazine, The Wesleyan,* and the *Provincial Wesleyan,* files of which are in Mount Allison Library, are valuable guides to the growth of Methodism after 1838 in the eastern provinces. Similarly the *Methodist Magazine* (U.S.A.) and the *Arminian* [later *Methodist*] *Magazine* (London), which are held by the United Church Archives, contain much information about the missionary effort of the two parent sections of the Methodist Connexion. The student should not need to be reminded of the importance of secular newspapers such as the *Acadian Recorder,* the *Novascotian,* the *Colonial Advocate,* the *Globe,* and the Toronto *Examiner.*

Finally, attention should be drawn to some modern works related to this subject. In the Canadian field, mention should be made of S. D. Clark's *Church and Sect in Canada* (Toronto: University of Toronto Press, 1948), his *Movements of Political Protest in Canada* (Toronto: University of Toronto Press, 1959), G. W. Brown's articles on Upper Canada and its Methodists in the *Canadian Historical Review* (1939), and the *Canadian Historical Association Reports* (1938), H. H. Walsh's *The Christian Church in Canada* (Toronto: Ryerson, 1956), and J. S. Moir's *Church and State in Canada West 1841-1867* (Toronto: University of Toronto Press, 1959). Similarly, students of American Methodism should not overlook the numerous studies published by W. W. Sweet. The standard history of English Methodism is *A New History of Methodism* by W. J. Townsend, H. B. Workman and G. Eayrs (2 vols.; London: Hodder and Stoughton, 1909). The serious student might also consult J. S. Simon, *John Wesley and the Methodist Societies* (5 vols.; London: Epworth, 1921-1934), and G. G. Findlay and W. W. Holdsworth, *The History of the Wesleyan Methodist Missionary Society* (5 vols.; London: Epworth, 1921). Among the numerous biographies of Wesley two may be singled out: M. Piette, *John Wesley in the Evolution of Protestantism* (New York: Sheed and Ward, 1937), a distinguished study by a Franciscan friar, and U. Lee, *John Wesley and Modern Religion* (Nashville: Cokesbury Press, 1936), written from the standpoint of a liberal Methodist theologian. *The Young Mr. Wesley* by V. H. H. Green (Toronto: Macmillan, 1961), incorporating new material about Wesley's spiritual development, appeared too late to be used in this book.

INDEX

Aberdeen, Earl of, 266
Acadia College, 94, *100*
Acadian Recorder, 290
Adelaide Street Church, 252
Adolphustown, 55
Albany, 44
Alder, Robert, character defined, 59-60, 62, 65; appointed missionary secretary, 87-8; meeting on *The Wesleyan,* 92-3; conversation with Bamford, 95; education and church questions, 95; warning against political involvement, 96; 1832 trip to Canada, 134, 136-41; visits Upper Canada in 1834, 146, 148-150; on duties of government, 178; 1839 visit to Upper Canada, 179-181; renewal of grant, 184-187, 224; urges reunion in maritimes, 196; tours American districts in 1847, 198-9; reunion negotiations, 225, 227-228, 250, 252; general comment, 279
Aldersgate, 3, 4
Alline, Henry, 30-2, 49
Allison, Charles F., 94-5, 203
America. *See* United States
American(s), 39, 41, 45-6, 48, 68-9, 74, 105, 107-9, 137, 139, 176, 189, 219, 258, 288
American Methodist Societies, viii, 1, 16-8, 29, 33-4, 36, 38, 41, *49,* 56, 65, 67, 69-70, 74, 95, 105
American General Conference, 16-20, 23, 27, 33, 35, 46, *50,* 54, 70-7, 101-2, 134, 138, 289
American Revolution, 17, 30, 40
Anderson, Alexander, 37, *50, 51*
Anderson, Joseph, 37, *51*
Anglican(s), vii, 1, 4, 6, 18, 21, 36-7, 30, 41, 43, *52,* 54, 59, 62, 66, 89-90, 93-4, 95, 104, 106, 110-4, 119-20, 122, 124-5, 135, 174-5, 183, 205-7, 210-11, 234, 236, 238-40, 255, 260, 270, 282, 285-6. *See also Church of England; Church, Established*

Annand, William, 206
Annapolis, 37, 64, 86, *97*
Annual Conference(s), 20, 28, 75, 102, 249, 289
Anti-Americanism, 63, 68-9, 101, 109, 139, 172
Anti-Calvinism, 31
Antinomianism, 38
Apostolic Succession, 25, 112
Aristocracy, 30, 41, 93, 122, 125, 142, 172, 190, 220
Arthur, Sir George, 172, 174, 176-7, 178-80, 184, 224, 230
Articles of Religion, 20
Arminian Magazine, 290
Arminian(s), 21, 66
Army, 36, 58, 106
Asbury, Bishop Francis, 18-21, 23, 27-8, 32-4, *49, 53,* 71, 102, 289
Assembly, Upper Canada, 66, 111, 113, 118, 120, 122, 124, 152, 154-6, 158, 160, 171, 174, 176, 238, 240, 260, 264, 266
Assembly, New Brunswick, 205
Assembly, Nova Scotia, 206, 208
Atheism, 209, 234, 237
Attwood, Thomas, 143
Augusta, 156-7
Authority, 12-3, 19, 27, 34, 38, 40, 55-6, 58, 61, 65-6, 71, 88-9, 96, 107, 109-10, 116-8, 139, 141, 159, 171, 176, 188, 200, 223, 226, 231, 233, 254, 256
Autocracy, 15-17, 19-20, 23, 75, 87

Bagot, Sir Charles, 224, 229
Baldwin, Robert, 118, 163, 182, 229-31, 236, 238, 261, 267, 269-70
Bamford, Stephen, 57-8, 61, 66, 86, 89, *95, 98*
Bathurst, Earl, 74
Baltimore Conference, 16-8, 28-9, 33
Bangs, Nathan, 43, 46, *49, 58,* 76, 101, *128,* 288, 289
Baptism of the Holy Ghost, 45
Baptist(s), 90-4, 205-7, 211, 285

291

Barry, John, 64, 66, 146
Barry, Robert, 32, 37
Beals, W. C., 210
Beatty, John, 152
Bedeque, 64
Beecham, John, 87, *98*, 200-1
Belleville, 127, 148, 156, 160, 187, 233, 266
Bennett, William, 54, 57, 60, 71-2, 86
Bible, 1-3, 6-8, 10-12, 14, 30-2, 36, 39, 45, 48, 58, 61, 66, 77-8, 88, 90, 96-7, 112, 115, 118, 155, 172, 178, 208, 227, 232, 235, 284, 287
Bidwell, M. S., 145, 171, 173, 288
Bigotry, 62, 68, 95, 125, 142, 278
Bishop(s), 19, 27, 34, 70, 74-6, 101-2, 121, 149, 175
Black, William, missionary to Nova Scotia, vii; attends Baltimore Conference, 17; conversion and early career, 29, 31-2, 33-5, 38, 39, 41; turns to English Conference, 54-55; type of message preached, 48; retirement, 58; administration, 64, 66; Methodist controversy in Canadas, 71-72; in semi-retirement, 86; general comment, 279; source material, 288-9
Boardman, Richard, 16
Book Committee, 181-3, 218, 279
Book Room, 222
Book Steward, 256
Bowdoin College, 90
Breckenridge, David, 75-6
Bridgetown, 91
Bristol, 3, 24, 250
Britain. *See* England
British Colonist, 230-1
British Conference. *See* Wesleyan Conference
British North America, vii, 23, 29, 33, 39, 56-9, 71, 87, 135, 196, 201, 221, 226, 278-9, 283-4
British North American Conference, 198-200, 225, 272
British North American Wesleyan Methodist Magazine, 200, *213*, 290
Brockville, 157
Bunting, Jabez, 87, *98*, 250
Burch, Thomas, 71
Burwell, Rev. A. H., 126
Busby, Sampson, 202

Calvinism, 5, 21, 31, 110
Canada Conference (1824), 74, 76-7, 101-2, 114
Canada East, 230. *See also* Lower Canada, Quebec
Canada West, 198-200, 209, 218, 222, 224, 226-8, 230, 232, 234, 236, 241-2, 250, 252-3, 257, 259, 267, 269, 271, 278-9, 283. *See also* Upper Canada
Canadian Alliance, 150-1
Canadian Conference. *See* Wesleyan Methodist Church in Upper Canada, 1833
Canadian Wesleyan Methodist Church (Ryanite), 76, 117, *165*, 217
Cape Breton, 62
Cape Tormentine, 202
Caput, 236, 239
Carroll, John, 86, 97, 104-6, 157, 217-9, 232, 248, 255, 257-8, 262, 289
Case, William, early years, 43-6; presiding elder in Upper Canada, 69-70; criticized by Wesleyans, 72-3; elected acting general superintendent, 102; career as superintendent, 105; brings Corson into ministry, 106; his influence wanes, *129*; union negotiations, 135, 139, 141; mediates between E. Ryerson and J. Richardson, 152; condemns Ryerson's editorial policy, 187; president of special conference 1840, 217; joins Wesleyans, 218-19; union negotiations, 1847, 251-2; his death, 279; source material, 288-9
Casual and Territorial Fund, 158-9, 184-5, 187
Cataraqui, 42, 47
Catterick, Thomas, 72
Caughey, James, 258
Cazenovia Seminary, 219
Champlain, Lake, 39
Chapel(s), 6, 47, 59, 65, 71, 91, *98*, 101, 159, 202, *214*, 222, 225, 253
Charity, 15-17, 34, 45, 87, 226, 253
Charlottetown, 64, 92
Charter (university), 121-2, 124, 234-7, 267

292

Christianity, 1-7, 14-6, 31-5, 38, 41, 44, 46, 55, 57-9, 61, 73-4, 88, 93, 95, 112, 115-6, 119, 123, 125, 142-3, 154, 159, 161, 177, 189, 202-3, 209-10, 223, 226-7, 229, 231-2, 235-7, 249-50, 260-1, 268, 270, 279-80, 282, 287

Christian Guardian, 105, 115-7, 120, 123-7, *129,* 139-63, *166,* 172-88, 190, *193,* 200, 218-21, 225-32, 234-41, 248-50, 256, 258, 260-7, 269-71, 285-6, 290

Church, 234, *244*

Church, Established, 30, 41, *49,* 54, 62, 95, 109-12, 114, 117, 120, 122, 124, 126, 154, 159-60, 175, 178, 180-1, 184, 188, 281, 284. *See also* Church of England; Anglican

Church of England, 2, 4, 7-11, 15, 18, 21, 23, 25, 28, 30, 37, 41, *51, 54,* 55, 59, 62, 108, 110-2, 119-20, 122-3, 125-6, 128, 134-6, 145, 160, *165,* 172, 177-9, 180, 183-4, 202, 205, *213,* 220, 225-7, 231, 236-9, 260, 262, 264-5, 281. *See also* Church, Established; Anglican

Church of Scotland, 41, 110-11, 117, 160, 183-4, 220, 236, 238, 262, 264. *See also* Presbyterian(s)

Church-state relations, 87, 95, 109-12, 117-19, 125, 139-40, 151, 153-4, 157, 159-60, 162-3, *165,* 172, 174, 177-8, 180, 183, 188, 190, 205-7, 211, 220-4, 226, 235-7, 254-5, 257, 269-71, 278, 281-2, 284-5, 287

Churchill, Charles, 91, *98*

Circuits, 9, 17, 19-20, 33-5, 37, 39, 41-2, 44, 47, *53,* 56-9, 64-5, 67-8, 70-1, 73, 75, 86-8, 91, 98, 106, 184, 199, 201-2, 218-9, 248, 251, 253-4, 256-7. *See also* Itinerancy

Clark, S. D., vii, 290

Clear Grits, 262

Clergy, 18, 30, 37, 62, 110-11, 113, 119, 123, 142, 145, 176, 236-7, 240, 257, 266, 289. *See also* Ministry, Missionaries, Itinerants, Preachers

Clergy reserves, 110-14, 117, 119-21, 125, 127, 144-5, 151, 153, 156-60, 162, 171-2, 174-88, 191, 220, 223, 239, 241, 254, 259, 262-7, 269-70, 281-2, 285-6

Coate, Samuel, 43

Cobourg, 250

Coke, Bishop Thomas, 16, 18, 21, 25-6, 28-9, 33, *49, 50,* 54, 56-7, 70, 79

Cokesbury College, 23, 28

Colborne, Sir John, 120, 123, 126, 135-6, 138, 140, 143, 145, 150, 154

Colebrooke, Sir William, 205-6

Colonial Advocate, 112, 143-4, 290

Colonial Office, 114, 117, 136, 150, 153, 158-9, 163, 176, 179, 185-6, 224, 288

Colonial Secretary, 120-1, 160, 176, 224, 266

Colony(s), 29-30, 40, 55, 57, 62, 68, 87, 89, 112, 120, 122, 126, 139, 143, 155, 180, 184, 188, 190, 199, 207, 221, 227-9, 255, 267, 271, 280, 284

Committee, the. *See* Missionary Committee

Committee, Book. *See* Book Committee

Compact theory, 115, *155,* 175

Conference, Annual. *See* Annual Conference

Conference, the, in Upper Canada. *See* Wesleyan Methodist Church in Upper Canada

Conference Contingent Fund, 253

Congregation(s), 30, 44, 46, 60, 105, 107, 198, 202-3, 207, 252, 265. *See also* Societies

Congregational Churches, 30-1, 41, 52, 90, 240

Connecticut, 42

Connexion(s), the, 1, 4-17, 20, 23, 33, 39, 51, 54-5, 56, 60, 64-5, 71-2, 77, 89, 92, 101-2, 128, 136-7, 139, 147, 150, 171, 174, 178, 187, 189, 199, 201, 218, 224-5, 229, 240-2

Conservatism, viii, 11, 13, 16-17, 23, 30, 55, 58-9, 61, 66, 68-9, 74, 96, 104, 108, 115, 125, 145, 147, 150-1, 153, 160, 162, 182, 197, 207, 210, 224, 233, 254-5, 257, 266, 280, 284-5. *See also* Tory

Constitution, 115, 119, 125, 143, 154-5, 161, 164, 172, 175-6, 180, 188, 190, 227, 229, 233, 262-4, 280, 284

Conversion, 8, 15, 22, 29, 32, 36, 38, 43-4, 46-7, 70, 74, 77-8, 90, 92, 103, 105-6, 137, 225, 231, 285

Constitutional Act, 110

Cooney, Robert, 96

293

Cornwall, 24, 72
Cornwallis, 37
Corson, Robert, 106-7, *129*
Cromwell, James, 33
Croscombe, William, 57-8, 89, 94, 95
Crosthwaite, Thomas, 91
Cumberland County, 29, 32-3, 37, *48*
Crown, British, 4, 38, 40, 59-61, 66, 70, 96, 114, 117, 119-21, 126, 136, 154-5, 160-1, 174, 188, 190, 227, 230, 233, 264

Dalhousie College, 94, 206
Dalhousie, Lord, 94
Daly, Dominick, 259
Davidson, J. C., 217-8
"Declaration of Independence of Certain Methodists", 75
Deed of Declaration, 11, 23, 26
Democracy, 12, 15, 17, 41, 70, 75, 96, 103, 109, 189, 203, 227, 257, 284
Denomination(s), 93, 111, 118, 124, 126, 160, 162, 177, 183, 204-11, 219, 228, 234-41, 259, 263-4, 266-71, 281-2, 287
Dependence, 48, 55, 65, 67, 79, 88, 196, 211
Derby, Earl of, 266
Desbrisay, Albert, 204
Detroit, 39, 47
Devonshire, 58, 89
Devotion, 35, 57, 59-60, 78, 89, 108
Dewolfe, Charles, 199, 203, 206
Diderot, Denis, 59
Discipline(s), 14, 17, 20, 22, 36, 42, 44-5, 56, 61, 66, 74, 87, 92, 105-6, 112, 141, 146, 148, 161, 181, 201, 230, 253
Dissent, 31, *52*, 62-3, 93, *99*, 111-3, 118, 126-7, 235, 238
District chairmen, 58, 65, 86, 88-9, 95-6, 156, 198, 253-4, 256-7
District Meeting. *See* Meeting(s), District
Divinity, 236, 239
Dixon, Dr. James, 263
Doctrine, 10-11, 18, 22, 31, 35, 40, 45, 56-7, 59, 63, 74, 76, 92, 96, 102-3, 108, 112, 115-6, 119, 161, 172, 180, 201-2, 237, 253; of assurance, 22; of election, 15, 21, 91; of purgatory, 91
Draper, Hetty, 38

Draper, W. H., 174, 179, 238-40
Drunkenness, 22, 45, 58, 70
Dunbar, George, 66
Dunham, Darius, 42-3, 47, 76-7
Durham, Earl of, 24, 173-4, 182, 189, 191, *192*, 229, 280
Durham Report, 182, 189-90, *192*, 280
"Duty of Constant Communion, The," 7

Eastern British America, Conference of, 55, *79*, 95, 201, *214*, 279, 289. *See also* Methodists, Maritimes
Editor(s), 92-3, 115, 117, 123-4, *129*, 144-5, 148-9, 152, 154, 172, 174, 179-81, 187, 199, 208-9, 219, 226, 231, 234, 237, 239, 249, 260-1, 264-6
Education, viii, 5, 19, 23, 32, 44, 90, 104, 106, 129, 147; New Brunswick, 87, 93-6, 197, 199, 204-6, 209-11, *215*; Nova Scotia, 87, 93-6, 197, 199, 203-11, *215*; Upper Canada, 109-10, 114, 116-7, 120-5, 127, *129*, 152, 159-60, 162-3, 174-6, 181-2, 219, 226, 228, 230, 234-41, 259-65, 267-71. *See also* University
Education Act (Canada West), 234-9
Elders, presiding, 19, 20, 27, 34, 39, 44, 46, *50*, *53*, 70-1, 75, 77, 102, 156, 254
Elections, 1830—116, 118, 127-8; 1834—150; 1836—vii, 96, 154-8; 1844—207, 230, 233; 1847-8—259, 261-2, 267, 271; 1851—265; 1854—266
Elgin, Earl of, 259, 263-4
Elizabethtown, 70, 75
Emigration, 62, 86, 197
England, 12, 18, 36-7, 40-1, 46, 54, 56, 59, 62-4, 68-9, 73-4, 77, 88, 96, 101, 109, 111, 119-22, 134-5, 137, 139, 143, 145, 154-5, 164, 173-4, 176, 178, 180, 184, 188-9, 198, 211, 219, 221, 226, 239, 255, 264-5, 278, 284
English, in Canada, 29, 31, 41, 57, 61, 64, 70-1, 87, 89-90, 105, 112, 124, 135-6, 140, 191, 203, 229
Episcopate, 18-21, 27, 102, 139, 151
Episcopalian(s). *See* Church of England
Equality, 16, 22, 40, 47, *51*, 103, 109, 115, 118-9, 124-6, 128, 140, 208, 220, 234, 238, 241, 260, 263-5, 269-70, 281-2

Ethic(s), 15, 22, 31, 108
Evangelism, vii, 4-7, 15, 17, 21-3, 32, 38, 41, 43, 55, 61, 65, 67, 77, 90, 104, 106, 142, 202-3, 205, 218-9, 258-9, 278, 287
Evans, Ephraim, 152-3, 159, *170*, 172-3, 177, 181, 187, 200-2, 207, 209, 218-9, 221-2, 224-5, 251, 260
Examiner (Toronto), 191, 230, 290
Executive Council (Upper Canada), 122, 154

Faith, 3-4, 7, 11, 14, 31, 36, 41, 43, 45, 58, 60-1, 71, 93, 104, 108, 118, 220, 223, 281
Family Compact, 109, 259
Farming, 29, 40, 62, 68, 106-7, 163, 219
Fenton, John, 134
Ferguson, George, 106-7, 157, 219, 232
Fidler, Daniel, 34-5, 50, *51*, 90
Fisk, Wilbur, 102
Fisher, Charles, 210
Fletcher, John, 12, 21, 25
Flint, Billa, 257
Free Church, 240
Freedom, 5, 32, 40, 102-3, 116, 120, 144, 146, 196, 281. *See also* Liberty
Fredericton, 37, 89-90, 93-4, *98, 99*, 197, 202, 205, 278
Friends of Religious Liberty Committee, 118-9, 121, 124

Garrettson, Freeborn, 33, 35, 39, *49*
General Wesleyan Methodist Missionary Society, 56-8, 64, 73, 134-5, 142, 178, 184-5, 200-1, 218, 221, 253-4, 263-4, 267
Genesee Conference, 42, 67, 69-71, 73, 75
George, Bishop Enoch, 70, 76
Glenelg, Lord, 156, 160
Globe, 290
Goderich, Viscount (Earl of Ripon), 120, 124, 136, 140, 143
Gospel. *See* Bible
Gourlay, Robert, 69
Great Britain. *See* England
Green, Anson, character described, 104; conversion and career, 105; political involvement, 107, 157, 276; moves acceptance of union, 141; attitude to clergy reserves, 160; attitude to Richey's charges against Ryerson, 187; opinions on *Christian Guardian*, 114-5, 172-3; chairmanship of Augusta district, 156; participation in missionary tour, 221; secretary of Conference, *1841*, 223; opinion of Baldwin-Lafontaine ministry, 229; opinion of Draper Bill, *1845*, 239; district chairman, 218-9; attitude to reunion, 225, 226, 252; delegate to British Conference, *1846*, 249, 255; appointed Book Steward, 256; attitude to grants, 263; "Help to all or Help to none," 265; comment, 279
Grievances, Seventh Report on, 151, 154
Grindrod, Edward, 149
Grey, Earl, 264, 266
Guardian. See Christian Guardian

Hagerman, Christopher, 120, 135, 236
Halifax, 33, 35, 37, *51, 52*, 64, 86, 92, 94, 199, 202, 278
Hallowell, 145
Hamilton, 157, 180, 220-1, 227, 255
Harrison, William, 86
Harvard, W. M., 159, 161-2, 171-3
Head, Sir Francis Bond, 154-8, 171, 174
Hedding, Bishop Elijah, 76
Hennigar, James, 86
Hetherington, John P., 146
Hincks, Francis, 155, 182-4, 191, 230, 265, 269-70
Holiness, 5-6, 10, 14-16, 22, 34, 38, 45, 59-60, 77-8, 96-7, 103, 106-7, 141, 258, 265, 287
Holy Club, 2
Holy Communion, 7, 22, 46
Holy Living and Holy Dying, Rules and Exercises of, 2
Holy Spirit, 4, 6, 14, 22, 45, 61, 91
Hoole, Elijah, 87, *98*, 188
Hopkey, Sophia, 24
Horton (Baptist) Academy, 93
Horton, 37, 59, 95
House of Commons, 114, 118, 120, 126
House of Lords, 174, 263
Howe, Joseph, 206-7, 210, 278
Hume, Joseph, 126, 143, 150
Hurlburt, Jesse, 219

295

Immigrants, from U.S. to Canada, 41, 68, 105, 107, *129*; from Europe and British Isles, 62, 64, 68-9, 77, 107-8, *129*, 135-7, 197, 221, 278
Imperial relations, 40-1, 60, 63, 109-14, 118, 120, 128, 134, 153-4, 158, 163, 171, 174-7, 186, 188-90, 201, 205, 220, 224, 229, 233, 264, 270-1, 280. *See also* Colony(s)
"Impressions Made By Our Late Visit to England", 142-5, 171
Indians, North American, 72, 78, 105, *129*, 135-6, 142, 159, 162, 187, 224, 242, 279
Inglis, Bishop Charles, 37
Inglis, Bishop John, 62
Irish in Canada, 60, 63-4, 68, 91, 107-8
Irish Conference, 250
Itinerancy, 9, 19-22, 27, 29, 33-7, 42-8, 54, 58-61, 64, 67-8, 75-7, 86, 89-90, 103, 106-8, 112-3, *129*, 141, 148-9, 172, 198, 200, 202, 219-20, 223, *242*, 257. *See also* Ministers, Missionaries, Preachers, Circuits

Jackson, George, 61
Jacobin(s), 70
Jessop, William, 34-5, 50
Johnston, J. W., 206
Jones, Peter, 135, 221
Jones, Richard, 218-9, 230, 258
Journalism. *See* Press

Keeler, Sylvanus, 76
Kennedy, W. P. M., vii, 155
Ketchum, Jesse, 119
King. *See* Crown
King's College, N.B., 59, 93, 205-6
King's College, N.S., 93, *99*
King's College, York, 121, 124, 234-5, 237-8, 240, 260, 271, 286
Kingston, 52, 72, 74, 101, 146-7, 149, 157, 160, *166*, 173, 225, 234, 236, 266, *274*
Kingswood School, 49
Knight, Richard, 89, 197-8, 200, 202, 207
Knox College, 238

Ladies' Academy, The (Sackville), 204
Lafontaine, Louis H., 229, 261, 267

Laity, 9-11, 16, 20-1, 27, 46, 56, 75, 86, 95, 102-3, 114, 123, 146, 148, *193*, 200-1, 206, 210-11, 230, 236, 240, 248-9, 257-9, 262, 270, 284, 289
Land, 52, 110-11, 119, 121, 253, 268. *See also* Clergy reserves
Law, William, 2
Lecky, W. E. H., 3
Legislative Council (Upper Canada), 114
Legal Hundred, 11, 55
Leggatt, William, 92, 96, 202
Lennox and Addington County, 155
Liberalism, viii, 11, 13, 23, 55, 59, 66, 104-5, 109, 115, 117, 119, 121, 125, 127, 139, 150, 152, 156-8, 162-3, 174, 181-2, 210-11, 234, 236, 240, 242, 254, 256, 259-61, 280, 284-5. *See also* Whigs
Liberty, civil and religious, vii, 12, 18, 66, 96, 118, 119, 124-5, 137, 160, 162, 164, 172, 176-7, 234, 281-2, 285
Liturgy, 18, 21, 60
Liverpool, N.S., 33, 37-8, *50, 51*, 64-5
Local preachers, 46, 58, 64, 75-6, 87, 106, 139, 141-2, 148-52, 161, *166, 167*
London, England, 1, 3, 10, 24, 88, 92, 185-6, 249-50, 288
London, University of, 205, 269
London, Upper Canada, 156-7, 220-1, 233
Lord, William, 151-3, 158, *169*
Losee, William, vii, 39, 42, 47, 52
Lount, Samuel, 171
Loyalists, 29-32, 35-8, 40-2, 47, *51, 52, 53*, 63-4, 68, 104, 108, 125, *129*, 190, 197
Lower Canada, 41, 53, 69, 72-3, 86, 89, 96, 134-5, 137, 143, 146, 220. *See also* Quebec
Lowry, James, 54
Lunenburg, 64
Lunn, William, 146
Luther, Martin, 1
Lutheran(s), 52

Macaulay, J., 288
Macdonald, John A., 259-61, 266, 270
Mackenzie, W. L., 126-7, 143-4, 149-51, 163, 184, 190
MacNab, Sir Allan, 266

296

Magazine(s). *See* Periodicals
Magistrates, 37-8, 116-7
Maitland, Sir Peregrine, 121, 134
Mann, James, 35-6, 38, 41, *50*, *51*, 57, 201
Mann, John, 35-6, 38, *50*, *51*, 57, 201
Maritime Provinces, viii-ix, 29-39, 41-2, 48, 54-7, 59-64, 66-7, 78-9, 86-97, 196-212, 217, 278-81, 283, 285, 287. *See* also Nova Scotia, New Brunswick, Newfoundland, Prince Edward Island
Marsden, George, 141
Marsden, Joshua, 54, 61
Matthews, Peter, 171
McColl, Duncan, 35-6, 38, *51*, 86, 288
McCulloch, Dr. Thomas, 94
McKendree, Bishop William, 19, 27, 74-5, 102
McLeod, Alexander, 90, 92, 198-9
McNab, Alexander, 219
Meetings, camp, 22, 28, 46, 91, 202-3, 220, 258; Class, 8-9, 20, 22, 32, 45-6, 52, 202, 220, 258, *274*; District, 56-7, 59-60, 64-6, 88-9, 92, 94-5, 137, 148, 200-1, 202, 208, 210, 220, 249, 251, 253, 288; Tea, 202; Protracted, 91-2, 202
Membership, American Societies, 17; Maritimes, 37, 64, 86, 90, 198, 201; Upper Canada, 47, 70, 107, 129, 157, 171, 223, 271
Methodism, general, 1, 5-16, 29, 66, 68, 70-1, 78, 86, 89-90, 92, 96, 103, 105-7, 110, 113, 115-6, 118, 126, 137, 139-42, 147, 152, 157, 162-3, 174, 177, 201, 220-2, 224-6, 229, 231-2, 248, 252-3, 256, 258, 278-9, 283-5, 287, 288-9
Methodist(s), American, vii, 1, 16-23, 29, 33, 48, 67, 70, 89, 95, 102, 105, 134, 289-90; British North America, viii, ix, 1, 17, 20, 23, 29, 32, 36-7, 41-4, 48, 54, 56, 58, 63, 65-7, 69-72, 74-6, 86-7, 135, 146, 150-1, 163, 180, 196, 249, 278-82, 285, 287, 288; Maritimes, vii-ix, 29-39, 41-2, 48-9, 54, 62-3, 66-7, 78, 86-97, 196-212, 278-85, 288-90; Upper Canada, vii-ix, 29, 33-4, 39-48, 67-79, 101-2, 107, 112-3, 115, 117-8, 122-7, 134, 137, 140-1, 144-8, 150-1, 155-64, 171, 173, 179, 182-3, 189-91, 200, 202, 217-9, 221-2, 224, 228-39, 241-2, 248, 258, 260-6, 269-71, 278-82, 285, 288, 290
Methodist Episcopal Church, (1834), ix, 148-151, 153, 171, 248; in Upper Canada, 1828 (Canada Conference), 101-3, 108, 115-7, 119, 124-5, 127, 134, 136-9, 141-2; of America (American Conference), ix, 17-23, 25, 28-9, 33-4, 39, 42, 50, 54, 72, 74-5, 102, 134, 289
Methodist Magazine, 290
Millerism, 226
Ministry, 8, 12, 17-19, 30-1, 33, 36, 39, 43-4, 45, *53*, 54-5, 58-9, 66-7, 74, 76-7, 88, 90, 92, 104-5, 107, 112, 114, 118-20, 126, 139-40, 154, 156, 159-60, 175, 196, 201-2, 206, 210, 217, 220, 225-6, 230, 232-3, 236, 256-8, 262, 265, 268, 279. *See also* Clergy, Missionaries, Pastors, Itinerants, Preachers
Missionaries (Anglican), 30, 37
Missionaries (Methodist), 2, 16-7, 29, 32, 34, 38, 42, 44, 46, *48*, 54, 56-7, 60-1, 63-7, 71-4, 76, 79, 86-7, 91, 94-5, *97*, *98*, 134-5, 146, 149, 181, 198-9, 201, 220-2, 226-7, 251, 253, 267
Mission(s), 33-4, 39, 42, 55-7, 67, 71, 77-8, 105, *129*, 134-7, 147, 162, 185-7, 200, 220, 228, 242, *243*, 248, 253, 255, 267, 279
Mission House, 56, 59
Missionary Board (Upper Canada), 135-6, 138
Missionary Committee, 56-8, 60-1, 64-7, 71, 73, 86-7, 89, 92-5, *97*, *98*, 134-7, 140-1, 146-7, 149, 150, 152-3, 159, 173, 178, 181, 185-6, 188, 196-201, 203-4, 210, 225-7, 250, 261, 290
Missionary Society (Upper Canada), 142
Mobocracy, 116, 126, 161
Moderate(s), 32, 60, 107, 109, 142-3, 146, 158, 231, 259, 266, 286
Monarchy. *See* Crown
"Money, Wesley's Sermon on the Use of," 13
Montgomery, Mr., 71
Montreal, 59, 70-1, *193*, 259
Mountain, Bishop Jacob, 110-11
Moravians, 3

297

Morin, Augustin N., 265-6
Morrison, Dr. T. D., 118, 151
Mount Allison Academy. *See* Sackville Academy

Napanee, 134, 148
Nationalism, 197, 271, 278, 287
Neutralism, political, 2, 10, 218, 231, 240, 248
Nelles, S. S., 268
New Brunswick, 29, 34-40, *49, 52*, 54, 60, 62-3, 86-7, 89, 91-6, *97*, 196-8, 201-2, 204-6, 209-11, 255, 260, 278, 282, 284
New Brunswick, College of. *See* King's College, N.B.
New Brunswick District, 86-9, 91, 94-5, *97*, 198, 202, 210
New Brunswick, University of. *See* King's College, N.B.
New England, 29-30, 40, 43, 62-4, 90
New Connexion Methodists, 248, *271*
Newfoundland, 29, 89, *212*
Newlight movement, 31, 37-8, 41, 63, 65, 91
Newspaper. *See* Press
New Testament, 14; notes on, 25
Newton, Frank, 38
Newton, Joshua, 37-8, *51*
New York Christian Advocate, 140
New York Conference, 39, 42, *52*, 222
New York State, 16, 32, 35, 42, 105, *129*
Niagara, 156-7; Peninsula, 39-40, 43, 47, *53*, 70, 145
Non-Anglican, 41, 206, 232, 237. *See also* Dissent
Normanby, Marquis of, 176, 179
North America, 40, 61, 87, 89, 107-9, 111, 119, 198, 212, 278, 284, 288
Nova Scotia and New Brunswick Wesleyan Methodist Magazine, 92
Nova Scotia District(s), vii, 17, 29-39, 41, 45, *50, 52*, 54, 57-9, 62, 64, 79, 86-9, 92-5, 196-8, 200-1, 210
Nova Scotia, 59-60, 62-3, 79, 87, 92-3, 96, 203-4, 206-11, 255, 268, 278, 280, 282, 284-5, 288
Novascotian, 290

Oligarchy, 30, 69, 98, 109, 259, 279
Olivant, Thomas, 54

Ordained ministry, 17-8, 25, 31, 33-4, 36, 39, 50, 139, 141, 149
Ottawa, 71
Oxford University, 2
Oxley, George, 32

Papineau, Louis, 190
Parrsboro, 64
Pastor(s), 67, 89, 104. *See also* Ministers, Clergy, Missionaries, Itinerants, Preachers
Peel, Sir Robert, 224
Pension Fund, 87. *See also* Superannuation
Periodicals. *See* Press
Perkins, Simeon, 35, 37, *50, 51,* 57, 61, *79*, 288
Petition(s), 114, 116-8, 120-1, 124, 127, 160, 174, 176, 207, 260, 263
Perronet, Vincent, 25
Perry, Peter, 155
Pickard, Humphrey, 90, 198-9, 204
Pictou Academy, 93-4
Pilmoor, Joseph, 16
Playter, George, 218-9, 221, 231-2, 248-9, 252, 257, 289
Politics, Maritimes, 37, 55, 66-7, 93, 95-7, 197, 203-4, 206-11; Upper Canada, vii-viii, 40-1, 45, 47-8, 69, 71-2, 74, 78, 101, 103-9, 111, 114-8, 121, 123, 125-8, 134-8, 142-7, 150-1, 153-4, 156-9, 161, 163, 171-3, 176-7, 179-82, 185-6, 188, 190, 217-22, 225-32, 240-42, 248, 254-5, 259, 261-2, 265-7, 269, 271
Pope, Rev. Henry, 72
Poverty, 7-8, 24, 42, 63, 65, 68, 92-3, 106, 142, 196, 208, 253
Prayer, 7-8, 10, 32, 43-4, 46, 58, 67, 71, 91, 96, 160, 251-2, 258, 265, 268
Preachers (general), 17-23, 25; Maritimes, 29-38, 54, 56-67, 86-92, 95-6, 198, 200, 207, 210; Upper Canada, 40-7, 67-78, 102-7, 112, 115-6, 119, 127, 134, 140, 142, 147, 149-53, 156, 161-2, 172-3, 187-8, 217-9, 222-3, 225, 230, 248-9, 251-9, 264. *See also* Clergy, Ministers, Pastors, Missionaries, Itinerants
Presbyterian(s), 52, 60, 68, 92-3, 110-11, 113, 158, 205, 211, 236, 238, 240, 259-61, 270, 285, 288. *See also* Church of Scotland

298

Press, 42, 90, 92, 95, 114, 116, 122, 126, 139-40, 143, 146, 150, 155, 160, 172-88, 191, 193, 199-200, 208-9, 213, 221, 226, 231, 248, 256-7, 263-6, 290. *See also* Individual papers
Proudfoot, Rev. William, 288
Price, J. H., 264
Priestley, James, 57-8, 60, 79
Prince Edward Island, 37, *52*, 62, 86, 97
Probationer(s), 57-8, 86, 105
Protestant(s), 15, 110, 112, 119, 234-5, 250, 264, 278. *See also* Individual denominations
Provincial Wesleyan (formerly *The Wesleyan*), 290
Protestant Episcopal Church, 28
Puseyism, 227, 237, 248

Quaker(s), 34, *52*
Quarterly Meeting or Conference, 10, 19-20, 22, 46, 72, 102, 148, 160, 251
Quebec (City), 71, 173; Province, 52, 110, 121, 220. *See also* Lower Canada
Queen's College, University of (Queen's University), 236-8, 260, 271
Quinté, Bay of, 39, 44, 47, *53*, 70, 76, *129*, 156

Radicalism, vii, 13, 96, 109, 115, 117, 125-6, 143, 145, 147-9, 154, 156-7, 159, 162-3, 173, 190, 232, 240, 257, 280, 285, 287
Rankin, Thomas, 27
Rebellion of 1837, 160-1, 171
Reform, vii, 16, 75, 96, 107, 109-10, 112-4, 116-9, 123, 125-7, 137, 143, 145-6, 150-8, 162-3, 171, 173-4, 176, 182-4, 190-1, 202, 206-7, 210-11, 229-33, 239, 241, 259, 261-3, 266, 280, 284-5
Reform Association of Canada, 230
Reform Party (Province of Canada), 229-30, 259, 262
Regiopolis College, 236-7, 260
Representative legislative conference, 249
Republicanism, 41, 61, 73, 111, 113, 117, 143, 158, 163, 178, 190
Reserves Act, 223

Responsible government, 182, 190, 207, 228-30, 259, 278, 280, 286. *See also* Self-government
Revival(s), 32, 65, 70, 76, 92, 202, 220, 258
Reynolds, John, 127
Rice, S. D., 90, *99*, 199
Richardson, Bishop James, 76, 104-5, 107, 112, 115, 117, 126, *129*, 141, 149, 151-3, 156, *169*
Richey, Matthew, early career, 60, 158; Principal of Upper Canada Academy, 158; views on *Guardian*, 181; controversy with Canadian Methodists, 184-5, 187-8; encourages Maritimes reunion, 201; suggested as Principal of Sackville Academy, 203; Alder's representative in Halifax, 199; district meeting secretary, 220; conditions of reunion in U.C., 222-3; visit to Bagot about grant, 224; defends Wesleyan interest in Canada West, 220, 222-4, 226-7, 250-1, 253; co-delegate and president, 255; views on university bills, 260; actions with regard to grant, 263; involvement in university plans, 268; resignation, *273*; general comment, 279; source material, 288-9
Roach, Thomas, 64
Robinson, John Beverley, 236, 288
Rolph, John, 145
Roman Catholic(s), 6, 15, 21, 68, 158, 207, 209-10, *215*, 225, 227, 234-6, 248, 250, 261, 278, 282
Russell, Lord John, 182
Ryan, Henry, 43, 46, *53*, 69, 71-3, 75-8, 86, 101-2, 105-6, 117
Ryerson, Egerton, Methodism and politics, 103; character described, 104-5; George Ferguson's opinion, 106; independence of outlook, 107; "review" of Strachan's sermon, 112-3; open letters to Strachan, 114; appointed editor, 115; comments on politics, 115-6; comments on clergy reserves, 117-9; presents reserves petition, 121; comments on education, 122-4; comment by Burwell, 126; union negotiations, 135-6, 139-42; resumes editorship

299

of *Guardian*, 141; publishes "Impressions," 142-4; contends with W. L. Mackenzie, 144, 146; defends union of 1833, 149-50; quarrels with Richardson, 151-2; resigns from *Guardian*, 152; writes open letters on Canadian politics, 155-6; negotiates with imperial government for Academy, 158; suggests division of reserves, 159; defines attitude to Rebellion of 1837, 160-1, 171-2; defends M. S. Bidwell, 171; resumes editorship of *Guardian*, 172-3; defines Methodists' political position, 176-7; defends Canadian Methodists, 180-2; contends for reserves settlement, 174-6; defends Thomson administration, 182-4; defines financial relationship with Wesleyans, 184; defends Canadian Methodist interests, 187-9, 217; his work evaluated, 189-91; appointed to Toronto circuit, 218; on missionary tour, 221; eulogy of Sydenham, 228; defends Metcalfe, 229-31; Richey's opinion of Ryerson, 233; involvement in education, 230, 234-41; censured by Toronto Methodists, 248; educational preoccupation, 256; puts forward compromise solution on district chairmen, 257; views on class meetings, 258; views on payment of grant, 263; works on university question, 268-9; general comment, 278, 280; source material, 288

Ryerson, George, 114, 119-20, 124, 126, *129*, 135, 137

Ryerson, John, comments on General Conference, *1828*, 101; character described, 104, 107; comments on Methodist influence, 127; union negotiations, *1832*, 134, 138; opinion of "Impressions", 145; views on union, 146, 149; Egerton's retirement as editor, 152; on 1836 election, 156-7; comments on clergy reserves, 158-9; comments on Sir F. B. Head, 171-2; views on *Guardian* editorship, 172-3; comments on tories, 173; visits E.B.A. Conference, 201; Book Steward, 218; position in Connexion, 219; missionary tour, 220-1; negotiates with Wesleyans, 222-3, 225; attitude toward Baldwin-Lafontaine ministry, 229, 248; views on college issue, 237, 239, 262, 268; reunion negotiations, 249-54; district chairman and co-delegate, 255-7, 263

Ryerson, Col. Joseph, 104

Ryerson, William, character described, 104; on trial as preacher, 106; independent opinions, 107; protest committee member, 113; urges reply to Strachan, 114; opinion of "Impressions", 145; consolidation of Kingston Societies, 146; views on local preachers' ordination, 149; opinion of Richardson, 152; district chairmanships, 156, 218; comment on "rectory question", 157; views on political prisoners, 172; comments on union, 172; mission to English Conference, 188; support for Egerton, 217-8; Canada Conference, 1841, president, 223; elected president of Conference, *1847*, 252; decline of influence, 256; motion for secularization of reserves, 266; views on affiliation of Victoria, 268; general comment, 279

Right(s), civil and religious, 117-9, 125-6, 139, 154-5, 161, 177, 180-1, 232, 237-8, 253, 265, 281

Sackville, 94, 199, 203-4
Sackville Wesleyan Academy (later Mount Allison University), 203-7, 209, 211, 288-90
Sacraments, 18-9, 46, 91, 161
Saint(s), 31, 35
Saint John, 29, 37, *51*, 59-60, 62-6, 89-90, *99*, 197, 199, 204
Saint John Grammar School, 60, 90
Salvation, 2-4, 15, 31, 36, 38, 43, 45, 48, 61, 67, 73, 91, 103, 107, 162, 287; by faith, 3
Sanctification, 5, 15, 22, 43, 45-8, 60, 103, 202
Sawyer, Joseph, *53*, 76-7
Scots (in Canada), 29, 36, 41, 68, *129*, 190
Scott, Jonathan, 218-9, 231

Secularism, viii-ix, 4, 9, 11, 14, 16-7, 21, 38, 46-7, 61, 78-9, 97, 103-5, 107-8, 111, 127, 137, 139, 158-9, 162, 174-5, 180-1, 183, 191, 205, 208, 211-2, 231, 234, 236-8, 240-1, 254, 256-7, 259-67, 269-71, 279, 281-2, 284, 287, 290

Sect(s), 90, 93-4, 111, 116, 122, 124-6, 134, 158, 206-9, 235, 239, 282

Self-government, 189, 191, 196-7, 201-2, 211, 217, 229, 269, 280-1, 284. *See also* Responsible Government

Sermon(s), 3, 7, 28, 36, 42-4, 46, 70, 104, 106, 111-2; Wesley's, 3, 7, 13, 25, 77

Settler(s), 29, 32, 40-1, 43, 47, 52, 68-9, 111, 135, 142, 159

Seventh Report on Grievances, 151, 154

Sherwood, Henry, 259, 261

Simcoe, John Graves, 41, 110, 121

Sissons, C. B., viii, 288

Slavery, 26, 28

Slight, Benjamin, *195*, 222, 288

Smith, T. W., 289

Snowball, John, 61

Society(s), 8-20, 32-7, 42, *50*, 54-7, 65, 67-8, 70, 72-4, 76-8, 86, 90, 96, 107, 114, 117, 137, 141, 146, 148, 150-1, 156-7, 171, 177, 202-3, 211, 217-20, 223-5, 231-2, 257, 288

Society and social questions, 5, 11, 13-4, 16-7, 22-3, 29-30, 36-7, 40-2, 47-8, 55, 61-7, 77, 87, 97, 103, 107-9, 114, 116, 118, 122, 125-6, 137, 163-4, 173-4, 176, 182, 190, 197-8, 203, 211, 219-20, 241, 252, 259, 279, 282-4, 286-7

Society for the Propagation of the Gospel, The, 110

Spencer, James, 219

Spiritual matters, 7, 15, 17, 22, 38-9, 43-5, 47-8, *53*, 54-5, 59, 61, 70, 74, 77, 87-9, 97, 106-8, 171, 173, 210, 220, 231, 249, 251

Squire, William, 152

Stanley, E. G. (later Lord Derby), 224

Stephen, James, 159

Stephen, Leslie, 4

Stevens, Abel, 290

Steward(s), 10, 14, 20, 65, 201, 279

Stinson, Joseph, character and appearance, 147; Canadian union, 149-51; difficulties of Upper Canada Academy, 152-3; attitude toward Rebellion of 1837, 160-1; supports E. Ryerson for *Guardian*, 172; address in *Guardian*, 176-7; growing conflict with Canadian leaders, 177-8, 181-5, 188; relations with Canadian Methodists after 1840, 220-4, 250

Strachan, Bishop John, member of provincial élite, 40; comment on Methodism, 53; lobbying about clergy reserves and education, 110-2; president of Board of Education, 121-2; comment on Methodists and establishment, 126; urges Wesleyans to return to Upper Canada, 134; letter for Thomas Turner, 138; campaigns for better terms on clergy reserves, 183; King's College opening, 236; views on Baldwin's university bill, 237-9; general comment, 278; source material, 288

Strong, John B., 71, 89

Sullivan, R. B., 230

Sunday School(s), 258

Sunday School Guardian, 258

Switzer's Chapel, 101

Sydenham, Baron. *See* C. P. Thomson

Taylor, Jeremy, 2

Taylor, Samuel, 25

Temple, William, 59-62, 64-6, 86, 89, 92, 94, *98*, 198, 203

Thames Valley, 40, 43

Thomson, Charles P. (Lord Sydenham), 173-4, 182-5, 189-91, *192*, *193*, 220, 224, 228-9, 263, 280

Toronto. *See* York

Toronto Patriot, 177, 179-80

Toronto Periodical Journal, 248

Toronto, University of, 236-7, 267-71

Tory(s), vii, 4, 75, 109-10, 112, 118, 126-8, 142, 144-5, 150, 154, 157-8, 162-4, 171-4, 176-7, 179, 190-1, 206-7, 210, 233, 240-1, 255, 259, 261-2, 266, 280. *See also* Conservatism

Tract Society, 258

Tractarian(s), 226

Trinity College, 271, *277*
Turner, Thomas, 135, 138
Twining, Thomas, 37

United Associate Synod, 288
Union movements, 138-41, 144, 146-53, 171-2, 178-81, 183-7, 196, *212*, 218, 220-8, 248-56, 259, 263, *273*
University(s), 94, 121-2, 205, 209, 219, 234-41, 259-62, 267-71, 282, 286. *See also individual titles;* Education
University College, Toronto, 268-9, 271
United States, 16, 21, 32, 46, 69, 71, 74, 102, 109, 111-3, 126, *129*, 135, 140, 172-3, 189, 208, 221, 239, 260, 284, 289
United Church Archives, 289-90
Upper Canada (general), *see also Canada West,* vii-viii, 54, 67, 95-6, 211; church-state, 109-20, 150-63, 171-91, 223-4, 227-33, 261-7; education, 121-8, 227, 234-9, 259-60, 267-9; Methodist activity, 17, 39-48, 67, 69-79, 101-8, 134-50, 171-3, 196, 217-23, 225-7, 240-1, 248-59, 269-71; politics, vii-viii, 40-1, 45, 47-8, 69, 71-2, 74, 78, 101, 103-9, 111, 114-8, 121, 123, 125-8, 134-8, 142-7, 150-1, 153-4, 156-9, 161, 163, 171-3, 176-7, 179-82, 185-6, 188-91, 217-22, 225-32, 240-42, 248, 254-5, 259, 261-2, 265-7, 269, 271
Upper Canada Academy (later Victoria College), 124, 140, 152-3, 158-9, 162, *169,* 171, 179, 183, 219, 222, 236, 282
Upper Canada Assembly. *See* Assembly, Upper Canada
Upper Canada College, 124, 152
Upper Canada Herald, 114
Upper Canada, University of, 238

Varley Wesleyan Day School, 204
Victoria College (Upper Canada Academy, Victoria University), 225, 236-8, 240, 260, 267-71, 282, 288
Voltaire, 59

War of 1812, 39, *53,* 54, 67-72, 76, 101
Washington, George, 22

Watson, Richard, 135-6, 196
Wentworth, Sir John, *52*
Wesley, Charles, 25
Wesley, John, family background and religious development, 1-4; theology, 5-6; as evangelist, 6-8; organization of his Connexion, 8-11; political opinions, 11-13; ethical ideas, 13-14; his societies described, 14-16; promotes Methodist expansion in America, 16-18; encourages W. Black, 29, 32-3; changes after his death, 55; his views invoked by Ryerson, 161; Bagot's relationship, 224; sources, 289
Wesley, Rev. Samuel, 1
Wesley, Susanna, 1, 2, 4
Wesleyan Methodist Church in Canada West, 1840 (Canada Conference), 217-21, 223, 225-32, 240-1, 248-52; in Canada West, *1847,* 253-8, 260, 262-7, 269-71, 279-83, 285-6, 288-9; in Upper Canada, 1833; Canadian Conference, or the Conference, 146, 148-57, 159-60, 162-3, 171, 173-4, 177-82, 184-8, 191, 196; in England, or Wesleyan Conference, or English Conference, or British Conference, 10-11, 15, 17-20, 26-8, 33, 51, 54-6, 59, 67, 70-3, 75, 79, 86-7, 94, 101-2, 134-42, 149-50, 172, 179-81, 184-5, 188, 201, 210-11, 218, 220-7, 248-56, 259-6, 264, 267, 269, 271, 279, 283, 287, 289
Wesleyan Methodist Episcopal Canadian Church, 76
Wesleyans, 73-4, 77-8, 87, 90, 92, 95-6, 134-7, 139, 141-53, 156-9, 161-2, 172-88, 196, 200-1, 203-4, 206-12, 217-29, 232-3, 240, 248-52, 254, 256, 259, 261-3, 268, 270, 279, 282-3, 287-8
Wesleyan, The, later *Provincial Wesleyan,* 92-3, 96, 200, 208-9, 290
Westminster Confession, 236
Whatcoat, Bishop Richard, 27
Whig(s), 143, 250. *See also* Liberalism
Whitehead, Thomas, 217-8
Wilkinson, Henry, 218-9, 230, 258

Williams, Richard, 71, 86, 89
Wilmot, Judge L. A., 95, 202, 205-6, 210, 278
Wood, Enoch, described by Carroll, 89; editorship with Temple, 92-3; "the plan of independence," 197; chairman of N.B. district, 198; attitude toward Maritimes conference, 198-201; principalship for Pickard, 203-4; attitude toward Governor Colebrooke, 205; views on King's College, N.B., 205-6; appointed missions superintendent (Canada West) in 1847, 255-7; describes union services, 256; views on district chairmanship, 256-7; political views, 260-2, 266; government grants, 263, 266; on the college question, 267-8

Wooster, Calvin, 43
Wray, James, 35, 50
Wright, David, 106, 129, 145, 156-7

"Yankeeism," 139, 147, 151, 177
York, Upper Canada (later Toronto), 44, 52, 72, 105, 110, 112-3, 118, 121, 134-5, 138, 145-7, 149, 156-7, 159, 177-8, 181, 218, 221, 223, 225-6, 230, 240, 248, 251-2, 255-6, 267-8
Youmans, David, 72

Date Due

DEC 6 1977		DEC 1 1 2000
		DEC 1 1 2000
		MAR 1 1 2006
MAR 7 1978		FEB 2 7 2006
AUG 1 8 1985		
MAY 3 0 1990		
MAY 1 5 1994		
DEC 1 7 1993		

BX 8356 .C2 F7
French, Goldwin Sylvester
Parsons & politics; the role o   010101 000   c.2

0 1163 02151596
TRENT UNIVERSITY

BX8356   .C2F7   cop.2

French, Goldwin
  Parsons & politics

261001

| DATE | ISSUED TO |

261001

CPSIA information can be obtained
at www.ICGtesting.com
Printed in the USA
BVHW032146080622
639322BV00009B/131

9 781014 973245